ELEMENTS OF LOGIC

ELEMENTS OF LOGIC

Richard Whately, D.D.

international debate education association

New York • Amsterdam • Brussels

Published by:
The International Debate Education Association
400 West 59th Street
New York, NY 10019

Library of Congress Control Number: 2008933856

Printed in the USA

IDEBATE PRESS

KEY TITLES IN RHETORIC, ARGUMENTATION, AND DEBATE makes available important texts and monographs that have long been unavailable. Revised or reissued with new prefaces, the books in this series are significant texts that offer teachers valuable resources long missing from their classrooms.

Books in the series include:

- *Logical Self-Defense* by Ralph H. Johnson and J. Anthony Blair
- *Perspectives on Argumentation: Essays in Honor of Wayne Brockriede* by Robert Trapp and Janice Schuetz
- *Elements of Logic* by Richard Whately
- *Decision by Debate* by Douglas Ehninger and Wayne Brockriede

IDEBATE Press is actively soliciting other volumes for this series. If you know of a valuable text that we should reissue, please send us your suggestions. If you are the author of an out-of-print text you think might be appropriate, please contact us. You can reach us at:
IDEA@willamette.edu.

For books from IDEBATE Press, go to:
http://www.idebate.org/main/books.asp

Preface to the IDEBATE Press reissue of *Elements of Logic*

Most of us first encountered Richard Whately's *Elements of Logic* as a passing mention in an undergraduate survey of rhetorical theory or an argumentation and debate course. Graduate level coverage of Whately's work frequently attaches little significance to the *Logic*. Following the lead of Wilbur Samuel Howell,[1] Whately has been dismissed as someone who merely reaffirmed Aristotle's doctrine of syllogistic reasoning. Whately's treatment of logic and reasoning is cast as standing in opposition to the new logic of scientific induction that dominated the modern era of logic and rhetoric. By the twentieth century, the new logic of the scientific method was the standard for teaching reasoning and critical thinking. Richard Whately's adaptation of Aristotle's system of logic seemed nothing more than an antiquarian view, simply one more treatise from the past.

Why, then, preserve a work based on a seemingly long-discarded reasoning process? Richard Whately's *Elements of Logic* has great utility for twenty-first century scholars and teachers as we face the daunting need to adapt and create models of reasoning that respond to the ways information is now encountered and processed. The *Logic* has much to offer those who will write the new textbooks for argumentation and critical thinking and for those who must find viable methods of teaching students whose thought patterns are increasingly becoming non-linear.

Richard Whately possessed an instinct and natural talent for teaching, a quality that underlies his work in logic and rhetoric. His use of Aristotle's syllogistic reasoning is more appropriately understood as neo-Aristotlean[2] and reflects his talent for teach-

1. Wilbur Samuel Howell, *Eighteenth-Century British Logic and Rhetoric* (Princeton, NJ: Princeton University Press, 1971), 700–702.
2. Ray E. McKerrow, "Richard Whately's Theory of Rhetoric," in *Explorations in Rhetoric: Studies in Honor of Douglas Ehninger*, ed. Ray E. McKerrow (Glenview, IL: Scott, Foresman, 1982), 138–139.

ing. In 1826, the first edition of the *Logic* compiled Whately's lectures on reasoning and critical thinking, the product of his tenure as an Oxford don at Oriel College. Whately understood that when teaching undergraduates, theory is best taught in terms of *praxis*. He "abjured philosophical niceties" and offered "plain, unadorned advice" for applying logic to the practical matters of the day.[3]

The *Logic* offers a number of useful principles for teaching reasoning and critical thinking to undergraduates today. First, Whately held that the chief impediment to acquiring knowledge and being able to function intellectually was the need to understand, and then always remember, that *reasoning is reasoning*. We do not have a different kind of reasoning process for every subject or case. The *Logic* provides an easily adaptable statement of this principle that we can employ to help our students understand that common reasoning patterns are a constant across subjects and contexts.

Second, contrary to Howell's opinion that Whately's devotion to Aristotle excludes inductive reasoning, Whately did not reject induction and the scientific method.[4] The *Logic* provides an explanation of the function of induction, and Whately teaches that induction is the process for finding the data necessary to create arguments. "Induction is a prior inventional tool, not to be confused with the rigor of the reasoning process itself."[5] This interpretation is especially applicable to teaching undergraduates today. The ease with which they can "cut and paste" from Internet sites causes many of them to believe that once they have found information, nothing more is required for creating arguments.

Third, Whately may have selected Aristotle's syllogism as the basis for teaching form in reasoning because he was seeking an all-purpose model that would function for teaching the basics of how to reason. In this sense, his approach was not unlike that of Stephen Toulmin's creation of a model for understanding the

3. McKerrow, 139.
4. McKerrow, 144.
5. McKerrow, 144.

reasoning process. Foreshadowing Toulmin, Whately offers the syllogism as the simple framework for creating arguments. The *Logic* explains the need for such a core model of structure for any kind of argument. While we may opt for the Toulmin model over the syllogism, or some other universal model, Whately's defense of the syllogistic model can easily be applied to our explanation of the need for a universal model to our students.

Fourth, the *Logic* provides justification for teaching students to learn and use the appropriate terminology of reasoning. For all who have struggled with explaining to students why it is essential to learn and use "technical terms," Whately offers help. He taught that terminology does not have to be a barrier to understanding if the student will learn it and use it. Whately has a cogent explanation of the value of terminology that any of us can employ in our teaching.

Whately's *Logic* offers a great deal more on language use that can be applied to how we teach reasoning and critical thinking. One of his principles is that using logic requires using language. His discussion of the properties of language, the need to define terms, and the difficulties that ambiguity and vagueness create for arguers is very contemporary. His connection of grammar to logic is especially useful today. E-mail, instant messaging, and other technological influences are creating students who do not know how to write or think in complete sentences. The *Logic* includes a very useful explanation of why knowing the parts of speech and the structure of sentences, and the role of the declarative sentence, is so necessary to being able to reason.

Finally, Whately's personal facility with analogy may be a useful feature of the *Logic* for developing instructional technique. One of the greatest challenges any teacher faces is making his or her students understand an abstract concept. Whately responded to that challenge by using analogies. Although many may seem time bound, how he used suitable analogies based on the common experience and knowledge base of his students and his placement of analogies as a means of illustrating the abstract principles of logic serve as an effective model for teaching by analogy.

In addition to the usefulness of the *Logic* as an aid to teaching argumentation and critical thinking, Whately's focus on Aristotle's syllogism as a universal model of argument can guide the generation of scholars who now must deal with the challenges to reasoning and critical thinking created by technology. We are now confronted by the need to teach reasoning techniques to students who do not acquire most of what they accept as fact by reading complete texts of source material and who do not learn the discipline of thought by substantive writing. Information comes in snippets and factoids downloaded from randomly organized electronic data-bases. Further, most of this information is no longer compiled, edited, or evaluated by credentialed reviewers.

The linear reasoning patterns of the inductive scientific method are fading. Students are constantly exposed to and seek out information that comes in short bursts and is dominated by visual and aural stimuli. While a return to Aristotle's syllogistic model may not be the solution, those who must create new models of reasoning to fit ever-evolving forms of electronic media may find guidance and inspiration in Richard Whately's *Elements of Logic*. Whately made an old form new by reinventing the syllogism to fit the new science of his day. Why and how he recast the syllogism as an all-purpose model of reasoning that incorporated the old with the new can be the starting point for developing new models to teach reasoning and critical thinking to students whose lives are increasingly dominated by new media.

Dr. Karyn Charles Rybacki
Northern Michigan University

TO

THE RIGHT REVEREND

EDWARD COPLESTON, D.D.

LORD BISHOP OF LLANDAFF,

&c. &c.

My Dear Lord,

To enumerate the advantages I have derived from your instructions, both in regular lectures and in private conversation, would be needless to those acquainted with the parties, and to the Public, uninteresting. My object at present is simply to acknowledge how greatly I am indebted to you in respect of the present Work; not merely as having originally imparted to me the principles of the Science, but also as having contributed remarks, explanations, and illustrations, relative to the most important points, to so great an amount that I can hardly consider myself as the Author of more than half of such portions of the treatise as are not borrowed from former publications. I could have wished, indeed, to acknowledge this more explicitly, by marking with some note of distinction those parts which are least my own. But I found it could not be done. In most instances there is something belonging to each of us; and even in those parts where your share is the largest, it would not be fair that you should be made responsible for any thing that is not entirely your own. Nor is it possible, in the case of a Science, to remember distinctly how far one has been, in each instance, indebted to the suggestions of another. Information, as to matters of fact, may easily be referred in the mind to the person from whom we have derived it: but scientific truths, when thoroughly embraced, become much more a part of the mind, as it were; since they rest, not on the authority of the instructor, but on reasoning from data, which we ourselves furnish;* they are scions engrafted on the stems previously rooted in our own soil; and we are apt to confound them with its indigenous productions.

You yourself also, I have reason to believe, have forgotten the greater part of the assistance you have afforded in the course of conversations on the subject; as I have found, more than once, that ideas which I distinctly remembered to have received from you, have not been recognized by you when read or

* See B. IV. Ch. ii. § 1.

repeated. As far, however, as I can recollect, though there is no part of the following pages in which I have not, more or less, received valuable suggestions from you, I believe you have contributed less to the Analytical Outline, and to the Treatise on Fallacies, and more, to the subjoined Dissertation, than to the rest of the Work.

I take this opportunity of publicly declaring, that as, on the one hand, you are not responsible for any thing contained in this Work, so, on the other hand, should you ever favour the world with a publication of your own on the subject, the coincidence which will doubtless be found in it with many things here brought forward as my own, is not to be regarded as any indication of plagiarism, at least on your side.

Believe me to be,

My dear Lord,

Your obliged and affectionate

Pupil and Friend,

RICHARD WHATELY.

PREFACE.

The following Treatise contains the substance of the Article "Logic" in the *Encyclopædia Metropolitana*. It was suggested to me that a separate publication of it might prove acceptable, not only to some who are not subscribers to that work, but also to several who are; but who, for convenience of reference, would prefer a more portable volume. In fact a number of individuals had actually formed a design (prevented only by this publication) of joining together to have the Article reprinted for their own private use.

I accordingly revised it, and made such additions, chiefly in the form of Notes, as I thought likely to increase its utility.

When applied to to contribute the Article, I asked and obtained permission from Dr. Copleston (now Bishop of Llandaff) to make use of manuscripts compiled in great measure from what I had heard from him in conversations on the subject, or which he had read to me from his common-place book, interspersed with observations of my own. These manuscripts I had drawn up and was in the habit of employing, for the use of my own pupils.

In throwing them into a form suitable for the Encyclopædia, and in subsequently enlarging the Article into the present volume, I have taken without scruple whatever appeared most valuable from the works of former writers; especially the concise, but in general accurate, treatise of Aldrich. But while I acknowledge my obligations to my predecessors, of whose labours I have largely availed myself, I do not profess to be altogether satisfied with any of the treatises that have yet appeared; nor have I accordingly judged it any unreasonable presumption to point out what seem to me the errors they contain. Indeed, whatever deference an Author may profess for the authority of those who have preceded him, the very circumstance of his publishing a work on the same subject, proves that he thinks theirs open to improvement. In censuring, however, as I have had occasion to do, several of the doctrines and explanations of logical writers, and of Aldrich in particular, I wish it to be understood that this is not from my having formed a low estimate of the merits of the Compendium drawn up by the Author just mentioned, but, on the contrary, from its popularity, (it being the one commonly used at Oxford) —from the impossibility of noticing particularly all the points in which we agree,—and from the consideration that errors are the more carefully to be pointed out in proportion to the authority by which they are sanctioned.

I have to acknowledge assistance received from several friends who have at various times suggested remarks and alterations. But I cannot avoid particularizing the Rev. J. Newman, Fellow of Oriel College, who actually composed a considerable portion of the work as it now stands, from manuscripts not designed for publication, and who is the original author of several pages. Some valuable illustrations of the importance of attending to the ambiguity of the terms used in Political Economy, were furnished by the kindness of my friend and former pupil, Mr. Senior, of Magdalen College, and now Master in Chancery, who preceded me in the office of Professor of Political Economy at Oxford, and afterwards was appointed to the same at King's College, London. They are printed in the Appendix. But the friend to whom it is inscribed has contributed far more, and that, in the most important parts, than all others together; so much, indeed, that, though there is in the treatise nothing of his which has not undergone such expansion or modification as leaves me solely responsible for the whole, there is not a little of which I cannot fairly claim to be the Author.

Each successive edition has been revised with the utmost care. But though the work has undergone not only the close examination of myself and several friends, but the severer scrutiny of determined opponents, I am happy to find that no material errors have been detected, nor any considerable alterations found necessary.

On the utility of Logic many writers have said much in which I cannot coincide, and which has tended to bring the study into unmerited disrepute.

By representing Logic as furnishing the sole instrument for the *discovery of truth* in all subjects, and as teaching the use of the *intellectual faculties* in general, they raised expectations which could not be realised, and which naturally led to a re-action. The whole system, whose unfounded pretensions had been thus blazoned forth, came to be commonly regarded as utterly futile and empty: like several of our most valuable medicines, which, when first introduced, were proclaimed, each, as a panacea, infallible in the most opposite disorders; and which consequently, in many instances, fell for a time into total disuse; though, after a long interval, they were established in their just estimation, and employed conformably to their real properties.

In one of Lord Dudley's (lately published) letters to Bishop Copleston, of the date of 1814, he adduces a presumption against the study of Logic, that it was sedulously cultivated during the dark periods in which the intellectual powers of mankind seemed nearly paralyzed,—when no discoveries were made, and when various errors were wide-spread and deep-rooted: and that when the mental activity of the world revived, and philosophical inquiry flourished and bore its fruits, logical studies fell into decay and contempt. And this I have introduced in the "Elements of Rhetoric," (Part II. Ch. iii. § 2,) among other examples of a *presumption* not in itself unreasonable, but capable of being *rebutted* by a counter-presumption. When any study has been unduly or unwisely cultivated to the neglect of others, and has even been intruded into their province, there is a *presumption* that a re-action* will ensue, and an equally excessive contempt, or dread, or disgust, succeed. And in the present instance, the mistaken and absurd cultivation of Logic during Ages of great intellectual darkness, might have been expected to produce, in a subsequent age of comparative light, an association in men's minds, of Logic, with the idea of apathetic ignorance, prejudice, and adherence to error; so that the legitimate uses, and just value of the science (supposing it to have any) would be likely to be scornfully overlooked. Our ancestors having neglected to raise fresh crops of corn, and contented themselves with vainly threshing over and over the same straw and winnowing the same chaff, it might have been anticipated that their descendants would, for a time, regard the very operations of threshing and winnowing with contempt, and would attempt to grind corn, straw, and chaff all together.

The *revival* of a study which had for a long time been regarded as an obsolete absurdity, would probably have appeared to many persons, thirty years ago, as an undertaking far more difficult than the introduction of some *new* study;—as resembling rather the attempt to restore life to one of the antediluvian fossil-plants, than the rearing of a young seedling into a tree.

It is a curious circumstance that the very person to whom the letter just alluded to was addressed should have lived to witness so great a change of public

* See "Charge," 1843.

opinion brought about (in a great degree through *his own* instrumentality*) within the short interval—indeed within a small portion of the interval—between the writing of that letter and its publication, that the whole ground of the presumption alluded to has been completely cut away. During that interval, the treatise which was with his aid composed, and by his permission inserted in the Encyclopædia, attracted so much attention as to occasion its separate publication, in a volume which has been frequently reprinted, not only in England, but in the United States of America; where it is in use, I believe, in every one of their Colleges. Add to which, the frequent allusions (compared with what could have been met with twenty or thirty years ago) to the subject of Logic, by writers on various subjects. And moreover several other treatises on the subject, either original works or abridgements, have been making their appearance with continually increased frequency of late years. Some indeed of these have little or nothing in common with the present work except the title. But even that very circumstance is so far encouraging, as indicating that the *name* of this science instead of exciting, as formerly, an almost universal prejudice, is considered as likely to prove a recommendation. Certainly Lord Dudley, were he *now* living, would not speak of the general neglect and contempt of Logic; though every branch of Science, Philosophy, and Literature, have flourished during the interval.

* See Dedication.

To explain fully the utility of Logic is what can be done only in the course of an explanation of the system itself. One preliminary observation only (for the original suggestion of which I am indebted to the same friend to whom this work is inscribed) it may be worth while to offer in this place. If it were inquired what is to be regarded as the most appropriate intellectual occupation of MAN, *as* man, what would be the answer? The Statesman is engaged with political affairs; the Soldier with military; the Mathematician, with the properties of numbers and magnitudes; the Merchant, with commercial concerns, &c.; but in what are *all* and each of these employed?—employed, I mean, as *men;* for there are many modes of exercise of the faculties, mental as well as bodily, which are in great measure common to us with the lower animals. Evidently, in *Reasoning*. They are all occupied in deducing, well or ill, Conclusions from Premises; each, concerning the subject of his own particular business. If, therefore, it be found that the process going on daily, in each of so many different minds, is, in any respect, the *same,* and if the principles on which it is conducted can be reduced to a regular system, and if rules can be deduced from that system, for the better conducting of the process, then, it can hardly be denied that such a system and such rules must be especially worthy the attention,—not of the members of this or that profession merely, but—of every one who is desirous of possessing a cultivated mind. To understand the theory of that which is the appropriate intellectual occupation of Man in general, and to learn to do that *well*, which every one will and *must* do, whether well or ill, may surely be considered as an essential part of a liberal education.

Even supposing that no practical improvement in argumentation resulted from the study of Logic, it would not by any means follow that it is unworthy of attention. The pursuit of knowledge on curious and interesting subjects, for its own sake, is usually reckoned no misemployment of time; and is considered as, incidentally, if not directly, useful to the individual, by the exercise thus afforded to the mental faculties. All who study Mathematics are not training themselves to become Surveyors or Mechanics; some knowledge of Anatomy and Chemistry is even expected in a man liberally educated, though without any view to his practising Surgery or Medicine. And the investigation of a process which is peculiarly and universally the occupation of Man, considered as Man, can hardly be reckoned a less philosophical pursuit than those just instanced.

It has usually been assumed, however, in the case of the present subject, that a theory which does not tend to the improvement of practice is utterly unworthy of regard; and then, it is contended that Logic has no such tendency, on the plea that men may and do reason correctly without it: an objection which would equally apply in the case of Grammar, Music, Chemistry, Mechanics, &c., in all of which systems the practice must have existed previously to the theory.

But many who allow the use of systematic principles in other things, are accustomed to cry up Common-

Sense as the sufficient and only safe guide in Reasoning. Now by Common-Sense is meant, I apprehend, (when the term is used with any distinct meaning,) an exercise of the judgment unaided by any Art or system of rules: such an exercise as we must necessarily employ in numberless cases of daily occurrence; in which, having no established principles to guide us,—no line of procedure, as it were, distinctly chalked out,—we must needs act on the best extemporaneous conjectures we can form. He who is eminently skilful in doing this, is said to possess a superior degree of Common-Sense. But that Common-Sense is only our *second-best* guide—that the rules of Art, if judiciously framed, are always desirable when they can be had, is an assertion, for the truth of which I may appeal to the testimony of mankind in general; which is so much the more valuable, inasmuch as it may be accounted the testimony of *adversaries*. For the generality have a strong predilection in favour of Common-Sense, except in those points in which they, respectively, possess the knowledge of a system of rules; but in these points they deride any one who trusts to unaided Common-Sense. A Sailor *e.g.* will, perhaps, despise the pretensions of medical men, and prefer treating a disease by Common-Sense: but he would ridicule the proposal of navigating a ship by Common-Sense, without regard to the maxims of nautical art. A Physician, again, will perhaps contemn Systems of Political-Economy,* of Logic, or Metaphysics, and insist on

* See Senior's Introductory Lecture on Political Economy, p. 28.

the superior wisdom of trusting to Common-Sense in such matters; but he would never approve of trusting to Common-Sense in the treatment of diseases. Neither, again, would the Architect recommend a reliance on Common-Sense alone, in building, nor the Musician, in music, to the neglect of those systems of rules, which, in their respective arts, have been deduced from scientific reasoning aided by experience. And the induction might be extended to every department of practice. Since, therefore, each gives the preference to unassisted Common-Sense only in those cases where he himself has nothing else to trust to, and invariably resorts to the rules of art, wherever he possesses the knowledge of them, it is plain that mankind universally bear their testimony, though unconsciously and often unwillingly, to the preferableness of systematic knowledge to conjectural judgments.

There is, however, abundant room for the employment of Common-Sense in the *application* of the system. To *bring* arguments, out of the form in which they are expressed in conversation and in books, into the regular logical shape, must be, of course, the business of Common-Sense, aided by practice; for such arguments are, by supposition, not as yet within the province of Science; else they would *not* be irregular, but would be already strict syllogisms. To exercise the learner in this operation, I have subjoined in the Appendix, some examples, both of insulated arguments, and (in the later editions) of the analysis of argumentative works. It should be added, however, that a large portion of what is usually introduced into

Logical treatises, relative to the finding of Arguments, —the different kinds of them, &c., I have referred to the head of *Rhetoric*, and treated of in a work on the Elements of that Art.

It was doubtless from a strong and deliberate conviction of the advantages, direct and indirect, accruing from an acquaintance with Logic, that the University of Oxford, when re-modelling their system, not only retained that branch of study, regardless of the clamours of many of the half-learned, but even assigned a prominent place to it, by making it an indispensable part of the Examination for the first Degree. This last circumstance, however, I am convinced, has, in a a great degree, produced an effect opposite to what was designed. It has contributed to lower instead of exalting, the estimation of the study; and to withhold from it the earnest attention of many who might have applied to it with profit. I am not so weak as to imagine that any System can ensure great proficiency in any pursuit whatever, either in all students, or in a very large proportion of them: "we sow many seeds to obtain a few flowers:" but it might have been expected (and doubtless was expected) that a majority at least of successful candidates would derive some benefit worth mentioning from their logical pursuits; and that a considerable proportion of the distinguished candidates would prove respectable, if not eminent logicians. Such expectations I do not censure as unreasonable, or such as I might not have formed myself, had I been called upon to judge at that period when our experience was all to come. Subsequently, however, experience has shown that those expectations have been very inadequately realized. The truth is, that a very small proportion, even of distinguished students, ever become proficients in Logic; and that by far the greater part pass through the University without knowing anything at all of the subject. I do not mean that they have not learned by rote a string of technical terms; but that they understand absolutely nothing whatever of the principles of the science.

I am aware that some injudicious friends of Oxford will censure the frankness of this avowal. I have only to reply that such is the truth; and that I think too well of, and know far too well, the University in which I have been employed in various academical occupations above a quarter of a century, to apprehend danger to her reputation from declaring the exact truth. With all its defects, and no human institution is perfect, the University would stand, I am convinced, higher in public estimation than it does, were the whole truth, and nothing but the truth, in all points respecting it, more fully known. But the scanty and partial success of the measures employed to promote logical studies is the consequence, I apprehend, of the *universality* of the requisition. That which *must* be done by *every one,* will, of course, often be done but indifferently; and when the belief is once fully established, which it certainly has long been, that anything which is indispensable to a testimonial, has little or nothing to do with the attainment of honors,* the lowest standard soon becomes the established one in the minds of the greater number; and provided that standard be once reached, so as to secure the candidate from rejection, a greater or less proficiency in any such branch of study is regarded as a matter of indifference, as far as any views of academical distinction are concerned.

Divinity is one of these branches, and to this also most of what has been said concerning Logic might be considered as equally applicable; but, in fact, there are several important differences between the two cases. In the first place, most of the students who are designed for the Church, and many who are not, have a value for theological knowledge, independently of the requisition of the schools; and on that ground do not confine their views to the lowest admissible degree of proficiency: whereas this can be said of very few in the case of Logic. And moreover, such as design to become candidates for holy Orders, know that another examination in Theology awaits them. But a consideration, which is still more to the present purpose, is, that Theology, not being a Science, admits of infinite *degrees* of proficiency, from that which is within the reach of a child, up to the highest that is attainable by the most exalted genius; every one of which degrees is inestimably valuable as far as it goes. If any one understands tolerably the Church-catechism, or even half of it, he knows *some-*

* In the last-framed Examination-statute an express declaration has been inserted, that proficiency in Logic is to have weight in the assignment of honors.

thing of divinity; and that something is incalculably preferable to nothing. But it is not so with a Science: one who does not understand the principles of Euclid's demonstrations, whatever number of questions and answers he may have learnt by rote, knows absolutely nothing of Geometry: unless he attain this point, all his labour is utterly lost; worse than lost, perhaps, if he is led to believe that he has learnt something of Mathematics, when, in truth, he has not. And the same is the case with Logic, or any other Science. It does not admit of such various degrees, as a knowledge of religion. Of course I am far from supposing that all who understand anything, much or little, of a certain Science, stand on the same level; but I mean, what is surely undeniable, that one who does not embrace the fundamental principles, of a Science, whatever he may have taken on authority, and learned by rote, knows, properly speaking, nothing of that science. And such, I have no hesitation in saying, is the case with a considerable proportion even of those candidates who obtain testimonials, including many who gain distinction. There are some persons (probably not so many as one in ten, of such as have in other respects tolerable abilities,) who are physically incapable of the degree of steady abstraction requisite for really embracing the principles of Logic or of any other Science, whatever pains may be taken by themselves or their teachers. But there is a much greater number to whom this is a great *difficulty*, though not an impossibility; and who having, of course, a strong disinclination to such a study, look naturally to the very lowest admissible standard. And the example of such examinations in Logic as must be expected in the case of men of these descriptions, tends, in combination with popular prejudice, to degrade the study altogether in the minds of the generality.

It was from these considerations, perhaps, that it was proposed, a few years ago, to leave the study of Logic altogether to the option of the candidates; but the suggestion was rejected; the majority appearing to think (in which opinion I most fully coincide) that, so strongly as the tide of popular opinion set against the study, the result would have been, within a few years, an almost universal neglect of that science. Matters were accordingly left, at that time, in respect of this point, on their former footing; which I am convinced was far preferable to the proposed alteration.

But a middle course between these two was suggested, which I was persuaded would be infinitely preferable to either; a persuasion which I had long entertained, and which is confirmed by every day's observations and reflections; of which, few persons, I believe, have bestowed more on this subject. Let the study of Logic, it was urged, be made *optional to those who are merely candidates for a degree*, but indispensable to the *attainment of academical honors;* and the consequence would be, that it would speedily begin and progressively continue, to rise in estimation and to be studied with real profit. The examination might then, it was urged, without any hardship, be made a strict one; since no one could complain that a certain moderate degree of scientific ability, and a resolution to apply to a certain prescribed study, should be the conditions of obtaining *distinction*. The far greater part would still study Logic; since there would be (as before) but few who would be willing to exclude themselves from the possibility of obtaining distinction; but it would be studied with a very different mind, when ennobled, as it were, by being made part of the passport to University honors, and when a proficiency in it came to be regarded generally as an honorable distinction. And in proportion as the number increased of those who really understood the science, the number, it was contended, would increase of such as would value it on higher and better grounds. It would in time come to be better known and better appreciated by all the well-informed part of society: and lectures in Logic at the University would then, perhaps, no longer consist exclusively of an explanation of the mere elements. This would be necessary indeed for beginners; but to the more advanced students, the tutors would no more think of lecturing in the bare rudiments, than of lecturing in the Latin or Greek Grammar; but, in the same manner as they exercise their pupils in Grammar, by reading with them Latin and Greek authors with continual reference to grammar-rules, so, they would exercise them in Logic by reading some argumentative work, requiring an analysis of it on logical principles.

These effects could not indeed, it was acknowledged, be expected to show themselves *fully* till after a considerable lapse of time; but that the change would *begin* to appear, (and that very decidedly) within three or four years, was confidently anticipated.

To this it was replied, that it was most desirable that no one should be allowed to obtain the Degree of B.A. without a knowledge of Logic. This answer carries a plausible appearance to those unacquainted with the actual state of the University; though in fact it is totally irrelevant. For it goes on the supposition, that hitherto this object *has been* accomplished; —that every one who passes his examination does possess a knowledge of Logic; which is notoriously not the fact, nor ever can be, without some important change in some part of our system. The question therefore is, not, as the above objection would seem to imply, whether a real, profitable knowledge of Logic shall be strictly required of every candidate for a Degree, (for this in fact never has been done) but whether, in the attempt to accomplish this by requiring the *form* of a logical examination from every candidate without exception, we shall continue to degrade the science, and to let this part of the examination be regarded as a mere form, by many who might otherwise have studied Logic in earnest, and with advantage:—whether the great majority of candidates, and those too of a more promising description, shall lose a real and important benefit, through the attempt, (which, after all, experience has proved to be a vain attempt) to comprehend in this benefit a very small number, and of the least promising.

Something of an approach to the proposed alteration, was introduced into the Examination-statute passed in 1830; in which, permission is granted to such as are candidates merely for a testimonial, to substitute for Logic a portion of Euclid. I fear, however, that little or nothing will be gained by this; unless indeed the Examiners resolve to make the examinations in Logic far stricter than those in Euclid. For since every one who is capable of really understanding Euclid must be also capable of Logic, the alteration does not meet the case of those whose inaptitude for Science is invincible; and these are the very description of men whose (so called) logical-examinations tend to depress the science. Those few who really are physically incapable of scientific reasoning, and the far greater number who fancy themselves so, or who at least will rather run a risk than surmount their aversion, and set themselves to study in earnest,—all these will be likely, when the alternative is proposed, to prefer Logic to Euclid; because in the latter, it is hardly possible, at least not near so easy as in Logic, to present the semblance of preparation by learning questions and answers by rote:—in the cant phrase of undergraduates, by getting crammed. Experience has proved this, in the case of the Responsion-examinations, where the alternative of Logic or Euclid has always been proposed to the candidates; of whom those most averse to Science, or incapable of it, are almost always found to prefer Logic.

The determination *may* indeed be formed, and acted on from henceforth, that all who do in reality know nothing, properly speaking, of any Science, shall be rejected: all I know is, that this has never been the case hitherto.

Still, it is a satisfaction to me, that attention has been called to the evil in question, and an experimental measure adopted for its abatement. A confident hope is thus afforded, that in the event (which I much fear) of the failure of the experiment, some other more effectual measure may be resorted to.*

I am sensible that many may object, that this is not the proper place for such remarks as the foregoing: what has the Public at large, they may say, to do with the statutes of the University of Oxford? To this it might fairly be replied, that not only all who think of sending their sons or other near relatives to Oxford, but all likewise who are placed under the ministry of such as have been educated there, are indirectly concerned, to a certain degree, in the system there pursued. But the consideration which had the chief share in inducing me to say what I have, is, that the vindication of Logic from the prevailing disregard and contempt under which it labours, would have been altogether incomplete without it. For let it be remembered that the science is judged of by the Public in this country, in a very great degree, from the specimens displayed, and the reports made, by those whom Oxford sends forth. Every one, on looking into the

* Since this was written, the experiment has been tried. In the first Examination-list under the new Statute (Easter, 1831), of 125 candidates who did *not* aspire to the higher classes, *twenty-five* presented Euclid for their examination, and *one hundred*, Logic!

University-Calendar or Statute-Book, feels himself justified in assuming, that whoever has graduated at Oxford must be a Logician: not, indeed, necessarily, a first-rate Logician; but such as to satisfy the public examiners that he has a competent knowledge of the science. Now, if a very large proportion of these persons neither are, nor think themselves at all benefited by their (so called) logical education, and if many of them treat the study with contempt, and represent it as a mere tissue of obsolete and empty jargon, which it is a mere waste of time to attend to, let any one judge what conclusions respecting the utility of the study, and the wisdom of the University in upholding it, are likely to be the result.

That prejudices so deeply-rooted as those I have alluded to, and supported by the authority of such eminent names, especially that of Locke, and (as is commonly, though not very correctly supposed) Bacon, should be overthrown at once by the present treatise, I am not so sanguine as to expect; but if I have been successful in refuting some of the most popular objections, and explaining some principles which are in general ill-understood, it may be hoped that just notions on the subject may continue (as they have begun) to gain ground more and more.

It may be permitted me to mention, that as I have addressed myself to various classes of students, from the most uninstructed tyro, to the furthest-advanced Logician, and have touched accordingly both on the most elementary principles, and on some of the most remote deductions from them, it must be expected that readers of each class will find some parts not well calculated for them. Some explanations will appear to the one too simple and puerile; and for another class, some of the disquisitions will be at first too abstruse. If to each description some portions are found interesting, it is as much as I can expect.

With regard to the style, I have considered *perspicuity* not only, as it always must be, the first point, but as one of such paramount importance in such a subject, as to justify the neglect of all others. Prolixity of explanation,—homeliness in illustration,—and baldness of expression, I have regarded as blemishes not worth thinking of, when anything was to be gained in respect of clearness. To some of my readers a temporary difficulty may occasionally occur from the use of some technical terms different, or differently applied, from what they have been accustomed to.* They must consider, however, that the attempt to conform in this point to the usage of *every* logical writer, would have been, on account of their variations from each other, utterly hopeless. I have endeavoured, in the terms employed, to make no wanton innovations, but to conform generally to established usage, except when there is some very strong objection to it;—where usage is divided, to prefer what may appear in each case the most convenient term;—and, above all, to explain distinctly the sense in which each is employed in the present work.

If any should complain of my not having given a

* See Book II. Chap. i. § 1.

history of all the senses in which each technical term has been used by each writer from its first introduction, and a review of the works of each, I can only reply that my design was not to write a Logical Archæology, or a Commentary on the works of former Logicians, but an elementary introduction to the science. And few, I suppose, would consider a treatise, for instance, on Agriculture, as incomplete, which should leave untouched the questions of, who was the inventor of the plough,—what successive alterations that implement has undergone,—and from what region wheat was first introduced.

And if again any should complain of the omission of such metaphysical disquisitions on the laws of thought, and the constitution of the human mind generally, as they have been accustomed to include under the head of *Logic*, my answer must be, that that term has been employed by me in a different sense; for reasons which I have stated in several parts of this treatise, and especially in Book IV. Chap. iii.; and that I am therefore only to be censured, at the utmost, as not having undertaken a work of a different kind, and on a different subject.

I would not, on the other hand, be understood as complaining of those who have used the word Logic in a more extended sense, or as underrating the value of their works. Only, the reader should be cautioned against the mistake — much commoner, I believe, than is generally thought—of confounding the extension of the *application of a name*, with the enlargement of the boundaries of a science.

It is proper however to mention that the first Part of the "Elements of Rhetoric" contains a discussion of such points as many writers have treated of under the department of Logic.

The technical language employed in this treatise, is, throughout, with the exception of a very few cases where some departure from ancient usage appeared indispensable, that of the older works on the subject. Some degree of prejudice perhaps might have been, in the outset, avoided, and a far greater *appearance* of originality produced, by adopting novel forms of expression. There are also many writers who have found fault with the established technical language, as cumbrous and perplexing. I have always found however that the phraseology they adopt in its stead consists of far more tedious circumlocution than that which they censure; while it is often less clear and less correct.

It should be observed however that all technical language (as well as all rules of art) must be expected to present, at first, a difficulty for the learner to surmount; though in the end, it will greatly facilitate his procedure. But with this view it is necessary that such language and rules should be not only distinctly *understood*, but also learnt, and *remembered* as familiarly as the Alphabet, and employed *constantly*, and with scrupulous *exactness*. Otherwise technical language will prove an encumbrance instead of an advantage; just as a suit of clothes would be, if instead of putting them on and *wearing* them, one should carry them about in his hands.

Of the correctness of the fundamental doctrines maintained in the work, I may be allowed to feel some confidence; not so much from the length of time that I have been more or less occupied with it,—enjoying at the same time the advantage of frequent suggestions and corrections from several judicious friends,—as from the nature of the subject. In works of taste, an author cannot be sure that the judgment of the Public will coincide with his own; and if he fail to give pleasure, he fails of his sole or most appropriate object. But in the case of truths which admit of scientific demonstration, it is possible to arrive by reasoning at as full an assurance of the justness of the conclusions established, as the imperfection of the human faculties will admit; and experience, accompanied with attentive observation, and with repeated trials of various methods, may enable one long accustomed to tuition, to ascertain with considerable certainty what explanations are the best comprehended. Many parts of the detail, however, may probably be open to objections; but if (as experience now authorizes me the more confidently to hope) no errors are discovered, which materially affect the substantial utility of the work, but only such as detract from the credit of the author, the object will have been attained which I *ought* to have had principally in view.

No credit, I am aware, is given to an author's own disclaimer of personal motives, and profession of exclusive regard for public utility; since even sincerity cannot, on this point, secure him from deceiving himself; but it may be allowable to observe, that one whose object was the increase of his reputation as a writer, could hardly have chosen a subject less suitable for his purpose than the present. At the time of the first publication, the study was neither popular, nor, apparently, likely soon to become so. Ignorance, fortified by prejudice, opposed its reception, even in the minds of those who are considered as both candid and well-informed. And as, on the one hand, a large class of modern philosophers might be expected to raise a clamour against "obsolete prejudices;" "bigoted devotion to the decrees of Aristotle;" "confining the human mind in the trammels of the Schoolmen," &c., so, on the other hand, all such as really are thus bigoted to everything that has been long established, merely because it has been long established, were likely to exclaim against the presumption of an author, who presumes to depart in several points from the track of his predecessors.

There is another circumstance, also, which tends materially to diminish the credit of a writer on this and some other kindred subjects. We can make no discoveries of *striking novelties:* the senses of our readers are not struck, as with the return of a Comet which had been foretold, or the extinction of a taper in carbonic-acid gas: the materials we work upon are common and familiar to all, and, therefore, supposed to be well understood by all. And not only is any one's deficiency in the use of these materials, such as is generally unfelt by himself, but when it is removed by satisfactory explanations—when the notions, which had been perplexed and entangled, are cleared up by the introduction of a few simple and apparently obvious principles, he will generally forget that any explanation at all was needed, and consider all that has been said as mere truisms, which even a child could supply to himself. Such is the nature of the fundamental principles of a science—they are so fully *implied* in the most evident and well-known truths, that the moment they are fully embraced, it becomes a difficulty to conceive that we could ever have been not aware of them. And hence, the more simple, clear, and obvious any principle is rendered, the more likely is its exposition to elicit those common remarks, "of course! of course!" "no one could ever doubt that;" "this is all very true, but there is nothing *new* brought to light;—nothing that was not familiar to every one," "there needs no ghost to tell us that." I am convinced that a verbose, mystical, and partially obscure way of writing on such a subject, is the most likely to catch the attention of the multitude. The generality verify the observation of Tacitus, "omne ignotum pro mirifico:" and when any thing is made very plain to them, are apt to fancy that they knew it already; so that the explanations of scientific truths are likely, for a considerable time at least, to be, by most men, underrated the more, the more perfectly they accomplish their object.

A very slow progress, therefore, towards popularity (far slower indeed than has in fact taken place) is the utmost that I expected for such a treatise as I have endeavoured to make the present. I felt myself bound, however, not only as a member of Society, but more especially as a Minister of the Gospel, to use my endeavours towards promoting an object which to me appears highly important, and (what is much more) whose importance was appreciated by very few besides. The cause of Truth universally, and not least, of religious Truth, is benefited by every thing that tends to promote sound reasoning, and facilitate the detection of fallacy. The adversaries of our Faith would, I am convinced, have been on many occasions more satisfactorily answered, and would have had fewer openings for cavil, had a thorough acquaintance with Logic been a more common *qualification than it is*. In lending my endeavours, therefore, whether with greater or less success, towards this object, I trust that I am neither uselessly nor unsuitably employed.

Those who are engaged in, or designed for the Sacred Ministry, and all others who are sensible that the cause of true Religion is not a concern of the Ministry alone, should remember that this is no time to forego any of the advantages which that cause may derive from an active and judicious cultivation of the faculties. Among the enemies of Christianity in the present day, are included, if I mistake not, a very different description of persons from those who were chiefly to be met with a century, or even half a century ago: what were called "men of wit and pleasure about town;"—ignorant, shallow, flippant declaimers, or dull and powerless pretenders to Philosophy. Among the enemies of the Gospel now, are to be found men not only of learning and ingenuity, but of *cultivated argumentative powers*, and not unversed in the principles of Logic. If the advocates of our Religion think proper to disregard this help, they will find, on careful inquiry, that *their opponents do not.* And let them not trust too carelessly to the strength of their cause. Truth will, indeed, prevail, where all other points are nearly equal; but it may suffer a temporary discomfiture, if hasty assumptions, unsound arguments, and vague and empty declamation, occupy the place of a train of close, accurate, and luminous reasoning.

It is not, however, solely, or chiefly, for polemical purposes, that the cultivation of the reasoning-faculty is desirable; in persuading, in investigating, in learning, or teaching, in all the multitude of cases in which it is our object to arrive at just conclusions, or to lead others to them, it is most important. A knowledge of logical rules will not indeed supply the want of other knowledge; nor was it ever proposed, by any one who really understood this science, to substitute it for any other: but it is no less true that no other can be substituted for this; that it is valuable in every branch of study; and that it enables us to use to the greatest advantage the knowledge we possess. It is to be hoped, therefore, that those Academical Bodies, who have been wise enough to retain this science, will, instead of being persuaded to abandon it, give their attention rather to its improvement and more effectual cultivation.

ADVERTISEMENT

TO

THE EIGHTH EDITION.

In the present edition several passages have been transferred from the parts of the work in which they had formerly been placed, to others; and some have been altered in expression.

The reader will please to observe that the angular brackets are used to indicate that the word [thus] enclosed is equivalent in sense to that which precedes it.

CONTENTS.

ELEMENTS OF LOGIC.

INTRODUCTION.

Definition of Logic.

§ 1. Logic, in the most extensive sense in which it has been thought advisable to employ the name, may be considered as the Science, and also as the Art, of Reasoning. It investigates the principles on which argumentation is conducted, and furnishes such rules as may be derived from those principles, for guarding against erroneous deductions. Its most appropriate office, however, is that of instituting an analysis of the process of the mind in Reasoning; and in this point of view it is, as I have said, strictly a *Science:* while, considered in reference to the practical rules above mentioned, it may be called the *Art* of Reasoning. For it is to be remembered, that as a *science* is conversant about speculative *knowledge only,* and *art* is the *application* of knowledge to *practice,* hence, Logic (as well as any other system of knowledge) becomes, when applied to practice, an *art;* while confined to the *theory* of reasoning, it is strictly a *science:* and it is as such that it occupies the higher place in point of dignity, since it professes to develop some of the most interesting and curious intellectual phenomena.*

Prevailing Mistakes respecting Logic.

Considering how early Logic attracted the attention of philosophers, it may appear surprising that so little progress should have been

* It is surely strange, therefore, to find in a treatise on Logic, (Aldrich's) a distinct dissertation to prove that it is an Art, and *not* a Science!

made, as is confessedly the case, in developing its principles, and perfecting the detail of the system; and this circumstance has been brought forward as a proof of the barrenness and futility of the study. But a similar argument might have been urged with no less plausibility, at a period not very remote, against the study of Natural Philosophy; and, very recently, against that of Chemistry. No science can be expected to make any considerable progress, which is not cultivated on right principles. Whatever may be the inherent vigour of the plant, it will neither be flourishing nor fruitful till it meet with a suitable soil and culture: and in no case is the remark more applicable than in the present; the greatest mistakes having always prevailed respecting the nature of Logic; and its province having in consequence been extended by many writers to subjects with which it has no proper connexion. Indeed, with the exception perhaps of Aristotle, (who is himself, however, not entirely exempt from the errors in question,) hardly a writer on Logic can be mentioned who has clearly perceived, and steadily kept in view throughout, its real nature and object. Before his time, no distinction was drawn between the science of which we are speaking, and that which is now usually called Metaphysics; a circumstance which alone shows how small was the progress made in earlier times. Indeed, those who first turned their attention to the subject, hardly thought of inquiring into the process of Reasoning itself, but confined themselves almost entirely to certain preliminary points, the discussion of which is (if logically considered) subordinate to that of the main inquiry.

History of Logic distinct from the teaching of the science.

To give even a very condensed account of the lives and works of all the principal writers on Logic,—of the technical terms introduced by each, and the senses in which each employed them,—and of the improvements or corruptions that were from time to time introduced,—in short, to write the History and Antiquities of Logical Science,—would be foreign to my present design. Such a work, if undertaken by a competent writer, would be, though not of a popular character, yet highly interesting and instructive to a limited class of students. But the extensive research which would form one indispensable qualification for such a task, would be only one out of many, even less common, qualifications, without which such a work would be worse than useless. The author should be one thoroughly on his guard against the common error of confounding together, or leading his readers to confound, an intimate acquaintance with many *books* on a given subject, and a clear insight into the subject itself. With ability and industry for investigating a multitude of minute particulars, he should possess the power of rightly estimating each according to its intrinsic importance, and not (as is very commonly done,) according to the degree of *laborious research* it may have cost him, or the *rarity* of the knowledge he may in any case have acquired. And he should be careful, while recording the opinions and expressions of various authors on points of science, to guard both himself and his readers against the mistake of taking anything on *authority*, that ought to be evinced by scientific reasoning; or of regarding each technical term as having a sort of prescriptive right to retain for ever the meaning attached to it by those who first introduced it. In no subject, in short, is it more important for an author to be free from all tinge of *antiquarian pedantry*.

But if I felt myself as fully competent to the task of writing such a history of Logic as I have alluded to, as I am conscious of not being so, I should still decidedly prefer keeping such a work altogether distinct from a treatise on the science; because the combination of the two in a single volume would render it the more difficult to avoid the blending of them confusedly together; and also because, on such a plan, the distinction could not be so easily preserved between Logic, in the sense in which I am here using that title, and various metaphysical disquisitions to which several writers have given the same name.

For these reasons I have thought it best to take only a slight and rapid glance of the series of logical writers down to the present day, and of the general tendency of their labours.

Early writers on Logic.

§ 2. Zeno the Eleatic, whom most accounts represent as the earliest systematic writer on the subject of Logic, or, as it was then called, Dialectics, divided his work into three parts; the first of which (upon Consequences) is censured by Socrates [Plato, *Parmen.*] for obscurity and confusion. In his second part, however, he furnished that interrogatory method of disputation [ἐρώτησις] which Socrates adopted, and which has since borne his name. The third part of his work was devoted to what may not be improperly termed the art of wrangling [ἐριστική], which supplied the disputant with a collection of sophistical questions, so contrived, that the concession of some point that seemed unavoidable, immediately involved some glaring absurdity. This, if it is to be esteemed as at all falling within the province of Logic, is certainly not to be regarded (as some have ignorantly or heedlessly represented it) as its principal or proper business. The Greek philosophers generally have unfortunately devoted too much attention to it; but we must beware of falling into the vulgar error of supposing the ancients to have regarded as a serious and intrinsically important study, that which in fact they considered as an ingenious recreation. The disputants diverted themselves in their leisure-hours by making trial of their own and their adversary's acuteness, in the endeavour mutually to perplex each other with subtle fallacies; much in the same way as men amuse themselves with propounding and guessing riddles, or with the game of chess; to each of which diversions the sportive disputations of the ancients bore much resemblance. They were closely analogous to the wrestling and other exercises of the Gymnasium; these last being reckoned conducive to bodily vigour and activity, as the former were to habits of intellectual acuteness; but the *immediate* object in each was a sportive, not a serious contest; though doubtless fashion and emulation often occasioned an undue importance to be attached to success in each.

Zeno.

Zeno, then, is hardly to be regarded as any further a logician than as to what respects his *erotetic* method of disputation; a course of argument constructed on this principle being properly an hypothetical Sorites, which may easily be reduced into a series of syllogisms.

Euclid and Antisthenes.

To Zeno succeeded Euclid of Megara, and Antisthenes; both pupils of Socrates. The former of these prosecuted the subject of the third part of his predecessor's treatise, and is said to have been the author of many of the fallacies attributed to the Stoical school. Of the writings of the latter nothing certain is known; if, however, we suppose the above-mentioned sect to be his disciples in this study, and to have retained his principles, he certainly took a more correct view of the subject than Euclid. The Stoics divided all λεκτὰ,—every thing that could be said,—into three classes; 1st, the Simple Term; 2d, the Proposition; 3d, the Syllogism; *viz.* the *hypothetical;* for they seem to have had little notion of a more rigorous analysis of argument than into that familiar form.

Archytas.

We must not here omit to notice the merits of Archytas, to whom we are indebted (as he himself probably was, in a great degree, to older writers) for the doctrines of the Categories. He, however, (as well as the other writers on the subject) appears to have had no distinct view of the proper object and just limits of the science of Logic; but to have blended with it metaphysical discussions not strictly connected with it, and to have dwelt on the investigation of the nature of Terms and Propositions, without maintaining a constant reference to the principles of Reasoning; to which all the rest should be made subservient.

Aristotle. The state, then, in which Aristotle found the science (if, indeed, it can properly be said to have existed at all before his time) appears to have been nearly this: the division into Simple Terms, Propositions, and Syllogisms, had been slightly sketched out; the doctrine of the Categories, and perhaps that of the Opposition of propositions, had been laid down; and, as some believe, the analysis of Species into Genus and Differentia had been introduced by Socrates. These, at best, were rather the materials of the system, than the system itself; the foundation of which indeed he distinctly claims the merit of having laid, and which remains fundamentally the same as he left it.

It has been remarked, that the logical system is one of those few theories which have been begun and completed by the same individual. The history of its discovery, as far as the main principles of the science are concerned, properly commences and ends with Aristotle; and this may perhaps in part account for the subsequent perversions of it. The brevity and simplicity of its fundamental truths (to which point indeed all real Science is perpetually tending) has probably led many to suppose that something much more complex, abstruse, and mysterious, remained to be discovered. The vanity, too, by which all men are prompted unduly to magnify their own pursuits, has led unphilosophical minds, not in this case alone, but in many others, to extend the boundaries of their respective sciences, not by the patient development and just application of the principles of those sciences, but by wandering into irrelevant subjects. The mystical employment of *numbers* by Pythagoras, in matters utterly foreign to arithmetic, is perhaps the earliest instance of the kind. A more curious and important one is the degeneracy of Astronomy into judicial Astrology; but none is more striking than the misapplication of Logic, by those who have treated of it as "the art of rightly employing the rational faculties," or who have intruded it into the province of Natural Philosophy, and regarded the Syllogism as an engine for the investigation of nature; while they overlooked the extensive field that was before them within the legitimate limits of the science; and perceived not the importance and difficulty of the task, of completing and properly filling up the masterly sketch before them.

The writings of Aristotle were not only for the most part absolutely lost to the world for about two centuries, but seem to have been but little studied for a long time after their recovery. An art, however, of Logic, derived from the principles traditionally preserved by his disciples, seems to have been generally known, and to have been employed by Cicero in his philosophical works; but the pursuit of the science seems to have been abandoned for a long time. As early in the Christian era as the second and third centuries, the Peripatetic doctrines experienced a considerable revival; and we meet with the names of Galen, Ammonius, (who seems to have taken the lead among the commentators on Aristotle) Alexander of Aphrodisias, and Porphyry, as logicians; but it is not till the close of the fifth century, or the beginning of the sixth, that Aristotle's logical works were translated into Latin by the celebrated Boethius.* Not one of these seems to have made any considerable advances in developing the theory of reasoning. Of the labours of Galen (who added the insignificant fourth Figure to the three recognised by Aristotle) little is known; and Porphyry's principal work is merely on the *predicables*. We have little of

Galen, Ammonius, Alexander, Porphyry.

Boethius.

* Born about A.D. 475, and died about A.D. 524.

the science till the revival of learning among the Arabians, by whom Aristotle's treatises on this as well as on other subjects, were eagerly studied.

Schoolmen. § 3. Passing by the names of some Byzantine writers of no great importance, we come to the times of the Schoolmen; whose waste of ingenuity, and frivolous subtilty of disputation, have been often made the subject of complaints, into the justice of which it is unnecessary here fully to inquire. It may be sufficient to observe, that their fault did not lie in their diligent study of Logic, and the high value they set upon it, but in their utterly mistaking the true nature and object of the science; and by the attempt to employ it for the purpose of physical discoveries, involving every subject in a mist of words, to the exclusion of sound philosophical investigation.* Their errors may serve to account for the strong terms in which Bacon sometimes appears to censure logical pursuits; but that this censure was intended to bear against the extravagant perversions, not the legitimate cultivation, of the science, may be proved from his own observations on the subject, in his *Advancement of Learning.* *Bacon.* "Had Bacon lived in the present day, I am inclined to think he would have made his chief complaint against unmethodized inquiry and illogical reasoning. Certainly he would *not* have complained of *Dialectics* as corrupting Philosophy. To guard *now* against the evils prevalent in *his* time, would be to fortify a town against battering-rams, instead of against cannon."†

Locke. His moderation, however, was not imitated in other quarters. Even Locke confounds in one sweeping censure the Aristotelic theory, with the absurd misapplications and perversions of it in later years. His objection to the science, as unserviceable in the *discovery*

* Of the character of the School-*divinity*, Dr. Hampden's Bampton Lectures furnish the best view that has, perhaps, ever appeared.

† Pol. Econ. Lect. ix. p. 237.

of truth (which has of late been often repeated), while it holds good in reference to many (misnamed) logicians, indicates that, with regard to the true nature of the science itself, he had no clearer notions than they have, of the just limits of logical science, as confined to the theory of Reasoning; and of the distinct character of that operation from the observations and experiments which are essential to the study of Nature.

For instance, in chap. xvii. "on Reason," (which, by the way, he perpetually confounds with *Reasoning*,) he says, in § 4, "If syllogisms must be taken for the only proper instrument of reason and means of knowledge, it will follow, that before Aristotle there was not one man that did or could know any thing by reason; and that since the invention of syllogisms there is not one in ten thousand that doth. But God has not been so sparing to men to make them barely two-legged creatures, and left it to Aristotle to make them rational, *i. e.* those few of them that he could get so to examine the grounds of syllogisms, as to see that in above threescore ways that three propositions may be laid together, there are but fourteen wherein one may be sure that the conclusion is right," *&c.* "God has been more bountiful to mankind than so: He has given them a mind that can reason without being instructed in methods of syllogizing," *&c.* All this is not at all less absurd than if any one, on being told of the discoveries of modern chemists respecting caloric, and on hearing described the process by which it is conducted through a boiler into the water, which it converts into a gas of sufficient elasticity to overcome the pressure of the atmosphere, *&c.*, should reply, "If all this were so, it would follow that before the time of these chemists no one ever did or could make any liquor boil."

He presently after inserts an encomium upon Aristotle, in which he is equally unfortunate; he praises him for the "*invention* of syllogisms:" to which he certainly had no more claim than Linnæus to the *creation* of plants and animals;

or Harvey, to the praise of having *made the blood circulate;* or Lavoisier, to that of having *formed the atmosphere* we breathe. And the utility of this invention consists, according to him, in the great service done against "those who were not ashamed to deny anything;" a service which never could have been performed, had syllogisms been an invention or discovery of Aristotle's; for what sophist could ever have consented to *restrict himself to one particular kind of arguments, dictated by his opponent?*

In an ordinary, obscure, and trifling writer, all this confusion of thought and common-place declamation might as well have been left unnoticed; but it is due to the general ability and to the celebrity of such an author as Locke, that errors of this kind should be exposed.

Watts.

An error apparently different, but substantially the same, pervades the treatises of Watts, and some other modern writers on the subject. Perceiving the inadequacy of the syllogistic theory to the vast purposes to which others had attempted to apply it, he still craved after the attainment of some equally comprehensive and all-powerful system; which he accordingly attempted to construct under the title of *The Right Use of Reason,*—which was to be a method of invigorating and properly directing all the powers of the mind:—a most magnificent object indeed, but one which not only does not fall under the province of Logic, but cannot be accomplished by any *one* science or system that can even be conceived to exist. The attempt to comprehend so wide a field, is no extension of science, but a mere verbal generalization, which leads only to vague and barren declamation.

It is not perhaps much to be wondered at, that in still later times several ingenious writers, forming their notions of the science itself from professed masters in it, such as have just been alluded to, and judging of its value from their failures, should have treated the Aristotelic system with so much reprobation and scorn.

Extravagant expectations of some writers.

The vague aspirations of some of these writers after a "true"—"rational"—"philosophical system of Logic," which, year after year, and generation after generation, is talked of, and hoped for, and almost promised, but which is acknowledged to have never yet existed,* may recall to one's mind the gorgeous visions which floated before the imagination of the Alchemists, of the Philosopher's Stone, and the Universal Medicine; and which made them regard with impatience and with scorn the humble labours of existing Metallurgy and Pharmacy. I believe that in respect of the present subject, the views I am alluding to arise in great measure from men's not perceiving that *Language*,† of some kind or other, is (as will be more fully shown hereafter) an *indispensable instrument* of all Reasoning that properly deserves the name.

Tendency to Realism.

And hence it is that one may find such writers as I allude to speaking disdainfully of "rules applicable merely to *reasoning in words*;"—representing Language as serviceable only "in *conveying* arguments to another;" and even as "limiting the play of our faculties;" and again as "rendering the mental perception of all abstract truths obscure and confused, in so far as the rude symbol of each idea is taken in the stead of the idea itself;" with other such expressions, emanating from that which is in truth the ancient and still prevalent doctrine of "Realism."

Incorrect views of the nature of the science.

The Syllogistic theory has usually been considered by these objectors as professing to furnish a *peculiar* method of reasoning, instead

* I have even seen a complaint made, that the introduction of some such perfect system has been prevented, by the application of the term Logic to that which is commonly so called. We do not find, however, that the application of the names of Astronomy and Chemistry to the studies formerly so called, prevented the origination of more philosophical systems.

† Hobbes, who has very clearly pointed this out, has unhappily diminished the benefit that might have been derived from much that he has written, by the prejudice he has raised against himself through his exceptionable doctrines in Morals, Politics, and Religion.

of a method of analyzing that mental process which must *invariably* take place in all correct reasoning; and accordingly they have contrasted the ordinary mode of reasoning with the syllogistic, and have brought forward with an air of triumph the argumentative skill of many who never learned the system; a mistake no less gross than if any one should regard Grammar as a peculiar Language, and should contend against its utility, on the ground that many speak correctly who never studied the principles of grammar. For Logic, which is, as it were, the Grammar of Reasoning, does not bring forward the regular Syllogism as a *distinct mode of argumentation*, designed to be *substituted* for any other mode;* but as the form to which *all* correct reasoning may be ultimately reduced: and which, consequently, serves the purpose (when we are employing Logic as an *art*) of a test to try the validity of any argument; in the same manner as by chemical analysis we develop and submit to a distinct examination the elements of which any compound body is composed, and are thus enabled to detect any latent sophistication and impurity.

§ 4. Many misconceptions not very dissimilar to those of Locke, which continue to prevail, more or less, in the present day, will be hereafter noticed, as far as is needful, in appropriate places. In this Introduction it would be unsuitable to advert to them except very briefly, and that, only with a view to caution the learner, unused to these studies, against being disheartened in the outset, by hearing, generally, that objections have been raised against the

* Strange as it may seem, there are some, (I suspect not a few,) who even go a step further, and consider Logic as something *opposed* to right reasoning, I have seen a Review, of a work which the Reviewer characterised as the production of an able *Logician*, and which he *therefore* concluded was likely to have influence with such as will *not* reason! The "not" might naturally have been regarded as a misprint, but that the context shows that such was the reviewer's real meaning.

On seeing such a passage written in the 19th century, who can wonder that in the Middle Ages, Grammar ("Gramarye") was regarded as a kind of magical art?

leading principles of the science, by writers of considerable repute; objections which he will hardly suppose to be, in so great a degree as they really are, either founded on mistake, or unimportant, and turning, in reality, on mere verbal questions.

For instance, some, he may be told, have maintained that men reason,—or that they may reason,—from a *single* premiss, without any other being either expressed or understood;—that men may, and do, reason from *one individual* case to another, without the intervention of any *general* [universal] proposition, whether stated or implied;—that the inferences from *Induction* are not drawn by any process that is, in substance, Syllogistic;—that the conclusion of a Syllogism is *not* really inferred from the Premises;—that a Syllogism is nothing but a kind of *trap* for ensnaring the incautious; and that it necessarily involves the *fallacy* of "begging the question;" with other such formidably-sounding objections; which, when simply spoken of as being afloat, and as maintained by able men, are likely to be supposed far more powerful than they will be found on a closer examination.

Of those who speak of a *single* premiss being sufficient to warrant a conclusion, some, it will be found, were confining their thoughts to such flat and puerile examples as Logical writers are too apt to employ exclusively; as "Socrates is a man; therefore he is a living-creature, &c.;" in which the conclusion had been already stated in the *one* premiss, to any one who does but *understand the meaning of the words;* "living-creature" being a part of what is signified in the very term "Man." But in such an instance as this; "He has swallowed a cup of laurel-water, therefore he has taken poison," the inference is one which no one could draw who should be ignorant—as *everybody* was, less than a century ago (though using the *word* in the *same sense* as now, to signify a "liquor distilled from laurel-leaves") that this liquor is poisonous.

Others again, when they speak of reasoning from one individual instance to another, without any universal premiss, mean sometimes, that no such premiss is *expressed,* (which is the case oftener than not) and that perhaps even the reasoner himself, if possessed of no great command of language, might be at a loss to state it correctly.* And indeed it continually happens that even long trains of reasoning will flash through the mind with such rapidity that the process is performed unconsciously, or at least leaves no trace in the memory, any more than the motions of the muscles of the throat and mouth in speaking, or the judgments by which we decide as to the *distances* of visible objects:† so that a conclusion may be supposed to be seized by intuition, which in reality is the result of rapid inference.

Some, again, appear to include under the title of "reasoning" every case in which a person believes one thing in consequence of his believing another thing; however far he may be from having any good grounds to warrant the

* It may be added, that in inward solitary reasoning, many, and perhaps most persons, but especially those not much accustomed to read or speak concerning the subjects that occupy their thoughts, make use, partly, of signs that are *not arbitrary* and *conventional,* but which consist of mental-*conceptions* of individual objects; taken, each, as a representative of a Class. *E. g.* a person practically conversant with mechanical operations, but not with discussions of them in words, may form a conception of—in colloquial phrase, "figure to himself"—a certain field or room, with whose shape he is familiar, and may employ this, in his inward trains of thought, as a Sign, to represent, for instance, "parallelogram" or "trapezium," &c.; or he may "figure to himself" a man raising a weight by means of a pole, and may use this conception as a general sign, in place of the term "lever;" and the terms themselves he may be unacquainted with; in which case he will be at a loss to impart distinctly to others his own reasonings; and in the attempt, will often express himself (as one may frequently observe in practical men unused to reading and speaking) not only indistinctly, but even erroneously. See below, § 5. Hence, partly, may have arisen the belief in those supposed "abstract ideas" which will be hereafter alluded to, and in the possibility of reasoning without the use of any Signs at all.

† The distance of an object having been, till a comparatively late period, supposed to be directly perceived by the eye.

inference: and they accordingly include those processes which take place in the minds of infants and of brutes; which are apt to *associate* with the appearance of an object before them the remembered impression of something that formerly accompanied it. Such a process is alluded to in the familiar proverbs that "A burnt child dreads the fire;" or as it is expressed in another form, "The scalded cat fears cold water;" or again in the Hebrew proverb, "He who has been bitten by a serpent is afraid of a rope." Most logical writers however have confined the name of "reasoning" to *valid* argument; which cannot exist without a universal premiss, implied, if not expressed. For whenever there are not two premises which, taken jointly, do imply, and virtually assert, the conclusion,—the alleged premiss or premises being such that a person may without inconsistency believe them true and yet not believe the conclusion,—then, we have what Logicians have been accustomed to call an *apparent*, but *not real* argument.

Some however have denied that the conclusion is inferred from the universal premiss. But then, they acknowledge that the truth of that premiss is an indispensable *condition* of such inference: an admission which would satisfy most Logicians. For if any botanical physiologist for instance, were to deny that the branches of a tree derive nourishment from the roots, saying that the branches are nourished by the juices of the earth, but admitting that the roots are an indispensable condition, and that if they are destroyed, the branches will wither, this would not be reckoned as substantially any new doctrine. And so also if any one chuse to maintain that the conclusion is drawn *from* the one premiss, *by*, or *through*, the other premiss, this would be accounted merely a needless and unimportant innovation in phraseölogy.

So also when inferences from Induction are spoken of as not being — or not necessarily being — substantially Syllogistic, the learner might at first sight be startled and perplexed, till he found it at the same time admitted that we have to decide, in each case of Induction, the question, whether the instances adduced be "sufficient" to warrant the inference;—whether it be "allowable" to draw the conclusion. And the decision of this question in the affirmative,—*i. e.* the decision that the procedure is not a mere random guess,—is, if expressed in words, *the very premiss* necessary to complete the Syllogism. (See B. iv. ch. i. § 1.)

So also it will be seen that the alleged *entrapping* character of a Syllogism, merely amounts to this; that whoever perceives the validity of an argument, has no mode of escape from the "snare" (so called) *except by the way he entered,* viz. the *premisses.* He has only the alternative of allowing one of *them* to be false, or else, the conclusion to be true. And it is a matter of daily occurrence, that a man is undeceived as to some principle he had incautiously admitted, by perceiving what it would lead to.

Complaints against Logic.

§ 5. Complaints have also been made that Logic leaves untouched the greatest difficulties, and those which are the sources of the chief errors in reasoning; *viz.* the ambiguity or indistinctness of Terms, and the doubts respecting the degrees of evidence in various Propositions: an objection which is not to be removed by any such attempt as that of Watts to lay down "rules for forming clear ideas," and, for "guiding the judgment;" but by replying that no art is to be censured for not teaching more than falls within its province, and indeed more than can be taught by any conceivable art. Such a system of universal knowledge as should instruct us in the full meaning or meanings of every term, and the truth or falsity,—certainty or uncertainty,—of every proposition, thus superseding all other studies, it is most unphilosophical to expect, or even to imagine. And to find fault with Logic for not performing this, is as if one should object to the science of Optics for not giving sight to the blind; or as if (like the man of whom Warburton tells a story in his *Div. Leg.*) one should complain of a reading-glass for being of no service to a person who had never learned to read.

In fact, the difficulties and errors above alluded to are *not* in the process of Reasoning itself (which alone is the appropriate province of Logic), but in the *subject-matter* about which it is employed. This process will have been correctly conducted if it have conformed to the logical rules, which preclude the possibility of any error creeping in *between* the principles assumed, and the conclusions we deduce from them. But still that conclusion may be false, if the principles we start from are so; and the known falsity of a conclusion will often serve (as has been above remarked) to correct a mistake made in the outset. In like manner, no arithmetical skill will secure a correct result to a calculation, unless the data are correct from which we calculate; nor does any one on that account undervalue Arithmetic; and yet the objection against Logic rests on no better foundation.

There is in fact a striking analogy in this respect between the two sciences. All Numbers (which are the subject of Arithmetic) must be numbers of *some things*, whether coins, persons, measures, or any thing else; but to introduce into the science any notice of the *things* respecting which calculations are made, would be evidently irrelevant, and would destroy its scientific character: we proceed therefore with arbitrary signs, representing numbers in the abstract. So also does Logic pronounce on the validity of a regularly-constructed argument, equally well, though arbitrary *symbols* may have been substituted for the Terms; and, consequently, without any regard to the things signified by those Terms. And the possibility of doing this (though the employment of such arbitrary symbols has been absurdly objected to, even by writers who understood not only Arithmetic but Algebra) is a proof of the strictly scientific character of the system. But many professed logical writers, not attending to the circumstances which have been just mentioned, have wandered into disquisitions on various branches of knowledge; disquisitions which must evidently be as boundless as human knowledge itself, since there is no subject on which Reasoning is not employed, and to which, consequently, Logic may not be *applied.* The error lies in regarding every thing as the *proper province* of Logic to which it is *applicable.**

Many however who do not fall altogether into that error, yet censure any logical treatise which, like the present, professes to be wholly conversant about *Language;* and speak of the science as treating, properly, of the comparison of "abstract *Ideas,*" of which, Language, they say, merely supplies the *names.* It may be sufficient at present to reply, that, supposing there really exist in the mind—or in some minds—certain "abstract ideas," by means of which *a train of reasoning may be carried on independently of Common-terms* [*or Signs* of any kind,]—for this is the real point at issue—and that a system of Logic may be devised, having reference to such reasoning,—supposing this,—still, as I profess not to know anything of these "abstract ideas," or of any "Universals" except *Signs,* or to be conscious of any such reasoning-process, I at least must confine myself to the attempt to teach the only Logic I do pretend to understand. Many, again, who speak slightingly of Logic altogether, on the ground of its being "conversant only about *words,*" entertain fundamentally the same views as the above; that is, they take for granted that Reasoning may be carried on *altogether independently of Language;* which they regard (as was above remarked) merely as a means of *communicating* it to others. And a Science or Art which they suppose to be confined to *this* office, they accordingly rank very low.

* A similar error is complained of by Aristotle, as having taken place with respect to Rhetoric; of which, indeed, we find specimens in the arguments of several of the interlocutors in *Cic. de Oratore.*

Such a view I believe to be very prevalent. The majority of men would probably say, if asked, that the use of Language is peculiar to *Man;* and that its office is to express to one another our thoughts and feelings. But neither of these is strictly true. Brutes do possess in some degree the power of being taught to understand what is said to them, and some of them even to utter sounds expressive of what is passing within them. But they all seem to be incapable of another, very important use of language, which does characterize Man; viz. the employment of "Common-terms" ("general-terms") formed by Abstraction, as *instruments of thought;* by which alone *a train of Reasoning* may be carried on.

And accordingly, a *Deaf-mute,* before he has been taught a Language,—either the Finger-language, or Reading,—cannot carry on a train of Reasoning, any more than a Brute. He differs indeed from a Brute in possessing the mental *capability* of employing Language; but he can no more *make use* of that capability, till he is in possession of some *System of arbitrary general-signs,* than a person born blind from Cataract can make use of his capacity of Seeing, till the Cataract is removed.

Hence, it will be found by any one who will question a Deaf-mute who has been taught Language after having grown up, that no such thing as a train of Reasoning had ever passed through his mind before he was taught.

If indeed we did reason by means of those "Abstract-ideas" which some persons talk of, and if the Language we use served *merely* to *communicate* with other men, then, a person would be able to reason, who had no knowledge of any *arbitrary Signs.* But there are no grounds for believing that this is possible; nor consequently, that "Abstract-ideas" (in that sense of the word) have any existence at all.*

* There have been some very interesting accounts published, by travellers in America, and by persons residing there, of a girl named Laura Bridgeman,

§ 6. From what has been said, it will be evident that there is hardly any subject to which it is so difficult to introduce the student in a clear and satisfactory manner, as the one we are now engaged in. In any other branch of knowledge, the reader, if he have any previous acquaintance with the subject, will usually be so far the better prepared for comprehending the exposition of the principles; or if he be entirely a stranger to it, will at least come to the study with a mind unbiassed, and free from prejudices and misconceptions: whereas, in the present case, it cannot but happen, that many who have given some attention to logical pursuits (or what are usually considered as such) will have rather been bewildered by fundamentally erroneous views, than prepared, by the acquisition of just principles, for ulterior progress; and that not a few who pretend not to any acquaintance whatever with the science, will yet have imbibed either such prejudices against it, or

who has been, from birth, not only Deaf-and-Dumb, but also Blind. She has however been taught the finger-language, and even to read what is printed in raised characters, and also to write.

The remarkable circumstance in reference to the present subject, is, that when she is alone, her *fingers are generally observed to be moving*, though the signs are so slight and imperfect that others cannot make out what she is thinking of. But if they inquire of her, she will tell them.

It seems that, having once learnt the use of *Signs*, she finds the necessity of them as an *Instrument of thought*, when thinking of anything beyond mere individual objects of sense.

And doubtless every one else does the same; though in *our* case, no one can (as in the case of Laura Bridgeman) *see* the operation: nor, in general, can it be *heard;* though some few persons have a habit of occasionally audibly talking to themselves; or as it is called, "thinking aloud." But the Signs we commonly use in silent reflection are merely mental *conceptions*, usually, of uttered words: and these doubtless, are such as could be hardly at all understood by another, even if uttered audibly. For we usually think in a kind of *short-hand*, (if one may use the expression) like the notes one sometimes takes down on paper to help the memory, which consist of a word or two,—or even a letter,—to suggest a whole sentence; so that such notes would be unintelligible to any one else.

It has been observed also that this girl, when asleep, and doubtless dreaming, has her fingers frequently in motion: being in fact talking in her sleep. See above, § 4.

such false notions respecting its nature, as cannot but prove obstacles in their study of it.

Difficulty attending abstract pursuits.

There is, however, a difficulty which exists more or less in all abstract pursuits; though it is perhaps more felt in this, and often occasions it to be rejected by beginners as dry and tedious; *viz.* the difficulty of perceiving to what ultimate end,—to what practical or interesting application—the abstract principles lead, which are first laid before the student; so that he will often have to work his way patiently through the most laborious part of the system, before he can gain any clear idea of the drift and intention of it.

Analytical & synthetical procedure.

This complaint has often been made by chemical students; who are wearied with descriptions of Oxygen, Hydrogen, and other invisible Elements, before they have any knowledge respecting such bodies as commonly present themselves to the senses. And accordingly some teachers of chemistry obviate in a great degree this objection, by adopting the *analytical* instead of the *synthetical* mode of procedure, when they are first introducing the subject to beginners; *i. e.* instead of synthetically enumerating the elementary substances, — proceeding next to the simplest combinations of these,—and concluding with those more complex substances which are of the most common occurrence, they begin by *analyzing* these last, and resolving them step by step into their simple elements; thus at once presenting the subject in an interesting point of view, and clearly setting forth the object of it. The synthetical form of teaching is indeed sufficiently interesting to one who has made considerable progress in any study; and being more concise, regular, and systematic, is the form in which our knowledge naturally arranges itself in the mind, and is retained by the memory: but the analytical is the more interesting, easy, and natural kind of *introduction;* as being the form in which the first invention or discovery of any kind of system must originally have taken place.

It may be advisable, therefore, to begin by giving a slight sketch, in this form, of the logical system, before we enter regularly upon the details of it. The reader will thus be presented with a kind of imaginary history of the course of inquiry by which that system may be conceived to have occurred to a philosophical mind.

BOOK I.

ANALYTICAL OUTLINE OF THE SCIENCE.

§ 1.

In every instance in which we *reason,* in the strict sense of the word, *i.e.* make use of arguments, (I mean *real,* i.e. *valid* arguments) whether for the sake of refuting an adversary, or of conveying instruction, or of satisfying our own minds on any point, whatever may be the subject we are engaged on, a certain process takes place in the mind which is one and the same in all cases, provided it be correctly conducted.

Of course it cannot be supposed that every one is even conscious of this process in his own mind; much less, is competent to explain the principles on which it proceeds. This indeed is, and cannot but be, the case with every other process respecting which any system has been formed; the practice not only may exist independently of the theory, but *must* have preceded the theory. There must have been Language before a system of Grammar could be devised; and musical compositions, previous to the Science of Music. This, by the way, will serve to expose the futility of the popular objection against Logic, that men may reason very well who know nothing of it. The parallel instances adduced, show that such an objection might be applied in many other cases, where its absurdity would be obvious; and that there is no ground for deciding thence, either that the system has no tendency to improve practice, or that even if it had not, it might not still be a dignified and interesting pursuit.

Reasoning process similar in all subjects.

One of the chief impediments to the attainment of a just view of the nature and object of Logic, is the not fully understanding, or not sufficiently keeping in mind, the SAMENESS of the reasoning-process in all cases. If, as the ordinary mode of speaking would seem to indicate, Mathematical reasoning, and Theological, and Metaphysical, and Political, *&c.* were essentially different from each other, *i.e.* different *kinds of reasoning*, it would follow, that supposing there could be at all any such science as we have described Logic, there must be so many different species, or at least different branches, of Logic. And such is perhaps the most prevailing notion. Nor is this much to be wondered at: since it is evident to all, that some men converse and write, in an argumentative way, very justly on one subject, and very erroneously on another; in which again others excel, who fail in the former. This error may be at once illustrated and removed, by considering the parallel instance of Arithmetic; in which every one is aware that the process of a calculation is not affected by the nature of the objects, whose numbers are before us: but that (*e.g.*) the multiplication of a number is the very same operation, whether it be a number of men, of miles, or of pounds; though nevertheless persons may perhaps be found who are accurate in the results of their calculations relative to natural-philosophy, and incorrect in those of political-economy, from their different degrees of skill in the subjects of these two sciences; not surely because there are different arts of Arithmetic applicable to each of these respectively.

Others again, who are aware that the simple system of Logic may be applied to all subjects whatever, are yet disposed to view it as a *peculiar method* of reasoning, and not, as it is, a method of unfolding and analyzing our reasoning: whence many have been led (*e.g.* the author of the Philosophy of Rhetoric) to talk of comparing Syllogistic-reasoning with Moral-reasoning; taking it for granted that it is possible to reason correctly without reasoning logically; which is, in fact, as great a blunder as if any one were to mistake *grammar* for a peculiar *language*, and to suppose it possible to speak correctly without speaking grammatically. They have in short considered Logic as *an* art of reasoning; whereas (so far as it is an art) it is *the* art of reasoning; the logician's object being, not to lay down principles by which one *may* reason, but, by which all *must* reason, even though they are not distinctly aware of them:—to lay down rules, not which *may* be followed with advantage, but which cannot possibly be *departed* from in sound reasoning. These misapprehensions and objections being such as lie on the very threshold of the subject, it would have been hardly possible, without noticing them, to convey any just notion of the nature and design of the logical system.

§ 2.

Origin of Logic.

Supposing it then to have been perceived that the operation of Reasoning is in all cases the same, the analysis of that operation could not fail to strike the mind as an interesting matter of inquiry. And moreover, since (apparent) arguments which are unsound and inconclusive, are so often employed, either from error or design; and since even those who are not misled by these fallacies, are so often at a loss to detect and expose them in a manner satisfactory to others, or even to themselves; it could not but appear desirable to lay down some general rules of reasoning applicable to all cases; by which a person might be enabled the more readily and clearly to state the grounds of his own conviction, or of his objection to the arguments of an opponent; instead of arguing at random, without any fixed and acknowledged principles to guide his procedure. Such rules would be analogous to those of Arithmetic, which obviate the tediousness and uncertainty of calculations in the head; wherein, after much labour, different persons might arrive at different results, without any of them being able distinctly to point out the error of the rest. A system of such rules, it is obvious, must, instead of deserving to be called the "art of wrangling," be more justly characterised as the "art of cutting short wrangling," by bringing the parties to issue at once, if not to agreement; and thus saving a waste of ingenuity.

Analysis of argument.

In pursuing the supposed investigation, it will be found that every Conclusion is deduced, in reality, from two other propositions; (thence called *Premises;*) for though one of these may be, and commonly is, suppressed, it must nevertheless be understood as admitted; as may easily be made evident by supposing the *denial* of the suppressed premiss; which will at once invalidate the argument; *e. g.* if any one, from perceiving that "the world exhibits marks of design," infers that "it must have had an intelligent author," though he may not be aware in his own mind of the existence of any other premiss, he will readily understand, if it be *denied* that "whatever exhibits marks of design must have had an intelligent author," that the affirmative of that proposition is necessary to the validity of the argument.* Or again, if any one on meeting with "an animal which has horns on the head" infers that "it is a ruminant," he will easily perceive that this would be no argument to any one who should not be aware of the general fact that "all horned animals ruminate."

Syllogism.

An argument thus stated regularly and at full length, is called a Syllogism; which therefore is evidently not a peculiar *kind of argument,* but only

* Some chuse to call this proposition not a *premiss* but merely a *condition.* This however is, substantially, (as has been formerly remarked) just what Logicians mean. Whoever has any good ground for believing his inference to be a just one, must believe this condition to exist.

a peculiar *form* of expression, in which every argument may be stated.*

When one of the premises is suppressed, (which for brevity's sake it usually is) the argument is called an Enthymeme. And it may be worth while to remark, that when the argument is in this state, the objections of an opponent are (or rather appear to be) of two kinds; *viz.* either objections to the *assertion* itself, or objections to its *force* as an argument. *E. G.* In one of the above instances, an atheist may be conceived either denying† that the world *does* exhibit marks of design, or denying ‡ that it *follows* from thence that it had an intelligent author. Now it is important to keep in mind that the only difference in the two cases is, that in the one, the *expressed* premiss is denied, in the other the *suppressed;* for the *force as an argument* of either premiss depends on the *other* premiss: if both be admitted, the conclusion legitimately connected with them cannot be denied.

Reason.

It is evidently immaterial to the argument whether the Conclusion be placed first or last;

* Some writers, and Locke among others, who profess to despise what they call "syllogistic reasoning," distinctly admit—as Locke does *e. g.* in ch. xvii. that "*all* right reasoning may be reduced to the form of Syllogism;" (which is admitting the utmost that I conceive any Logician maintains) only, there are, he says, other and better "ways of reasoning:" that is, as he proceeds to explain, people do not always, or usually, *express* their reasoning in a *syllogistic form:* as if any one had ever doubted *that!* Except indeed it be a writer in the Edinburgh Review, (in 1839) who in deprecating and deriding all attempts to adduce *evidences* of the truth of Christianity, as useless, and even dangerous, for the mass of mankind, (a discovery, by the way, which its first promulgators were not enlightened enough to make) gives as a reason, that "the Gospel has been the stay of countless millions who never framed a *syllogism.*" And very probable it is, that Nicodemus for instance, and those who deputed him, when he said "we know that thou art a teacher sent from God; for no man can do these miracles that thou doest except God be with him," though he spoke grammatically and reasoned conclusively, may have never heard of syllogisms, or even of nouns and verbs.

† As the ancient atheists did.

‡ As the modern atheists do.

but it may be proper to remark, that a Premiss placed *after* its Conclusion is called the *Reason* * of it, and is introduced by one of those conjunctions which are called *causal; viz.* "since," "because," *&c.* which may indeed be employed to designate a Premiss, whether it came first or last. The *illative* conjunctions, "therefore," *&c.* designate the Conclusion.

Proof and cause.

It is a circumstance which often occasions error and perplexity, that both these classes of conjunctions have also another signification, being employed to denote, respectively, *Cause* and *Effect*, as well as *Premiss* and *Conclusion: e.g.* If I say, "this ground is rich, *because* the trees on it are flourishing," or "the trees are flourishing, and *therefore* the soil must be rich," I employ these conjunctions to denote the connexion of *Premiss* and *Conclusion;* for it is plain that the luxuriance of the trees is not the cause of the soil's fertility, but only the cause of *my knowing* it. If again I say, "the trees flourish, *because* the ground is rich," or "the ground is rich, and *therefore* the trees flourish," I am using the very same conjunctions to denote the connexion of *cause* and *effect;* for in this case, the luxuriance of the trees, being evident to the eye, would hardly need to be *proved,* but might need to be *accounted* for.

There are, however, many cases, in which the Cause is employed to *prove* the existence of its Effect; especially in arguments relating to *future* events; as *e.g.* when from favourable weather any one argues that the crops are likely to be abundant:† the *cause* and the *reason,* in that case, coincide. And this contributes to their being so often confounded together in other cases.

* The Major-premiss is often called the *Principle;* and the word *Reason* is then confined to the Minor.

† See Appendix, No. I. art. *Reason.* See also *Rhetoric,* Part I. ch. 2, § ii.

§ 3.

In an argument, such as the examples above given, it is, as has been said, impossible for any one, who admits both Premises, to avoid admitting the Conclusion.

A man may perhaps deny, or doubt, and require proof, that all animals that are horned do ruminate. Nay, it is conceivable that he may even not clearly understand what "*ruminant*" means; but still it will be not the less clear to him, that, *supposing* these Premises granted, the Conclusion must be admitted.

And even if you suppose a case where one or both of the Premises shall be manifestly false and absurd, this will not alter the *conclusiveness* of the Reasoning; though the *conclusion* itself may perhaps be absurd also. For instance, "All the Ape-tribe are originally descended from Reptiles or Insects: Mankind are of the Ape-tribe; therefore Mankind are originally descended from Reptiles or Insects:" here, every one * would perceive the falsity of all three of these propositions. But it is not the less true that the conclusion *follows* from those premises, and that *if* they were true, it would be true also.

Apparent arguments.

But there will be frequently an *apparent* connexion of Premises with a Conclusion which does not in reality follow from them, though to the inattentive or unskilful, the argument may appear to be valid. And there are many other cases in which a doubt may exist whether the argument be valid or not: *i. e.* whether it be possible or not to admit the Premises, and yet deny the Conclusion. It is of the highest importance, therefore, to lay down some regular form to which every valid argument may be reduced, and to devise a rule which shall show the validity of every argument in that form, and consequently the unsoundness of any apparent argument which cannot be reduced to it. *E. G.* If such

* Except certain French Naturalists.

an argument as this be proposed, "every rational agent is accountable; brutes are not rational agents; therefore they are not accountable:" or again, "all wise legislators suit their laws to the genius of their nation; Solon did this; therefore he was a wise legislator:" there are some, perhaps, who would not perceive any fallacy in such arguments, especially if enveloped in a cloud of words; and still more, when the conclusion is true, or (which comes to the same point) if they are disposed to believe it: and others might perceive indeed, but might be at a loss to explain, the fallacy. Now these (apparent) arguments exactly correspond, respectively, with the following, the absurdity of the conclusions from which is manifest: "every horse is an animal; sheep are not horses; therefore they are not animals;" and, "all vegetables grow; an animal grows; therefore it is a vegetable." These last examples, I have said, correspond exactly (considered as arguments) with the former; the question respecting the validity of an Argument, being, not whether the conclusion be *true*, but whether it *follows* from the premises adduced.

This mode of exposing a fallacy, by bringing forward a similar one whose conclusion is obviously absurd, is often, and very advantageously, resorted to in addressing those who are ignorant of Logical rules;* but to lay down such rules, and employ *them* as a test, is evidently a safer and more compendious, as well as a more philosophical mode of proceeding. To attain these, it would plainly be neces-

* An exposure of some of Hume's fallacies in his "Essay on Miracles" and elsewhere, was attempted, on this plan, a few years ago, in a pamphlet (published anonymously, as the nature of the argument required, but which I see no reason against acknowledging) entitled "Historic Doubts relative to Napoleon Buonaparte;" in which it was shown that the existence of that extraordinary person could not, on Hume's principles, be received as a well-authenticated fact; since it rests on evidence less strong than that which supports the Scripture-histories.

For a clear development of the mode in which this last evidence operates on most minds, see "Hinds on Inspiration," p. 30—46.

sary to analyze some clear and valid arguments, and to observe in what their conclusiveness consists.

Analysis of an argument.

Let us then examine and analyze such an example as one of those first given: for instance, "Every animal that has horns on the head is ruminant; the Elk has horns on the head; therefore the Elk is ruminant." It will easily be seen that the validity [or "conclusiveness;" or "soundness"] of the Argument does not at all depend on our conviction of the truth of either of the Premises; or even on our understanding the meaning of them. For if we substitute for one of the things we are speaking about, some unmeaning Symbol, (such as a letter of the alphabet) which may stand for anything that may be agreed on, the Reasoning remains the same.

For instance, suppose we say, (instead of "animal that has horns on the head,") "Every X is ruminant; the Elk is X; therefore the Elk is ruminant;" the Argument is equally valid.

And again, instead of the word "ruminant," let us put the letter "Y:" then the argument "Every X is Y; the Elk is X; therefore the Elk is Y;" would be a valid argument as before.

And the same would be the case if you were to put "Z" for "the Elk:" for the syllogism "Every X is Y; Z is X; therefore Z is Y," is completely valid, whatever you suppose the Symbols X, Y, and Z to stand for.

Any one may try the experiment, by substituting for X, Y, and Z, respectively, any words he pleases; and he will find that, if he does but preserve the same *form* of expression, it will be impossible to admit the truth of the Premises, without admitting also the truth of the Conclusion.

An Argument may be understood though its Terms are not.

And it is worth observing here, that nothing is so likely to lead to that—very common, though seemingly strange—error, of supposing ourselves to understand distinctly what in reality we understand but very imperfectly, or not at all, as the want of attention to what has been just explained.

A man reads—or even writes—many pages perhaps, of an argumentative work, in which one or more of the terms employed convey nothing distinct to his mind: and yet he is liable to overlook this circumstance, from finding that he clearly understands the *Arguments.* He may be said, in one sense, *to understand what he is reading;* because he can perfectly follow the *train of Reasoning,* itself. But *this,* perhaps, he might equally well do, if he were to substitute for one of the words employed, X, or Z, or any other such unknown Symbol; as in the examples above. But a man will often confound together, the *understanding of the Arguments,* in themselves, and the *understanding of the words employed,* and of the nature of the things those words denote.

It appears then, that valid Reasoning, when regularly expressed, has its validity [or conclusiveness] made evident from the mere *form of the expression* itself, independently of any regard to the sense of the words.

In examining this form, in such an example as that just given, you will observe that in the first Premise ("X is Y,") it is assumed universally of the *Class* of things (whatever it may be) which "X" denotes, that "Y" may be affirmed of them: and in the other Premise, ("Z is X") that "Z" (whatever it may stand for) is *referred* to that Class, as *comprehended* in it. Now it is evident that whatever is said of the *whole* of a Class, may be said of anything that is comprehended [or "included," or "contained,"] in that Class: so that we are thus authorized to say (in the conclusion) that "Z" is "Y."

Thus also, in the example first given, having assumed universally, of the Class of "Things which exhibit marks of design," that they "had an intelligent maker," and then, in the other Premiss, having referred "The world" to that

Class, we conclude that it may be asserted of "The world" that "it had an intelligent maker."

And the process is the same when anything is *denied* of a whole Class. We are equally authorized to deny the same, of whatever is comprehended under that Class. For instance, if I say, "No liar is deserving of trust; this man is a liar; therefore he is not deserving of trust;" I here deny "deserving of trust," of the whole Class denoted by the word "liar;" and then I refer "this man" to that Class; whence it follows that "deserving of trust" may be denied of him.

This argument also will be as manifestly valid, if (as in the former case) you substitute for the words which have a known meaning, any undetermined Symbols, such as letters of the alphabet. "No X is Y; Z is X; therefore Z is not Y," is as perfect a syllogism as the other with the affirmative conclusion.

Meaning of the word Class.

And here it is to be observed, that by "*Class*" is meant throughout this treatise, not merely a "Head" or "general-description" to which several things are *actually* referred, but one to which an indefinite number of things *might conceivably* be referred; viz. as many as (in the colloquial phrase) may "*answer* to the *description.*" E.G. One may conceive that when the first-created man existed alone, some superhuman Beings may have contemplated him not merely as an individual bearing the *proper-name* of *Adam*, but also, by Abstraction, simply, as possessing those attributes which we call collectively "humanity" ["human-nature;"] and may have applied to him a name,—such as "Man"—implying those attributes, [that description] and which would consequently suit equally well any of his descendants.

When then anything is said to be "referred to such and such a *Class*" this is to be understood either of an *actual*, or what may be called a *potential* Class: *i. e.* the word Class is used whether there actually exist, or not, *several* things to which the description will apply. For it is evident, that, in any case, we refer something to a certain Class *in consequence* of that thing's possessing certain attributes, and not, *vice versâ*. And this being kept in mind, there is a convenience in employing the word "Class" instead of introducing circumlocution by always speaking of "description."

It will be found, then, on examination, that all valid arguments whatever may be easily reduced to such a form as that of the foregoing syllogisms; and that consequently the principle on which they are constructed is the UNIVERSAL PRINCIPLE of Reasoning. So elliptical, indeed, is the ordinary mode of expression, even of those who are considered as prolix writers,—*i.e.* so much is implied and left to be understood in the course of argument, in comparison of what is actually stated, (most men being impatient, even to excess, of any appearance of unnecessary and tedious formality of statement), that a single sentence will often be found, though perhaps considered as a single argument, to contain, compressed into a short compass, a chain of several distinct arguments. But if each of these be fully developed, and the whole of what the author intended to imply be stated expressly, it will be found that all the steps even of the longest and most complex train of reasoning, may be reduced into the above form.*

Meaning of "logical reasoning."

It is a mistake (which might appear scarcely worthy of notice, had not so many, even esteemed writers, fallen into it) to imagine that Aristotle and other logicians meant to propose that this prolix form of unfolding arguments should universally supersede, in argumentative discourses, the common forms of expression; and that, "to reason logically,"

* One of the ancients is reported to have compared Logic to the closed fist, and Rhetoric to the open hand. To me it appears that the *reverse* of this comparison would be more correct.

means, to state all arguments at full length in the syllogistic form; and Aristotle has even been charged with inconsistency for not doing so. It has been said that "in his *Treatises of Ethics, Politics, &c.* he argues like a rational creature, and never attempts to bring his own system into practice."* As well might a chemist be charged with inconsistency for making use of any of the compound substances that are commonly employed, without previously analyzing and resolving them into their simple elements; as well might it be imagined that, "to speak grammatically," means, to *parse* every sentence we utter. The chemist (to pursue the illustration) keeps by him his tests and his method of analysis, to be employed when any substance is offered to his notice, the composition of which has not been ascertained, or in which adulteration is suspected. Now a fallacy may aptly be compared to some adulterated compound; "it consists of an ingenious mixture of truth " and falsehood, so entangled,—so intimately blended,— " that the falsehood is (in the chemical phrase) *held in* " *solution:* one drop of sound logic is that test which imme- " diately disunites them, makes the Foreign substance " visible, and precipitates it to the bottom."†

§ 4.

Aristotle's Dictum.

But to resume the investigation of the principles of Reasoning: the Maxim resulting from the examination of a syllogism in the foregoing form, and of the application of which, every valid argument is in reality an instance, is, " that whatever is predicated (*i.e.* affirmed or denied) universally, of any Class of things, may be predicated, in like manner, (*viz.* affirmed or denied) of

* Lord Kames.

† This excellent illustration is cited from a passage in an anonymous pamphlet, "An Examination of Kett's Logic." The author displays, though in a hasty production, great reach of thought, as well as knowledge of his subject.

any thing comprehended in that Class." This is the principle, commonly called the *dictum de omni et nullo*, for the indication of which we are indebted to Aristotle, and which is the keystone of his whole logical system.

It is remarkable that some, otherwise judicious writers, should have been so carried away by their zeal against that philosopher, as to speak with scorn and ridicule of this principle, on account of its obviousness and simplicity; though they would probably perceive at once, in any other case, that it is the greatest triumph of philosophy to refer many, and seemingly very various, phenomena to one, or a very few, simple principles; and that the more simple and evident such a principle is, provided it be truly applicable to all the cases in question, the greater is its value and scientific beauty. If, indeed, any principle be regarded as *not* thus applicable, *that* is an objection to it of a different kind. Such an objection against Aristotle's Dictum, no one has ever attempted to *establish* by any kind of proof; but it has often been *taken for granted;* it being (as has been stated) very commonly supposed, without examination, that the syllogism is a *distinct kind of argument*, and that the rules of it accordingly do not apply, nor were intended to apply, to all reasoning whatever. Dr. Campbell * endeavours, under this misapprehension, with some ingenuity, and not without an air of plausibility, to show that every syllogism must be futile and worthless, because the Premises virtually assert the Conclusion: little dreaming, of course, that his objections, however specious, lie against the *process of reasoning itself*, universally; and will, therefore, of course, apply to those very arguments which he is himself adducing. He should have been reminded of the story of the woodman, who had mounted a tree, and was so earnestly employed in lopping the boughs, that he unconsciously cut off the bough on which he was standing.

It is still more extraordinary to find other eminent

* "Philosophy of Rhetoric."

authors * adopting, expressly, the very same objections, and yet distinctly admitting the possibility of reducing every course of argument to a series of syllogisms.

Mistake respecting the meaning of the Dictum.

One of these writers brings an objection against the Dictum of Aristotle, which it may be worth while to notice briefly, for the sake of setting in a clearer light the real character and object of that Principle. Its application being, as has been seen, to a regular and conclusive Syllogism, he supposes it intended to prove and *make evident* the conclusiveness of such a syllogism; and remarks how unphilosophical it is to attempt giving a *demonstration of a demonstration*. And certainly the charge would be just, if we could imagine the logician's object to be, to *increase the certainty* of a conclusion which we are supposed to have already arrived at by the clearest possible mode of proof. But it is very strange that such an idea should ever have occurred to one who had even the slightest tincture of Natural-philosophy: for it might as well be imagined that a natural-philosopher's or a chemist's design is to strengthen the testimony of our senses by *à priori* reasoning, and to convince us that a stone when thrown will fall to the ground, and that gunpowder will explode when fired; because they show that according to their principles those phenomena must take place as they do. But it would be reckoned a mark of the grossest ignorance and stupidity not to be aware that their object is not to *prove* the existence of an individual phenomenon, which our eyes have witnessed, but (as the phrase is) to *account* for it: *i. e.* to show according to what *principle* it takes place;—to refer, in short, the *individual case* to a *general law* of nature. The object of Aristotle's Dictum is precisely analogous; he had, doubtless, no thought of adding to the force of any individual syllogism; his design was to point out the *general principle* on which that process is conducted which takes

* As Dugald Stewart: Philosophy, vol. ii.: and Locke, vol. ii. ch. 17. § 4.

place in each syllogism. And as the Laws* of nature (as they are called) are in reality merely *generalized facts*, of which all the phenomena coming under them are particular instances; so, the proof drawn from Aristotle's Dictum is not a distinct demonstration brought to confirm another demonstration, but is merely a generalized and abstract statement of *all* demonstration whatever; and is, therefore, in fact, *the very demonstration* which (*mutatis mutandis*) accommodated to the various subject-matters, is actually employed in each particular case.

The Dictum, a statement of argument in the abstract.

In order to trace more distinctly the different steps of the abstracting process, by which any particular argument may be brought into the most general form, we may first take a syllogism (*i.e.* an argument stated accurately and at full length), such as the example formerly given, "whatever exhibits marks of design, *&c.*," and then somewhat generalize the expression, by substituting (as in algebra) arbitrary unmeaning symbols for the significant terms that were originally used; the syllogism will then stand thus; "every B is A; C is B; therefore C is A." The reasoning, when thus stated, is no less evidently valid, whatever terms, A, B, and C, respectively, may be supposed to stand for. Such terms may indeed be inserted as to make all or some of the assertions *false;* but it will still be no less impossible for any one who *admits* the truth of the *premises,* in an argument thus constructed, to deny the conclusion; and this it is that constitutes the conclusiveness of an argument.

Viewing then the syllogism thus expressed, it appears clearly, that "A stands for *any thing whatever* that is affirmed of a certain entire Class," (*viz.* of *every* B) "which class comprehends or contains in it *something else*," *viz.* C. (of which B is, in the second premiss, affirmed); and that, consequently, the first term (A) is, in the conclusion, predicated of the third C.

* Appendix, No. I. art. *Law.*

Now to assert the validity of this process, now before us, is to *state the very Dictum* we are treating of, with hardly even a verbal alteration: *viz.:*

1. Any thing whatever, predicated of a whole class,
2. Under which class something else is contained,
3. May be predicated of that which is so contained.

The three members into which the Maxim is here distributed, correspond to the three propositions of the syllogism to which they are intended respectively to apply.*

Utility of non-significant symbols.

The advantage of substituting for the terms, in a regular syllogism, arbitrary unmeaning symbols, such as letters of the alphabet, is much the same as in Geometry: the Reasoning itself is then considered, by itself, clearly, and without any risk of our being misled by the truth or falsity of the conclusion; which is, in fact, accidental and variable; the essential point being, as far as the *argument* is concerned, the *connexion between* the premises and the conclusion. We are thus enabled to embrace the general principle of all reasoning, and to perceive its applicability to an indefinite number of individual cases. That Aristotle, therefore, should have been accused of making use of these symbols for the purpose of *darkening* his demonstrations, and that too by persons not unacquainted with Geometry and Algebra, is truly astonishing. If a geometer, instead of designating the four angles of a square by four letters, were to call them *north, south, east,* and *west,* he would not render the demonstration of a theorem the easier; and the learner would be much more likely to be perplexed in the application of it.

It belongs then exclusively to a Syllogism, properly so called (*i. e.* a valid argument, so stated that its conclusiveness is evident from the mere *form* of the expression), that if letters, or any other unmeaning symbols, be substituted for the several terms, the validity of the argument shall

* See Book iv. ch. iii. § 1.

still be evident. Whenever this is not the case, the supposed argument is either unsound and sophistical, or else may be reduced (without any alteration of its meaning) into the syllogistic form; in which form, the test just mentioned may be applied to it.

True character of the Dictum.

Some persons have remarked of the "Dictum" (meaning it as a disparagement) that it is merely a somewhat circuitous *explanation of what is meant by a Class.* It is, in truth, just such an explanation of this as is needful to the student, and which must be kept before his mind in reasoning. For we should recollect that not only every Class [the Sign of which is, a "Common-term"] comprehends under it an indefinite number of individuals,—and often of other Classes—differing in many respects from each other, but also most of those individuals and classes may be referred, each, to an indefinite number of classes according as we *chuse to abstract* this point or that, from each.

Now to *remind* one, on each occasion, that so and so is referable to such and such a Class, and that the class which happens to be before us comprehends such and such things, —this is *precisely all that is ever accomplished by Reasoning.*

For one may plainly perceive, on looking at any of the examples above, that when we assert *both* the Premises taken in conjunction, we have, virtually, implied the Conclusion. Else, indeed, it would *not* be impossible (as it is) for any one to deny the Conclusion, who admits both Premises.*

* Hence, some have considered it as a disparagement to a Syllogism (which they imagine to be *one kind* of Argument) that you can gain no *new truth* from it; the Conclusions it establishes being in fact known already, by every one who has admitted the Premises.

Since, however, a Syllogism is not a certain distinct kind of argument, but *any* argument whatever, stated in a regular form, the complaint, such as it is, lies against Reasoning altogether. In B. iv. ch. 2, this point is more fully explained.

Detection of unsound arguments.

What is called an unsound or fallacious argument (*i. e.* an *apparent* argument, which is, in reality, none) cannot, of course, be reduced into this form; but when stated in the form most nearly approaching to this that is possible, its fallaciousness becomes more evident, from its nonconformity to the foregoing rule: *e. g.* "whoever is capable of deliberate crime is responsible; an infant is not capable of deliberate crime; therefore, an infant is not responsible," (see § 3): here the term "responsible" is affirmed universally of "those capable of deliberate crime;" it might, therefore, according to Aristotle's Dictum, have been affirmed of any thing contained under that class; but, in the instance before us, *nothing* is mentioned as contained under that class; only, the term "infant" is *excluded* from that class; and though what is affirmed of a whole class may be affirmed of any thing that *is* contained under it, there is no ground for supposing that it may be *denied* of whatever is *not* so contained; for it is evidently possible that it may be applicable to a whole class and to something else besides. To say, *e.g.* that all trees are vegetables, does not imply that *nothing else* is a vegetable; nor, when it is said, that "all who are capable of deliberate crime are responsible," does this imply, that "no others are responsible;" for though this may be very *true*, it has not been asserted in the premiss before us; and in the analysis of an argument, we are to discard all consideration of what *might* be asserted; contemplating only what *actually is* laid down in the premises. It is evident, therefore, that such an apparent argument as the above does not comply with the rule laid down, nor can be so stated as to comply with it; and is consequently invalid.

Again, in this instance, "food is necessary to life; corn is food; therefore, corn is necessary to life:" the term "necessary to life" is affirmed of food, but *not universally;* for it is not said of *every kind of food:* the meaning of the assertion being manifestly that "*some* food is necessary to life;" so that, expressed in symbols, the apparent argument might stand thus; "Some X is Y; Z is X; therefore Z is Y." Here again, therefore, the rule has not been complied with, since that which has been predicated, [affirmed or denied] not of the *whole*, but of a *part* only of a certain class, cannot be, on that ground, predicated of *whatever* is contained under that class.

There is an argument against miracles by the well-known Mr. Hume, which has perplexed many persons, and which exactly corresponds to the above. It may be stated thus: "Testimony is a kind of evidence more likely to be false, than a miracle to be true;" (or, as it may be expressed in other words, we have more reason to expect that a witness should lie, than that a miracle should occur) "the evidence on which the Christian miracles are believed, is testimony; therefore the evidence on which the Christian miracles are believed is more likely to be false than a miracle to be true."

Here it is evident that what is spoken of in the first of these Premises, is, "*some* testimony;" not "all testimony," [or *any whatever*,] and by "a witness" we understand, "*some* witness," not, "*every* witness:" so that this apparent argument has exactly the same fault as the one above.*

§ 5.

The fallacy in these last cases is, what is usually described in logical language as consisting in the "non-distribution of the middle term:" *i. e.* its not being employed to denote *all* the objects to which it is applicable. In order to understand this phrase, it is necessary to observe, that a *Proposition* being an expression in which one thing is said, *i. e.* affirmed or denied of another, (*e. g.* "A is B,") both that of which something is said, and that which is said of it (*i. e.* both A and B), are called "terms;" from their being (in their nature) the extremes or *boundaries* of the Propo-

* See Appendix ii. Example No. 26.

sition: and there are, of course, two, and but two, terms in a proposition (though it may so happen that either of them may consist either of one *word*, or of several); and a term is said to be "distributed," when it is taken universally, so as to stand for every thing it is capable of being applied to; and consequently "undistributed," when it stands for a portion only of the things signified by it: thus, "*all* food," or *every* kind of food, are expressions which imply the distribution of the term "food;" "*some* food" would imply its non-distribution. And it is also to be observed that the term of which, in one premiss, something is affirmed or denied, and to which, in the other premiss, something else is referred as contained in it, is called the "middle" term in the syllogism, as standing *between* the other two (*viz.* the two terms of the conclusion), and being the medium of proof. Now it is plain, that if in each premiss a *part* only of this middle-term is employed, *i. e.* if it be not at all distributed, no conclusion can be drawn. Hence, if, in the example formerly adduced, it had been merely stated that "*something*" (not "*whatever*," or "*everything*") "which exhibits marks of design, is the work of an intelligent author," it would not have followed, from the world's exhibiting marks of design, that that is the work of an intelligent author.

Distribution of terms.

It is to be observed, also, that the words "all" and "every," which mark the distribution of a term, and "some," which marks its non-distribution, are not always expressed: they are frequently understood, and left to be supplied by the context; *e. g.* "food is necessary;" viz. "*some* food;" "man is mortal;" viz. "*every* man."

Propositions thus expressed are called by logicians "*indefinite*," because it is left undetermined by the form of the expression whether the "subject" (the term of which something is affirmed or denied being called the "subject" of the proposition, and that which is said of it, the "predi-

Indefinite Propositions.

cate") be distributed or not. Nevertheless it is plain that in every proposition the Subject either is, or is not, meant to be distributed; though it be not declared whether it is or not. Consequently, every proposition, whether expressed indefinitely or not, must be understood as either "universal" or "particular;" those being called Universal in which the predicate is said of the whole of the subject (or, in other words, where the subject is distributed); and those, Particular, in which it is said only of a part of the subject: *e.g.* "All men are sinful," is universal; "some men are sinful," particular. And this division of propositions is, in logical language, said to be according to their "*quantity.*"

Quantity and quality of propositions.

But the distribution or non-distribution of the *predicate* is entirely independent of the *quantity* of the proposition; nor are the signs "all" and "some" ever affixed to the predicate; because its distribution depends upon, and is indicated by, the "*quality*" of the proposition; *i.e.* its being *affirmative* or *negative;* it being a universal rule, that the predicate of a negative proposition is distributed, and of an affirmative, undistributed. The reason of this may easily be understood, by considering that a term which stands for a whole Class may be applied to (*i. e. affirmed* of) any thing that is comprehended under that class, though the term of which it is thus affirmed may be of much narrower extent than that other, and may, therefore, be far from coinciding with the *whole* of it. Thus it may be said with truth, that "the Negroes are uncivilized," though the term uncivilized be of much wider extent than "Negroes," comprehending, besides them, Hottentots, *&c.*; so that it would not be allowable to assert, that "*all* who are uncivilized are Negroes;" it is evident, therefore, that it is a *part* only of the term "uncivilized" that has been affirmed of "Negroes:" and the same reasoning applies to every affirmative proposition; for though it may so happen that the subject and predicate coincide; *i. e.* are of equal extent, as, *e.g.* "all men are rational animals;" "all equilateral triangles are equiangular;" (it being equally true, that "all rational animals are men," and that "all equiangular triangles are equilateral;) yet this is not *implied by the form of the expression;* since it would be no less true, that "all men are rational animals," even if there were other rational animals besides Man.

It is plain, therefore, that if *any part* of the predicate is applicable to the subject, it may be affirmed, and, of course, cannot be denied, of that subject; and consequently, when the predicate *is denied* of the subject, this implies that *no part* of that predicate is applicable to that subject; *i.e.* that the *whole* of the predicate is denied of the subject; for to say, *e.g.* that "no beasts of prey ruminate," implies that beasts of prey are excluded from the *whole class* of ruminant animals, and consequently that "no ruminant animals are beasts of prey." And hence results the above-mentioned rule, that the distribution of the predicate is implied in negative propositions, and its non-distribution, in affirmatives.

Non-distribution of the predicate in affirmatives.

The learner may perhaps be startled at being told that the predicate of an affirmative is *never* distributed; especially as Aldrich has admitted that accidentally this *may* take place: as in such a proposition as "all equilateral triangles are equiangular:" but this is not accurate: he might have said that in such a proposition as the above the predicate is *distributable*, but not that it is actually distributed: *i.e.* it so *happens* that "all equiangular triangles *are* equilateral;" but this is *not implied* in the previous assertion; and the point to be considered is, not what *might be* said with truth, but what actually *has been* said. And accordingly mathematicians give distinct demonstrations of the above two propositions.

If it happen to be my object to assert that the Predicate as well as the Subject of a certain affirmative proposition is to be understood as distributed—and if I say, for instance, "all equilateral triangles, *and no others*, are equiangular,"—I am asserting, in reality, not *one* proposition, merely, but *two*. And this is the case whenever the proposition I state is understood (whether from the meaning of the words employed, or from the general drift of the discourse) to imply that the whole of the Predicate is meant to be affirmed of the Subject.

Thus, if I say of one number—suppose 100—that it is the Square of another, as 10, then, this is understood by every one, from his *knowledge of the nature of numbers*, to imply, what are, in reality, the *two* propositions, that 100 is "the Square of 10," and also that "the Square of 10 is 100." So also, if I say that "Romulus was the first king of Rome," this implies, from the peculiar *signification of the words*, that "the first king of Rome was Romulus."

Terms thus related to each other are called in technical language, "*convertible*" [or "equivalent"] terms. But then, you are to observe that when you not only affirm one term of another, but also affirm (or imply) that these *are* "*convertible*" terms, you are making not merely *one* assertion, but *two*.

Distribution of middle terms.

It is to be remembered, then, that it is not sufficient for the middle term to *occur* in a Universal-proposition; since if that proposition be an affirmative, and the middle-term be the *predicate* of it, it will not be distributed: *e.g.* if in the example formerly given, it had been merely asserted, that "all the works of an intelligent author show marks of design," and that "the universe shows marks of design," nothing could have been proved; since, though both these propositions are universal, the middle-term is made the predicate in each, and both are affirmative; and accordingly, the rule of Aristotle is not here complied with, since the term "work of an intelligent author," which is to be proved applicable to "the universe," would *not* have been affirmed of the middle-term ("what shows marks of design") under which "universe" is contained; but the middle-term, on the contrary, would have been affirmed of it.

If, however, one of the premises be negative, the middle-term may then be made the predicate of that, and will thus, according to the above remark, be distributed; *e.g.* "no ruminant animals are predacious; the lion is predacious; therefore the lion is not ruminant:" this is a valid syllogism; and the middle term (predacious) is distributed by being made the predicate of a negative proposition. The form, indeed, of the syllogism is not that prescribed by the Dictum, but it may easily be reduced to that form, by stating the first proposition thus: "no predacious animals are ruminant;" which is manifestly implied (as was above remarked) in the assertion that "no ruminant animals are predacious." The syllogism will thus appear in the form to which the Dictum applies.

The Dictum universally applicable.

It is not every argument, indeed, that can be reduced to this form by so short and simple an alteration as in the case before us: a longer and more complex process will often be required; and rules will hereafter be laid down to facilitate this process in certain cases: but there is no sound argument but what *can* be reduced into this form, without at all departing from the real meaning and drift of it; and the form will be found (though more prolix than is needed for ordinary use) the most perspicuous in which an argument can be exhibited.

All Reasoning whatever, then, rests on the one simple Principle laid down by Aristotle, that "what is predicated, either affirmatively or negatively, of a term distributed, may be predicated in like manner (*i. e.* affirmatively or negatively) of any thing contained under that term." So that when our object is to prove any proposition, *i. e.* to show that one term may rightly be affirmed or denied of another, the process which really takes place in our minds is, that we *refer* that term (of which the other is to be thus predicated) to some class* (*i. e.* middle-term) of which that other may be affirmed, or denied, as the case may be.

Whatever the subject-matter of an argument may be, the Reasoning itself, considered by itself, is in every case the same process; and if the writers against Logic had kept this in mind, they would have been cautious of expressing their contempt of what they call "syllogistic reasoning," which is in truth *all* reasoning; and instead of ridiculing Aristotle's Principle for its obviousness and simplicity, would have perceived that these are, in fact, its highest praise: the easiest, shortest, and most evident theory, provided it answer the purpose of explanation, being ever the best.

§ 6.

If we conceive an inquirer to have reached, in his investigation of the theory of Reasoning, the point to which we have now arrived, a question which would be likely next to engage his attention, is that of *Predication; i. e.* since in reasoning we are to find a middle-term which may be predicated affirmatively of the Subject in question, we are led to inquire what terms may be affirmed, and what denied, of what others.

Common and singular terms.

It is evident that a proper-name, or any other term which denotes but a single individual, as "Cæsar," "the Thames," the Conqueror of Pompey," "this river" (hence called in Logic a "Singular-term") cannot be affirmed of any thing besides that individual, and may therefore be denied of any thing else; we may say, "this river is the Thames," or "Cæsar was the conqueror of Pompey;" but we cannot say of any thing else that it is the Thames, *&c.*

On the other hand, those terms which are called "*Common*," as denoting any one individual of a whole class, as

* That is, either an *actual*, or a *potential* class. See above, § 3.

"river," "conqueror," may of course be affirmed of any, or all that belong to that class: [of any thing answering to a certain *description*] as, "the Thames is a river;" "the Rhine and the Danube are rivers."

Common-terms, therefore, are called "predicables" (viz. *affirmatively*-predicable), from their capability of being affirmed of others: a Singular-term, on the contrary, may be the Subject of a proposition, but never the Predicate, unless it be of a negative proposition; (as *e. g.* the first-born of Isaac was not Jacob;) or, unless the Subject and Predicate be only two expressions for the same individual object; as in some of the above instances.

Abstraction & generalization.

The process by which the mind arrives at the notions expressed by these "common" (or in popular language, "general") terms, is properly called "Generalization;" though it is usually (and truly) said to be the business of *abstraction;* for Generalization is one of the purposes to which Abstraction is applied. When we *draw off*, and *contemplate separately* any part of an object presented to the mind, disregarding the rest of it, we are said to *abstract* that part. Thus, a person might, when a rose was before his eyes or mind, make the scent a distinct object of attention, laying aside all thought of the colour, form, *&c.*; and thus, even though it were the *only* rose he had ever met with, he would be employing the faculty of Abstraction; but if, in contemplating *several* objects, and finding that they agree in certain points, we abstract the circumstances of agreement, disregarding the differences, and give to all and each of these objects a name applicable to them in respect of this agreement, *i. e.* a common name, as "rose,"—or again, if we give a name to some attribute wherein they agree, as "fragrance" or "redness,"—we are then said to *generalize*. Abstraction, therefore, does not necessarily imply Generalization, though Generalization implies Abstraction.

Much needless difficulty has been raised respecting the

results of this process; many having contended, and perhaps more having taken for granted, that there must be some really-existing *thing*,* corresponding to each of those "general" [or "common"] terms, and of which such term is the name, standing for and representing it: *e. g.* that as there is a really existing Being corresponding to the proper name, "Ætna," and signified by it, so, the common-term, "mountain," must also have some one really existing thing corresponding to it; and of course *distinct* from each individual mountain (since the term is not Singular but Common), yet existing *in* each, since the term is applicable to each of them. "When many different men," it is said, "are at the same time thinking or speaking about a 'mountain,' *i. e.* not any particular one, but 'a mountain, generally,' their minds must be all employed on *something;* which must also be *one* thing, and not several, and yet cannot be any one individual." And hence a vast train of mystical disquisitions about Ideas, *&c.* has arisen, which are at best nugatory, and tend to obscure our view of the process which actually takes place in the mind.

Notions expressed by common terms.

The fact is, the notion expressed by a Common-term is merely an inadequate [incomplete] notion of an Individual; and from the very circumstance of its inadequacy, it will apply equally well to any one of an indefinite number of individuals of the same description;—to any one, in short, possessing the attribute or attributes that have been abstracted, and which are designated by that Common-term. *E. G.* if I omit the mention and the consideration of every circumstance which distinguishes Ætna from any other mountain, I then form a notion (expressed by the Common-term "Mountain") which *inadequately* designates Ætna (*i. e.* which does not imply any of its peculiarities, nor its numerical singleness), and is equally applicable to any one of several other individuals.

* See the subjoined Dissertation, Book IV. Chap. v.

Generalization, it is plain, may be indefinitely extended by a further abstraction applied to common-terms: *e. g.* as by abstraction from the term Socrates we obtain the common-term "Philosopher;" so, from "philosopher," by a similar process, we arrive at the more general-term "man;" from "man" we advance to "animal," *&c.* And so also, you may advance from any "ten" objects before you, (for instance, the fingers; from which doubtless arose the custom of reckoning by tens) to the general-term,—the number "ten;" and thence again, to the more general-term, "number;" and ultimately to the term "quantity."*

Different abstractions from the same object.

We are thus enabled, not only to separate, and consider singly one part of an object presented to the mind, but also to fix arbitrarily upon whatever part we please, according as may suit the purpose we happen to have in view. *E. G.* any individual person to whom we may direct our attention, may be considered either in a political point of view, and accordingly referred to the class of Merchant, Farmer, Lawyer, *&c.* as the case may be; or physiologically, as Negro, or White-man; or theologically, as Pagan, Mahometan, Christian, *&c.*; or geographically, as European, American, *&c.* And so, in respect of anything else that may be the subject of our reasoning: we arbitrarily fix upon and abstract that point which is essential to the purpose in hand; so that the same object may be referred

* The employment of this faculty at pleasure has been regarded, and perhaps with good reason, as the characteristic distinction of the human mind from that of the Brutes. Accordingly, even the most intelligent Brutes seem incapable of forming any distinct notion of *number*: to do which evidently depends on Abstraction. For in order to *count* any objects, you must withdraw your thoughts from all *differences* between them, and regard them simply as *units*. And accordingly, the Savage Tribes (who are less removed than we are from the Brutes) are remarked for a great deficiency in their notions of *number*. Few of them can count beyond ten, or twenty; and some of the rudest Savages have no words to express any numbers beyond five. See Dr. Taylor's "Natural-history of Society."

to various different classes, according to the occasion. Not, of course, that we are allowed to refer anything to a class to which it does *not* really belong; which would be pretending to abstract from it something that was *no* part of it; but that we arbitrarily fix on *any part* of it which we chuse to abstract from the rest.

It is important to notice this, because men are often disposed to consider each object as *really* and properly belonging to some *one* class alone;* from their having been accustomed, in the course of their own pursuits, to consider, in one point of view only, things which may with equal propriety be considered in other points of view also: *i. e.* referred to various Classes, (or predicates.) And this is that which chiefly constitutes what is called narrowness-of-mind. *E. G.* a mere botanist might be astonished at hearing such plants as Clover and Lucerne included, in the language of a farmer, under the term "grasses," which he has been accustomed to limit to a tribe of plants widely different in all botanical characteristics; and the mere farmer might be no less surprised to find the troublesome "weed," (as he has been accustomed to call it,) known by the name of Couch-grass, and which he has been used to class with nettles and thistles, to which it has no *botanical* affinity, ranked by the botanist as a species of Wheat, (*Triticum Repens.*) And yet neither of these classifications is in itself erroneous or irrational; though it would be absurd, in a botanical treatise, to class plants according to their agricultural use; or, in an agricultural treatise, according to the structure of their flowers. So also, a Diamond would be classed by a jeweller along with the ruby, emerald, &c., as a *precious stone:* while the chemist classes it, along with plumbago and coal, as one of the forms of *carbon.*

Different modes of classification.

The utility of these considerations, with a view to the present subject, will be readily estimated, by recurring to

* See the subjoined Dissertation, Book IV. Chap. v.

the account which has been already given of the process of Reasoning; the analysis of which shows that it consists in referring the term we are speaking of to some class, *viz.* a middle term; which term again is referred to, or excluded from (as the case may be) another class, *viz.* the term which we wish to affirm or deny of the Subject of the Conclusion. So that the quality of our reasoning in any case must depend on our being able correctly, clearly, and promptly, to *abstract* from the Subject in question that which may furnish a Middle-term suitable to the occasion.

Utility of the analytical form.

The imperfect and irregular sketch which has here been attempted, of the logical system, may suffice (even though some parts of it should not be at once fully understood by those who are entirely strangers to the study) to point out the general drift and purpose of the science, and to render the details of it both more interesting and more intelligible. The Analytical form, which has here been adopted, is, generally speaking, better suited for *introducing* any science in the plainest and most interesting form; though the Synthetical, which will henceforth be employed, is the more regular, and the more compendious form for storing it up in the memory.

It is to be observed, however, that technical terms and rules will be rather an encumbrance than a help, unless we take care not only to understand them thoroughly, but also to learn them so perfectly that they may be as readily and as correctly employed as the names of the most familiar objects around us.

But if any one will take the trouble to do this *once for all,* he will find that in the end, much trouble will have been saved. For, the explanations given of such technical-terms and general rules, when thoroughly learnt, once, will save the necessity of going through nearly the *same* explanation, *over and over again* on each separate occasion.

In short, the advantage of technical-terms is just like

what we derive from the use of *any other* Common-terms. When, for instance, we have once accurately learnt the definition of a "Circle," or have had fully described to us what sort of creature an "Elephant" is, to say "I drew a Circle," or, "I saw an Elephant," would be sufficiently intelligible, without any need of giving the description or definition at full length, over and over again, on every separate occasion.

BOOK II.

SYNTHETICAL COMPENDIUM.

CHAP. I.—*Of the Operations of the Mind and of Terms.*

§ 1.

Operations of the Mind.

THERE are three operations [or states] of the mind which are immediately concerned in Argument; which are called by logical writers —1st. Simple-apprehension; 2d. Judgment; 3d. Discourse or Reasoning.*

Simple-apprehension.

1st. Simple-apprehension they define to be that act or condition of the mind in which it receives a notion of any object; and which is analogous to the perception of the senses. It is either Incomplex or Complex: † Incomplex-apprehension is of one object, or of several without any relation being perceived between them, as of "a man," "a horse," "cards:" Com-

* Logical writers have in general begun by laying down that there are, *in all*, three operations of the mind: (*in universum tres*) an assertion by no means incontrovertible, and which, if admitted, is nothing to the present purpose. Our business is with *argumentation*, expressed in words, and the operations of the mind implied in that; what others there may be, or whether any are irrelevant questions.

The opening of a treatise with a statement respecting the operations of the mind universally, tends to foster the prevailing error (from which probably the minds of the writers were not exempt) of supposing that Logic professes to teach "the use of the mental faculties in general;"—the "right use of reason," according to Watts.

† With respect to the technical terms employed in this work, see the Preface.

plex, is of several *with* such a relation, as of "a man on horseback," "a pack of cards."

Judgment. 2d. Judgment is the comparing together in the mind two of the notions [or ideas] which are the objects of Apprehension, whether complex or incomplex, and pronouncing that they *agree* or *disagree* with each other: [or that one of them *belongs* or does not belong to the other.] Judgment, therefore, is either *affirmative* or *negative*.

Discourse. 3d. Reasoning [or "discourse"] is the act of proceeding from certain Judgments to another *founded* upon them, [or the result of them.]

§ 2.

Language. Language affords the *signs* by which these operations of the mind are not only expressed, and communicated to others, but even, for the most part, carried on by ourselves. The notion obtained in an act of *apprehension*, is called, when expressed in language, a *term;* an act of *judgment* is expressed by a *proposition;* an act of *reasoning*, by an *argument;* (which, when *regularly* expressed, is a syllogism;) as *e. g.*

"Every dispensation of Providence is beneficial;
Afflictions are dispensations of Providence,
Therefore they are beneficial:"

is a Syllogism; the act of reasoning being indicated by the word "*therefore*." It consists of three *propositions*, each of which has (necessarily) two *terms*, as "beneficial," "dispensations of Providence," *&c.*

In introducing the mention of *language* previously to the definition of Logic, I have departed from established practice, in order that it may be clearly understood, that Logic is *entirely conversant about language.* If any process of reasoning *can* take place, in the mind, without any employment of language, orally or mentally, (a metaphysical question which I shall not here discuss) such a process does not come within the province of the science here treated of.* This truth, most writers on the subject, if indeed they were fully aware of it themselves, have certainly not taken due care to impress on their readers.

Purposes for which Language is employed.

Language is employed for various purposes. It is the province of the historian, for instance, to convey *information* by means of language, —of the Poet, to afford a certain kind of *gratification*,—of the orator, to *persuade*, &c. &c.; while it belongs to the argumentative writer or speaker, as such, to *convince* the understanding. And as Grammar is conversant about language universally, for whatever purpose it is employed, so, it is only so far as it is employed for this last purpose, *viz.* that of *reasoning*, that it falls under the cognizance of Logic.

Terms. Propositions. Syllogisms.

And whereas, in reasoning, *terms* are liable to be *indistinct*, (*i. e.* without any clear, determinate meaning,) *propositions* to be *false*, and *arguments inconclusive*, Logic undertakes directly and completely to guard against *this last* defect, and, incidentally, and in a certain degree, against the others, as far as can be done by the *proper use of language*. It is, therefore, (when regarded as an *art*) "the Art of employing language properly for the purpose of Reasoning; and of distinguishing what is properly and truly an Argument, from spurious imitations of it." The importance of such a study no one can rightly estimate who has not long and attentively considered how much our thoughts are influenced by expressions, and how much error, perplexity, and labour are occasioned by a faulty use of language; and many who are not unaware of *that*, have yet failed to observe that "*signs*" (such as Language supplies) are an indispensable *instrument* of all Reasoning, strictly so called.

* See Introduction, § 5.

Degree and manner in which the several defects are to be guarded against.

In reference however to the above-mentioned defects, two important distinctions are to be observed. 1st. It is to be remembered that that which is, *really*, a Term, may be *indistinctly* apprehended by the person employing it, or by his hearer; and so also, a Proposition which is *false*, is not the less a *real Proposition:* but, on the other hand, any expression or statement which does not really *prove* anything, is *not*, *really*, an Argument at all, though it may be brought forward and passed off as such.

2dly, It is to be remembered that (as it is evident from what has been formerly said) no rules can be devised that will *equally* guard against *all three* of the above-mentioned defects.

To arrive at a distinct apprehension of everything that may be expressed by any Term whatever, and again, to ascertain the truth or falsity of every conceivable Proposition, is manifestly beyond the reach of any system of rules. But on the other hand, it *is* possible to exhibit any pretended Argument whatever in such a form as to be able to *pronounce decisively* on its validity or its fallaciousness.

So that the *last* of the three defects alluded to (though not, the two former) may be *directly* and *completely* obviated by the application of suitable rules. But the other two defects can be guarded against (as will presently be shown) only *indirectly*, and to a certain degree.

In other words, rules may be framed that will enable us to decide, what is, or is not, *really* a "Term,"—really, a "Proposition"—or really, an "Argument:" and to do this, is to guard *completely* against the defect of *inconclusiveness;* since nothing that is inconclusive, is, really, an "Argument;" though that may be *really a* "Term" of which you do not *distinctly* apprehend the meaning; and that which is *really a* "*Proposition*," may be a *false* Proposition.

Analysis of Syllogism & Proposition.

A Syllogism being, as aforesaid, resolvable into three Propositions, and each Proposition containing two Terms; of these terms, that which is spoken of is called the *subject;* that which is said of it, the *predicate;* and these two are called the *terms* [or extremes] because, logically, the Subject is placed *first,* and the Predicate *last;** and, in the middle, the Copula, which indicates the act of Judgment, as by it the Predicate is affirmed or denied of the Subject. The Copula must be either IS or IS NOT; which expressions indicate simply that you affirm or deny the Predicate, of the Subject. The substantive-verb is the only *verb* recognised by Logic; inasmuch as all others are compound; being resolvable, by means of the verb, "to be," and a participle or adjective: *e.g.* "the Romans conquered:" the word conquered is both copula and predicate, being equivalent to "*were* (Cop.) *victorious*" (Pred.)

It is proper to observe, that the Copula, as such, has no relation to *time;* but expresses merely the agreement or disagreement of two given terms: hence, if any other *tense* of the substantive-verb besides the present, is used, it is either understood as the same in sense, (the difference of tense being regarded as a matter of grammatical propriety only;) or else, if the circumstance of *time* really do *modify the sense* of the whole proposition, so as to make the use of that tense an essential, then, this circumstance is to be regarded as a part of one of the terms: "*at that time,*" or some such expression, being understood: as "this man *was* honest;" *i. e.* "he is one formerly-honest." In such cases, an emphasis, accompanied with a peculiar tone, is usually laid on the substantive-verb.†

* In Greek and in Latin, very often, and, not unfrequently, in English, the predicate is, actually, put first: as "great is Diana of the Ephesians."

† Strange to say, there are persons who thus understand our Lord's declaration to Pilate: "my kingdom *is* not of this world;" viz. "*now;*" meaning (secretly) that it was to become so HEREAFTER, when his followers should have

Sometimes the substantive-verb is both Copula and Predicate; *i. e.* where *existence* only is predicated: *e. g.* Deus *est*, "there is a God." "One of Jacob's sons is not." And observe, that the Copula, merely as such, does not imply *real existence: e. g.* "a faultless man is a Being feigned by the Stoics, and which one must not expect to meet with."

§ 3.

It is evident that a Term may consist either of one Word or of several; and that it is not every word that is *categorematic*, i. e. capable of being employed by itself as a Term. Adverbs, Prepositions, *&c.* and also Nouns in any other case besides the nominative, are *syncategorematic*, i. e. can only form part of a term. A nominative Noun may be by itself a term. A Verb (all except the substantive-verb used as the copula) is a *mixed* word, being resolvable into the Copula and Predicate, to which it is equivalent; and, indeed, is often so resolved in the mere rendering out of one language into another; as "*ipse adest*," "he is present."

Categorematic.

Syncategorematic.

Mixed.

Infinitives. It is to be observed, however, that under "verb," we do not include the Infinitive, which is properly a Noun-substantive, nor the Participle, which is a Noun-adjective. They are *verbals;* being related to their respective verbs in respect of *the things they signify:* but not *verbs,* inasmuch as they differ entirely in their *mode of signification.* It is worth observing, that an Infinitive (though it often comes last in the sentence) is *never the predicate,* except when another Infinitive is the Subject: *e. g.*

subj. pred.

"I hope to succeed:" *i. e.* "to succeed is what I hope."
"Not to advance is to fall back."

attained greater strength! What can be the *moral* sentiments of those who can believe such to have been the *secret sense* of the words of a divine messenger who is to be our model of truth and of all virtue!

It is to be observed, also, that in English there are two infinitives, one in "*ing*," the same in sound and spelling as the Participle-present; from which, however, it should be carefully distinguished; *e.g.* "rising early is healthful," and "it is healthful to rise early," are equivalent.

Grammarians have produced much needless perplexity by speaking of the *participle in* "*ing*," being *employed* so and so; when it is manifest that that very employment of the word constitutes it, to all intents and purposes, an *infinitive* and not a participle.

The advantage of the infinitive in *ing*, is, that it may be used either in the nominative or in any oblique case; not (as some suppose) that it necessarily implies a *habit; e.g.* "Seeing is believing:" "there is glory in dying for one's country:" "a *habit* of observing," *&c.*

If I say "he is riding," and again "riding is pleasant," in the former sentence "riding" is an Adjective, and is the Predicate; in the latter it is a Substantive and is the Subject; the sentence being equivalent to "it is pleasant to ride."

In this, and in many other cases, the English word IT serves as a *representative* of the Subject when that is put last: *e.g.*

pred. subj.

"It is to be hoped that we shall succeed."

An adjective (including participles) cannot, by itself, be made the Subject of a proposition; but is often employed as a Predicate: as "Crassus was rich;" though some chuse to consider some substantive as understood in every such case, (*e.g.* rich man) and consequently do not reckon adjectives among Simple-terms; [*i. e.* words which are capable, singly, of being employed as terms.] This, however, is a question of no practical consequence; but I have thought it best to adhere to Aristotle's mode of statement. (*See* his Categ.)

Of Simple-terms, then, (which are what the first part of Logic treats of) there are many *Simple-terms.*

divisions; of which, however, one will be sufficient for the present purpose; *viz.* into *singular* and *common:* because, though any term whatever may be a *subject,* none but a *common* term can be affirmatively *predicated* of *several* others. A Singular-term stands for *one individual,* as "Cæsar," "the Thames:" these, it is plain, cannot be said [predicated] *affirmatively,* of any thing but those individuals respectively. A Common-term is one that may stand for any of an indefinite number of individuals, which are called its *significates: i. e.* can be *applied* to any of them, as comprehending them in its *single signification;* as "man," "river," "great."

Singular and common terms.

The learner who has gone through the Analytical Outline, will now be enabled to proceed to the Second and Third Chapters either with or without the study of the remainder of what is usually placed in the First Chapter, but which I have subjoined as a Supplement. See Chap. V.

Chap. II.—*Of Propositions.*

§ 1.

The second part of Logic treats of the *Proposition;* which is, "*Judgment expressed in words.*"

Definition of Proposition.

A Proposition is defined logically "*a Sentence indicative,*" [or "asserting"] i. e. which "*affirms* or *denies.*"* It is this that distinguishes a *Proposition* from a *Question,* a *Command,* &c.

Logical Writers are accustomed to add, in explanation

* "Sentence" being, in logical language, the *Genus,* and "indicative" the "Differentia," [or distinguishing-quality.] See Ch. V. § 6.

of this definition, that a "Proposition" must not be *ambiguous;* inasmuch as that which has more than one *meaning,* is in reality not *one,* but *several* propositions. And they also add that it must not be imperfect or ungrammatical; which is only saying that any combination of words that does not really form a "Sentence" cannot be a "Proposition;" though one may perhaps conjecture from it what it was that the speaker meant to assert.

Categorical and hypothetical propositions.

Propositions considered merely as *Sentences,* are distinguished into "Categorical" and "Hypothetical."

The Categorical asserts simply that the Predicate does, or does not, apply to the Subject: as "The world had an intelligent maker:" "Man is not capable of raising himself, unassisted, from the savage to the civilized state." The Hypothetical [called by some writers, "Compound"] makes its assertion under a *Condition,* or with an *Alternative;* as "If the world is not the work of chance, it must have had an intelligent maker:" "Either mankind are capable of rising into civilization unassisted, or the first beginning of civilization must have come from above."

The former of these two last examples is of that kind called "Conditional-propositions;"* the "*condition*" being denoted by "if," or some such word. The latter example is of the kind called "Disjunctive;" the *alternative* being denoted by "either" and "or."

The division of Propositions into Categorical and Hypothetical, is, as has been said, a division of them considered merely as *Sentences;* for a like distinction might be extended to other kinds of Sentences also. Thus, "Are men capable of raising themselves to civilization?" "Go and study books of travels," are what might be called *catego-*

* Or "hypothetical," according to those writers who use the word "compound" where we have used "hypothetical."

rical sentences, though not *propositions.* "If man is incapable of civilizing himself, whence came the first beginning of civilization?" might be considered as a *conditional question:* and "Either admit the conclusion, or refute the argument," as a *disjunctive command.*

Categorical propositions are subdivided into the *pure,* which asserts *simply* [*purely*] that the subject does or does not agree with the predicate, and the *modal,* which expresses in what *mode* [or manner] it agrees; *e. g.* "An intemperate man will be sickly;" "Brutus killed Cæsar;" are *pure.* "An intemperate man will *probably* be sickly;" "Brutus killed Cæsar *justly;*" are *modal.* At present we speak only of *pure categorical* propositions.

Substance of a Proposition. The above division of Propositions (into Categorical and Hypothetical) is called in the phraseology of Logical writers, a "division of them according to their *substance;*" *i. e.* considered simply as *sentences.*

The "characteristic-*quality*" [Differentia] of a Proposition being its "*asserting,*"—*i. e.* "affirming or denying" something, hence Propositions are divided, according to their "*Quality,*" into "affirmative" and "negative." The division of them again, into "true" and "false," is also called a division according to their "quality;" namely, the "quality of the *Matter:*" (as it has relation to the subject-matter one is treating of) while the other kind of quality (a proposition's being *affirmative* or *negative*) is "the quality of the *expression.*"

Quality.

The "quality of the matter" is considered (in relation to our present inquiries) as *accidental,* and the "quality of the expression" as *essential.* For though the truth or falsity of a proposition—for instance, in Natural-history, is the most essential point *in reference to Natural-history,* and of a *mathematical* proposition, in reference to *Mathematics,* and so in other cases,—this is merely accidental in reference to an inquiry (such as the present) only as to *forms of expression.* In reference to *that,* the essential difference is that between affirmation and negation.

And here it should be remarked by the way, that as, on the one hand, every *Proposition* must be either true or false, so, on the other hand, *nothing else* can be, strictly speaking, either true or false. In colloquial language however, "true" and "false" are often more loosely applied; as when men speak of the "*true* cause" of any-thing; meaning, "the *real* cause;"—the "true heir," that is, the *rightful* heir; —a "*false* prophet,"—that is, a *pretended* prophet, or one who *utters falsehoods;*—a "true" or "false" argument; meaning a *valid,* [real] or an *apparent*-argument;—a man "true," or "false" to his friend; *i. e. faithful* or unfaithful, &c.

A Proposition, it is to be observed, is Affirmative or Negative, according to its *Copula; i. e.* according as the Predicate is affirmed or denied of the Subject. Thus, "Not to advance, is to fall back," is *affirmative:* "No miser is truly rich" [or "a miser is not truly rich"] is a *negative.* "*A few* of the sailors were saved," is an affirmative; "*Few* of the sailors were saved," is properly a negative; for it would be understood that you were speaking of "most of the sailors," and *denying* that they were saved.

Quantity.

Another division* of propositions is according to their *quantity* [or extent.] If the Predicate is said of the *whole* of the Subject, the proposition is *Universal:* if of *part* of it only, the proposition is *Particular* (or partial:) *e. g.* "Britain is an island;" "all tyrants are miserable;" "no miser is rich;" are *Universal* propositions, and their subjects are therefore said to be *distributed;* being understood to stand, each, for *the whole* of its Significates: but, "*some* islands are fertile;" "all tyrants are not assassinated;" are *Particular,* and their subjects, consequently,

* See Chap. V. § 3.

not *distributed*, being taken to stand for a *part* only of their Significates.

As every proposition must be either *Affirmative* or *Negative*, and must also be either *universal* or *particular*, we reckon, in all, four kinds of pure categorical propositions, (*i. e.* considered as to their quantity and quality *both;*) *viz.* Universal Affirmative, whose symbol (used for brevity) is *A;* Universal Negative, *E;* Particular affirmative, *I;* Particular Negative, *O.*

§ 2.

When the subject of a proposition is a Common-term, the *universal signs* ("all, no, every") are used to indicate that it is distributed, (the proposition being consequently then universal;) the *particular signs* ("some, *&c.*") the contrary. Should there be *no sign* at all to the common term, the quantity of the proposition (which is called an *Indefinite* proposition) is ascertained by the *matter; i. e.* the nature of the connexion between the extremes: which is either Necessary, Impossible, or Contingent. In necessary and in impossible Matter, an Indefinite is *understood as a universal: e. g.* "birds have wings;" *i. e. all:* "birds are not quadrupeds;" *i. e. none:* in contingent matter, (*i. e.* where the terms partly [sometimes] agree, and partly not) an Indefinite is understood as a Particular; *e. g.* "food is necessary to life;" *i. e. some* food; "birds sing;" *i. e. some* do; "birds are not carnivorous;" *i. e. some* are not, or, all are not.

Indefinite.

It is very perplexing to the learner, and needlessly so, to reckon *indefinites* as one class of propositions in respect of quantity.* They must *be* either universal or particular, though it is not *declared* which. The person, indeed, who utters the indefinite proposition, may be mistaken as to this

* Such a mode of classification resembles that of some grammarians, who, among the Genders, enumerate the *doubtful gender!*

point, and may mean to speak universally in a case where the proposition is not universally true. And the hearer may be in doubt *which* was meant, or *ought* to be meant; but the speaker must mean either the one or the other.

Of course the determination of a question relating to the "matter," *i. e. when* we are authorized to use the universal, and when, the particular sign,—when, an affirmative, and when a negative,—is what cannot be determined by *Logic.*

Singular propositions.

As for *singular* propositions, (*viz.* those whose subject is either a *proper name,* or a common term with a *singular* sign) they are reckoned as Universals, (see Book IV. Ch. IV. § 2.) because in them we speak of the *whole* of the subject; *e. g.* when we say, "Brutus was a Roman," we mean the *whole* of Brutus. This is the general rule; but some Singular-propositions may fairly be reckoned *particular; i. e.* when some qualifying word is inserted, which indicates that you are *not* speaking of the whole of the subject; *e. g.* "Cæsar was not *wholly* a tyrant;" "this man is *occasionally* intemperate;" "non *omnis* moriar."

It is not meant that these *may* not be, and that, the most naturally, accounted Universals; but it is only by viewing them in the other light, that we can regularly state the *Contradictory* to a Singular proposition. Strictly speaking, when we regard such propositions as admitting of a variation in Quantity, they are not properly considered as Singular; the subject being, *e. g.* not *Cæsar,* but the *parts* of his character.

Distribution of terms.

It is evident that the *subject* is *distributed* in every *universal* proposition, and never in a *particular:* (that being the very difference between universal and particular propositions:) but the distribution or non-distribution of the *predicate,* depends (not on the *quantity,* but) on the *quality,* of the proposition; for, if any *part of the predicate* agrees with the Subject, it must be *affirmed* and not *denied* of the Subject; therefore, for an Affirmative-proposition to be true, it is *sufficient* that some *part of the predicate* agrees with the Subject; and (for the same reason) for a Negative to be true, it is necessary that the *whole* of the predicate should *disagree* with the Subject: *e. g.* it is true that "learning is useful" though the whole of the term "useful" does not agree with the term "learning" (for many things are useful besides learning;) but "no vice is useful," would be false if any part of the term "useful" agreed with the term "vice;" *i. e.* if you could find any one useful thing which was a vice.

And this holds good equally whether the negative proposition be "universal" or "particular." For to say that "Some X is not Y" (or—which is the same in sense—that "All X is not Y") is to imply that there is *no part* of the term "Y" [no part of the class which "Y" stands *for*] that is applicable to the *whole without exception*, of the term "X;"—in short, that there is *some part* of the term "X" to which "Y" is *wholly* inapplicable.

Thus, if I say, "some of the men found on that island are not sailors of the ship that was wrecked there," or, in other words, "the men found on that island are *not, all of them,* sailors of the ship, &c." I imply that the term "sailors, &c." is *wholly* inapplicable to *some* of the "men on the island;" though it might perhaps be applicable to others of them.

Again, if I say "some coin is made of silver," and "some coin is not made of silver," (or in other words, that "all coin is not made of silver") in the former of these propositions I imply, that in *some portion* (at least) of the Class of "things made of silver," is found [or comprehended] "some coin:" in the latter proposition I imply that there is "some coin" which is contained in *no* portion of the Class of "things made of silver;" or (in other words) which is *excluded* from the *whole* of that Class. So that the term "made of silver" is distributed in this latter proposition, and not, in the former.

The two practical rules then to be observed respecting distribution, are,

1st. All universal propositions (and no particular) distribute the *subject*.

2d. All *negative* (and no affirmative) the predicate.*

It *may happen* indeed, that the whole of the predicate in an affirmative may agree with the subject; *e. g.* it is equally true, that "all men are rational animals;" and "all rational animals are men;" but this is merely *accidental*, and is not at all *implied* in the *form of expression*, which alone is regarded in Logic.†

* Hence, it is matter of common remark, that it is difficult to prove a Negative. At first sight this appears very obvious, from the circumstance that a Negative has one more Term distributed than the corresponding Affirmative. But then, again, a difficulty may be felt in accounting for this, inasmuch as any Negative may be expressed (as we shall see presently) as an Affirmative, and *vice versâ*. The proposition, *e. g.* that "such a one is not in the Town," might be expressed by the use of an equivalent term, "he is absent from the Town."

The fact is, however, that in every case where the observation as to the difficulty of proving a Negative holds good, it will be found that the proposition in question is contrasted with one which has really a term the less, distributed; or a term of less extensive sense. *E. G.* It is easier to prove that a man has proposed wise measures, than that he has never proposed an unwise measure. In fact, the one would be to prove that "*Some* of his measures are wise;" the other, that "*All* his measures are wise." And numberless such examples are to be found.

But it will very often happen that there shall be Negative propositions much more easily established than certain Affirmative ones on the same subject. *E. G.* That "The cause of animal-heat is *not* respiration," is said to have been established by experiments; but *what* the cause *is* remains doubtful. See Note to Chap. III. § 5.

† When, however, a Singular Term is the Predicate, it must, of course, be co-extensive with the Subject; as "Romulus was the founder of Rome." In this and also in some other cases (see B. I. § 5.) we judge, not from the *form* of the *expression*, but from the *signification* of the terms, that they are "equivalent" ["*convertible*"] terms.

Of Opposition.

§ 3.

Two propositions are said to be *opposed* to each other, when, having the same Subject and Predicate, they differ, in *quantity*, or *quality*, or *both*.* It is evident, that with any given subject and predicate, you may state four distinct propositions, *viz.* A, E, I, and O; any two of which are said to be *opposed*;† hence there are four different kinds of opposition, *viz.* 1st. the two universals (A and E) are called *contraries* to each other; 2d. the two particular, (I and O) *subcontraries*; 3d. A and I, or E and O, *subalterns*; 4th. A and O, or E and I, *contradictories*.

Contraries. *Subcontraries.* *Subalterns.* *Contradictories.*

As it is evident, that the truth or falsity of any proposition (its quantity and quality being known) must depend on the *matter* of it, we must bear in mind, that, "*in necessary matter, all affirmatives are true, and negatives false; in impossible matter, vice versâ; in contingent matter, all universals, false, and particulars true;*" *e. g.* "*all* islands (or *some* islands) are surrounded by water," must be true, because the *matter is necessary*: to say, "*no* islands, or some—*not*, &c." would have been false: again, "*some* islands are fertile;" "*some* are not fertile," are both true, because it is Contingent Matter: put "*all*" or "no" instead of "*some*," and the propositions will be false.

Hence it will be evident, that Contraries will be *both false* in Contingent matter, but never *both true*: Subcontraries, *both true* in Contingent matter, but never *both false*: Contradictories, always *one true* and *the other false*, &c. with other observations, which will be immediately made on viewing

* For Opposition of *Terms*, see Chap. V.

† In ordinary language however, and in some logical treatises, propositions which do not differ in *Quality* (viz. *Subalterns*) are not reckoned as "opposed."

the scheme; in which the four propositions are denoted by their symbols, the different kinds of matter by the initials, n, i, c, and the *truth* or *falsity* of each proposition in each matter, by the letter v. for *(verum)* true, f. for *(falsum)* false.

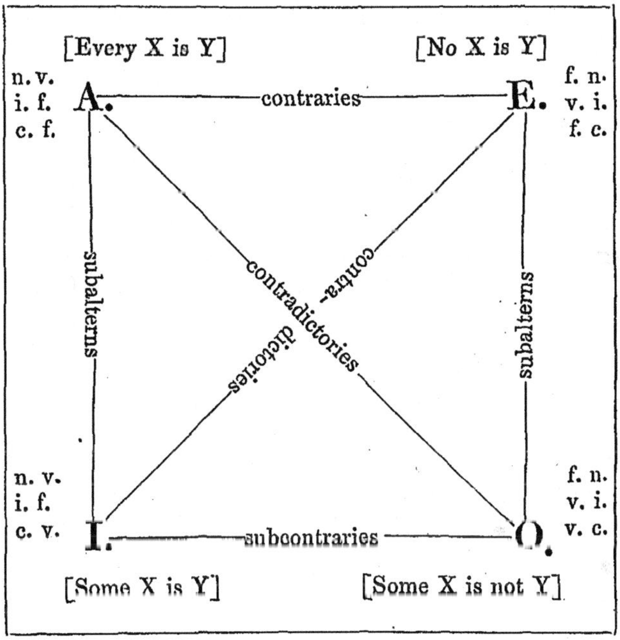

You may substitute for the unmeaning Symbols X, Y (which stand for the Terms of the above Propositions) whatever significant Terms you will; and on their meaning, of course, will depend the truth or falsity of each proposition.

For instance, Naturalists have observed that "animals having horns on the head are universally ruminant;" that, of "carnivorous animals" none are ruminant; and that, of "animals with hoofs," some are ruminant, and some, not. Let us take then instead of "X," "animals with horns on the head," and for "Y," "ruminant:" here, the real connexion of the Terms in respect of their meaning—which Connexion is called the "*matter*" of a proposition—is such that the Predicate may be affirmed universally of the Subject; and of course the *affirmatives* (whether Universal or Particular) will be true, and the "negatives" false. In this case the "matter" is technically called "necessary;" inasmuch as we *cannot avoid believing* the Predicate to be applicable to the Subject.

Again, let "X" represent "carnivorous-animal," and "Y" "ruminant:" this is a case of what is called "impossible matter;" (*i.e.* where we *cannot possibly conceive* the Predicate to be applicable to the Subject) being just the reverse of the foregoing; and, of course, both the Affirmatives will here be false, and both Negatives true.

And lastly, as an instance of what is called "contingent matter,"—*i.e.* where the Predicate can neither be affirmed universally, nor denied universally, of the Subject, take "hoofed-animal" for "X" and "ruminant" for "Y;" and of course the Universals will both be false, and the Particulars, true: that is, it is equally true that "some hoofed animals are ruminant," and that "some are not."

By a careful study of the above Scheme, bearing in mind and applying the rule concerning *matter*, the learner will easily elicit all the maxims relating to "Opposition;" as that, in the Subalterns, the truth of the Particular (which is called the *subalternate*) follows from the truth of the Universal *(subalternans)*, and the falsity of the Universal from the falsity of the Particular: that Subalterns differ in *quantity alone;* Contraries, and also Subcontraries, in *quality alone;* Contradictories, in both: and hence, that if any proposition is known to be true, we infer that its Contradictory is false; if false, its Contradictory true, *&c.*

Belief and disbelief coincide.

"Contradictory-opposition" is the kind most frequently alluded to, because (as is evident from what has been just said) to *deny*,—or to *disbelieve*,—a proposition, is to *assert*, or to *believe*, its Contradictory; and of course, to *assent* to, or *maintain* a proposition, is to reject its Contradictory. Belief therefore, and Disbelief, are not *two different* states of the mind, but the *same*, only considered in reference to two Contradictory propositions. And consequently, *Credulity* and *Incredulity* are not opposite habits, but the same; in reference to some class of propositions, and to their contradictories.

For instance, he who is the most *incredulous* respecting a certain person's *guilt*, is, in other words, the most ready to believe him *not guilty;* he who is the most credulous* as to certain works being within the reach of Magic, is the most incredulous [or " slow of heart to believe"] that they are *not* within the reach of Magic; and so, in all cases.

The reverse of *believing this or that individual* proposition, is, no doubt, to *disbelieve that same* proposition: but the reverse of *belief generally*, is (not disbelief; since that implies belief; but) *doubt.* †

Of course the learner must remember, as above observed, that the determination of the " matter" is out of the province of Logic. The rules of Opposition merely pronounce on the truth or falsity of each proposition, *given*, the " matter."

* As the Jews, in the time of Jesus, in respect of his works.

† And there may even be cases in which *doubt* itself may amount to the most extravagant credulity. For instance, if any one should " doubt whether there is any such Country as Egypt," he would be in fact *believing* this most incredible proposition; that "it is *possible* for many thousands of persons, unconnected with each other, to have agreed, for successive Ages, in bearing witness to the existence of a fictitious Country, without being detected, contradicted, or suspected."

All this, though self-evident, is, in practice, frequently lost sight of: the more, on account of our employing, in reference to the Christian Religion, the words "*Believer* and *Un*believer;" whence, unthinking persons are led to take for granted that the rejection of Christianity implies a less *easy belief* than its reception.

The only way to be safe from credulity on a given subject, is, either to examine carefully and dispassionately, and decide *according to the evidence*, or else to withdraw your thoughts from it altogether. *E. G.* in some legal trial which does not concern or interest us, we neither pronounce that the

Of Conversion.

§ 4.

A proposition is said to be *converted* when its Terms are *transposed; i. e.* when the Subject is made the Predicate, and the Predicate the Subject. When nothing more is done, this is called *simple* conversion.

Illative conversion. No conversion is employed for any logical purpose, unless it be *illative;* i. e. when the truth of the converse is implied by* the truth of the Exposita, (or proposition given ;) *e.g.*

"No virtuous man is a rebel, *therefore*
No rebel is a virtuous man."

"No Christian is an astronomer, *therefore*
No astronomer is a Christian." †

"Some boasters are cowards, *therefore*
Some cowards are boasters."

The "conversion" of such a proposition as this, "No

plaintiff *has* a just title to the property he claims, nor again that he has *not* a just title, nor yet, that there *is no sufficient evidence* to show whether his title is just or not; but we disregard the whole question.

Hence we may perceive that "*private-judgment,*" the *right*, and the *duty* of which have long been warmly debated, is a thing *unavoidable*, in any matter concerning which one takes an interest. For if a man resolves that he will implicitly receive, *e.g.* in Religious points, all the decisions of a certain Pastor, Church, or Party, he *has*, in so doing, performed *one* act of private-judgment, which includes all the rest: just as if a man, distrusting his own skill in the management of property, should make over his whole estate to trustees; in doing which he *has* exercised an act of ownership; for which act, generally, and for the choice of such and such particular trustees, he is *responsible.* (See Essay ii. On the Kingdom of Christ, § 26.)

* The reader must not suppose from the use of the word "illative," that this conversion is a process of *reasoning:* it is in fact only stating the *same* Judgment in another form.

† When Galileo's persecutors endeavoured to bring about the former of these, they forgot that it implied the latter. And the same may be said of some opponents of Geology at the present day.

one [is happy who] is anxious for change," would be effected by altering the arrangement of the words in brackets, into "who is happy."

Strictly speaking, *that* is not a *real* "conversion,"—but only an "*apparent* conversion"—which is not "illative." For, (as has been above said) there is not a *mere transposition* of the terms, but a *new term* introduced, when a term which was undistributed in the "exposita," is distributed [taken universally] in the Converse. But as it is usual, in common discourse, to speak of "an *unsound* argument,"—meaning "an *apparent*-argument, which is in reality *not* an argument," so, in this case also, it is common to say, for instance, that "Euclid proves first that all equilateral triangles are equiangular, and afterwards he proves the *Converse*, that all equiangular triangles are equilateral:" or again, to say, "It is true that all money is wealth; but I deny the *Converse*, (in reality, the *apparent*-converse) that all wealth is money."

Conversion then, strictly so called,—that is, "illative-conversion,"—can only take place when no term is distributed in the Converse, which was undistributed in the "Exposita."

Hence, since E [Universal-negative] distributes both terms, and I, [Particular-affirmative] neither, these may both be simply-converted illatively; as in the examples above. But as A does not distribute the Predicate, its simple-conversion would not be illative; (*e. g.* from "all birds are animals," you cannot infer that "all animals are birds,") as there would be a term distributed in the Converse, which was not before. We must therefore *limit its quantity* from universal to particular, and the Conversion will be illative: (*e. g.* "*some* animals are birds;") this might be fairly named conversion by *limitation;* but is commonly called "*Conversion per accidens.*" E may thus be converted also. But in O, whether the quantity be changed or not, there will still be a term (the predicate of the converse) distributed, which

Conversion per accidens.

was not before: you can therefore only convert it illatively, by changing the quality; *i. e.* considering the negative as attached to the *predicate instead of to the copula*, and thus regarding it as I. One of the terms will then not be the same as before; but the proposition will be equipollent (*i. e.* convey the same meaning); *e. g.* "some who possess wealth are not happy:" you may consider "*not-happy*" as the predicate, instead of "*happy;*" the proposition will then be I, and of course may be simply converted; "some who are not happy possess wealth:" or, (as such a proposition is often expressed) "one may possess wealth *without* being happy."* This

Contraposition.

Ambiguity of the words "may," "must," &c.

* It is worth remarking by the way, that in such examples as the above, the words, "may," "can," "cannot," &c. have no reference (as they sometimes have) to *power*, as exercised by an agent; but merely to the *distribution* or *non-distribution of Terms:* or to the *confidence* or *doubtfulness* we feel respecting some supposition.

To say, for instance, that "a man who has the plague *may* recover," does not mean that "it is in his *power* to recover if he chuses;" but it is only a form of stating a *particular-proposition:* [I] namely, that "*Some* who have the plague recover." And again to say, "there *may* be a bed of coal in this district," means merely "The existence of a bed of coal in this district—is—a thing which I cannot confidently deny or affirm."

So also to say "a virtuous man *cannot* betray his Country" [or "it is *impossible* that a virtuous man should betray, &c."] does not mean that he lacks the *power*, (for there is no *virtue* in not doing what is out of one's power) but merely that "not betraying one's country" *forms an essential part of the notion* conveyed by the *term* "virtuous." We mean in short that it is as much out of *our* power to *conceive* a virtuous man who should be a traitor, as to conceive "a Square with *unequal sides;*" that is, a square which is *not* a square. The expression therefore is merely a way of stating the Universal-proposition [E] "No virtuous man betrays his Country."

So again, to say, "a weary traveller in the deserts of Arabia *must* eagerly drink when he comes to a Spring," does not mean that *he* is *compelled* to drink, but that *I* cannot *avoid believing* that he will;—that there is no *doubt* in my mind.

In these and many other such instances, the words "may," "must," "can," "impossible," &c. have reference, not to *power* or *absence of power in an agent,* but only to *universality* or absence of universality in the *expression;* or, to *doubt or absence of doubt* in our own mind, respecting what is asserted. See Appendix, No. 1, Art. *May*.

may be named conversion by *negation;* or as it is commonly called, by *contraposition.**

A may also be fairly converted in this way, *e. g.*

> " Every poet is a man of genius; *therefore*
> He who is not a man of genius is not a poet:"
> (or, " None but a man of genius can be a poet:"
> or, " A man of genius alone can be a poet:"
> or, " One cannot be a poet without being a man of genius."

For (since it is the same thing to *affirm* some attribute of the subject, or to *deny* the *absence* of that attribute) the original proposition [Exposita] is precisely equipollent to this,

> subj. pred.
> " No poet is not-a-man-of-genius;"

which, being E, may of course be simply converted. Thus, in one of these three ways, every proposition may be illatively converted: viz. *E, I, Simply; A, O, by Negation; A, E,—Limitation.*

Convertible terms.

Note, that as it was remarked that, in some affirmatives, the whole of the Predicate does actually agree with the Subject, so, when this is the case, A being converted simply, the Converse will be *true:* but still, as its truth does not *follow* from that of the original proposition [" exposita"] the Conversion is not *illative.* Many propositions in mathematics are of this description: *e. g.*

> " All equilateral triangles are equiangular;" and
> " All equiangular triangles are equilateral."

Though both these propositions are true, the one does not

* No mention is made by Aldrich of this kind of conversion; but it has been thought advisable to insert it, as being in frequent use, and also as being employed in this treatise for the direct reduction of Baroko and Bokardo.

follow from the other; and mathematicians accordingly give a distinct proof of each.

As the simple converse of A can then only be true when the subject and predicate are exactly equivalent (or, as they are called, *convertible* terms); and as this must always be the case in a *just definition*, so the correctness of a definition may be tried by this test. *E. G.* "A good government is that which has the happiness of the governed for its object;" if this be a *right definition*, it will follow that "a government which has the happiness of the governed for its object is a good one." But to assert a proposition, and to add, or imply, that *it is a just definition*, is to make, *not one* assertion, but *two.*

Chap. III.—*Of Arguments.*

§ 1.

Syllogisms.

The third operation of the mind, viz. *reasoning*, [or "discourse"] expressed in words, is *argument;* and an argument stated *at full length*, and in its *regular form*, is called a *syllogism.* The third part of Logic therefore treats of the *syllogism.* Every Argument * consists of two parts; that which *is proved;* and that *by means of which* it is proved. The former is called, *before* it is proved, the *question; when proved*, the *conclusion* [or *inference;*] that which is used to prove it, if stated *last* (as is often done in *common discourse*,) is called the *reason*, and is introduced by "*because*," or some other *causal* conjunction; *e. g.* "Cæsar deserved death, *because* he was a tyrant, and all tyrants deserve death." If the Conclusion be stated

* I mean, in the strict technical sense; for in popular use the word Argument is often employed to denote the latter of these two parts alone: *e. g.* "This is an *Argument* to prove so and so;" "this conclusion is established by the *Argument:*" *i. e.* Premises.—See Appendix, No. I. art. *Argument.*

last (which is the strict *logical form,* to which all Reasoning may be reduced) then, that which is employed to prove it is called the *premises,** and the Conclusion is then introduced by some *illative* conjunction, as "therefore," *e. g.*

> "All tyrants deserve death:
> Cæsar was a tyrant;
> *therefore* he deserved death." †

Since, then, an argument is an expression in which "*from something laid down and granted as true (i. e. the Premises) something else (i. e. the Conclusion) beyond this must be admitted to be true, as following necessarily [resulting] from the other;* and since Logic is wholly concerned in the use of language, it follows that a Syllogism (which is an argument stated in a regular logical form) must be "an argument so expressed, that the conclusiveness of it is manifest from *the mere force of the expression,*" *i. e.* without considering the *meaning of the terms: e. g.* in

Definition of Argument.

Definition of Syllogism.

* Both the premises together are sometimes called the *antecedent.*

† It may be observed that the definition here given of an *argument,* is in the common treatises of Logic laid down as the definition of a *syllogism;* a word which I have confined to a more restricted sense. There cannot evidently be any *argument,* whether regularly or irregularly expressed, to which the definition given by Aldrich, for instance, would not apply; so that he appears to employ "syllogism" as synonymous with "argument." But besides that it is clearer and more convenient, when we have these two words at hand, to employ them in the two senses respectively which we want to express, the truth is, that in so doing I have actually conformed to Aldrich's *practice:* for he generally, if not always, employs the term "syllogism" in the very sense to which I have confined it: *viz.* to denote an argument *stated in regular logical form;* as, *e. g.* in a part of his work (omitted in the late editions) in which he is objecting to a certain pretended syllogism in the work of another writer, he says, "valet certe *argumentum; syllogismus* tamen est falsissimus," &c. Now (waiving the exception that might be taken at this use of "*falsissimus,*" nothing being, strictly, true or false, but a *proposition*) it is plain that he limits the word "syllogism" to the sense in which it is here defined, and is consequently inconsistent with his own definition of it.

this Syllogism, "Every Y is X, Z is Y, therefore Z is X:" the Conclusion is inevitable, whatever terms X, Y, and Z, respectively are understood to stand for. And to this form all legitimate Arguments may ultimately be brought.

Necessary & probable conclusions.

One circumstance which has misled some persons into the notion that there may be Reasoning that is not, substantially, syllogistic, is this; that in a Syllogism we see the Conclusion following *certainly* [or *necessarily*] from the Premises; and again, in any apparent-syllogism which on examination is found to be (as we have seen in some of the examples) not a *real* one [not "valid"] the Conclusion *does not follow at all;* and the whole is a mere deception. And yet we often hear of Arguments which have *some* weight, and yet are not quite *decisive;*—of Conclusions which are rendered *probable,* but not absolutely *certain,* &c. And hence some are apt to imagine that the *conclusiveness* of an Argument admits of *degrees;* and that sometimes a conclusion may, *probably and partially,*—though not *certainly and completely*—follow from its Premises.

This mistake arises from men's forgetting that the *Premises themselves* will very often be *doubtful;* and then, the Conclusion also will be doubtful.

As was shown formerly, one or both of the Premises of a perfectly valid Syllogism may be utterly false and absurd: and then, the Conclusion, though inevitably following from them, may be either true or false, we cannot tell which. And if one or both of the Premises be merely probable, we can infer from them only a *probable* Conclusion; though the *conclusiveness,*—that is, the connexion between the Premises and the Conclusion—is perfectly certain.

For instance, assuming that "every month has 30 days" (which is palpably false) then, from the minor-premise that "April is a month," it follows (which happens to be true) that "April has 30 days:" and from the minor-premiss that "February is a month," it follows that "February has

30 days;" which is false. In each case the conclusiveness of the Argument is the same; but in every case, when we have ascertained the falsity of one of the Premises, we know nothing (as far as *that argument* is concerned) of the truth or falsity of the Conclusion.

When however we are satisfied of the falsity of some *Conclusion*, we may, of course, be sure that (at least) one of the Premises is false; since if they had both been true, the Conclusion would have been true.

And this—which is called the "*indirect*" mode of proof—is often employed (even in Mathematics) for establishing what we maintain: that is, we prove the *falsity* of some Proposition (in other words, the *truth* of its *contradictory*) by shewing that if assumed as a Premiss, along with another Premiss known to be true, it leads to a Conclusion manifestly false. For though, from a false assumption, either falsehood or truth may follow, from a true assumption, truth only can follow.

§ 2.

Aristotle's dictum.

The Rule or Maxim (commonly called "*dictum de omni et nullo*") by which Aristotle explains the validity of the above Argument (every Y is X, Z is Y, therefore Z is X), is this: *whatever is predicated of a term distributed, whether affirmatively or negatively, may be predicated in like manner of every thing contained under it.*" Thus, in the examples above, X is predicated of Y distributed, and Z is contained under Y (*i. e.* is its Subject;) therefore X is predicated of Z: so "all tyrants," *&c.* (§ 1.) This Rule may be *ultimately* applied to all arguments; (and their validity ultimately rests on their conformity thereto) but it cannot be *directly and immediately* applied to *all* even of pure *categorical* syllogisms; for the sake of brevity, therefore, some other Axioms are commonly applied in practice, to avoid the occasional tediousness of reducing all syllogisms to that form in which Aristotle's *dictum* is applicable.*

Canons of categorical-syllogisms.

We will speak first of pure categorical syllogisms; and the Axioms or Canons by which their validity is to be explained: *viz.* first, *if two terms agree with one and the same third, they agree with each other:* secondly, *if one term agrees and another disagrees with one and the same third, these two disagree with each other.* On the former of these Canons rests the validity of *affirmative* conclusions; on the latter, of *negative:* for no categorical syllogism can be faulty which does not violate these Canons; none correct which does: hence on these two Canons are built the rules or cautions which are to be observed with respect to syllogisms, for the purpose of ascertaining whether those Canons have been strictly observed or not.

1st. *Every syllogism has three, and only three terms: viz.* the middle-term, and the two terms (or *extremes,* as they are commonly called) of the Conclusion [or Question]. Of these, 1st, the *subject* of the Conclusion is called the *minor-term;* 2d, its *predicate,* the *major-term;* and 3d, the *middle-term,* (called by the older logicians "Argumentum,") is that with which each of them is separately compared, in order to judge of their agreement or disagreement with each other. If therefore there were *two* middle-terms, the *extremes* (or

* Instead of following the usual arrangement, in laying down first the Canons which apply to all the figures of categorical syllogisms, and then going back to the "dictum of Aristotle" which applies to only one of them, I have pursued what appears a simpler and more philosophical arrangement, and more likely to impress on the learner's mind a just view of the science: viz. 1st, to give the rule (Aristotle's Dictum) which applies to the most clearly and regularly-constructed argument, the Syllogism in the first Figure, to which *all* reasoning may be reduced: then, the canons applicable to all *categoricals;* then, those belonging to the *hypotheticals;* and lastly, to treat of the *Sorites;* which is improperly placed by Aldrich *before* the hypotheticals. By this plan the province of strict Logic is extended as far as it can be; every kind of argument which is of a *syllogistic* character, and accordingly, directly cognizable by the rules of Logic, being enumerated in natural order.

terms of conclusion) not being both compared to the *same*, could not be conclusively compared to each other.

2d. *Every syllogism has three, and only three propositions; viz.* 1st, the *major-premiss* (in which the *major term* is compared with the *middle*:) 2d, the *minor-premiss* (in which the *minor-term* is compared with the *middle*;) and 3d, the Conclusion, in which the Minor-term is compared with the Major.*

3d. Note, that *if the middle-term is ambiguous, there are in reality two middle-terms, in sense,* though but one in *sound.* An ambiguous Middle-term is either an *equivocal* term used in different senses in the two premises: (*e. g.*

> "*Light* is contrary to darkness;
> Feathers are *light*; therefore
> Feathers are contrary to darkness:")

or a term *not distributed*: for as it is then used to stand for a *part* only of its *significates*, it may happen that one of the Extremes may have been compared with *one part* of it, and the other with another part of it; *e. g.*

> "White is a colour,
> Black is a colour; therefore
> Black is white."——Again,

> "Some animals are beasts,
> Some animals are birds; therefore
> Some birds are beasts."

The middle-term therefore must be distributed once, at least, in the premises; (*i. e.* by being the Subject of an Univer-

* In some logical treatises the Major premiss is called simply "*Propositio*;" and the Minor, "*Assumptio.*" In ordinary discourse, the word "Principle" is often used to denote the Major-premiss, and "Reason," the Minor.

sal, or Predicate of a Negative, Chap. ii. §. 2,) and once is sufficient; since if one extreme has been compared to a *part* of the middle-term, and another to the *whole* of it, they must have been both compared to the same.

4th. *No term must be distributed in the conclusion which was not distributed in one of the premises;* for that (which is called an *illicit* process, either of the Major or the Minor term) would be to employ the *whole* of a term in the Conclusion, when you had employed only a *part* of it in the Premiss; and thus, in reality, to introduce a fourth term: *e. g.*

"All quadrupeds are animals,
A bird is not a quadruped; therefore
It is not an animal."—Illicit process of the major.

Again, "What is related in the Talmud is unworthy of credit: Miraculous stories are related in the Talmud; therefore Miraculous stories are unworthy of credit." If this conclusion be taken as A, there will be an "illicit process of the Minor-term;" (since every one would understand the Minor-premiss as particular) but a *particular* conclusion may fairly be inferred. In the case of an illicit-process of the *Major*, on the contrary, the premises do not warrant *any* conclusion at all.

5th. *From negative premises you can infer nothing.* For in them the Middle is pronounced *to disagree with both extremes;* not, to *agree with both;* or, to agree with one, and *disagree* with the other; therefore they cannot be compared together; *e. g.*

"A fish is not a quadruped;"
"A bird is not a quadruped," proves nothing.

6th. *If one premiss be negative, the conclusion must be negative;* for in that premiss the middle-term is pronounced to disagree with one of the Extremes, and in the other premiss (which of course is affirmative by the preceding rule) to agree with the other extreme; therefore the Extremes disagreeing with each other, the Conclusion is negative. In the same manner it may be shewn, that *to prove a negative conclusion one of the Premises must be a negative.*

* By these six rules all categorical Syllogisms are to be tried; and from them it will be evident; 1st, that *nothing can be proved from two particular Premises;* (since you will then have *either the middle Term undistributed,* or an *illicit process.* For if each premiss were I, there would be no distribution of any term at all: and if the premises were I and O, as

> "Some animals are sagacious:
> Some beasts are not sagacious:
> Some beasts are not animals,"

there would be but one term—the predicate of O—distributed; and supposing that one to be the Middle, then, the conclusion (being of course negative, by rule 6th) would have its predicate,—the Major-term—distributed, which was undistributed in the premiss. And, for the same reason, 2dly, that if one of the Premises be particular, the Conclusion must be particular; *e.g.*

> "All who fight bravely deserve reward;
> Some soldiers fight bravely;" you can only infer that
> "Some soldiers deserve reward:"

* Others have given twelve rules, which I found might more conveniently be reduced to six. No syllogism can be faulty which violates none of these six rules. It is much less perplexing to a learner not to lay down as a distinct rule, that, *e.g.* against *particular premises:* which is properly a *result* of the foregoing; since a syllogism with two particular premises would offend against either R. 3. or R. 4.

for to infer a universal Conclusion would be an "illicit-process of the Minor." But from two universal Premises you cannot always infer a universal Conclusion; *e. g.*

"All gold is precious;
All gold is a mineral: therefore
Some mineral is precious."

And even when we *can* infer a universal, we are always *at liberty* to infer a particular; since what is predicated of *all* may *of course be* predicated of some.*

Of Moods.

§ 3.

When we designate the three propositions of a syllogism in their order, according to their respective "Quantity" and "Quality" (indicated by their *symbols*) we are said to determine the *mood* of the syllogism. *E. G.* the example just above, "all gold, *&c.*" is in the Mood A, A, I.

As there are four kinds of propositions, and three propositions in each syllogism, all the possible ways of combining these four, (A, E, I, O,) by threes, are sixty-four. For, any one of these four may be the major-premiss; each of these four majors may have four different minors; and of these sixteen pairs of premises, each may have four different conclusions. $4 \times 4 (= 16) \times 4 = 64$. This is a mere arithmetical calculation of the Moods, without any regard to the logical rules; for many of these Moods are inadmissible in practice, from

* The memorial-lines in which some of the Logical-writers summed up the foregoing rules, were,

"*Distribus Medium, nec quartus terminus adsit;*"
"*Utraque nec præmissa negans, nec particularis;*"
"*Sectetur partem Conclusio deteriorem;*" (*i. e.* the Particular being regarded as *inferior* to the Universal; and the Negative, to the Affirmative)
"*Et non distribuat nisi cum Præmissa, negetve.*"

violating some of those rules; *e.g.* the Mood E, E, E, must be rejected as having *negative premises;* I, O, O, for *particular premises;* and many others for the same faults; to which must be added I, E, O, for an "illicit-process of the major," in every Figure; since the Conclusion, being negative, would distribute the Major-term, while the Major-premiss, being I, would distribute no term. By examination then of all, it will be found that, of the sixty-four there remain but eleven Moods which can be used in a legitimate syllogism, *viz.* A, A, A, A, A, I, A, E, E, A, E, O, A, I, I, A, O, O, E, A, E, E, A, O, E, I, O, I, A, I, O, A, O.

Of Figure.

§ 4.

The Figure of a syllogism consists in the situation of the Middle-term with respect to the Extremes of the Conclusion, [*i. e. the major and minor term.*] When the Middle-term is made the *subject of the major premiss, and the predicate of the minor,* that is called the first Figure; which is far the most natural and clear of all, as to this alone Aristotle's dictum may be *at once* applied. In the Second-Figure the Middle-term is the *predicate* of *both* premises: in the Third, the *subject* of both: in the Fourth, the *predicate of the Major premiss, and the subject of the Minor.* This Figure is the most awkward and unnatural of all, being the very reverse of the first.

Note, that the *proper order* * is to place the Major premiss *first*, and the Minor *second;* but this does not *constitute* the Major and Minor premises; for that premiss (wherever

* *Proper, i. e.* in a *Treatise on Logic,* or in a *logical analysis;* not, necessarily in *ordinary discourse.* This remark may appear superfluous, but that I have known a writer, generally acute and intelligent, fall into the strange misapprehension alluded to. The *proper* collocation of plants in a botanical herbarium, and in a flower-garden, and again, on a farm, would be widely different.

placed) is the Major, which *contains the major term,* and the Minor, the minor (v. R. 2. § 2.)

Each of the allowable moods mentioned above will not be allowable in every Figure; since it may violate some of the foregoing rules, in one Figure, though not in another: *e. g.* I, A, I, is an allowable mood in the third Figure; but in the first it would have an *undistributed middle.** So A, E, E, would in the first Figure have an *illicit process of the major,* but is allowable in the second; and A, A, A, which in the first Figure is allowable, would in the third have an *illicit process of the minor:* all which may be ascertained by trying the different Moods in each figure, as per scheme.

Let X represent the Major term, Z the Minor, Y the Middle.

1st Fig.	2d Fig.	3d Fig.	4th Fig.
Y, X,	X, Y,	Y, X,	X, Y,
Z, Y,	Z, Y,	Y, Z,	Y, Z,
Z, X,	Z, X,	Z, X,	Z, X.

The Terms alone being here stated, the *quantity and quality* of each Proposition (and consequently the Mood of the whole Syllogism) is left to be filled up: (*i. e.* between Y and X, we may place either a *negative* or *affirmative* Copula: and we may prefix either a *universal* or *particular* sign to Y.) By applying the Moods then to each Figure, it will be found that each figure will admit six Moods only, as not violating the rules against *undistributed middle,* and against *illicit process:* and of the Moods so admitted, several (though valid) are *useless,* as having a particular

* *e. g.* Some restraint is salutary (I): all restraint is unpleasant (A): something unpleasant is salutary (I). Again: Some herbs are fit for food (I): nightshade is an herb (A): some nightshade is fit for food (I).

Conclusion, when a *universal might have* been drawn; *e. g.* A, A, I, in the first Figure,

> "All human creatures are entitled to liberty;
> All slaves are human creatures; therefore
> *Some* slaves are entitled to liberty."

Of the twenty-four Moods, then, (six in each Figure) five are for this reason neglected: for the remaining nineteen, logicians have devised names to distinguish both the Mood itself, and the Figure in which it is found; since when one Mood (*i. e. one in itself,* without regard to Figure) occurs in two different Figures, (as E, A, E, in the first and second) the mere letters denoting the *mood* would not inform us concerning the *figure.* In these names, then, the *three vowels* denote the propositions of which the Syllogism is composed: the consonants (besides their other uses, of which hereafter) serve to keep in mind the Figure of the Syllogism.

Fig. 1. { bArbArA, cElArEnt, dArII, fErIOque prioris.

Fig. 2. { cEsArE, cAmEstrEs, fEstInO, bArOkO,* secundæ.

Fig. 3. { tertia, dArAptI, dIsAmIs, dAtIsI, fElAptOn, bOkArdO, † fErIsO, habet: quarta insuper addit.

Fig. 4. { brAmAntIp, cAmEnEs, dImArIs, fEsApO, frEsIsOn.

By a careful study of these mnemonic lines (which must be committed to memory) you will perceive that A can only be proved in the First-Figure, in which also every other Proposition may be proved; that the Second proves only *negatives:* the Third only *particulars:* that the First-

* Or, Fakoro, see § 7. † Or, Dokamo, see § 7.

Figure requires the major-premiss to be *universal,* and the minor, *affirmative, &c.;* with many other such observations, which will readily be made, (on trial of several Syllogisms, in different Moods) and the reasons for which will be found in the foregoing rules. *E. G.* to shew why the Second-figure has only Negative Conclusions, we have only to consider, that in it the middle-term being the *predicate in both premises,* would not be *distributed* unless one premiss were *negative;* (Chap. ii. § 2.) therefore the Conclusion must be negative also, by Chap. iii. § 2, Rule 6. One Mood in each figure may suffice in this place by way of example:

First, *Barbara, viz.* (bAr.) "Every Y is X; (bA) every Z is Y; therefore (rA) every Z is X:" *e. g.* let the major-term (which is represented by X) be "one who possesses all virtue;" the minor-term (Z) "every man who possesses one virtue;" and the middle-term (Y) "every one who possesses prudence;" and you will have the celebrated argument of Aristotle, *Eth.* sixth book, to prove that the virtues are inseparable; *viz.*

> "He who possesses prudence, possesses all virtue;
> He who possesses one virtue, must possess prudence;
> therefore
> He who possesses one, possesses all."

Second, *Camestres,* (cAm) "every X is Y; (Es) no Z is Y; (trEs) no Z is X." Let the major-term (X) be "true philosophers," the minor (Z) "the Epicureans;" the middle (Y) "reckoning virtue a good in itself;" and this will be part of the reasoning of Cicero, *Off.* book first and third, against the Epicureans.

Third, *Darapti, viz.* (*dA*) "every Y is X; (*rAp*) every Y is Z; therefore (*tI*) some Z is X:" *e. g.*

> "Prudence has for its object the benefit of individuals; but prudence is a virtue: therefore some virtue has for its object the benefit of the individual,"

is part of Adam Smith's reasoning (*Moral Sentiments*) against Hutcheson and others, who placed all virtue in benevolence.

Fourth, *Camenes, viz.* (*cAm*) "every X is Y; (*En*) no Y is Z; therefore (*Es*) no Z is X:" *e. g.*

> "Whatever is expedient, is conformable to nature;
> Whatever is conformable to nature, is not hurtful to society; therefore
> What is hurtful to society is never expedient;"

is part of Cicero's argument in *Off.* Lib. iii.; but it is an inverted and clumsy way of stating what would much more naturally fall into the First-Figure; for if you examine the Propositions of a Syllogism in the Fourth-Figure, *beginning* at the *Conclusion*, you will see that as the major-term is predicated of the minor, so is the minor of the middle, and that again of the major; so that the major appears to be merely *predicated of itself.* Hence the five Moods in this Figure are seldom or never used; some one of the fourteen (*moods with names*) in the first three Figures, being the forms into which all arguments may most readily be thrown: but of these, the four in the First Figure are the clearest and most natural; as to them Aristotle's Dictum will *immediately* apply.

With respect to the use of the first three Figures (for the Fourth is never employed but by an accidental awkwardness of expression) it may be remarked, that the First is that into which an argument will be found to fall the most naturally, except in the following cases:—First, When we have to *disprove* something that has been maintained, or is likely to be believed, our arguments will usually be found to take most conveniently the form of the Second Figure: *viz.* we prove that the thing we are speaking of cannot belong to such a Class, either because it

Use of the Second - Figure.

wants what belongs to the whole of that Class, (Cesare) or because it *has* something of which that class is destitute; (Camestres) *e. g.* "No impostor would have warned his followers (as Jesus did) of the persecutions they would have to submit to;" and again, "An enthusiast would have expatiated (which Jesus and his followers did not) on the particulars of a future state."

The same observations will apply, *mutatis mutandis,* when a Particular Conclusion is sought; as in Festino and Baroko.

The arguments used in the process called the "Abscissio Infiniti," will in general be the most easily referred to this Figure. (See Chap. v. § 1. subsection 6.) The phrase was applied by some logical writers to a series of arguments used in any inquiry in which we go on *excluding,* one by one, certain suppositions, or certain classes of things, from that whose real nature we are seeking to ascertain.

Thus, certain symptoms, suppose, exclude "*small-pox;*" that is, prove this *not* to be the patient's disorder; other symptoms, suppose, exclude "*Scarlatina,*" &c., and so one may proceed by gradually narrowing the range of possible suppositions. Hence, the Second Figure might be called the "*exclusive*" Figure.

Use of the Third - Figure.

The Third Figure is, of course, the one employed when the Middle-Term is *Singular,* since a Singular term can only be a Subject. This is also the form into which most arguments will naturally fall that are used to establish an *objection* (Enstasis of Aristotle) to an opponent's Premiss, when his argument is such as to require that premiss to be Universal. It might be called, therefore, the "*Enstatic*" Figure. *E. G.* If any one contends that "this or that doctrine ought not to be admitted, because it cannot be explained or comprehended," his suppressed major-premiss may be refuted by the argument that "the connexion of the Body and Soul cannot be explained or comprehended." Thus again you might prove by the example of a certain individual,* the contradictory of a Proposition (which would seem to most persons a very probable conjecture) that a deaf and dumb person, born blind, cannot be taught *language*.

A great part of the reasoning of Butler's Analogy may be exhibited in this form.

Reduction of Syllogisms.

As it is on the Dictum above-mentioned that all Reasoning *ultimately* depends, so, all arguments may be in one way or other brought into some one of the four Moods in the First-Figure: and a Syllogism is, in that case, said to be *reduced: (i. e. to the first figure.)* These four are called the *perfect* moods, and all the rest *imperfect*.

Ostensive Reduction.

§ 5.

In reducing a Syllogism, we are not, of course, allowed to introduce any new Term or Proposition, having nothing granted but the truth of the Premises; but these Premises are allowed to be *illatively converted* (because the truth of any Proposition *implies* that of its illative Converse) *or transposed:* by taking advantage of this liberty, where there is need, we deduce (in Figure 1st,) from the Premises originally given, either the *very same Conclusion* as the original one, or another from which the *original Conclusion* follows by illative *Conversion*. *E. G. Darapti*,

" All wits are dreaded;
All wits are admired;
Some who are admired are dreaded,"

is reduced into *Darii*, by converting "by limitation" *(per accidens)* the minor Premiss.

* Laura Bridgeman, alluded to above.

"All wits are dreaded;
Some who are admired are wits; therefore
Some who are admired are dreaded."

And *Camestres,—e. g.*

"All true philosophers account virtue a good in itself;
The advocates of pleasure do not account, *&c.*
Therefore they are not true philosophers,"

is reduced to *Celarent,* by simply converting the Minor, and then transposing the Premises.

"Those who account virtue a good in itself, are not advocates of pleasure;
All true philosophers account virtue, *&c.:* therefore
No true philosophers are advocates of pleasure."

This Conclusion may be *illatively converted* into the original one.

So, *Baroko;** *e. g.*

Reduction by means of conversion by negation.

"Every true patriot is a friend to religion;
Some great statesmen are not friends to religion;
Some great statesmen are not true patriots,"

to *Ferio,* by converting the major *by negation,* ["contraposition,"] vide Chap. ii. § 4.

"He who is not a friend to religion, is not a true patriot;
Some great statesmen," *&c.*

and the rest of the Syllogism remains the same: only that

* Or Fakoro, considered *i.e.* as Festino. See note at the end of this chapter.

the minor Premiss must be considered as affirmative, because you take "not-a-friend-to-religion," as the middle term. In the same manner *Bokardo* * to *Darii*; *e. g.*

> "Some slaves are not discontented;
> All slaves are wronged; therefore
> Some who are wronged are not discontented."

Convert the major "by negation" ("contraposition") and then transpose them; the Conclusion will be the *converse by negation of the original one,* which therefore may be inferred from it; *e. g.*

> "All slaves are wronged;
> Some who are not discontented are slaves;
> Some who are not discontented are wronged."

In these ways (by what is called *Ostensive Reduction,* because you prove, in the first figure, either the *very same* Conclusion as before, or one *which implies it*) all the imperfect Moods may be reduced to the four perfect ones. But there is also another way, called *Indirect*-reduction, or

Reductio ad impossibile.

§ 6.

By which we prove (in the First-Figure) not, directly, that the original Conclusion is *true,* but that it *cannot be false;* *i. e.* that an absurdity would follow from the supposition of its being false; *e. g.*

> "All true patriots are friends to religion;
> Some great statesmen are not friends to religion;
> Some great statesmen are not true patriots:"

* Or Dokamo, considered *i. e.* as Disamis. See note at the end of this chapter.

if this Conclusion be not true, its contradictory must be true; *viz.*

"All great statesmen are true patriots:"

let this then be assumed, in the place of the minor Premiss of the original Syllogism, and a false conclusion will be proved; *e.g.*

bAr, "All true patriots are friends to religion;
bA, All great statesmen are true patriots;
rA, *All great statesmen are friends to religion:*"

for as this Conclusion is the Contradictory of the original minor Premiss, it must be false, since the Premises are always supposed to be granted; therefore one of the *Premises* (by which it has been correctly proved) must be false also; but the major Premiss (being one of those originally granted) is *true;* therefore the *falsity must be in the minor Premiss;* which is the *contradictory* of the original-Conclusion; therefore the original-Conclusion must be true. This is the *indirect* mode of Reasoning. (See *Rhetoric,* Part I. Ch. ii. § 1.)

§ 7.

Signification of the names of the Moods.

This kind of Reduction is seldom employed but for *Baroko* and *Bokardo,* which are thus reduced by those who confine themselves to *simple* Conversion, and Conversion by limitation, *(per accidens;)* and they framed the names of their Moods, with a view to point out the manner in which each is to be reduced; *viz.* B, C, D, F, which are the initial letters of all the Moods, indicate to which Mood of the first figure *(Barbara, Celarent, Darii,* and *Ferio)* each of the others is to be reduced: *m* indicates that the Premises are to be *transposed; s* and *p,* that the Proposition denoted by the vowel immediately preceding, is to be *con-*

verted; s, simply, *p, per accidens*, [by limitation:] thus, in *Camestres*, (see example,) the *C* indicates that it must be reduced to *Celarent;* the two *ss*, that the minor Premiss and Conclusion must be *converted simply;* the *m*, that the Premises must be *transposed.* The *P*, in the mood Bramantip, denotes that the Premises warrant a Universal-conclusion in place of a Particular. The *I*, though of course it cannot be illatively converted *per accidens, viz.:* so as to become A, yet is thus converted in the Conclusion, because as soon as the Premises are transposed (as denoted by *m*,) it appears that a Universal Conclusion follows from them.

K (which indicates the reduction *ad impossibile*) is a sign that the Proposition, denoted by the vowel immediately before it, must be left out, and the contradictory of the Conclusion substituted; *viz.* for the *minor* Premiss in *Baroko* and the *major* in *Bokardo.* But it has been already shown (§ 5) that the Conversion by "contraposition," [by "negation"] will enable us to reduce these two Moods, *ostensively.**

CHAP. IV.

SUPPLEMENT TO CHAP. III.

Of Modal Syllogisms, and of all Arguments besides regular and pure-Categorical Syllogisms.

Of Modals.

§ 1.

Hitherto we have treated of *pure* categorical Propositions, and the Syllogisms composed of such. A *pure* categorical

* If any one should chuse that the names of these moods should indicate this, he might make K the index of conversion by negation; and then the names would be, by a slight change, *Fakoro* and *Dokamo.*

proposition is styled by some logicians a proposition "*de inesse*," from its asserting simply that the Predicate is or is not (in our conception) contained in the Subject; as "John killed Thomas." A modal proposition asserts that the predicate is or is not contained in the Subject in a certain *mode*, or manner; as, "accidentally," "wilfully," *&c.*

A *Modal* proposition may be stated as a *pure* one, by *attaching the mode to one of the Terms:* and the Proposition will in all respects fall under the foregoing rules; *e.g.* "John killed Thomas *wilfully* and *maliciously*;" here the Mode is to be regarded as part of the Predicate. "It is *probable* that all knowledge is useful;" "probably useful" is here the Predicate. But when the Mode is only used to express the necessary, contingent, or impossible connexion of the Terms, it may as well be attached to the *Subject: e.g.* "man is *necessarily* mortal;" is the same as "*all* men are mortal:" "injustice is *in no case* expedient," corresponds to "no injustice is expedient:" and "this man is *occasionally* intemperate," has the force of a *particular:* (vide Chap. ii. § 2. note.) It is thus, and thus only, that two singular Propositions may be contradictories; *e.g.* "this man is *never* intemperate," will be the *contradictory* of the foregoing. Indeed every sign (of universality or particularity) may be considered as a *Mode.*

Since, however, in all Modal Propositions, you assert that the dictum (*i.e.* the *assertion itself*) and the *Mode*, agree together, or disagree, so, in some cases, this may be the most convenient way of stating a Modal, purely:

subj. cop. pred. subject

e.g. "It *is* *impossible* that all men should be virtuous."

sub. cop.

Such is a proposition of the Apostle Paul's: "This is

pred. subject.

a faithful saying, *&c.* that Jesus Christ came into the

subj.

world to save sinners."* In these cases one of your *Terms* (the subject) is itself *an entire Proposition.*

In English, the word IN is often used in expressing one proposition combined with another in such a manner as to make the two, one proposition: *e.g.* "You will have a formidable opponent to encounter *in* the Emperor:" this involves two propositions; 1st, "You will have to encounter the Emperor;" 2d, "He will prove a formidable opponent:" this last is implied by the word *in*, which denotes (agreeably to the expression of Logicians mentioned above when they speak of a proposition "de *in*esse") that that Predicate is *contained in* that Subject.

Drift of a Proposition.

It may be proper to remark in this place, that we may often meet with a Proposition whose *drift* and force will be very different, according as we regard this or that as its Predicate.† Indeed, properly speaking, it may be considered as several different Propositions, each indeed implying the *truth* of all the rest, but each having a distinct Predicate; the division of the sentence being varied in each case; and the variations marked, either by the collocation of the words, the intonation of the voice, or by the designation of the emphatic words, [*viz.*: the Predicate,] as scored under, or printed in italics. *E. G.* "The Organon[1] of Bacon[2] was not[3] designed[4] to supersede[5] the Organon of Aristotle[6]:" this might be regarded as, at least, six different propositions: if the word numbered (1) were in italics, it would leave us at liberty to suppose that Bacon might have

* See Rhetoric, Part iii. Ch. 2. § 2.

† On the logical analysis of propositions Mr. Greenlaw has founded a very ingenious, and as it appears to me, correct and useful grammatical theory, of the use of the *Latin Subjunctive.* His work is well worth the notice of Students of Logic as well as of Latinity.

designed to supersede by *some* work of his, the Organon of Aristotle; but not by his own *Organon;* if No. 2 were in Italics, we should understand the author to be contending, that whether or no any *other* author had composed an Organon with such a design, *Bacon* at least did not: if No. 3, then, we should understand him to maintain that whether Bacon's Organon does or does not supersede Aristotle's, no such *design* at least was entertained: and so with the rest. Each of these is a distinct Proposition; and though each of them implies the truth of all the rest, (as may easily be seen by examining the example given) one of them may be, in one case, and another, in another, the one which it is important to insist on.

We should consider in each case what *Question* it is that is proposed, and what answer to it would, in the instance before us, be the most *opposite* or *contrasted* to the one to be examined. *E.G.* "You will find this doctrine in Bacon," may be contrasted, either with, "You will find in Bacon a *different* doctrine," or with, "You will find this doctrine in a *different author.*"

Emphatic words.

And observe, that when a proposition is contrasted with one which has a *different predicate,* the Predicate is the emphatic word; as "this man is a *murderer;*" *i.e.* not one who has slain another *accidentally,* or in *self-defence:* "this man *is* a murderer," with the Copula for the emphatic word, stands opposed to "he is *not* a murderer;" a proposition with the *same terms,* but a different Copula.*

* Thus if any one reads (as many are apt to do) "Thou shalt *not* steal,"—"Thou shalt *not* commit adultery," he implies the question to be, whether we are commanded to steal or to forbear: but the question really is, *what things* are forbidden; and the answer is "Thou shalt not *steal;*" "Thou shalt not commit *adultery,*" &c.

The connexion between Logic and correct Delivery is further pointed out in *Rhet.* App. 1.

Strictly speaking, the two cases I have mentioned coincide; for when the "is" or the "not" is emphatic, it becomes properly the Predicate: *viz.* "the statement of this man's being a murderer, is *true,*" or, "is *false.*"

It will often happen that several of the Propositions which are thus stated in a single sentence, may require, each, to be distinctly stated and proved: *e.g.* the Advocate may have to prove, first the *fact*, that "John killed Thomas;" and then, the character of the act, that "the killing was wilful and malicious." See Praxis, at the end of the vol. See also *Elements of Rhetoric*, Part I. Ch. iii. § 5.

Of Hypotheticals.

§ 2.

A Hypothetical* Proposition is defined to be *two or more categoricals united by a Copula* [conjunction]: and the different kinds of Hypothetical Propositions are named from their respective conjunctions; *viz.* conditional, disjunctive, causal, *&c.*

When a hypothetical conclusion is inferred from a hypothetical Premiss, so that the force of the Reasoning does not turn on the hypothesis, then the Hypothesis (as in Modals) *must* be considered *as part of one of the Terms;* so that the *Reasoning* will be, in effect, categorical: *e.g.*

predicate.

"Every conqueror is either a hero or a villain:
Cæsar was a conqueror; therefore

predicate.

He was *either a hero or a villain.*"

"Whatever comes from God is entitled to reverence;

subject.

If the Scriptures are not wholly false, they must come from God;
If they are not wholly false, they are entitled to reverence."

* *Compound*, according to some writers.

But when the *Reasoning* itself *rests* on the hypothesis (in which way a *categorical* Conclusion may be drawn from a hypothetical Premiss,) this is what is called a *hypothetical Syllogism;* and rules have been devised for ascertaining the validity of such Arguments at once, without bringing them into the categorical form. (And note, that in these Syllogisms, the *hypothetical Premiss* is called the *major*, and the *categorical one* the *minor*.) They are of two kinds, *conditional* and *disjunctive.*

Of Conditionals.

§ 3.

A *Conditional** Proposition has in it an *illative force; i. e.* it contains two, and only two categorical Propositions, whereof one *results* from the other [or follows from it,] *e. g.*

antecedent.

" If the Scriptures are not wholly false,

consequent.

they are entitled to respect."

That from which the other results is called the *Antecedent; that which results from it*, the *Consequent* (*consequens;*) and the *connexion* between the two (expressed by the word "if") the *Consequence* (*consequentia.*)

The natural order is, that the Antecedent should come *before* the Consequent; but this is frequently reversed: *e. g.* "The husbandman is well off if he knows his own advantages." (Virg. *Geor.*)

Every Conditional-proposition may be considered as an Universal-*affirmative*, whether the members of which it consists be Universal or Particular, Negative or Affirma-

* Called *Hypothetical* by those writers who use the word *Compound* to denote what I have called Hypothetical.

tive. And the truth or falsity of a Conditional-Proposition depends entirely on the *consequence: e. g.* "if Logic is useless, it deserves to be neglected;" here both Antecedent and Consequent are *false:* yet the whole Proposition is *true; i. e.* it is true that the Consequent *follows* from the Antecedent. "If Cromwell was an Englishman, he was an usurper," is just the reverse case: for though it is true that "Cromwell was an Englishman," and also that "he was an usurper," yet it is not true that the latter of these Propositions *depends on* the former; the whole Proposition, therefore, is false, (or at least absurd,—see next section) though both Antecedent and Consequent are true.

It is to be observed, however, that a false, or at least nugatory, Conditional-Proposition of *this* kind, *viz.:* in which each *member* is a true categorical,—is such, that, though itself absurd, no *false conclusion* can be drawn from it; as may be seen from the instance just given.

A Conditional Proposition, in short, may be considered as an assertion of the *validity* of a certain Argument; since to assert that an argument is *valid,* is to assert that the Conclusion necessarily results from the Premises, whether those Premises be *true* or not.

The meaning, then, of a Conditional Proposition,—which is, that *the antecedent being granted, the consequent* is granted, may be considered in two points of view: first, "if the Antecedent *be* true, the Consequent *must* be true;" hence the first rule; *the antecedent being granted, the consequent may be inferred:* secondly, "if the Antecedent *were* true, the Consequent *would* be true;" hence the second rule; *the consequent being denied, the antecedent may be denied;* for the Antecedent must in that case be false; since if it were true, the Consequent (which is granted to be false) would be true also. *E. G.* "If this man has a fever, he is not fit to travel;" here if you *grant the antecedent,* the first rule applies, and you infer the truth of the

Constructive & destructive.

Consequent; "he has a fever; therefore he is not fit to travel." If A is B, C is D; but A is B, therefore C is D; and this is called a *constructive* Conditional Syllogism. But if you *deny the consequent* (*i. e.* grant its *contradictory*) the second rule applies, and you infer the *contradictory of the antecedent;* "he is fit to travel; therefore he has not a fever;" this is the *destructive* Conditional Syllogism. If A is B, C is D; C is not D, therefore A is not B. Again, "If the crops are not bad, corn must be cheap," for a major; then, "but the crops are not bad, therefore corn must be cheap," is Constructive. "Corn is not cheap, therefore the crops are bad," is Destructive. "If every increase of population is desirable, some misery is desirable; but no misery is desirable; therefore some increase of population is not desirable," is Destructive.

But if you *affirm* the *consequent* or *deny* the *antecedent,* you can infer nothing; for the same Consequent may *follow from other* Antecedents: *e. g.* in the example above, a man may be unfit to travel *from other* disorders besides a fever; therefore it does not follow, from his being unfit to travel, that he has a fever; or (for the same reason) from his *not* having a fever, that he is *not* unfit to travel.

Fallacies in categorical & in hypothetical form, correspond.

And it is to be observed that these fallacies correspond respectively with those mentioned in treating of Categorical Syllogisms. The assertion of the Consequent, and inferring thence the truth of the Antecedent, answers to the fallacy of "undistributed-Middle," or to that of "negative-premises." *E. G.* "He who has a fever is unfit to travel;" (or, "is not fit to travel.") "This man is unfit" (or, "is not fit") "to travel; therefore he has a fever." The fallacy again of denying the Antecedent, and thence inferring the Contradictory of the Consequent, corresponds either to that of negative-premises, or to "illicit-process of the Major," or that of introducing, palpably, "more than three terms." *E. G.* "He who has a fever is unfit to travel; this man has not a fever," &c.*

There are, then, two, and only two, kinds of Conditional Syllogisms; the *constructive,* founded on the first rule, and answering to *direct* Reasoning; and the *destructive,* on the second, answering to *indirect;* being in fact a mode of throwing the indirect form of reasoning into the direct: *e. g.* If C be not the centre of the circle, some other point must be; which is impossible: therefore C is the centre. (Euclid, B. III. Pr. 1.)

Conversion of Conditionals.

And note, that a Conditional Proposition may (like the categorical A) be *converted by negation; i. e.* you may take the *contradictory of the consequent,* as an *antecedent,* and the *contradictory of the antecedent,* as a *consequent: e. g.* "If this man is fit to travel, he has not a fever." By this conversion of the major Premiss, a Constructive Syllogism may be reduced to a Destructive, and *vice versâ.* (See § 6. Ch. iii.)

Of Disjunctives.

§ 4.

A Disjunctive Proposition is one that consists of two or more categoricals, connected by the conjunctions "either" and "or," the force of which is, to *state an alternative; i. e.* to imply that *some one* of the categoricals thus connected must be true: *e. g.* "either A is B, or C is D" will not be a true proposition unless one of the two members of it be true.

On the other hand, one of the members may be true, and yet they may have no such natural *connexion* together as to warrant their being proposed as an alternative; as "either Britain is an island, or a triangle is a square." Such a proposition would rather be called nugatory and

* Virtually, all these fallacies do really amount to the introduction of a fourth term. See § 2. Ch. iii.

absurd, than false; since no false *conclusion* could be deduced from it; as was remarked in the last section concerning such a Conditional as this might be reduced to: *e. g.* "If Britain is not an island," &c. Such propositions are often colloquially uttered in a kind of jest.

If, therefore, one or more of these categoricals be denied (*i. e.* granted to be false) you may infer that the remaining one, or (if several) *some one* of the remaining ones, is true. *E. G.* "Either the world is eternal, or the work of chance, or the work of an intelligent Being; it is not eternal, nor the work of chance, therefore it is the work of an intelligent Being." "It is either spring, summer, autumn, or winter; but it is neither spring nor summer; therefore it is either autumn or winter." Either A is B, or C is D; but A is not B, therefore C is D.

Exclusive disjunctives.

Observe, that in these examples (as well as in most others) it is implied not only that *one* of the members (the categorical Propositions) must be *true,* but that *only one* can be true; so that, in such cases, if one or more members be *affirmed,* the rest may be *denied;* [the members may then be called *exclusive*:] *e. g.* "It is summer, therefore it is neither spring, autumn, nor winter;" "either A is B, or C is D; but A is B, therefore C is not D." But this is by no means universally the case; *e. g.* "Virtue tends to procure us either the esteem of mankind, or the favour of God:" here both members are true, and consequently from one being affirmed we are not authorized to deny the other. Of course we are left to conjecture in each case, from the context, whether it is meant to be implied that the members are or are not "exclusive."

Disjunctive reducible to conditional.

It is evident that a disjunctive Syllogism may easily be reduced to a *conditional,* by taking as an Antecedent the *contradictory* of one or more of the members: *e. g.* if it is not spring or summer, it is either autumn or winter, &c.

Hypothetical propositions always affirmative.

It is to be observed of Hypothetical [compound] Propositions, whether Conditional or Disjunctive, that they are always *affirmative:* *i. e.* it is always affirmed, not denied, that the connexion between the several categorical members, denoted, respectively, by the conjunctions employed, does exist. Accordingly, the *contradiction* of any hypothetical proposition is *not* made by a *hypothetical.* If I assert that "if A is B, C is D," you might deny that, by saying "it does not follow that if A is B, C must be D;" or in some such expression. So the contradiction of this, "either A is B or C is D," would be by *two categorical* negatives; "neither is A, B, nor is C, D:" or, it is *possible* that neither A is B, nor C, D. The conjunctions "neither" and "nor," it should be observed, do not correspond in their nature with "either" and "or;" since these last are disjunctive, which the others are not.

The Dilemma,

§ 5,

is a complex kind of Conditional Syllogism. The account usually given of the Dilemma in Logical treatises is singularly perplexed and unscientific. And it is remarkable that all the rules they usually give respecting it, and the faults against which they caution us, relate exclusively to the *Subject-matter:* as if one were to lay down as rules respecting a Syllogism in *Barbara,* "1st. Care must be taken that the major Premiss be true: 2dly. that the minor Premiss be true!"

Most, if not all, writers on this point either omit to tell us whether the Dilemma is a kind of *conditional,* or of *disjunctive* argument; or else refer it to the latter class, on account of its having one disjunctive Premiss; though it clearly belongs to the class of Conditionals.

1st. If you have in the *major* Premiss *several antecedents* all with the *same consequent*, then, these Antecedents, being (in the *minor*) *disjunctively granted* (*i. e.* it being granted that *some one* of them is true,) the one *common consequent* may be inferred, (as in the case of a simple Constructive Syllogism:) *e. g.* if A is B, C is D; and if X is Y, C is D; but either A is B, or X is Y: therefore C is D. "If the blest in heaven have no desires, they will be perfectly content: so they will, if their desires are fully gratified; but either they will have no desires, or have them fully gratified; therefore they will be perfectly content." Note, in this case, the two Conditionals which make up the major Premiss may be united into one Proposition by means of the word "*whether*:" *e. g.* "whether the blest, *&c.* have no desires, or have their desires gratified, they will be content."

Simple constructive Dilemma.

2d. But if the *several antecedents* have each a *different consequent*, then the Antecedents, being, as before, disjunctively granted, you can only *disjunctively* infer the consequents: *e. g.* if A is B, C is D; and if X is Y, E is F; but either A is B, or X is Y; therefore either C is D, or E is F. "If Æschines joined in the public rejoicings, he is inconsistent; if he did not, he is unpatriotic: but he either joined, or not: therefore he is either inconsistent or unpatriotic."* This case, as well as the foregoing, is evidently *constructive*.

Complex constructive Dilemma.

In the Destructive form, whether you have one Antecedent with several Consequents, or several Antecedents, either with one, or with several Consequents; in all these cases, if you deny the *whole* of the Consequent, or Consequents, you may in the conclusion deny the *whole* of the Antecedent or Antecedents: *e. g.* "If the world were eternal, the most useful arts, such as printing, *&c.* would be of unknown antiquity: and on the same supposition, there

Arguments that are not properly Dilemmas.

* Demost. *For the Crown.*

would be records long prior to the Mosaic; and likewise the sea and land, in all parts of the globe, might be expected to maintain the same relative situations now as formerly: but none of these is the fact: therefore the world is not eternal." Again, "If the world existed from eternity, there would be records prior to the Mosaic; and if it were produced by chance, it would not bear marks of design: there are no records prior to the Mosaic: and the world does bear marks of design: therefore it neither existed from eternity, nor is the work of chance." These are sometimes called Dilemmas, but hardly differ from *simple* conditional Syllogisms, two or more being expressed together.

Nor is the case different if you have *one* antecedent with several consequents, which consequents you *disjunctively* deny; for that comes to the same thing as *wholly* denying them; since if they be not *all* true, the *one antecedent* must equally fall to the ground; and the Syllogism will be equally simple: *e. g.* "If we admit the popular objections against Political Economy, we must admit that it tends to an excessive increase of wealth; and also, that it tends to impoverishment: but it cannot do *both* of these; (*i. e.* either not the one, or, not the other) therefore we cannot admit the popular objections," *&c.*; which is evidently a simple Destructive.

The true Dilemma is, "*a conditional Syllogism with several* antecedents in the major, and a disjunctive minor*;" hence,

Destructive Dilemma.

3d. That is most properly called a *destructive Dilemma,* which has (like the constructive ones) a *disjunctive minor Premiss; i. e.* when you have several Antecedents with each a different Consequent; which Consequents (instead of wholly denying

* The name Dilemma implies precisely *two* antecedents; and hence it is common to speak of "the horns of a dilemma;" but it is evident there may be either two or more.

them, as in the case lately mentioned) you *disjunctively* deny; and thence, in the Conclusion, deny disjunctively the Antecedents: *e. g.* if A is B, C is D; and if X is Y, E is F: but either C is not D, or E is not F; therefore, either A is not B, or X is not Y. "If this man were wise, he would not speak irreverently of Scripture in jest; and if he were good, he would not do so in earnest; but he does it, either in jest, or earnest; therefore he is either not wise, or not good." Or again, you may have a Dilemma partly *constructive* and partly *destructive:* as the above example would be, if you were to *convert* one of the conditionals, (see § 3.) into "if C is not D, A is not B:" for the Minor-Premiss would then assert that either the Antecedent of one of the Conditionals is true, or the Consequent of the other, false.

Resolution of a Dilemma. Every Dilemma may be reduced into two or more simple Conditional-Syllogisms: *e. g.* "If Æschines joined, *&c.* he is inconsistent; he *did* join, *&c.* therefore he is inconsistent;" and again, "If Æschines did not join, *&c.* he is unpatriotic; he *did not, &c.* therefore he is unpatriotic." Now an opponent might deny *either* of the minor Premises in the above Syllogisms, but he could not deny *both;* and therefore he must admit one or the other of the Conclusions; for, when a Dilemma is employed, it is supposed that *some one* of the Antecedents must be true (or, in the destructive kind, *some one* of the Consequents false), but that we cannot tell *which* of them is so; and this is the reason why the argument is stated in the form of a Dilemma.

Sometimes it may happen that *both* antecedents may be true, and that *we* may be aware of this; and yet there may be an advantage in stating (either separately or conjointly) both arguments, even when each proves the same conclusion, so as not to derive any additional confirmation from the other;—still, I say, it may sometimes be advisable to state both, because, of two propositions equally true, one man may deny or be ignorant of the one, while he admits the other; and another man, *vice versâ*.

From what has been said, it may easily be seen that all Dilemmas are in fact *conditional syllogisms;* and that Disjunctive Syllogisms may also be reduced to the form of Conditionals; but as it has been remarked, that all Reasoning whatever may *ultimately* be brought to the one test of Aristotle's "Dictum," it remains to show how a Conditional Syllogism may be thrown into such a form, that that test will at once apply to it; and this is called the

*Reduction of Hypotheticals.**

§ 6.

For this purpose we must consider every Conditional Proposition as a Universal-affirmative categorical Pro-

* Aldrich has stated, somewhat rashly, that Aristotle utterly despised Hypothetical Syllogisms, and thence made no mention of them. We cannot, however, considering how large a portion of his works is lost, draw any conclusion from the mere absence of a treatise on this branch, in the portion which has come down to us.

Aldrich observes, that no hypothetical argument is valid which cannot be reduced to a categorical form; and this is evidently agreeable to what has been said at the beginning of chap. iii.; but then he has unfortunately omitted to teach us *how* to reduce Hypotheticals to this form; except in the case where the Antecedent and Consequent chance to have each the *same* Subject; in which case, he tells us to take the minor Premiss and Conclusion as an Enthymeme, and fill that up categorically; *e.g.* "If Cæsar was a tyrant, he deserved death: he was a tyrant, therefore he deserved death;" which may easily be reduced to a categorical form, by taking as a major Premiss, "all tyrants deserve death." But when (as is often the case) the Antecedent and Consequent have not each the same Subject, (as in the very example he gives, "if A is B, C is D,") he gives no rule for reducing such a Syllogism as has a Premiss of this kind; and indeed leads us to suppose that it is to be rejected as invalid, though he has just before demonstrated its validity.

And this is likely to have been one among the various causes which occasion many learners to regard the whole system of Logic as a string of idle reveries, having nothing true, substantial, or practically useful in it; but of the same character with the dreams of Alchymy, Demonology, and judicial-Astrology. Such a mistake is surely the less inexcusable in a learner, when sition, of which the Terms are entire Propositions, *viz.* the antecedent answering to the *Subject*, and the consequent to the *Predicate*. *E.G.* The Proposition "if A is B, X is Y" may be considered as amounting to this; "The case [or supposition] of A being B, is a case of X being Y." And then, to say (as in the Minor-premiss and the Conclusion, of a constructive-conditional syllogism) "A is B; and therefore X is Y," is equivalent to saying "the present [or the existing] case is a case of A being B: therefore this is a case of X being Y." Again, to say, "if Louis is a good king, France is likely to prosper," is equivalent to saying, "The case of Louis being a good king, is a case of France being likely to prosper:" and if it be granted as a minor Premiss to the Conditional Syllogism, that "Louis is a good king;" that is equivalent to saying, "the present case is the case of Louis being a good king;" from which you will draw a conclusion in *Barbara*. (*viz.* "the present case is a case of France being likely to prosper,") exactly equivalent to the original Conclusion of the Conditional Syllogism: *viz.* "France is likely to prosper." As the Constructive Conditional may thus be reduced to *Barbara*, so may the Destructive, in like manner, to *Celarent: e.g.* "If the Stoics are right, pain is no evil: but pain is an evil; therefore the Stoics are not right;" is equivalent to— "The case of the Stoics being right, is the case of pain being no evil; the present case is not the case of pain being no evil; therefore the present case is not the case of the Stoics being right." This is *Camestres*, which, of course, is easily reduced to *Celarent*. Or, if you will, all Conditional Syllogisms may be reduced to *Barbara*, by con-

his master first *demonstrates* the validity of a certain argument, and then tells him that after all it is good for nothing; (*prorsus repudiandum.*)

In the late editions of Aldrich's Logic, all that he says of the reduction of Hypotheticals is omitted; which certainly would have been an improvement, if a more correct one had been substituted; but as it is, there is a complete hiatus in the system.

sidering them all as Constructive; which may be done, as mentioned above, by "converting by negation" [contraposition] the major Premiss. (See § 3.)

Abridged forms of reduction of hypotheticals.

The reduction of Hypotheticals may always be effected in the manner above stated; but as it produces a circuitous awkwardness of expression, a more convenient form may in some cases be substituted. *E.G.* in the example above, it may be convenient to take "*true*" for one of the Terms: "that pain is no evil is not true; that pain is no evil is asserted by the Stoics; therefore something asserted by the Stoics is not true." Sometimes again it may be better to unfold the argument into two Syllogisms: *e.g.* in a former example; first, "Louis is a good king; the governor of France is Louis; therefore the governor of France is a good king." And then, second, "every country governed by a good king is likely to prosper," *&c.*

A Dilemma may of course (see § 5,) be reduced into two or more categorical Syllogisms.

When the Antecedent and Consequent of a Conditional have each the *same* Subject, you may sometimes reduce the Conditional by merely substituting a categorical Major-Premiss for the conditional one: *e.g.* instead of "if Cæsar was a tyrant, he deserved death; he was a tyrant, therefore he deserved death;" you may put for a major, "all tyrants deserve death;" *&c.* But it is of no great consequence, whether Hypotheticals are reduced in the most *neat and concise* manner or not; since it is not intended that they should be reduced to Categoricals, in *ordinary practice*, as the *readiest way* of trying their validity, (their own rules being quite sufficient for that purpose;) but only *that we should be able*, if required, to subject any argument whatever to the test of Aristotle's Dictum, in order to show that all Reasoning turns upon one simple principle.

Of Enthymeme, Sorites, &c.

§ 7.

There are various abridged forms of Argument which may be easily expanded into regular Syllogisms; such as,

Enthymeme. 1st. The Enthymeme,* which is a Syllogism with one Premiss suppressed. As all the Terms will be found in the remaining Premiss and Conclusion, it will be easy to fill up the Syllogism by supplying the Premiss that is wanting, whether Major or Minor: *e.g.* "Cæsar was a tyrant; therefore he deserved death." "A free nation must be happy; therefore the English are happy."

This is the ordinary form of speaking and writing. It is evident that Enthymemes may be filled up hypothetically.

It is to be observed, that the Enthymeme is *not strictly syllogistic; i.e.* its conclusiveness is not apparent from the mere form of expression, till the suppressed Premiss shall have been, either actually or mentally, supplied. The *expressed* Premiss may be true, and yet the Conclusion false.

The Sorites, on the other hand, is strictly syllogistic; as may be seen by the examples. If the Premises *stated* be true, the Conclusion must be true. For,

2d. When you have a string of Syllogisms, in the first figure, in which the Conclusion of each is made the Premiss of the next, till you arrive at the main or ultimate Conclusion of all, you may sometimes state these briefly, in the

Sorites. form called *Sorites;* in which the Predicate of the first proposition is made the Subject of the next; and so on, to any length, till finally the Predicate of the last of the Premises is predicated (in the Conclusion) of the Subject of the first: *e.g.* A (either every A, or some A) is B, every B is C, every C is D, every D is E; therefore A is E; or else "no D is E; therefore A is

* The word Enthymeme is employed in a different sense from this, by Aristotle, in Rhet. B. i. See *Elements of Rhetoric*, Part I. Ch. ii. § 2.

not E." "The English are a brave people; a brave people are free; a free people are happy; therefore the English are happy." A Sorites, then, has as many Middle-terms as there are intermediate Propositions between the first and the last; and consequently, it may be drawn out into as many separate Syllogisms; of which the first will have, for its *major Premiss*, the *second*, and for its *minor*, the *first*, of the Propositions of the Sorites; as may be seen by the example. The reader will perceive also by examination of that example, and by framing others, that the first proposition in the Sorites is the only *minor* premiss that is expressed: when the whole is resolved into distinct syllogisms, each conclusion becomes the minor premiss of the succeeding syllogism. Hence, in a Sorites, the *first* proposition, and that alone, of all the premises, may be *particular;* because in the first Figure the minor may be particular, but not the major; (see Chap. iii. § 4.) and all the other propositions, prior to the conclusion, are major premises. It is also evident that there may be, in a Sorites, one, and only one, *negative* premiss, *viz.* the last: for if any of the others were negative, the result would be that one of the syllogisms of the Sorites would have a *negative minor* premiss; which is (in the 1st Fig.) incompatible with correctness. See Chap. iii. § 4.

Application of the Dictum to the Sorites.

To the Sorites the "Dictum" formerly treated of may be applied, with one small addition, which is self-evident. "Whatever is affirmed or denied of a whole Class, may be affirmed or denied of whatever is comprehended in [*any Class that is wholly comprehended in*] that Class." This sentence, omitting the portion enclosed in brackets, you will recognise as the "Dictum" originally laid down: and the words in brackets supply that extension of it which makes it applicable to a "Sorites," of whatever length; since it is manifest that that clause might be enlarged as far as you will, into "a Class that is wholly comprehended in a Class, which again is wholly comprehended in another Class, &c.

Hypothetical Sorites. A string of Conditional Syllogisms* may in like manner be abridged into a Sorites; *e. g.* if A is B, C is D; if C is D, E is F; if E is F, G is H; but A is B, therefore G is H. "If the Scriptures are the word of God, it is important that they should be well explained; if it is important, *&c.* they deserve to be diligently studied; if they deserve, *&c.* an order of men should be set aside for that purpose; but the Scriptures are the word, *&c.*; therefore an order of men should be set aside for the purpose, *&c.*" In a *destructive* Sorites, you, of course, go back from the denial of the last consequent to the denial of the first antecedent: "G is not H; therefore A is not B."

The foregoing are all the forms in which Reasoning can be exhibited *syllogistically;* i. e. so that its validity shall be manifest from the *mere form of expression.*

Induction. Example. Those who have spoken of *Induction* or of *Example,* as a distinct kind of Argument in a Logical point of view, have fallen into the common error of confounding *Logical* with *Rhetorical* distinctions, and have wandered from their subject as much as a writer on the orders of Architecture would do who should introduce the distinction between buildings of brick and of marble. Logic takes no cognizance of *Induction,* for instance, or of *à priori* reasoning, *&c.,* as distinct *Forms* of argument; for when thrown into the syllogistic form, and when letters of the alphabet are substituted for the Terms (and it is thus that an Argument is properly to be brought under the cognizance of Logic), there is no distinction between them. *E. G.* "a Property which belongs to the ox,

* Hence it is evident how injudicious an arrangement has been adopted by former writers on Logic, who have treated of the Sorites and Enthymeme before they entered on the subject of Hypotheticals.

sheep, deer, goat, and antelope, belongs to all horned animals; rumination belongs to these; therefore to all." This, which is an inductive argument, is evidently a Syllogism in *Barbara.* The essence of an inductive argument, as well as of the other kinds which are distinguished from it, consists not in the *form of the Argument*, but in the relation which the *Subject-matter* of the Premises bears to that of the Conclusion.*

Abbreviations.

3d. There are various other abbreviations commonly used, which are so obvious as hardly to call for explanation: as where one of the Premises of a Syllogism is itself the Conclusion of an Enthymeme, which is expressed at the same time: *e.g.* "All useful studies deserve encouragement; Logic is such *(since it helps us to reason accurately;)* therefore it deserves encouragement;" here the Minor-premiss is what is called an *Enthymematic sentence*.†

Hints suggesting arguments.

And it may be added, that such a sentence will sometimes be in the form, not of a *Proposition*, but of an *Exclamation*,—a *Question*,—or a *Command;* and yet will be such as readily to suggest to the mind a Proposition.

For instance, in some of the examples lately given, one might say (in place of one of the Propositions) "Chuse which you will of these two suppositions;" or "Who can doubt that so and so follows?"

The message to Pilate from his wife ‡ furnishes an instance of a single word ("*just*") suggesting a Major-premiss, while the Conclusion is stated in the form of an *exhortation:* "Have thou nothing to do with that *just* man." And the succeeding sentence must have been designed to convey

* See *Rhetoric,* Part I. Ch. ii. § 6. Nothing probably has tended more to foster the prevailing error of considering Syllogism as a *particular kind of argument,* than the inaccuracy just noticed; which appears in all or most of the logical works extant. See *Dissertation on the Province of Reasoning,* Ch. i.

† The *antecedent* in that Minor-premiss (*i. e.* that which *makes* it Enthymematic) is called by Aristotle the *Prosyllogism.*

‡ Matt. xxvii. 19.

a hint of Arguments for the Proof of each of the Premises on which that Conclusion rested.

And here it may be observed, that the usual practice of selecting for examples, in Logical treatises, such arguments as hardly even an ignorant clown, or a child, would need to state at full length, and which the slightest *hint* would sufficiently suggest to any one, has contributed to the prevailing mistake of supposing that Syllogisms, universally, are mere trifling; the fact, that all *arguments* are, substantially, syllogistic, being overlooked.

Things needing proof to one man, may be self-evident to another.

It is worth remarking however in this place, that the further any one advances, in intellectual cultivation, generally, or in any particular department, he will have less and less need (not, of argumentation altogether, but) of *such* arguments as are needful for a beginner. To this last, many propositions may need to be proved at full length, which, to one further advanced, require only to have the proofs *hinted* at, and which to one still more advanced need merely to be *stated as* propositions, or, ultimately, not even *that;* being sufficiently suggested to the mind by the mere mention of one of the terms. And hence the proverbial expression, that "a word is enough to the wise."

Equivalents.

It is evident that you may, for brevity, substitute for any term an *equivalent:* as in an example above, "*it*" for "Logic;" "*such*," for "a useful study," *&c.* The doctrine of Conversion, laid down in the Second Chapter, furnishes many equivalent propositions, since each is equivalent to its illative Converse. The division of nouns also (for which see Chap. v.) supplies many equivalents; *e. g.* if A is the *genus* of B, B must be a *species* of A: if A is the *cause* of B, B must be the *effect* of A, *&c.*

Syllogisms apparently incorrect.

4th. And many Syllogisms, which at first sight appear faulty, will often be found, on examination, to contain correct reasoning, and consequently, to be reducible to a regular form; *e. g.* when you have, *apparently, negative Premises,* it may happen, that by considering one of them as *affirmative,* (see Chap. ii. § 4,) the Syllogism will be regular: *e. g.* "no man is happy who is not secure: no tyrant is secure; therefore no tyrant is happy," is a Syllogism in *Celarent.* If this experiment be tried on a Syllogism which has *really* negative Premises, the only effect will be to change that fault into another: *viz.* an excess of Terms, or (which is substantially the same) an undistributed Middle; *e. g.* "an enslaved people is not happy; the English are not enslaved; therefore they are happy:" if "enslaved" be regarded as one of the Terms, and "not enslaved" as another, there will manifestly be four. Hence one may see how very little difference there is in reality between the different faults which are enumerated.

Sometimes there will appear to be too many terms; and yet there will be no fault in the Reasoning, only an irregularity in the expression: *e. g.* "no irrational agent could produce a work which manifests design; the universe is a work which manifests design; therefore no irrational agent could have produced the universe." Strictly speaking, this Syllogism has five terms; but if you look to the meaning, you will see, that in the first Premiss (considering it *as a part of this argument*) it is not, properly, "an irrational agent" that you are speaking of, and of which you predicate that it could not produce a work manifesting design; but rather it is this "work," *&c.* of which you are speaking, and of which it is predicated that it could not be produced by an irrational agent; if, then, you state the Propositions in that form, the Syllogism will be perfectly regular. (See above, § 1.)

Thus, such a Syllogism as this, "every true patriot is disinterested; few men are disinterested; therefore few men are true patriots;" might appear at first sight to be in the second Figure, and faulty; whereas it is *Barbara,* with the *Premises transposed:* for you do not really predicate of "few men," that they are "disinterested," but of "*disinterested persons*," that they are "few." Again, "none but candid men are good reasoners; few infidels are candid; few infidels are good reasoners." In this it will be most convenient to consider the Major-premiss as being, "all good reasoners are candid," (which of course is precisely equipollent to its illative converse by negation;) and the Minor-premiss and Conclusion may in like manner be fairly expressed thus—"most infidels are not candid; therefore most infidels are not good reasoners:" which is a regular Syllogism in *Camestres*.* Or, if you would state it in the first Figure, thus: "those who are not candid [or uncandid] are not good reasoners: most infidels are not candid; most infidels are not good reasoners."

Chap. V.

SUPPLEMENT TO CHAP. I.

[*This Supplement may be studied either before or after the preceding three Chapters.*]

§ 1.

Univocal, Equivocal, Analogous. The usual divisions of nouns into *univocal*, *equivocal*, and *analogous*, and into nouns of the *first* and *second intention*, are not, strictly speaking, divisions of *words*, but divisions of the *manner of employing* them; the *same* word may be employed either univocally, equivocally, or analogously; either in the First-intention, or in the Second. The ordinary logical treatises often occasion great perplexity to the learner, by not noticing this circumstance, but rather leading him to suppose the contrary. (See Book III. § 8.)

* The reader is to observe that the term employed as the Subject of the Minor-premiss, and of the conclusion, is "most-infidels:" he is not to suppose that "most" is a sign of distribution; it is merely a compendious expression for "the greater part of."

Some of those other divisions of nouns, which are the most commonly in use, though not appropriately and exclusively belonging to the Logical system,—*i. e.* to the theory of reasoning,—it may be worth while briefly to notice in this place.

Let it be observed, then, that a term expresses the view we take of an object. And its being viewed as *an* object, *i. e.* as one, or again as several, depends on our arbitrary choice; *e. g.* we may consider a "troop of cavalry" as one object; or we may make any single "horse with its rider," or any "separate man" or horse, or any limb of either, the subject of our thoughts.

Singular and Common terms.

1. When then any one object is considered according to its *actual existence*, as numerically *one*, the name denoting it is called *Singular*; as, "this tree," the "city of London," *&c.* When it is considered as to its nature and character only, as being *of such a description* as might equally apply to other single objects, the inadequate or incomplete view (see B. I. § 3, and § 6.) thus taken of an individual, is expressed by a Common-term; as "tree," "city," "minister-of-state."

Absolute and Relative.

2. When any object is considered as a part of a whole, viewed in reference to the whole or to another part, of a more complex object of thought, the name expressing this view is called *Relative*: and to Relative-term is opposed *Absolute*; as denoting an object considered as a whole, and without reference to any thing of which it is a part, or to any other part distinguished from it. Thus, "Father," and "Son," "Rider," "Commander," *&c.* are Relatives; being regarded, each as a part of the complex objects, Father-and-Son, *&c.*; the same object designated *absolutely*, would be termed a Man, Living-Being, *&c.*

Correlative.

Nouns are *Correlative* to each other, which denote objects related to each other, and viewed *as to* that relation. Thus, though a King is a ruler of *men*, "King" and "Man" are not correlative, but "King" and *Subject*, are.

Compatible and opposite.

3. When there are two views which cannot be taken of one single object at the same time, the terms expressing these views are said to be *Opposite*, or Inconsistent [repugnantia]; as, "black," and "white;" when both may be taken of the same object at the same time, they are called Consistent, or *Compatible* [convenientia]; as "white," and "cold." Relative terms are Opposite, only when applied with reference to the same Subject: as, one may be both Master and Servant; but not at the same time to the same person.

Concrete and abstract.

4. When the notion derived from the view taken of any object, is expressed with a reference to, or as in conjunction with, the object that furnished the notion, it is expressed by a *Concrete* term; as, "foolish," or "fool;" when without any such reference, by an *Abstract** term; as, "folly."

Attributive or Connotative, and Absolute or non-Connotative.

5. When a term applied to some object is such as to imply in its signification some "*attribute*" belonging to that object, such a term is called by some of the early logical writers "*Connotative*;" but would perhaps be more conveniently called "*Attributive*." It "connotes," *i. e.* "notes along with" the object [or *implies*] something considered as inherent therein: as "The capital of France;" "The founder of Rome." The founding of Rome, is, by that appellation, "*attributed*" to the person to whom it is applied.

A term which merely *denotes* an object without implying any attribute of that object, is called "*Absolute*" or "Non-connotative;" as "Paris;" "Romulus." The last terms *de*note respectively the same objects as the two former;

* It is unfortunate that some writers have introduced the fashion of calling *all* "Common-terms" *Abstract*-terms.

but do not, like them, *con*note [*imply* in their signification] any attribute of those individuals.

Every Concrete-common-term is "attributive," [connotative] whether in the adjective * or substantive form; as "Man," "human," "triangle," "triangular," "saint," "holy:" for, "man" *e. g.* or "human," are appellations denoting, not the *attribute itself* which we call "human-nature," but a Being to which such a term is applied in reference to, and *by virtue of*, its possessing that attribute. An Abstract-common-term, being the name of an Attribute-itself — as "human-nature," "triangularity," "holiness," — is "Absolute" [non-connotative] except where there is an attribute *of* an attribute implied in the term; as the term "fear" *e. g.* may be considered as implying some *hope* of escape; without which the apprehension of evil would be called "despair."

It is to be observed that many a term is employed—and to a certain degree, correctly employed, *i. e.* not *mis*applied—by persons who do not clearly and fully take in its signification;—who do not know, or do not bring before their minds, exactly what is implied [connoted] by it. *E. G.* a child learns to apply the term "money" to the bits of metal he sees pass from hand to hand, long before he has any clear notion (which some never fully attain) of what it is that constitutes "money," and is *implied* [connoted] by the term. So also it is conceivable that a person might, under certain circumstances, know perfectly *what individuals* are Aldermen, Senators, &c. while he had but a very vague and imperfect notion of the Office which such a term implies. And such a *familiarity* as this with any term, (together with one's being able to comprehend processes of *reasoning* in which it occurs) tends to

* Some logical writers confine the word to *adjectives;* but there seems no essential difference in reference to the present subject. Indeed, in Greek and in Latin it often happens that a word may be reckoned either adjective or substantive; as "stultus;" "hospes."

conceal from men their imperfect apprehension of its signification, and thus often leads to confusion of thought, and error. (See B. iv. ch. iv. § 2.)

Positive, Privative & Negative.

6. A term which denotes a certain view of an object as being actually taken of it, is called *Positive:* as, "*speech,*" "a man *speaking:*" a term denoting that this view *might* conceivably be taken of the object, but *is* not, is *Privative;* as "*dumbness,*" a "man *silent,*" *&c.** That which denotes that such a notion is not and *could* not be formed of the object, is called *Negative;* as, "a dumb statue," a "lifeless carcase," *&c.*

Many negative-terms which are such *in sense only*, have led to confusion of thought, from their real character being imperfectly perceived. *E. G.* "Liberty," which is a purely *negative* term, denoting merely "absence of restraint," is sometimes confounded with "Power."†

It is to be observed that the same term may be regarded either as Positive, or as Privative or Negative, according to the quality or character which we are referring to in our minds: thus, of "happy" and "miserable," we may regard the former as Positive, and the latter (*un*happy) as Privative; or *vice versâ;* according as we are thinking of enjoyment or of suffering.

* Many Privative epithets are such that by a little ingenuity the application of them may be represented as an absurdity. Thus, Wallis's remark (introduced in this treatise) that a jest is generally a mock-fallacy, *i. e.* a fallacy not designed to deceive, but so palpable as only to furnish amusement, might be speciously condemned as involving a contradiction: for "the *design to deceive,*" it might be said, "is essential to a fallacy." In the same way it might be argued that it is absurd to speak of "a dead man;" *e. g.* "every man is a living creature; nothing dead is a living creature; therefore no man is dead!"

† An extension of a man's power (as Tucker has observed in his "Light of Nature") may be the means of diminishing his "liberty;" as the liberty of a helpless paralytic is not abridged by locking the door of his room; though it would be, if he were to recover the use of his limbs. See a notice of the word "aperture" in § 5. Essay i. 1st Series.

Definite and indefinite.

7. A Privative or Negative term is also called *Indefinite* [infinitum] in respect of its not defining and marking out an object; in contradistinction to this, the Positive term is called Definite [finitum] because it does thus define or mark out. Thus, "organized Being," or "Cæsar," are called Definite, as marking out, and limiting our view to, one particular class of Beings, or one single person; "unorganized," or "not-Cæsar," are called Indefinite, as not restricting our view to any class, or individual, but only excluding *one*, and leaving it undetermined, what other individual the thing so spoken of may be, or what other class it may belong to.

Contradictory opposition of terms.

It is to be observed, that the most perfect opposition between terms exists between any two which differ only in respectively wanting and having the particle *not* (either expressly, or in sense) attached to them; as, "organized," and "not-organized;" "corporeal," and "incorporeal." For not only is it impossible for both these views to be taken at once of the same thing, but also, it is impossible but that *one or other* should be applicable to every object; as there is nothing that can be *both*, so there is nothing that can be *neither*. Every thing that can be even conceived, must be either "Cæsar," or "not-Cæsar;"—either "corporeal," or "incorporeal." And in this way a complete twofold division may be made of any subject, being certain (as the expression is) to *exhaust* it. And the repetition of this process, so as to carry on a subdivision as far as there is occasion, is thence called by Logicians "abscissio infiniti;" *i. e.* the repeated cutting off of that which the object to be examined is *not; e. g.* "1. This disorder either is, or is not, a dropsy; and for this or that reason, it is *not;* 2. Any other disease either is, or is not, gout; this is not: then, 3. It either is, or is not, consumption, *&c.*" This procedure is very common in Aristotle's works. (See B. ii. ch. 3. § 4.)

Such terms may be said to be in Contradictory-opposition to each other.

Contrary terms.

On the other hand, *Contrary* terms, *i. e.* those which, coming under some one class, are the *most* different of all that belong to that class, as "wise" and "foolish," both denoting mental habits, are opposed, but in a different manner: for though *both* cannot be applied to the same object, there may be other objects to which *neither* can be applied: nothing can be at once both "wise" and "foolish;" but a stone cannot be either.

§ 2.

The notions expressed by Common-terms, we are enabled (as has been remarked in the Analytical Outline) to form, by the faculty of *abstraction:* for by it, in contemplating any object (or objects,) we can attend exclusively to some particular circumstances belonging to it, [some certain parts of its nature as it were,] and quite withhold our attention from the rest. When, therefore, we are thus contemplating several individuals which *resemble* each other in some *part* of their nature, we can (by attending to *that part alone,* and not to those points wherein they differ) assign them *one common name,* which will express or stand for them merely as far as they all *agree;* and which, of course, will be applicable to all or any of them; (which process is called *generalization*) and each of these names is called a *common-term,* from its belonging to them *all alike;* or a *predicable,* because it may be predicated-affirmatively of them, or of any of them. (See B. i. § 3.)

Generalization.

Predicables.

Generalization (as has been remarked) implies Abstraction; but it is not the same thing; for there may be abstraction without generalization. When we are speaking of an Individual, it is usually an abstract notion that we form; *e. g.* suppose we are speaking of the present King of France; he must actually *be* either at Paris or elsewhere;

sitting, standing, or in some other posture; and in such and such a dress, *&c.* Yet many of these circumstances, (which are *separable* Accidents,* and consequently) which are regarded as *non-essential to the individual,* are quite disregarded by us; and we *abstract* from them what we consider as essential; thus forming an *abstract* notion of the Individual. Yet there is here no generalization.

§ 3.

The following is the account usually given in logical treatises of the different kinds [heads] of Predicables; but it cannot be admitted without some considerable modifications, explanations and corrections, which will be subjoined.

Whatever Term can be affirmed of several things, must express either their *whole essence,* which is called the *Species;* or a *part* of their essence (*viz.* either the *material* part, which is called the *Genus,* or the *formal* and *distinguishing part,* which is called *Differentia,* or in common discourse, *characteristic*) or something *joined* to the *essence;* whether *necessarily* (*i.e.* to the *whole* species, or, in other words, *universally,* to every individual of it), which is called a *Property:* or *contingently* (*i.e.* to *some* individuals only of the species), which is an *Accident.*

Species. *Genus.* *Differentia.* *Property.* *Accident.*

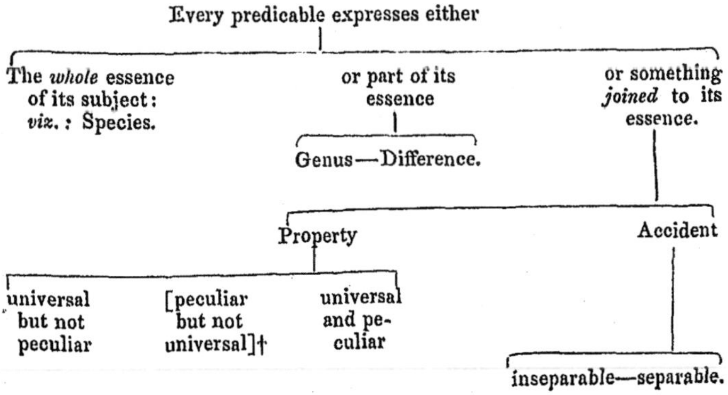

* See § 6.

† See below, § 4.

Of these predicables, genus and species are commonly said, in the language of logicians, to be *predicated in quid;* (τὶ) *i.e.* to answer to the question, "what?" as, "what is Cæsar?" Answer, "a man;" "what is a man?" Answer, "an animal;" Difference, in "*quale quid;*" (ποῖον τι) Property and Accident in *quale* (ποῖον.)

Genus and Species, each, a whole, in different senses.

It is evident from what has been said, that the Genus and Difference put together make up the Species. *E. G.* "rational" and "animal" constitute "man;" so that, *in reality,* the Species contains the Genus [*i.e. implies* it;] and when the Genus is called a *whole,* and is said to *contain* the Species, this is only a *metaphorical* expression, signifying that it *comprehends* the Species, in its own more *extensive* signification. If for instance I predicate the term "animal" of an individual man, as Alexander, I speak truth indeed, but only such *a portion* of the truth that I might equally predicate the same term of his horse Bucephalus. If I predicate the terms "Man" and "Horse" of Alexander and of Bucephalus respectively, I use a more full and *complete* expression for each than the term "animal;" and this last is accordingly the more *extensive,* as it contains, [or, more properly speaking, comprehends] and may be applied to, several different Species; *viz.:* "bird," "beast," "fish," *&c.*

In the same manner the name of a *species* is a more *extensive* [*i.e.* comprehensive] but less *full and complete* term than that of an *individual* (*viz.* a Singular-term;) since the Species may be predicated of each of these.

"The impression produced on the mind by a Singular Term, may be compared to the distinct view taken in by the eye, of any object (suppose some particular man) near at hand, in a clear light, which enables us to distinguish the features of the *individual:* in a fainter light, or rather further off, we merely perceive that the object is *a man:* this corresponds with the idea conveyed by the name of the Species: yet farther off, or in a still feebler light, we can distinguish merely some *living object;* and at length, merely *some* object; these views corresponding respectively with the terms denoting the Genera, less or more remote." *

Hence it is plain that when logicians speak of "Species" as "expressing the whole essence of its subjects," this is not strictly correct, unless we understand by the "whole essence" the "whole that any *common*-term *can* express;"—the "nearest approach to the whole essence of the individual that any term (not synonymous with the Subject) can denote." No predicate can express, strictly, the *whole* essence of its Subject, unless it be merely another name, of the very same import, and co-extensive with it; as "Cæsar was the conqueror of Pompey."

But when logicians speak of Species as a "whole," this is, properly, in reference to the Genus and the Difference; each of which denotes a "part" of that Species which we constitute by joining those two together. But then, it should be remembered that a Species is not a *predicable* in respect of its Genus and Difference (since it cannot be predicated of *them*) but only in respect of the Individuals, or lower Species, of which it can be predicated.

§ 4.

Subaltern genus and species.

A Species then, it is plain, when predicated of Individuals, stands in the same relation to *them*, as the Genus to the Species; and when predicated of other (lower) Species, it is then, in respect of these, a Genus, while it is a Species in respect of a higher Genus; as "quadruped," which is a species of "animal," is a Genus in respect of "horse;" which latter again may be predicated of Bucephalus and of other individuals. Such a term is called a *subaltern* Species or Genus; being each, in respect of different other terms, respectively.

* Rhet. Part. III. Chap. ii. § 1.

Highest Genus and lowest Species.

A Genus that is *not* considered as a *species* of anything, is called *summum* (the highest) Genus; a Species that is *not* considered as a *genus* of anything,—*i. e.* is regarded as containing under it only *individuals*,—is called *infima* (the lowest) Species.

When I say of a Magnet, that it is "a kind of *iron-ore*," that is called its *proximum*-genus, because it is the closest [or lowest] genus that is predicated of it: "mineral" is its more *remote* genus.

Specific Difference & Property.

When I say that the Differentia of a magnet is its "*attracting iron*," and that its Property is "*polarity*," these are called respectively a Specific Difference and Property; because magnet is (I have supposed) an *infima species* [*i. e. only* a species.]

When I say that the Differentia of iron ore is its "*containing iron*," and its Property, "*being attracted by the magnet*," these are called respectively, a *generic* Difference and Property, because "iron-ore" is a *subaltern* Species or Genus; being both the *genus* of *magnet*, and a *species* of *mineral*.

Generic Difference & Property.

It should be observed here, that when logicians speak of Property and Accident as predicables expressing, not the Essence or part of the Essence of a subject, but something *united to* the Essence, this must be understood as having reference not to the nature of things as they are in themselves, but to our conceptions of them. "Polarity" for instance is as much a part of the real nature of the substance we call "Magnet," as its "attraction of iron;" and again, a certain shape, colour, or specific gravity, as much belongs in reality to *those magnets which are of that* description, as either polarity, or attraction. But our modes of conceiving, and of expressing our conceptions, have reference to the relations in which objects stand to our own minds; and are influenced in each instance by the *parti-*

cular end we have in view. That, accordingly, is accounted a part of the Essence of anything, which is essential to *the notion of it formed in our minds.* Thus, if we have annexed such a notion to the term, Man, that "rationality" stands prominent in our minds, in distinguishing Man from other Animals, we call this, *the* "Difference," and a part of the "Essence" of the term Man; though "risibility" be an attribute which does not less really belong to Man. So, the *primary* and prominent distinction in our minds of a Triangle from other plane rectilineal Figures, is its having three sides; though the equality of its three angles to two right angles, be, in reality, no less essential to a triangle. But that this last is the fact, is demonstrated to the learner not till long after he is supposed to have become familiar with the notion of a Triangle.

Hence, in different sciences or arts, different attributes are fixed on, as essentially characterising each species, according as this or that is the most important in reference to the matter we are engaged in. In Navigation, for instance, the *polarity* of the Magnet is the essential quality; since if there could be any other substance which could possess this, without attracting iron, it would answer the same purpose: but to those manufacturers who employ Magnets for the purpose of more expeditiously picking up small bits of iron, and for shielding their faces from the noxious steel-dust, in the grinding of needles, the *attracting* power of the Magnet is the essential point.

Under the head of Property, logicians have enumerated, as may be seen in the preceding table, not only such as are strictly called Properties, as belonging each to the *whole* Species of which it is predicated, and to that *alone*, but also, such as belong to the *whole* Species, and to others besides; in other words, Properties which are *universal*, but not *peculiar*; as "to breathe air" belongs to every *man*; but not to man alone; and it is, therefore, strictly speaking, not so much a Property of the Species "man," as of the higher, (*i. e.* more comprehensive,) Species, which is the Genus of that, *viz.* of "land-animal." And it is this that logicians mean by *generic*-property.

Peculiar Accident.

Other Properties, as some logicians call them, are *peculiar* to a species, but do not belong to the whole of it; *e. g.* man *alone* can be a poet, but it is not *every* man that is so. These, however, are more commonly and more properly reckoned as *accidents.*

Some have also added a fourth kind of Property; *viz.* that which is peculiar to a Species, and belongs to every Individual of it, but *not at every time.* But this is, in fact, a contradiction; since whatever does not *always* belong to a Species, does not belong to it *universally.* It is through the ambiguity of words that they have fallen into this confusion of thought; *e. g.* the example commonly given is, "homini canescere;" "to become grey" being, they say, (though it is not) *peculiar* to man, and belonging to *every* individual, though not *always,* but only in old age, &c. Now, if by "canescere" be meant the *very state* of becoming grey, this manifestly does not belong to every man: if again it be meant to signify the *liability* to become grey at some time or other, this does belong *always* to man. And the same in other instances. Indeed the very Proprium fixed on by Aldrich, "risibility," is nearly parallel to the above. Man is "*always capable of laughing;*" but he is not "*capable of laughing always.*"

Accidents separable and inseparable.

That is most properly called an "Accident," which may be absent or present, the essence of the Species continuing the same; as, for a man to be "*walking,*" or a "*native of Paris.*" Of these two examples, the former is what logicians call a *separable* Accident, because it may be separated from the *individual:* (*e. g.* he may sit down;) the latter is an *inseparable* Accident, being not separable from the individual, (*i. e.* he who is a native of Paris can never be otherwise;)

" from the individual," I say, because *every accident* must be separable from the *species,* else it would be a *property.**

This seems to me a clearer and more correct description of the two kinds of Accident than the one given by Aldrich; *viz.* that a Separable-Accident may be *actually* separated, and an Inseparable, only *in thought,* " ut Mantuanum esse, a Virgilio." For surely " to be the author of the Æneid" was another Inseparable-Accident of the same individual; " to be a Roman citizen" another; and " to live in the days of Augustus" another; now can we *in thought* separate all these things from the essence of *that individual?* To do so would be to form the idea of a *different* individual. We can indeed conceive a *man,* and one who might chance to bear the *name* of Virgil, without any of these Accidents; but then it would plainly not be the *same* man. But Virgil, whether sitting or standing, &c. we regard as the same man; the abstract notion which we have formed of that individual being unaltered by the absence or presence of these separable accidents. (See above, § 2.)

Predicables relatively so called.

Let it here be observed, that both the general name " Predicable," and each of the classes of Predicables, (*viz.* Genus, Species, *&c.*) are *relative;* *i. e.* we cannot say *what predicable* any term is, or whether it is any at all, unless it be specified of *what* it is to be predicated: *e. g.* the term " red" would be considered a *genus,* in relation to the terms " pink," " scarlet," *&c.*: it might be regarded as the *differentia,* in relation to " red rose;"—as a *property* of " blood,"—as an *accident* of " a house," *&c.* And in

* In the Portuguese language there are two words, " ser" and " estar," both answering to the English " to be;" and foreigners, I have been told, are often much perplexed about the proper use of each. I soon found, however, that the rule is a logical one, easily remembered: " estar" furnishes the copula when the predicate is a *separable-accident,* and " ser," in *all other* cases. *E. G.* " *Estar* in Inghilterra" is " to be in England;" " *Ser* Inglez" is " to be an Englishman;" " Quem *e?*" " who is he?" " Quem *esta* la?" " who is there?" &c.

all cases accordingly, the Differences or Properties of any lower species will be *Accidents* in reference to the class they come under. *E. G.* "malleability" is an "accident" in reference to the term "metal;" but it is a "property" of gold and most other metals; as the absence of it,—brittleness,—is of Antimony and Arsenic, and several others, formerly called Semimetals.

A common-term not the name of one real thing.

And universally, it is to be steadily kept in mind, that no "common-terms" have, as the names of Individuals ["singular-terms"] have, any *real thing existing in nature* corresponding to each of them,* but that each of them is merely a sign denoting a certain *inadequate notion* which our minds have formed of an Individual, and which, consequently, not including the notion of "individuality" [*numerical*-unity] nor anything wherein that individual differs from certain others, is applicable equally well to all, or any of them. Thus "man" denotes no real thing (as the sect of the Realists maintained) distinct from each individual, but merely *any* man, viewed *inadequately*, *i. e.* so as to omit, and abstract from, all that is peculiar to each individual; by which means the term becomes applicable alike to any one of several individuals, or (in the plural) to several together.

Unity of a common-term belongs to the term itself only.

The *unity* [*singleness*] or *sameness* of what is denoted by a *common*-term, does not, as in the case of a *singular*-term, consist in the *object itself* being (in the *primary* sense) *one* and the same,† but in the oneness of the *Sign* itself; which is like a Stamp (for marking bales of goods, or cattle,) that impresses on each a *similar* mark; called, thence, in the *secondary* sense, *one and the same* mark. And just such a *stamp*, to the mind, is a Common-term; which

* Τόδε τι, as Aristotle expresses it; though he has been represented as the champion of the opposite opinion: vide *Catag.* c. 3.

† See Book IV. Chap. v. § 2. and Append. Art. "Same."

being, itself, one, conveys to each of an indefinite number of minds an impression precisely *similar*, and thence called —in the transferred sense, one and the *same* Idea.

And we arbitrarily fix on the circumstance which we in each instance chuse to abstract and consider separately, disregarding all the rest; so that the same individual may thus be referred to any of several different Species, and the same Species, to several Genera, as suits our purpose. Thus, it suits the Farmer's purpose to class his cattle with his ploughs, carts, and other possessions, under the name of "*stock*:" the Naturalist, suitably to *his* purpose, classes them as "*quadrupeds*," which term would include wolves, deer, *&c.*, which to the farmer would be a most improper classification: the Commissary, again, would class them with corn, cheese, fish, *&c.*, as "*provision*;" that which is most essential in one view, being subordinate in another.

Different modes of classification.

§ 5.

Division.

An *individual* is so called because it is incapable of *logical Division*; which is a metaphorical expression, to signify "the distinct [*i. e.* separate] enumeration of several things signified by one common name."

This operation is directly opposite to *generalization*, (which is performed by means of "Abstraction;") for as, in that, you *lay aside* the *differences* by which several things are distinguished, so as to call them all by one *common name*, so, in Division, you *add on* the Differences, so as to enumerate them by their *several distinct* names. Thus, "mineral" is said to be divided into "stones, metals," *&c.*; and metals again into "gold, iron," *&c.*; and these are called the Parts [or members] of the division.

Logical division, metaphorically so called.

"Division," in its primary sense, means separating from each other (either actually, or in enumeration) the parts of which some really-existing single object consists: as when you divide "an animal" (that is, any single animal) into its several members; or again, into its "bones, muscles, nerves, blood-vessels," &c. And so, with any single Vegetable, &c.

Now, each of the *parts* into which you thus "physically" (as it is called) divide "an animal," is strictly and properly a "part," and is *really* less than the whole: for you could not say of a bone, for instance, or of a limb, that it is "an Animal."

But when you "divide"—in the secondary sense of the word (or, as it is called, "metaphysically")—"Animal," that is, the *Genus* "Animal," into Beast, Bird, Fish, Reptile, Insect, &c. each of the *parts* [or "members"] is metaphorically called a "part," and is, in another sense, *more* than the whole [the Genus] that is thus divided. For you may say of a Beast or Bird that it is an "Animal;" and the term "Beast" implies not only the term "Animal," but something more besides; namely, whatever "Difference" *characterizes* "Beast," and separates it from "Bird," "Fish," &c.

And so also any Singular-term [denoting one individual] implies not only the whole of what is understood by the Species it belongs to, but also more; namely, whatever distinguishes that single object from others of the same Species: as "London" implies all that is denoted by the term "City," and also all that distinguishes that individual-city.

The "parts" ["members"] in that figurative sense with which we are now occupied, are each of them *less than the whole*, in another sense; that is, of *less comprehensive* signification. Thus, the Singular-term "Romulus" embracing only an individual-king, is *less extensive* than the Species

"King;" and that, again, less extensive than the Genus "Magistrate," &c.

An "*In*dividual" then is so called from its being *incapable of being* (in this figurative sense) *divided.*

And though the two senses of the word "Division" are easily distinguishable when explained, it is so commonly employed in each sense, that through inattention, confusion often ensues.

We speak as familiarly of the "division" of Mankind into the several races of "Europeans, Tartars, Hindoos, Negroes," &c. as of the "division" of the Earth into "Europe, Asia, Africa," &c. though "the Earth" [or "the World"] is a Singular-term, and denotes what we call *one Individual.* And it is plain we could not say of Europe, for instance, or of Asia, that it is "a World." But we can predicate "Man" of every individual European, Hindoo, &c.

And here observe that there is a common colloquial incorrectness (increasing the liability to confusion) in the use of the word "division," in each of these cases, to denote *one of the* "*parts*" into which the whole is divided. Thus you will sometimes hear a person speak of Europe as one "division" of the Earth; or of such and such a "division" of an Army: meaning "*portion.*" And so again a person will sometimes speak of "animals that belong to the *feline division* of the Carnivora" [flesh-eating-animals] meaning, that *portion of the Class* "Carnivora."

Schemes of Division.

It is usual when a long and complex course of Division is to be stated, to draw it out, for the sake of clearness and brevity, in a form like that of a genealogical "*Tree.*"* And by carefully examining any specimen of such a "Tree" (going over it repeatedly, and comparing each portion of it with the explanations above given) you will be able per-

* See the Division of Fallacies, Book III. § 4.

fectly to fix in your mind the technical terms we have been explaining.

Take for instance as a "Summum-genus" the mathematical-term

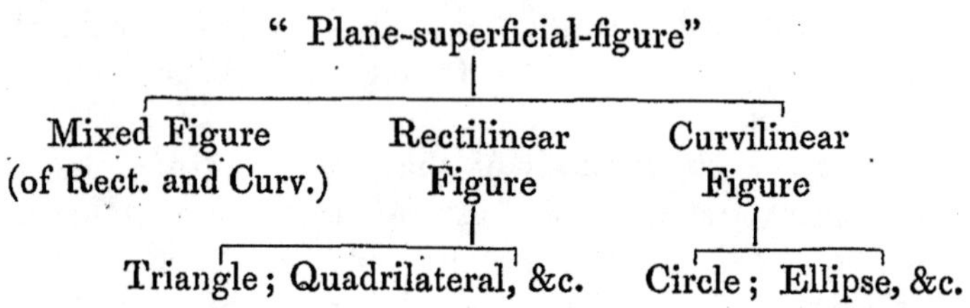

Such a "Tree of division" the Student may easily fill up for himself. And the employment of such a form will be found exceedingly useful in obtaining clear views in any study you are engaged in.

For instance, in the one we have been now occupied with, take for a Summum-Genus, "Expression;" (*i. e.* "expression-in-language" of any such mental-operation as those formerly noticed) you may then exhibit, thus, the division and subdivision of—

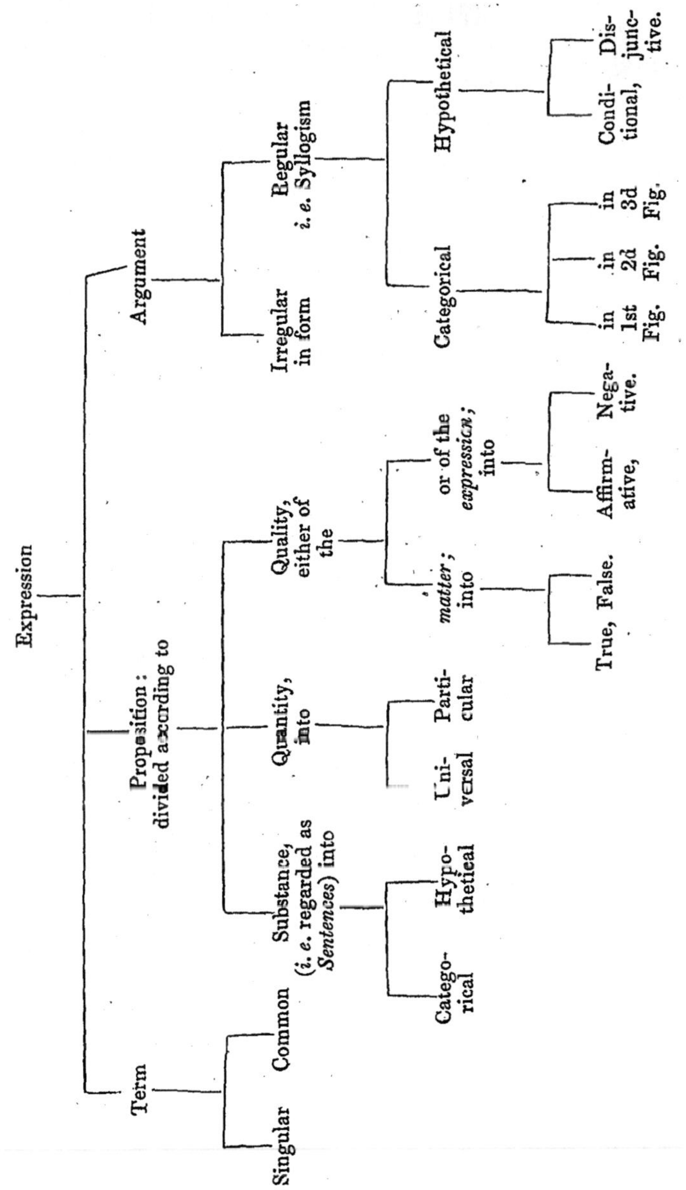
Expression
Term
Singular
Common
Proposition: divided according to
Substance, (i. e. regarded as Sentences) into
Catego-rical
Hypo-thetical
Quantity, into
Uni-versal
Parti-cular
Quality, either of the
matter; into
True,
False.
or of the expression; into
Affirm-ative,
Nega-tive.
Argument
Irregular in form
Regular i. e. Syllogism
Categorical
in 1st Fig.
in 2d Fig.
in 3d Fig.
Hypothetical
Condi-tional,
Dis-junc-tive.

Ordinary rules for division.

The rules ordinarily given for Division are three: 1st. each of the Parts, or any of them short of *all*, must *contain less* (*i. e.* have a narrower signification) than the thing divided. 2d. All the Parts together must be exactly equal to the thing divided; therefore we must be careful to ascertain that the *summum genus* may be predicated of *every* term placed under it, and of nothing *else*. 3d. The Parts or Members must be *opposed* [contradistinguished] *i. e.* must not be contained in one another: *e. g.* if you were to divide "book" into "poetical, historical, folio, quarto, french, latin," *&c.* the members would be contained in each other; for a french book may be a quarto, or octavo, and a quarto, french, english, *&c. &c.* You must be careful, therefore, to keep in mind the *principle of division* with which you set out: *e. g.* whether you begin dividing books according to their *matter*, their *language*, or their *size*, *&c.* all these being so many *cross-divisions*. And when anything is capable (as in the above instance) of being divided in several different ways, we are not to reckon one of these as the true, or real, or *right* one, without specifying what the object is which we have in view: for one mode of dividing may be the most suitable for one purpose, and another for another: as *e. g.* one of the above modes of dividing books would be the most suitable to a bookbinder; another in a philosophical, and the other in a philological view.

Cross-divisions.

It is a useful practical rule, whenever you find a discussion of any subject very perplexing, and seemingly confused, to examine whether some "Cross-division" has not crept in unobserved. For this is very apt to take place; (though of course such a *glaring* instance as that in the above example could not occur in practice) and there is no more fruitful source of indistinctness and confusion of thought.

When you have occasion to divide anything in several

different ways,—that is, "on several principles-of-division"—you should take care to state distinctly *how many* divisions you are making, and on what principle each proceeds.

For instance, in the "Tree" above given, it is stated, that "Propositions" are divided in different ways, "*according to*" this and that, &c. And thus the perplexity of Cross-division is avoided.

Additional caution.

Two other rules in addition to those above given, are needful to be kept in mind: viz. 4thly, A Division should not be "*arbitrary*;" that is, its Members should be *distinguished* from each other by "Differences" either expressed or readily understood; instead of being set apart from each other at random, or without any sufficient ground. For instance, if any one should divide "coins" into "gold-coins," "silver," and "copper," the ground of this distinction would be intelligible: but if he should, in proceeding to subdivide silver-coin, distinguish as two branches, on the one side, "shillings," and on the other "all silver-coins *except* shillings," this would be an *arbitrary* Division.

5thly, A Division should be *clearly arranged* as to its Members: that is, there should be as much *sub*division as the occasion may require; and not a mere catalogue of the "lowest-Species," omitting *intermediate* classes ["*subaltern*"] between these and the "highest-genus:" nor again an intermixture of the "subaltern," and "lowest-species," so as to have, in any two branches of the division, Species contradistinguished and placed opposite, of which the one ought naturally to be placed *higher up* [nearer the "Summum"] and the other, *lower down* in the Tree.

For instance, to divide "plane-figure" at once, into "equilateral-triangles, squares, circles, ellipses," &c., or again "vegetable," into "Elms, pear-trees, turnips, mushrooms," &c., or again to divide "Animal" into "Birds, Fishes, Reptiles, Horses, Lions." &c. would be a transgression of this rule.

And observe that, (as has been formerly remarked) although such *glaring* cases as are given by way of examples could not occur in practice, errors precisely corresponding to them, may, and often do occur; and produce much confusion of thought and error.

§ 6.

Definition.

Definition is another metaphorical word, which literally signifies, "laying down a boundary;" and is used in Logic to signify "an expression which explains any term, so as to *separate* it from everything else," as a boundary separates fields.

Essential and accidental definitions.

In reference to the several modes adopted for furnishing such explanation, Logicians distinguish [divide] Definitions into *essential* and *accidental.* They call that an "*essential*-definition" which states what are regarded as the "constituent parts of the essence" of that which is to be defined; and an "*accidental*-definition" [or *Description*] one which lays down what are regarded as "circumstances belonging to it;" viz. Properties or Accidents; such as causes, effects, &c.

Accidents in the narrowest sense, (as defined above, § 3) cannot, it is plain, be employed in a Description [accidental-definition] of any *Species;* since no Accident (in that sense) can belong to the *whole* of a Species, nor consequently furnish an adequate Definition thereof.

Definition of individuals.

In the "description" of an *individual,* on the contrary, we employ, not *Properties,* (which as they do belong to the whole of a Species, cannot serve to distinguish one individual of that Species from another) but Accidents—generally, *inseparable-accidents*—in conjunction with the Species: as "Philip was a
Sp.
king of Macedon, who subdued Greece;" "Britain is an
Sp.
Island, situated so and so," &c.

Physical and logical definitions.

The Essential-definition again is divided into *physical* [natural] and *logical* [metaphysical] definition: the physical-definition being made by an enumeration of such parts as are *actually* separable,—such as are the hull, masts, &c. of a "Ship;"—the root, trunk, branches, bark, &c. of a "Tree;" the Subject, Predicate, and Copula of a "Proposition."

The "*logical*-definition" consists of the "Genus" and "Difference;" which are called by some writers the "metaphysical" [ideal] parts; as being *not two real parts* into which an *individual*-object can (as in the former case) be actually divided, but only different views taken [notions formed] of a *class* of objects, by one mind. *E. G.* "A

Genus

Proposition" would be defined, logically, "a sentence

Difference. G.

affirming-or-denying:" A "Magnet" "an Iron-ore having

D.

attraction for iron;" a "Square," a "Rectangle" [right-

D.

angled parallelogram] having equal sides.

Nominal and real definitions.

Definitions again have been divided by Logicians into the *Nominal*, which explains merely the *meaning of the term* defined;* and *Real*, which explains the nature of the *thing signified* by that term.

This division is evidently according to the *object designed*

* Aldrich, having given as an instance of a Nominal Definition the absurd one of "homo, qui ex humo," has led some to conclude that the Nominal definition must be founded on the *etymology*; or at least that such was his meaning. But that it was not, is sufficiently plain from the circumstance that Wallis (from whose work his is almost entirely abridged) expressly says *the contrary*. Be this as it may, however, it is plain that the etymology of a term has nothing to do with any logical consideration of it. See § 8, Book III.

to be effected by each Definition: the former division, on the other hand—into Accidental, Physical and Logical—being a division according to the *means employed* by each to effect its object. These therefore are evidently two "cross-divisions;"* a circumstance which has been generally overlooked by Logical writers, who have thus introduced confusion and perplexity.

And here the question may naturally occur to the reader, whether there be properly any distinction between *nominal* and *real*-definition;—whether the *meaning* of a *Common-term*, and the *nature* of the *thing signified* by it, are not one and the same; since the object of our thoughts when we employ a Common-term, is—not any such "abstract idea" as some talk of, but—the *Term itself*, regarded as a Sign &c. as was formerly explained.

And in truth there are many cases in which there does exist this exact coincidence between the meaning of the term and the nature of the thing; so that the same definition which would be rightly styled "nominal," as explaining nothing beyond the exact meaning of the term, might also be considered as entitled to be called a "real-definition," as implying every attribute that *can* belong to the thing signified. Such are all definitions of mathematical

Technical terms.

and logical terms, and other technical terms of Science. There cannot *e. g.* be any property of a "Circle," or a "Square," that is not implied in the *definitions* of those terms. Some of these properties may not indeed at once occur to a beginner in Mathematics; and others, not even to one somewhat further advanced: but they must all be implied in the definitions: and it would be reckoned an impropriety to add *e. g.* to the definition of a Square that it is *bisected by its diagonal:* because though this might not at once occur to a beginner, and needs to be demonstrated, it is demonstrated *from* the

* See preceding §.

definition: to speak of "a Square divided by its diagonal into unequal parts," would be absurd, — unmeaning, — inconceivable. And the same, with other mathematical terms.

But it is otherwise with terms of a different character, which are the names of actually existing substances. There may be attributes of the thing signified that are not at all implied in the signification of the term. *E. G.* The term "laurel-water" is used by us in the same sense as by our ancestors, to signify "a liquor distilled from laurel-leaves;" though the *poisonous* quality of it was unknown a century ago. And so also many discoveries have been made, and others probably will be made, respecting several metals, heavenly-bodies, &c. though the words "iron," "gold," "star," are employed in the same sense as formerly;—a sense which does not imply the properties that have been discovered.

And any Definition which goes *beyond* a "nominal-definition," *i. e.* which explains anything *more* of the nature of the thing than is implied in the name, may be regarded, strictly speaking, as, so far, a "real-definition."

The very word "Definition" however is not usually employed in this sense; but rather, "*Description.*"

Logic is concerned with Nominal definitions alone.

Logic is concerned with *nominal*-definition alone; with a view to guard against *ambiguity* in the use of terms.*

To ascertain fully the various properties of animals and vegetables, belongs to Physiology;—of metals, earths, &c. to Chemistry; and so, with other things.

* And for this purpose it will often happen that a definition will be sufficient in reference to the *existing occasion,* even though it may fall short of expressing *all* that is implied by the term. See Book III. § 10.

We should however carefully guard against the common mistake, of supposing that any one who applies a term correctly in several instances, must of course understand fully its signification.

It is to be observed that the word "*Definition*" is sometimes used to denote the *whole sentence,* in which the term defined is conjoined with the explanation given of it; as when we say, "a triangle is a threesided figure:" sometimes it is used to signify merely *that which gives* the explanation; as when we say "three-sided figure" is *the definition* of "triangle."

In the former case, the sentence has the form of a *Proposition;* but what it is that such a proposition asserts, is not always implied in the mere expression, but is left to be collected from the supposed intention of the speaker.

Real existence not asserted by a definition.

Real *existence* is not necessarily implied: *e.g.* "A Phœnix is a bird fabled to live a thousand years," &c. implies merely that this is the *meaning* in which the word Phœnix has been used; not that any such bird ever did or could exist.

Sometimes again it is not implied even that the universal, or the ordinary, sense of the term is such as corresponds to the definition given; but merely that such is the sense in which the author intends to employ it.

Imperative form of definitions.

And in this case, the definition is sometimes stated in the *imperative* instead of the indicative form; as is frequently done in the works of Aristotle, who is accustomed thus to waive, in some cases, all questions as to the *ordinary* employment of a term by others; saying "*Let* so and so be taken to signify this or that."

In mathematical and other scientific definitions, whether expressed in the form of Propositions, or in the Imperative (or, as it might be called, *Postulate*) form, it is understood to be implied that the definition involves no self-contradiction,—no absurdity; but that the thing denoted by the term defined—whether believed actually to exist or not—is *conceivable,* and may, not irrationally, be made a subject of thought. *E. G.* Though a "mathematical-line" cannot be conceived to be actually drawn on paper,—though nothing could be exhibited to the senses as having length and *no* breadth, every one can make the distance *e. g.* between two towns, a separate subject of his thoughts, having his mind wholly withdrawn from the width of the road.

A mathematical Definition accordingly may be considered as involving a *Postulate;* and it would be very easy to express any of them in the form of Postulates. *E. G.* "Let a plane-figure bounded by a curve-line everywhere equidistant from a certain point within it, be called a Circle;" this would be understood to imply that such a figure is *conceivable*, and that the writer *intended to employ* that term to signify such a figure; which is precisely all that is meant to be asserted in the Definition of a Circle.

Rules for Definition.

The Rules or Cautions usually laid down by Logical writers for framing a Definition, are very obvious: *viz.* 1st. The definition must be *adequate; i. e.* neither too extensive nor too narrow for the thing defined; *e.g.* to define "fish," "an animal that lives in the water," would be too *extensive*, because many insects, *&c.* live in the water; to define it, "an animal that has an air-bladder," would be too *narrow;* because many fish are without any. Or again, if in a definition of "Money" you should specify its being "made of metal," that would be too *narrow*, as excluding the *shells* used as money in some parts of Africa: if again you would define it as an "article of value given in exchange for something else," that would be too *wide*, as it would include things exchanged by *barter;* as when a shoemaker who wants coals, makes an exchange with a collier who wants shoes.

Arbitrary exceptions.

And observe, that such a defect in a Definition cannot be remedied by making an *arbitrary exception;* (such as was alluded to above, § 5) as if for instance (and it is an instance which actually occurred) a person should give such a Definition of "Capital" as should include (which he did not mean to do) "Land;" and should then propose to remedy this by defining "Capital," any "property of such and such a description, *except Land.*"

2d. The Definition must be in itself plainer than the thing defined, else it would not *explain it:* I say, "in itself," (*i. e.* generally) because, to some particular person, the term defined may happen to be even more familiar and better understood, than the language of the Definition.

And this rule may be considered as including that which is usually given by Logicians as a third rule; *viz.* that a Definition should be couched in a *convenient number* of *appropriate* words (if such can be found suitable for the purpose): since *figurative* words (which are opposed to appropriate) are apt to produce ambiguity or indistinctness; too great *brevity* may occasion *obscurity;* and too great *prolixity*, *confusion.* But this perhaps is rather an admonition with respect to Style, than a strictly logical rule; nor can we accordingly determine with precision, in each case, whether it has been complied with or not; there is no drawing the line between "too long" and "too concise," *&c.* Nor would a definition unnecessarily prolix be censured as *incorrect,* but as *inelegant,* inconvenient, *&c.*

Tautology. If, however, a definition be chargeable with *Tautology,* (which is a distinct fault from prolixity or verbosity) it may justly be called incorrect, though without offending against the first two rules. Tautology consists in inserting too much, not in mere *words,* but in *sense;* yet not so as too much to narrow the definition (in opposition to Rule 1.) by excluding some things which belong to the class of the thing defined; but only, so as to state something which has been *already implied.* Thus, to define a Parallelogram "a four-sided figure whose opposite sides are parallel *and equal,*" would be tautological; because, though it is *true* that such a figure, and such alone, is a parallelogram, the *equality* of the sides is implied in their being *parallel*, and may be proved from it. Now the insertion of the words "and equal," leaves, and indeed leads, a reader to suppose that there may be a four-sided figure whose opposite sides are parallel but *not* equal. Though therefore such a definition asserts nothing false, it leads to a supposition of what is false; and consequently is to be regarded as an incorrect definition.

The inference just mentioned,—*viz.*: that you implied that a quadrangle might have its opposite sides parallel, and *not* equal,—would be drawn from such a definition, according to the principle of "exceptio probat regulam," *an exception proves a rule.** The force of the maxim (which is not properly confined to the case of an *exception*, strictly so called) is this; that "the mention of any circumstance introduced into the statement either of a definition, or of a precept, law, remark, *&c.* is to be presumed *necessary* to be inserted; so that the precept, *&c.* would *not hold good* if this circumstance were absent." In short, the word "*only*," or some such expression, is supposed to be understood. If *e. g.* it be laid down that he who breaks into an *empty* house shall receive a certain punishment, it would be inferred that this punishment would not be incurred by breaking into an *occupied* house: if it were told us that some celestial phenomenon could not be seen *by the naked*

* Thus it has been inferred,—and not without reason,—that the occasional Forms of Prayer and Thanksgivings which are put forth from time to time under the authority of "Orders in Council," are *illegal* and at variance with the "Act of Uniformity;" inasmuch as in that Act (prefixed to our Prayer-books) not only is conformity to the Book of Common-prayer enjoined, and no authority to make alterations or additions to the Service recognized, but there is an *Exception*, which, it is maintained, *proves the rule:* the King in Council being *expressly authorized* to insert and alter from time to time the "*names* of such of the Royal-family as are to be prayed *for*:" which plainly implies that no *other* alterations made by that authority were contemplated as allowable. See "Appeal on behalf of Church Government." Houlston and Co.

eye, it would be inferred that it would or might be visible through a *telescope:* if we are told that we are not to teach doctrines unwarranted by Scripture, *and which were not held by the early Fathers,* this would usually be understood to imply that any doctrine they *did* hold, might be taught, on their authority, even though not scriptural:* *&c.*

And much is often inferred in this manner, which was by no means in the Author's mind; from his having inaccurately inserted what chanced to be present to his thoughts. Thus, he who says that it is a crime for people to violate the property of a *humane* Landlord who *lives among them,* may perhaps not mean to imply that it is no crime to violate the property of an absentee-landlord, or of one who is not humane; but he leaves an opening for being so understood. Thus again in saying that "an animal which breathes through gills and *is scaly,* is a fish," though nothing false is asserted, a presumption is afforded that you mean to give a definition such as would be too *narrow;* in violation of Rule 1.

And *Tautology,* as above described, is sure to mislead any one who interprets what is said, conformably to the maxim that "an exception proves a rule."

Accidental circumstances mistaken for essential.

It often happens that one or more of the above rules is violated through men's proneness to introduce into their definitions, along with, or instead of, *essential* circumstances,

* "The maxim of 'abundans cautela nocet nemini' is by no means a safe one if applied without limitation. It is sometimes imprudent (and some of our Divines have, I think, committed this imprudence) to attempt to 'make assurance doubly sure' by bringing forward confirmatory reasons, which, though in themselves perfectly fair, may be interpreted unfairly, by representing them as an acknowledged *indispensable* foundation;—by assuming for instance, that an appeal to such and such of the ancient Fathers or Councils, in confirmation of some doctrine or practice, is to be understood as an admission that it would fall to the ground if *not* so confirmed."—*Kingdom of Christ,* Essay II. § 23, note.

such as are in the strict sense, *accidental.* I mean, that the notion they attach to each term, and the explanation they would give of it, shall embrace some circumstances, *generally, but not always,* connected with the thing they are speaking of; and which might, accordingly, (by the strict account of an "Accident") be "absent or present, the essential character of the subject remaining the same." A definition framed from such circumstances, though of course incorrect, and likely at some time or other to mislead us, will not unfrequently obtain reception, from its answering the purpose of a correct one, at a particular time and place.

"For instance, the Latin word *Meridies,* to denote the *southern* quarter, is etymologically suitable (and so would a definition founded on that etymology) *in our hemisphere;* while in the other, it would be found just the reverse. Or if any one should define the North Pole, that which is 'inclined towards the sun,' this would, *for half the year,* answer the purpose of a correct definition; and would be the opposite of the truth for the other half.

"Such glaring instances as these, which are never likely to occur in practice, serve best perhaps to illustrate the character of such mistakes as do occur. A specimen of that introduction of accidental circumstances which I have been describing, may be found, I think, in the language of a great number of writers, respecting Wealth and Value; who have usually made *Labour* an essential ingredient in their definitions. Now it is true, *it so happens,* by the appointment of Providence, that valuable articles are in *almost* all instances obtained by Labour; but still, this is an accidental, not an essential circumstance. If the aerolites which occasionally fall, were diamonds and pearls, and if these articles could be obtained in no other way, but were casually picked up, to the same amount as is now obtained by digging and diving, they would be of precisely the same value as now. In this, as in many other points in Political Economy, men are prone to confound *cause* and *effect*. It is not that pearls fetch a high price *because* men have dived for them; but on the contrary, men dive for them because they fetch a high price."*

* Pol. Econ. Lect. IX. p. 251—253.

BOOK III.

OF FALLACIES.

Introduction.

ALTHOUGH sundry instances of Fallacies have been from time to time noticed in the foregoing Books, it will be worth while to devote a more particular attention to the subject.

Definition of Fallacy.

By a Fallacy is commonly understood, "any unsound mode of arguing, which appears to demand our conviction, and to be decisive of the question in hand, when in fairness it is not." Considering the ready detection and clear exposure of Fallacies to be both more extensively important, and also more difficult, than many are aware of, I propose to take a Logical view of the subject; referring the different Fallacies to the most convenient heads, and giving a scientific analysis of the procedure which takes place in each.

After all, indeed, in the practical detection of each individual Fallacy, much must depend on natural and acquired acuteness; nor can any rules be given, the mere learning of which will enable us to *apply* them with mechanical certainty and readiness: but still we shall find that to take correct general views of the subject, and to be familiarized with scientific discussions of it, will tend, above all things, to *engender such a habit of mind*, as will best fit us for practice.

Indeed the case is the same with respect to Logic in general. Scarcely any one would, in ordinary practice, state to himself either his own or another's reasoning, in Syllogisms in Barbara at full length; yet a familiarity with Logical principles tends very much (as all feel, who are really well acquainted with them) to beget a habit of clear and sound reasoning. The truth is, in this, as in many other things, there are processes going on in the mind (when we are practising anything quite familiar to us) with such rapidity as to leave no trace in the memory; and we often apply principles which did not, as far as we are conscious, even occur to us at the time.

Inaccurate language of former writers.

It would be foreign, however, to the present purpose, to investigate fully the manner in which certain studies operate in remotely producing certain effects on the mind: it is sufficient to establish the *fact*, that habits of scientific analysis (besides the intrinsic beauty and dignity of such studies) lead to practical advantage. It is on Logical principles therefore that I propose to discuss the subject of Fallacies; and it may, indeed, seem to have been unnecessary to make any apology for so doing, after what has been formerly said, generally, in defence of Logic; but that the generality of Logical writers have usually followed so opposite a plan. Whenever they have to treat of any thing that is beyond the mere elements of Logic, they totally lay aside all reference to the principles they have been occupied in establishing and explaining, and have recourse to a loose, vague, and popular kind of language; such as would be the best suited indeed to an exoterical discourse, but seems strangely incongruous in a professed Logical treatise. What should we think of a Geometrical writer, who, after having gone through the Elements, with strict definitions and demonstrations, should, on proceeding to Mechanics, totally lay aside all reference to scientific principles,—all use of technical terms,—and treat of the subject in undefined terms, and with probable and popular arguments? It would be thought strange, if even a Botanist, when addressing those whom he had been instructing in the principles and the terms of his system, should totally lay these aside when he came to describe plants, and should adopt the language of the vulgar. Surely it affords but too much plausibility to the cavils of those who scoff at Logic altogether, that the very writers who profess to teach it should never themselves make any application of, or reference to, its principles, on those very occasions, when, and *when only*, such application and reference are to be expected. If the principles of any system are *well* laid down,—if its technical language is judiciously framed,—then, surely, those principles and that language will afford (for those who have once thoroughly learned them) the best, the most clear, simple, and concise method of treating any subject connected with that system. Yet even writers generally acute, in treating of the Dilemma and of the Fallacies, have very much forgotten the Logician, and assumed a loose and rhetorical style of writing, without making any application of the principles they had formerly laid down, but, on the contrary, sometimes departing widely from them.*

The most experienced teachers, when addressing those who are familiar with the elementary principles of Logic, think it requisite, not indeed to lead them, on each occasion, *through the whole detail* of those principles, when the process is quite obvious, but always to *put them on the road*, as it were, to those principles, that they may plainly see

* Aldrich (and the same may be said of several other writers) is far more confused in his discussion of Fallacies than in any other part of his treatise; of which this one instance may serve: after having distinguished Fallacies into those in the *expression*, and those in the *matter* ("in dictione," and "extra dictionem,") he observes of one or two of *these last*, that they are not properly called *Fallacies*, as not being *Syllogisms faulty in form*; ("Syllogisimi forma peccantes:") as if any one, that was such, could be "Fallacia *extra dictionem*."

their own way to the end, and take a scientific view of the subject: in the same manner as mathematical writers avoid indeed the occasional tediousness of going all through a very simple demonstration, which the learner, if he will, may easily supply; but yet always speak in strict mathematical language, and with reference to mathematical principles, though they do not always state them at full length. I would not profess, therefore, any more than they do, to write (on subjects connected with the science) in a language intelligible to those who are ignorant of its first rudiments. To do so, indeed, would imply that one was not taking a scientific view of the subject, nor availing one's-self of the principles that had been established, and the accurate and concise technical language that had been framed.

Mistakes as to the office of Logic.

The rules already given enable us to develop the principles on which all reasoning is conducted, whatever be the Subject-matter of it, and to ascertain the validity or fallaciousness of any apparent argument, as far as the *form of expression* is concerned; that being alone the proper province of Logic.

But it is evident that we may nevertheless remain liable to be deceived or perplexed in Argument by the assumption of *false or doubtful Premises*, or by the employment of *indistinct or ambiguous Terms;* and, accordingly, many Logical writers, wishing to make their systems appear as perfect as possible, have undertaken to give rules "for attaining clear ideas," and for "guiding the judgment;" and fancying or professing themselves successful in this, have consistently enough denominated Logic, the "Art of using the Reason;" which in truth it would be, and would nearly supersede all other studies, if it could of itself ascertain the *meaning* of every *Term*, and the *truth or falsity* of every *Proposition;* in the same manner as it actually can, the *validity* of every *Argument*. And they have been led into this, partly by the consideration that Logic is concerned about the "three Operations" of the mind—simple Apprehension, Judgment, and Reasoning; not observing that it is not *equally* concerned about all: the last Operation being alone its appropriate province; and the rest being treated of only in reference to that.

Discredit brought upon Logic.

The contempt justly due to such pretensions has most unjustly fallen on the Science itself; much in the same manner as Chemistry was brought into disrepute among the unthinking, by the extravagant pretensions of the Alchymists. And those Logical writers have been censured, not (as they should have been) for *making* such professions, but for not *fulfilling* them. It has been objected, especially, that the rules of Logic leave us still at a loss as to the most important and difficult point in reasoning; *viz.* the ascertaining the sense of the terms employed, and removing their ambiguity: a complaint resembling that made (according to a story told by Warburton,* and before alluded to) by a man who found fault with all the reading-glasses presented to him by the shopkeeper; the fact being that he had never *learnt to read.* In the present case, the complaint is the more unreasonable, inasmuch as there neither is, nor ever *can possibly be*, any such system devised as will effect the proposed object of clearing up the ambiguity of Terms. It is, however, no small advantage, that the rules of Logic, though they cannot, alone, ascertain and clear up ambiguity in any Term, yet do point out in *which* Term of an argument it is to be sought for: directing our attention to the *middle*-Term, as the one on the ambiguity of which a Fallacy is likely to be built.

It will be useful, however, to class and describe the different kinds of ambiguity which are to be met with; and also the various ways in which the insertion of false, or, at least, unduly assumed, Premises, is most likely to elude

* In his *Div. Leg.*

observation. And though the remarks which will be offered on these points may not be considered as strictly forming a *part* of Logic, they cannot be thought out of place, when it is considered how essentially they are connected with the *application* of it.

§ 1.

Division of Fallacies.

The division of Fallacies into those in the WORDS (IN DICTIONE,) and those in the MATTER (EXTRA DICTIONEM) has not been, by any writers hitherto, grounded on any distinct principle: at least, not on any that they have themselves adhered to. The confounding together, however, of these two classes is highly detrimental to all clear notions concerning Logic; being obviously allied to the prevailing erroneous views which make Logic the *art of employing the intellectual faculties in general*, having the *discovery of truth* for its object, and all kinds of knowledge for its proper subject-matter; with all that train of vague and groundless speculations which have led to such interminable confusion and mistakes, and afforded a pretext for such clamorous censures.

It is important, therefore, that rules should be given for a division of Fallacies into Logical and Non-logical, on such a principle as shall keep clear of all this indistinctness and perplexity.

If any one should object, that the division about to be adopted is in some degree arbitrary, placing under the one head, Fallacies which many might be disposed to place under the other, let him consider not only the indistinctness of all former divisions, but the utter impossibility of framing *any* that shall be completely secure from the objection urged, in a case where men have formed such various and vague notions, from the very want of some clear principle of division. Nay, from the elliptical form in which all reasoning is usually expressed, and the peculiarly involved and oblique form in which Fallacy is for the most part conveyed, it must of course be often a matter of doubt, or rather, of arbitrary *choice*, not only to which genus each *kind* of fallacy should be referred, but even to which kind to refer any *one individual* Fallacy.

Indeterminate character of Fallacies.

For, since, in any Argument, one Premiss is usually suppressed, it frequently happens, in the case of a Fallacy, that the hearers are left to the alternative of supplying *either* a Premiss which is *not true*, or *else*, one which *does not prove* the Conclusion. *E. G.* if a man expatiates on the distress of the country, and thence argues that the government is tyrannical, we must suppose him to assume *either* that "every distressed country is under a tyranny," which is a manifest falsehood, *or*, merely that "every country under a tyranny is distressed," which, however true, proves nothing, the Middle-Term being undistributed. Now, in the former case, the Fallacy would be referred to the head of "extra dictionem;" in the latter to that of "in dictione." Which are we to suppose the speaker meant us to understand? Surely just whichever each of his hearers might happen to prefer: some might assent to the false Premiss; others, allow the unsound Syllogism; to the Sophist himself it is indifferent, as long as they can but be brought to admit the Conclusion.

Without pretending, then, to conform to every one's mode of speaking on the subject, or to lay down rules which shall be in themselves (without any call for labour or skill in the person who employs them) readily applicable to, and decisive on, each individual case, I shall propose a division which is at least perfectly clear in its main principle, and coincides, perhaps, as nearly as possible, with the established notions of Logicians on the subject.

§ 2.

Logical Fallacies.

In every Fallacy, the Conclusion either *does*, or *does not follow from the Premises.* Where the Conclusion does not follow from the Premises, it is manifest that the fault is in the *Reasoning*, and in that alone; these, therefore, we call Logical Fallacies,* as being properly, violations of those rules of Reasoning which it is the province of Logic to lay down.

Of these, however, one kind are more *purely Logical,* as exhibiting their fallaciousness by the bare *form* of the expression, without any regard to the meaning of the Terms: to which class belong: 1st. Undistributed Middle; 2. Illicit Process; 3d. Negative Premises, or Affirmative Conclusion from a Negative Premiss, and *vice versâ:* to which may be added 4th. those which have palpably (*i.e. expressed)* more than three Terms.

Semi-Logical Fallacies.

The other kind may be most properly called *semi-logical; viz.* all the cases of ambiguous middle-Term except its non-distribution: for though in such cases the conclusion does not follow, and though the rules of Logic show that it does not, *as soon as the ambiguity of the middle Term is ascertained,* yet the discovery and ascertainment of this ambiguity requires attention to the *sense of the Term,* and knowledge of the Subject-matter; so that here, Logic teaches us not *how to find* the Fallacy, but only *where to search* for it, and on what principles to condemn it.

Accordingly it has been made a subject of bitter complaint against Logic, that it presupposes the most difficult point to be already accomplished, *viz.* the sense of the Terms to be ascertained. A similar objection might be urged against every other art in existence; *e.g.* against

* In the same manner as we call that a *criminal* court in which crimes are *judged.*

Agriculture, that all the precepts for the cultivation of land presuppose the possession of a farm; or against Perspective, that its rules are useless to a blind man. The objection is indeed peculiarly absurd when urged against Logic, because the object which it is blamed for not accomplishing *cannot* possibly be within the province of *any one* art whatever. Is it indeed possible or conceivable that there should be any method, science, or system, that should enable one to know the full and exact meaning of every term in existence? The utmost that can be done is to give some general rules that may assist us in this work; which is done in the first two chapters of Book II.*

Familiarity with a term distinct from clear apprehension of its meaning.

Nothing perhaps tends more to conceal from men their imperfect conception of the meaning of a term, than the circumstance of their being able fully to comprehend a *process of reasoning* in which it is involved, without attaching any distinct meaning at all to that term; as is evident when X Y Z are used to stand for Terms, in a regular Syllogism. Thus a man may be *familiarized* with a term, and never find himself *at a loss* from not comprehending it; from which he will be very likely to infer that he *does* comprehend it, when perhaps he does not, but employs it vaguely and incorrectly; which leads to fallacious Reasoning and confusion. It must be owned, however, that many Logical writers have, in great measure, brought on themselves the reproach in question, by calling Logic "the right use of Reason," laying down "rules for gaining clear ideas," and such-like ἀλαζωνεία, as Aristotle calls it; (*Rhet.* Book I. Chap. ii.)

* The very author of the objection says, "This (the comprehension of the meaning of general Terms) is a study which every individual must carry on for himself; and of which no rules of Logic (how useful soever they may be in directing our labours) can supersede the necessity." D. Stewart, *Phil.* Vol. II. chap. ii. s. 2.

§ 3.

Material Fallacies.

The remaining class (*viz.* where the Conclusion does follow from the Premises) may be called the Material, or Non-logical Fallacies: of these there are two kinds;* 1st. when the Premises are such as ought not to have been assumed; 2d. when the Conclusion is not the one required, but irrelevant; which Fallacy is commonly called "*ignoratio elenchi,*" because your Argument is not the "elenchus" (*i. e.* proof of the *contradictory*) of your opponent's assertion, which it should be; but proves, instead of that, some other proposition resembling it. Hence, since Logic defines what Contradiction is, some may chuse rather to range this with the *Logical* Fallacies, as it seems, so far, to come under the jurisdiction of that Art. Nevertheless, it is perhaps better to adhere to the original division, both on account of its clearness, and also because few would be inclined to apply to the Fallacy in question the accusation of being *inconclusive,* and consequently "illogical" reasoning; besides which, it seems an artificial and circuitous way of speaking, to suppose in all cases an *opponent* and a *contradiction;* the simple statement of the matter being this,—I am required, by the circumstances of the case, (no matter why) to prove a certain Conclusion; I prove, not that, but one which is likely to be mistaken for it;—in this lies the Fallacy.

Ignoratio elenchi.

It might be desirable therefore to lay aside the name of "*ignoratio elenchi,*" but that it is so generally adopted as to require some mention to be made of it. The other kind of Fallacies in the Matter will comprehend (as far as the vague and obscure language of Logical writers will allow us

* For it is manifest that the fault, if there be any, must be either 1st. in the *Premises,* or 2dly. in the *Conclusion,* or 3dly. in the *Connexion* between them.

to conjecture) the fallacy of "*non causa pro causa*," and that of "*petitio principii.*" Of these, the former is by them distinguished into "*a non vera pro vera*," and "*a non tali pro tali*;" this last would appear to mean arguing from a case *not parallel* as if it *were* so; which, in Logical language, is, having the *suppressed* Premiss false; for it is in *that* the *parallelism* is affirmed; and the "*non vera pro vera*" will in like manner signify the *expressed* Premiss being false; so that this Fallacy will turn out to be, in plain terms, neither more nor less than falsity (or unfair assumption) of a Premiss.

Non causa pro causa.

The remaining kind, "*petitio principii*," ["begging the question,"] takes place when a Premiss, whether true or false, is either plainly equivalent to the Conclusion, or depends on it for its own reception. It is to be observed, however, that in all correct Reasoning the Premises must, virtually, imply the Conclusion; so that it is not possible to mark precisely the distinction between the Fallacy in question and fair Argument; since that may be correct and fair Reasoning to one person, which would be, to another, "begging the question;" inasmuch as to one, the Conclusion might be more evident than the Premiss, and to the other, the reverse. The most plausible form of this Fallacy is arguing in a *circle;* and the *greater* the circle, the harder to detect.

Begging the question.

§ 4.

There is no Fallacy that may not properly be included under some of the foregoing heads: those which in the Logical treatises are separately enumerated, and contradistinguished from these, being in reality instances of them, and therefore more properly enumerated in the subdivision thereof; as in the scheme annexed:—

Fallacies.

- Logical. (*i. e.* when the fault is, strictly, in the very process of Reasoning; the Conclusion *not following* from the Premises.)
  - Purely-logical. (§ 7.) (*i. e.* where the fallaciousness is apparent from the mere *form of expression.*)
    - Undistributed middle.
    - Illicit process, &c.
  - Semi-logical. (the middle term being ambiguous *in sense.*)
    - in itself,
      - accidentally.
      - from some connexion between the different senses.
        - resemblance.
        - analogy.
        - cause and effect, &c.
    - *from the context,*
      - (§ 11.) Fallacy of Division and Composition.
      - (§ 12.) Fallacia accidentis, &c.
- Non-logical or Material. (*i. e.* when the Conclusion *does follow* from the Premises.)
  - Premiss unduly assumed.
    - (§ 13.) (*Petitio principii.*) Premiss depending on the Conclusion.
      - Circle.
      - assuming a proposition not the very same as the question, but unfairly implying it.
    - (§ 14.) Premiss false or unsupported.
  - Conclusion irrelevant. (*ignoratio elenchi.*)
    - (§ 17.) Fallacy of objections, &c.
    - (§ 16.) Fallacy of shifting ground.
      - to something wholly irrelevant.
      - from Premiss to Premiss alternately.
    - (§ 15.) Fallacy of using complex and general terms.
    - (§ 15.) Fallacy of appeals to the passions; *ad hominem; ad verecundiam, &c.*

§ 5.

On each of the Fallacies which have been thus enumerated and distinguished, I propose to offer some more particular remarks; but before I proceed to this, it will be proper to premise two general observations, 1st. on the *importance*, and 2d. the *difficulty*, of detecting and describing Fallacies. Both have been already slightly alluded to; but it is requisite that they should here be somewhat more fully and distinctly set forth.

Importance of detecting Fallacies.

1st. It seems by most persons to be taken for granted that a Fallacy is to be dreaded merely as a weapon fashioned and wielded by a skilful sophist; or, if they allow that a man may with honest intentions slide into one unconsciously, in the heat of *argument*, still they seem to suppose that where there is no *dispute*, there is no cause to dread Fallacy; whereas there is much danger, even in what may be called *solitary reasoning*, of sliding unawares into some Fallacy, by which one may be so far deceived as even to *act upon* the conclusion thus obtained. By "solitary reasoning" I mean the case in which one is not seeking for *arguments* to prove a *given question*, but labouring to elicit from one's previous stock of knowledge *some useful inference.**

Influence of words on thoughts.

To select one from innumerable examples that might be cited, and of which some more will occur in the subsequent part of this essay; it is not improbable that many indifferent sermons have been produced by the ambiguity of the word "*plain*." A young divine perceives the truth of the maxim, that "for the lower orders one's language cannot be too *plain*:" (*i. e. clear* and *perspicuous*, so as to require no learning nor inge-

* See the chapter on "inferring and proving," (Book IV. ch. iii.) in the Dissertation on the Province of Reasoning.

nuity to understand it,) and when he proceeds to practice, the word "*plain*" indistinctly flits before him, as it were, and often checks him in the use of *ornaments* of style, such as metaphor, epithet, antithesis, *&c.*, which are opposed to "plainness" in a totally different sense of the word; being by no means necessarily adverse to *perspicuity*, but rather, in many cases, conducive to it; as may be seen in several of the clearest of our Lord's discourses, which are the very ones that are the most richly adorned with figurative language. So far indeed is an ornamented style from being unfit for the vulgar, that they are pleased with it even in excess. Yet the desire to be "plain," combined with that dim and confused notion which the ambiguity of the word produces in such as do not separate in their minds, and set before themselves, the two meanings, often causes them to write in a dry and bald style, which has no advantage in point of perspicuity, and is least of all suited to the taste of the vulgar. The above instance is not drawn from mere conjecture, but from actual experience of the fact.

Another instance of the strong influence of words on our ideas may be adduced from a widely different subject: most persons feel a certain degree of *surprise* on first hearing of the result of some late experiments of the Agricultural-Chemists, by which they have ascertained that universally what are called *heavy* soils are specifically the lightest; and *vice versâ.* Whence this *surprise?* for no one ever *distinctly believed* the established names to be used in the literal and *primary* sense, in consequence of the respective soils having been *weighed* together; indeed it is obvious on a moment's reflection that *tenacious clay-soils* (as well as muddy roads) are *figuratively* called heavy, from the difficulty of ploughing, or passing over them, which produces an *effect like* that of bearing or dragging a heavy weight; yet still the terms "light" and "heavy," though used figuratively, have most undoubtedly introduced into men's minds something of the ideas expressed by them in their primitive sense. The same words, when applied to articles of diet, have produced important errors; many supposing some article of food to be *light of digestion* from its being *specifically light.* So true is the ingenious observation of Hobbes, that "words are the counters of wise men, and the money of fools."

"Men imagine," says Bacon, "that their minds have the command of Language; but it often happens that Language bears rule over their mind." Some of the weak and absurd arguments which are often urged against Suicide may be traced to the influence of words on thoughts. When a Christian moralist is called on for a direct *Scriptural precept* against suicide, instead of replying that the Bible is not meant for a complete code of *laws*, but for a system of *motives* and *principles*, the answer frequently given is "thou shalt do no *murder*;" and it is assumed in the arguments drawn from Reason, as well as in those from Revelation, that Suicide is a species of Murder; *viz.* because it is *called* self-*murder*; and thus, deluded by a name, many are led to rest on an unsound argument; which, like all other fallacies, does more harm than good, in the end, to the cause of truth. Suicide, if any one considers the nature and not the name of it, evidently wants the most essential characteristic of murder, *viz.* the *hurt and injury* done to one's neighbour, in depriving him of life, as well as to others by the *insecurity* they are in consequence liable to feel. And since no one can, strictly speaking, do *injustice* to himself, he cannot, in the literal and primary acceptation of the words, be said either to rob or to murder himself. He who deserts the post to which he is appointed by his great Master, and presumptuously cuts short the state of probation graciously allowed him for "working out his salvation," (whether by action or by patient endurance,) is guilty indeed of a grievous sin, but of one not the least analogous in its character to murder. It implies no inhumanity. It is much more closely allied to the sin of wasting life in indolence, or in trifling pursuits,—

that life which is bestowed as a seed-time for the harvest of immortality. What is called in familiar phrase "killing time," is, in truth, an approach, as far as it goes, to the destruction of one's own life: for "Time is the stuff life is made of."

"Time destroyed
Is suicide, where more than blood is spilt."—*Young*.*

Errors arising from the use of analogical terms.

More especially deserving of attention is the influence of Analogical Terms in leading men into erroneous notions in Theology; where the most important terms are analogical; and yet they are continually employed in Reasoning, without due attention (oftener through want of caution than by unfair design) to their analogical nature; and most of the errors into which theologians have fallen may be traced, in part, to this cause.†

Twofold danger from any false assumption.

In speaking of the importance of refuting Fallacies, (under which name I include, as will be seen, any false assumption employed as a Premiss) this consideration ought not to be overlooked; that an unsound Principle, which has been employed to establish some mischievously false Conclusion, does not at once become harmless, and too insignificant to be worth refuting, as soon as that Conclusion is given up, and the false Principle is no longer employed for that particular use. It may equally well lead to some *other* no less mischievous result. "A false

* It is surely wiser and safer to confine ourselves to such arguments as will bear the test of a close examination, than to resort to such as may indeed at the first glance be more specious and appear stronger, but which, when exposed, will too often leave a man a dupe to the fallacies on the opposite side. But it is especially the error of controvertialists to urge every thing that *can* be urged; to snatch up the first weapon that comes to hand; ("furor arma ministrat;") without waiting to consider what is TRUE.

† See the notes to Ch. v. § 1 of the Dissertation subjoined.

premiss, according as it is combined with this, or with that, true one, will lead to two different false conclusions. Thus, if the principle be admitted, that any *important* religious errors ought to be forcibly suppressed, this may lead either to *persecution* on the one side, or to latitudinarian *indifference* on the other. Some may be led to justify the suppression of heresies by the civil sword; and others, whose feelings revolt at such a procedure, and who see persecution reprobated and discountenanced by those around them, may be led by the same principle to regard religious errors as of little or no importance, and all religious persuasions as equally acceptable in the sight of God."*

Over-estimate of the effect of some fallacies.

It ought however to be observed on the other hand, that such effects are often attributed to some fallacy as it does not in fact produce. It shall have been perhaps triumphantly urged, and repeated again and again, and referred to by many as irrefragable; and yet shall have never convinced any one; but have been merely assented to by those already convinced. To many persons any two well-sounding phrases, which have a few words the same, and are in some manner connected with the same subject, will serve for Premiss and Conclusion: and when we hear a man profess to derive conviction from such arguments, we are naturally disposed to regard his case as hopeless. But it will often happen that in reality his reasoning faculties shall have been totally dormant; and equally so perhaps in another case, where he gives his assent to a process of sound reasoning, leading to a conclusion which he has already admitted. "The puerile fallacies which you may sometimes hear a man adduce on some subjects, are perhaps in reality no more *his own* than the sound arguments he employs on others; he may have given an indolent unthinking acquiescence to each; and if he can be excited

* See Essays, 3d Series, Ch. v. § 2. p. 228.

to exertion of thought, he may be very capable of distinguishing the sound from the unsound."*

Thus much, as to the extensive practical influence of Fallacies, and the consequent high importance of detecting and exposing them.

§ 6.

Difficulty of detecting Fallacies.

2dly. The second remark is, that while sound reasoning is ever the more readily admitted, the more clearly it is perceived to be such, Fallacy, on the contrary, being rejected as soon as perceived, will, of course, be the more likely to obtain reception, the more it is obscured and disguised by obliquity and complexity of expression. It is thus that it is the most likely either to slip accidentally from the careless reasoner, or to be brought forward deliberately by the Sophist. Not that he ever wishes this obscurity and complexity to be perceived; on the contrary, it is for his purpose that the expression should *appear* as clear and simple as possible, while in reality it is the most tangled net he can contrive.

Fallacies concealed by elliptical language.

Thus, whereas it is usual to express our reasoning *elliptically*, so that a Premiss (or even two or three entire steps in a course of argument) which may be readily supplied, as being perfectly obvious, shall be left to be understood, the Sophist in like manner suppresses what is *not* obvious, but is in reality the weakest part of the argument: and uses every other contrivance to withdraw our attention (his art closely resembling the juggler's) from the quarter where the Fallacy lies. Hence the uncertainty before mentioned, to which class any individual Fallacy is to be referred: and hence it is that the *difficulty* of detecting

* Pol. Econ. Lect. I. p. 15.

and exposing Fallacy, is so much greater than that of comprehending and developing a process of sound argument. It is like the detection and apprehension of a criminal in spite of all his arts of concealment and disguise; when this *is accomplished*, and he is *brought to trial* with all the evidence of his guilt produced, his conviction and punishment are easy; and this is precisely the case with those Fallacies which are given as examples in Logical treatises; they are in fact already detected, by being stated in a plain and regular form, and are, as it were, only brought up to *receive sentence*. Or again, fallacious reasoning may be compared to a perplexed and entangled mass of *accounts*, which it requires much sagacity and close attention to clear up, and display in a regular and intelligible form; though *when this is once accomplished*, the whole appears so perfectly *simple*, that the unthinking are apt to undervalue the skill and pains which have been employed upon it.

Fallacies concealed by lengthy discussion.

Moreover, it should be remembered, that a very *long* discussion is one of the most effectual veils of Fallacy. Sophistry, like poison, is at once detected, and nauseated, when presented to us in a concentrated form; but a Fallacy which when stated barely, in a few sentences, would not deceive a child, may deceive half the world, if *diluted* in a quarto volume. For, as in a calculation, one single figure incorrectly stated will enable us to arrive at any result whatever, though every other figure, and the whole of the operations, be correct, so, a single false assumption in any process of reasoning, though every other be true, will enable us to draw what conclusion we please; and the greater the number of true assumptions, the more likely it is that the false one will pass unnoticed. But when you single out one step in the course of the reasoning, and exhibit it as a Syllogism with one Premiss true and the other false, the sophistry is easily perceived. I have seen a long argument to prove that the potato is not a cheap article of food; in which there was an elaborate, and perhaps correct, calculation of the produce per acre, of potatoes, and of wheat,—the quantity lost in bran—expense of grinding, dressing, *&c.*, and an assumption slipped in, as it were incidentally, that *a given quantity of potatoes contains but one-tenth part of nutritive matter equal to bread:* from all which (and there is probably *but one* groundless assertion in the whole) a most triumphant result was deduced.*

To use another illustration; it is true in a course of argument, as in Mechanics, that "nothing is stronger than its weakest part;" and consequently a chain which has *one* faulty link will break: but though the number of the sound links adds nothing to the *strength* of the chain, it adds much to the chance of the faulty one's *escaping observation.* In such cases as I have been alluding to, one may often hear it observed that "there is a *great deal of truth* in what such a one has said:" *i. e.* perhaps it is *all* true, *except one* essential point.

Error of supposing all Fallacies to be easy of detection.

To speak, therefore, of all the Fallacies that have ever been enumerated as too glaring and obvious to need even being mentioned, because the simple instances given in logical treatises, and there stated in the plainest and consequently most easily detected form, are such as would (in that form) deceive no one;—this, surely, shows extreme weakness, or else unfairness. It may readily be allowed, indeed, that to detect *individual* Fallacies, and *bring them under* the general rules, is a harder

* This, however, gained the undoubting assent of a Review by no means friendly to the author, and usually noted more for scepticism than for ready assent! "All things," says an apocryphal writer, "are double, one against another, and nothing is made in vain:" unblushing assertors of falsehood seem to have a race of easy believers provided on purpose for their use: men who will not indeed believe the best established truths of religion, but are ready to believe any thing else.

task than to *lay down* those general rules; but this does not prove that the latter office is trifling or useless, or that it does not essentially conduce to the performance of the other. There may be more ingenuity shown in detecting and arresting a malefactor, and convicting him of the fact, than in laying down a law for the trial and punishment of such persons; but the latter office, *i.e.* that of a legislator, is surely neither unnecessary nor trifling.

It should be added that a close observation and Logical analysis of Fallacious arguments, as it tends (according to what has been already said) to form a habit of mind well suited for the practical detection of Fallacies; so, for that very reason, it will make us the more careful in making *allowance* for them: *i.e.* to bear in mind how much men in general are liable to be influenced by them. *E.G.* a *refuted* argument *ought* to go for *nothing*, (except where there is some ground for assuming that no *stronger* one could be adduced:)* but in *fact* it will generally prove *detrimental* to the cause, from the Fallacy which will be presently explained. Now, no one is more likely to be practically aware of this, and to take precautions accordingly, than he who is most versed in the whole theory of Fallacies; for the best Logician is the least likely to calculate on *men in general* being such.

§ 7.

Of Fallacies in form,

enough perhaps has already been said in the preceding Compendium: and it has been remarked above, that it is often left to our *choice* to refer an individual Fallacy to this head or to another.

It may be worth observing, however, that to the present class we may the most conveniently refer those Fallacies, so

* See Essay II. on Kingdom of Christ, § 22, note.

common in practice, of supposing the Conclusion false, because the Premiss is false, or because the Argument is unsound; and of inferring the truth of the Premiss from that of the Conclusion. *E.G.* if any one argues for the existence of a God, from its being universally believed, a man might perhaps be able to refute the argument by producing an instance of some nation destitute of such belief; the argument *ought* then (as has been observed above) to *go for nothing:* but many would go further, and think that this refutation had *disproved* the existence of a God; in which they would be guilty of an illicit process of the Major-term: *viz.* "whatever is universally believed must be true; the existence of a God is not universally believed; therefore it is not true." Others again, from being convinced of the truth of the Conclusion, would infer that of the Premises; which would amount to the Fallacy of an undistributed Middle: *viz.* "what is universally believed is true; the existence of a God is true; therefore it is universally believed." Or, these Fallacies might be stated in the hypothetical form; since the one evidently proceeds from the denial of the Antecedent to the denial of the Consequent; and the other from the establishing of the Consequent to the inferring of the Antecedent; which two Fallacies will usually be found to correspond respectively with those of Illicit process of the major, and Undistributed Middle.

Weak arguments practically detrimental.

Fallacies of this class are very much kept out of sight, being seldom perceived even by those who employ them; but of their practical importance there can be no doubt, since it is notorious that a weak argument is always, in practice, *detrimental;* and that there is no absurdity so gross which men will not readily admit, if it appears to lead to a conclusion of which they are already convinced. Even a candid and sensible writer is not unlikely to be, by this means, misled, when he is seeking for arguments to support a conclusion which he has long been fully convinced of himself; *i. e.* he will often use such arguments as would never have *convinced* himself, and are not likely to convince others, but rather (by the operation of the converse Fallacy) to *confirm* in their dissent those who before disagreed with him.

It is best therefore to endeavour to put yourself in the place of an *opponent* to your own arguments, and consider whether you could not find some objection to them. The applause of *one's own party* is a very unsafe ground for judging of the real force of an argumentative work, and consequently of its real utility. To satisfy those who were doubting, and to convince those who were opposed, are much better tests;* but *these* persons are seldom very loud in their applause, or very forward in bearing their testimony.

Of Ambiguous Middle.

§ 8.

That case in which the Middle is undistributed belongs of course to the preceding head; the fault being perfectly manifest from the mere form of the expression: in that case the Extremes are compared with *two parts of the same* term; but in the Fallacy which has been called semi-logical, (which we are now to speak of) the Extremes are compared with *two different* terms, the Middle being used in two different senses in the two Premises.†

And here it may be remarked, that when the argument is brought into the form of a *regular Syllogism*, the contrast between these two senses will usually appear very striking, from the two Premises being *placed together;* and hence the scorn with which many have treated the very mention

* The strongest, perhaps, of all external indications of the strength of an argument, is, the implied admission of those who nevertheless resolve *not* to admit the conclusion. See Appendix; Art. *Person,* last clause.

† For some instances of important ambiguities, see Appendix.

of the Fallacy of Equivocation, deriving their only notion of it from the *exposure* of it in Logical treatises; whereas, in practice it is common for the two Premises to be placed very far apart, and discussed in different parts of the discourse; by which means the inattentive hearer overlooks any ambiguity that may exist in the Middle-term. Hence the advantage of Logical habits, in fixing our attention strongly and steadily on the *important* terms of an argument.

And here it should be observed, that when we mean to charge any argument with the fault of "equivocal-middle," it is not enough to say that the Middle-term is a word or phrase which *admits* of more than one meaning; (for there are few that do not) but we must show, that in order for each premiss to be admitted, the Term in question must be understood in one sense (pointing out *what* that sense is) in one of the premises, and in another sense, in the other.

Importance of minute distinctions.

And if any one speaks contemptuously of "over exactness" in fixing the precise sense in which some term is used,—of attending to minute and subtle distinctions, &c. we may reply that these *minute* distinctions are exactly those which call for careful attention; since it is *only* through the neglect of *these* that Fallacies ever escape detection.

For, a very *glaring* and palpable equivocation could never mislead any one. To argue that "feathers dispel darkness, because they are *light*," or that "this man is agreeable, because he is *riding*, and *riding* is agreeable," is an equivocation which could never be employed but in jest. And yet however slight in any case may be the distinction between the two senses of a Middle-term in the two premises, the apparent-argument will be equally inconclusive; though its fallaciousness will be more likely to escape notice.

Even so, it is for want of attention to *minute* points, that houses are robbed, or set on fire. Burglars do not in general come and batter down the front-door; but climb in at some window whose fastenings have been neglected. And an incendiary, or a careless servant, does not kindle a tar-barrel in the middle of a room, but leaves a lighted turf, or a candle snuff, in the thatch, or in a heap of shavings.

In many cases, it is a good maxim, to "take care of little things, and great ones will take care of themselves."

Paronymous words.

One case, which may be regarded as coming under the head of Ambiguous middle, is, (what I believe logical writers mean by "*Fallacia Figuræ Dictionis*,") the Fallacy built on the grammatical structure of language, from men's usually taking for granted that *paronymous* [or *conjugate*] words—*i. e.* those belonging to each other, as the substantive, adjective, verb, *&c.* of the same root, have a precisely correspondent meaning; which is by no means universally the case. Such a fallacy could not indeed be even exhibited in strict Logical form, which would preclude even the attempt at it, since it has two middle terms in sound as well as sense. But nothing is more common in practice than to vary continually the terms employed, with a view to grammatical convenience; nor is there anything unfair in such a practice, as long as the *meaning* is preserved unaltered: *e. g.* "murder should be punished with death; this man is a murderer; therefore he deserves to die," *&c. &c.* Here we proceed on the assumption (in this case just) that to commit murder and to be a murderer,—to deserve death and to be one who ought to die, are, respectively, equivalent expressions: and it would frequently prove a heavy inconvenience to be debarred this kind of liberty; but the abuse of it gives rise to the Fallacy in question: *e. g.* "*projectors* are unfit to be trusted; this man has formed a *project*, therefore he is unfit to be trusted:"* here the Sophist

* Adam Smith's *Wealth of Nations*: Usury.

proceeds on the hypothesis that he who forms a *project* must be a *projector:* whereas the bad sense that commonly attaches to the latter word, is not at all implied in the former.

This Fallacy may often be considered as lying not in the Middle, but in one of the terms of the Conclusion; so that the Conclusion drawn shall not be, in reality, at all warranted by the Premises, though it will appear to be so, by means of the grammatical affinity of the words: *e. g.* "to be acquainted with the guilty is a *presumption* of guilt; this man is so acquainted; therefore we may *presume* that he is guilty:" this argument proceeds on the supposition of an exact correspondence between "*presume*" and "*presumption,*" which, however, does not really exist; for "presumption" is commonly used to express a kind of *slight suspicion;* whereas "to presume" amounts to *actual belief.*

The above remark will apply to some other cases of ambiguity of term; *viz.* the Conclusion will often contain a term, which (though not, as here, different *in expression* from the corresponding one in the Premiss, yet) is *liable* to be understood in a sense different from what it bears to the Premiss; though, of course, such a Fallacy is less common, because less likely to deceive, in *those* cases than in *this;* where the term used in the Conclusion, though professing to correspond with one in the Premiss, is not the very *same in expression,* and therefore is more *certain* to convey a different sense; which is what the Sophist wishes.

There are innumerable instances of a non-correspondence in paronymous words, similar to that above instanced; as between *art* and *artful, design* and *designing, faith* and *faithful, &c.;* and the more slight the variation of meaning, the more likely is the Fallacy to be successful; for when the words have become so widely removed in sense as "pity" and "pitiful," every one would perceive such a Fallacy, nor could it be employed but in jest.

This Fallacy cannot in practice be refuted, (except when

you are addressing regular logicians,) by stating merely the impossibility of reducing such an argument to the strict logical form. You must find some way of pointing out the *non-correspondence* of the terms in question; *e. g.* with respect to the example above, it might be remarked, that we speak of *strong* or *faint* "presumption," but we use no such expression in conjunction with the verb "presume," because the word itself *implies strength.*

No fallacy is more common in controversy than the present; since in this way the Sophist will often be able to misinterpret the propositions which his opponent admits or maintains, and so employ them against him. Thus in the examples just given, it is natural to conceive one of the Sophist's Premises to have been borrowed from his opponent.*

Etymology.

The present Fallacy is nearly allied to, or rather perhaps may be regarded as a branch of that founded on *etymology; viz.* when a term is used at one time, in its customary, and at another, in its etymological sense. Perhaps no example of this can be found that is more extensively and mischievously employed than in the case of the word *representative:* assuming that its right meaning must correspond exactly with the strict and original sense of the verb, "represent," the Sophist persuades the multitude, that a member of the House of Commons is bound to be guided in all points by the opinion of his constituents: and, in short, to be merely their *spokesman:* whereas law, and custom, which in this case may be considered as fixing the meaning of the Term, require no such thing, but enjoin the representative to act according to the best of his *own* judgment, and on his own responsibility.

Horne Tooke has furnished a whole magazine of such

* Perhaps a dictionary of such paronymous [conjugate] words as do not regularly correspond in meaning, would be nearly as useful as one of synonyms; *i. e.* properly speaking, of *pseudo-synonyms.*

N 2

weapons for any Sophist who may need them; and has furnished some specimens of the employment of them. He contends, that it is idle to speak of eternal or immutable "*Truth*," because the word is derived from to "trow," *i. e.* believe. He might on as good grounds have censured the absurdity of speaking of sending a letter by the "*post*," because a post, in its primary sense, is a pillar; or have insisted that "Sycophant" can never mean anything but "Fig-shewer."

§ 9.

Fallacy of Interrogations.

It is to be observed, that to the head of Ambiguous middle should be referred what is called "*Fallacia plurium Interrogationum*," which may be named, simply, "the Fallacy of Interrogation;" *viz.* the Fallacy of asking several questions which appear to be but one; so that whatever *one* answer is given, being of course applicable to one only of the implied questions, may be interpreted as applied to the other: the refutation is, of course, to reply *separately* to each question, *i. e.* to detect the ambiguity.

I have said, several "questions which *appear to be but one*," for else there is no *Fallacy;* such an example, therefore, as "*estne homo animal et lapis?*" which Aldrich gives, is foreign to the matter in hand; for there is nothing unfair in asking two distinct questions (any more than in asserting two distinct propositions) *distinctly and avowedly.*

This Fallacy may be referred, as has been said, to the head of Ambiguous middle. In all Reasoning it is very common to state one of the Premises in form of a question, and when that is admitted, or supposed to be admitted, then to fill up the rest: if then one of the Terms of that question be ambiguous, whichever sense the opponent replies to, the Sophist assumes the *other* sense of the Term in the remaining Premiss. It is therefore very common to state an equivocal argument, in form of a question so worded, that there shall be *little doubt which* reply will be given; but if there *be* such doubt, the Sophist must have *two* Fallacies of equivocation ready; *E. G.* the question "whether anything vicious is expedient," discussed in Cic. *Off.* Book III. (where, by the bye, he seems not a little perplexed with it himself) is of the character in question, from the ambiguity of the word, "*expedient*," which means sometimes, "conducive to temporal prosperity," sometimes "conducive to the greatest good:" whichever answer therefore was given, the Sophist might have a Fallacy of equivocation founded on this term; *viz.* if the answer be in the negative, his argument, Logically developed, will stand thus,—"what is vicious is not expedient; whatever conduces to the acquisition of wealth and aggrandizement is expedient; therefore it cannot be vicious:" if in the affirmative, then thus,—"whatever is expedient is desirable; something vicious is expedient, therefore desirable."*

Again, a witness was once asked by a Parliamentary Committee (in 1832) whether he knew "how long the practice had *ceased* in Ireland of dividing the tithes into four portions, one for the poor," *&c.* This resembles the hackneyed instance of asking a man "whether he had *left off* beating his father." [See Vol. of Charges and Tracts, p. 379.] King Charles II.'s celebrated inquiry—of the Royal Society (noticed below, § 14) may be referred to this head. He asked the cause why a dead fish does not (though a live fish does) add to the weight of a vessel of water. This implies *two* questions; the first of which many of the philosophers for

* Much of the declamation by which popular assemblies are often misled, against what is called, without any distinct meaning, the "doctrine of expediency," (as if the "right" and the "expedient" were in opposition) might be silenced by asking the simple question, "Do you then admit that the course you recommend is *in*expedient?"

a time overlooked: *viz.* 1st. is it a *fact?* 2dly. if it be a fact, what can cause it?*

Distribution and non-distribution.

This kind of Fallacy is frequently employed in such a manner, that the uncertainty shall be, not about the *meaning*, but the *extent* of a Term, *i. e.* whether it is *distributed* or not: *e.g.* "did A B in this case act from such and such a motive?" which may imply either, "was it his *sole* motive?" or "was it *one* of his motives?" in the former case the term [" that-which-actuated-A B "] is distributed; in the latter, not: now if he acted from a *mixture* of motives, whichever answer you give, may be misrepresented, and your conclusion thus disproved.

Again, those who dispute the right of a State to enforce the profession of a certain religion, have been met by the question, "has a State a right to enforce Laws?" If we answer in the negative, we may be interpreted as denying that *any* laws can rightfully be enforced; which would of course go to destroy the very existence of a Political-community: if, in the affirmative, we may be interpreted as sanctioning the enforcement of *any laws whatever* that the Legislature may see fit to enact: whether enjoining men to adore a Crucifix, or to trample on it;—to reverence Christ, or Mahomet, *&c.* The ambiguity of the question lies in "*Laws;*" understood either as "*some* laws," or, as "*any laws without exception.*"†

§ 10.

Intrinsic and incidental equivocations.

In some cases of ambiguous Middle, the Term in question may be considered as having *in itself*, from its own equivocal nature, two significations; (which apparently constitutes the "*Fallacia equivocationis*" of Logical

* See Historic Doubts relative to Napoleon.

† See "Essays on the Kingdom of Christ." Note A. to Essay I.

writers;) others again have a Middle-term which is ambiguous from the context, *i.e.* from what is *understood in conjunction* with it. This division will be found useful, though it is impossible to draw the line accurately in it.

The *elliptical* character of ordinary discourse causes many Terms to become practically ambiguous, which yet are not themselves employed in *different senses*, but with different *applications*, which are *understood*. Thus, "The Faith" would be used by a Christian writer to denote the Christian Faith, and by a Mussulman, the Mahometan; yet the word Faith, has not in these cases, *of itself*, two different significations. So ἐκλεκτοί, "elect," or "chosen," is sometimes applied to such as are "chosen," to certain *privileges* and *advantages*; (as the Israelites were, though "they were overthrown in the wilderness" for their disobedience; and as all Christians are frequently called in the New Testament) sometimes again to those who are "chosen," as fit to receive a *final reward*, having made a right use of those advantages; as when our Lord says, "many are called, but few chosen."

Amphibolia.

What Logicians have mentioned under the title of "Fallacia amphiboliæ" is referable to this last class; though in real practice it is not very likely to occur. An *amphibolous* sentence is one that is capable of two meanings, not from the double sense of any of the words, but from its admitting of a double *construction*: as in the instance Aldrich gives, which is untranslatable; "quod tangitur a Socrate, illud sentit;" where "illud" may be taken either as the nominative or accusative. So also the celebrated response of the oracle; "Aio te, Æacida, Romanos vincere posse:" "Pyrrhus the Romans shall, I say, subdue:" which closely resembles (as Shakspeare remarks) the witch-prophecy, "The Duke yet lives that Henry shall depose." This effect is produced by what the French call "construction louche," a squinting construction; *i.e.* where some word or words may be referred either to the former or latter clause of the sentence;

of which an instance occurs in the rubric prefixed to the service for the 30th January. "If this day shall happen to be Sunday [this form of prayer shall be used] and the fast kept the next day following:" the clause in brackets may belong either to the former or the latter part of the sentence. In the Nicene Creed, the words, "by whom all things were made," are grammatically referable either to the Father or the Son. And in the 2d Commandment, the clause "of them that hate me," is a genitive governed either by "children," or by "generation:" the latter being indicated by the ordinary mode of punctuation and of reading; which totally changes the real sense.* The following clause of a sentence from a newspaper, is a curious specimen of Amphibolia:—"For protecting and upholding such electors as refused, contrary to their desires and consciences, to vote for Messrs. A and B, regardless of threats, and unmindful of intimidation."

Accidental equivocation.

There are various ways in which words come to have two meanings:

1st. By *accident*; (*i. e.* when there is no perceptible connexion between the two meanings) as "*light*" signifies both the contrary to "heavy" and the contrary to "dark." Thus, such Proper-names as John or Thomas, *&c.* which happen to belong to several different persons, are ambiguous, because they have a different signification in each case where they are applied. Words which fall under this first head are what are the most strictly called *equivocal.*

First and second intention.

2dly. There are several terms in the use of which it is necessary to notice the distinction between *first* and *second intention.*† The "first-intention" of a Term, (according to

* See Rhetoric, Appendix.

† I am aware that there exists another opinion as to the meaning of the phrase "second intention;" and that Aldrich is understood by some persons to mean (as indeed his expression may very well be understood to imply) that

the usual acceptation of this phrase) is a certain *vague and general* signification of it, as opposed to one more *precise* and *limited*, which it bears in some particular art, science, or system, and which is called its "second-intention." Thus, among farmers, in some parts, the word "beast" is applied particularly and especially to the ox kind; and "bird," in the language of many sportsmen, is in like manner appropriated to the partridge: the common and general acceptation (which every one is well acquainted with) of each of those two words, is the First-intention of each; the other, its Second-intention.

For some remarks on the Second-intention of the word "Species," when applied to *organized beings* (*viz.* as denoting those plants or animals, which it is conceived may have descended from a common stock), see the subjoined Dissertation, Book IV. Chap. v. § 1.

It is evident that a Term may have several Second-intentions, according to the several systems into which it is introduced, and of which it is one of the technical Terms: thus "line" signifies, in the Art-military, a certain form of drawing up ships or troops: in Geography, a certain division of the earth; to the fisherman, a string to catch fish, *&c. &c.*; all which are so many distinct Second-intentions, in each of which there is a certain signification "of extension in length" which constitutes the First-intention, and which corresponds pretty nearly with the employment of the Term in Mathematics.

In a few instances the Second-intention, or philosophical employment of a Term, is more *extensive* than the First-intention, or popular use: thus "affection" is limited in popular use to "love;" "charity," to "almsgiving;"

every predicable must necessarily be employed in the Second-intention. I do not undertake to combat the doctrine alluded to, because I must confess that, after the most patient attention devoted to the explanations given of it, I have never been able to comprehend what it is that is meant by it. It is one, however, which, whether sound or unsound, appears not to be connected with any Logical processes, and therefore may be safely passed by on the present occasion.

"flower," to those flowers which have conspicuous petals; and fruit, to such as are eatable.

It will sometimes happen, that a Term shall be employed always in some one or other of its second intentions; and never, strictly in the first, though that first intention is a *part of its signification* in each case. It is evident, that the utmost care is requisite to avoid confounding together, either the first and second intentions, or the different second intentions with each other.

Resemblance and Analogy. 3dly. When two or more things are connected by *resemblance* or *analogy*, they will frequently have the same name. Thus a "*blade* of grass," and the contrivance in building called a "*dove-tail*," are so called from their *resemblance* to the *blade** of a sword, and the *tail* of a real dove. But two things may be connected by *analogy*, though they have in *themselves* no *resemblance:* for analogy is the resemblance of *ratios* (or relations:) thus, as a *sweet* taste *gratifies* the palate, so does a *sweet* sound *gratify* the ear; and hence the same word "*sweet*" is applied to both, though no flavour can resemble a sound in itself. So, the *leg of a table* does not resemble that of an animal; nor the foot of a mountain that of an animal; but *the leg answers the same purpose* to the table, as the leg of an animal to that animal; the foot of a mountain has the *same situation* relatively to the mountain, as the foot of an animal to the animal. This analogy therefore may be expressed like a mathematical analogy (or proportion); "leg : animal : : supporting-stick : table."

The words pertaining to *Mind* may in general be traced up, as borrowed (which no doubt they all were, originally) by Analogy, from those pertaining to *Matter:* though in many cases the primary sense has become obsolete.

Thus, "edify" † in its primary sense of "build up" ‡

* Unless, indeed, the primary application of the Term be to the leaf of grass, and the secondary to cutting instruments, which is perhaps more probable; but the question is unimportant in the present case.

† See 1 Peter ii. 5. ‡ See *Johnson's Dictionary*.

is disused, and the origin of it often forgotten; although the substantive "edifice" remains in common use in a corresponding sense.

When however we speak of "weighing" the reasons on both sides,—of "seeing," or "feeling" the force of an argument,—"imprinting" anything on the memory, &c. we are aware of these words being used analogically.

Primary and secondary senses.

In all these cases (of this 3d head) one of the meanings of the word is called by Logicians *proper, i. e.* original or primary; the other *improper,* secondary, or transferred: thus, *sweet* is originally and properly applied to *tastes;* secondarily and *improperly* (*i. e.* by analogy) to sounds: thus also, *dove-tail* is applied secondarily (though not by analogy, but by direct resemblance) to the contrivance in building so called.

When the secondary meaning of a word is founded on some *fanciful* analogy, and especially when it is introduced for ornament's sake, we call this a *metaphor;* as when we speak of "a ship's *ploughing* the deep;" the turning up of the surface being essential indeed to the plough, but accidental only, to the ship. But if the analogy be a more important and essential one, and especially if we have no other word to express our meaning but this transferred one, we then call it *merely* an *analogous* word (though the *metaphor* is analogous also) *e.g.* one would hardly call it *metaphorical* or *figurative* language to speak of the "leg of a table," or "mouth of a river."*

There are two kinds of error, each very common—which lead to confusion of thought in our use of analogical words:

i. The error of supposing the *things themselves* to be similar, from their having *similar relations* to other things.

ii. The still commoner error of supposing the Analogy to *extend further* than it does; [or, to be more *complete* than

* See Bp. Copleston's account of Analogy in the notes to his "Four Discourses."

it really is;] from not considering *in what* the Analogy in each case consists.

For instance, the "*Servants*" that we read of in the Bible, and in other translations of ancient books, are so called by Analogy to servants among us: and that Analogy consists in the offices which a "servant" performs, in waiting on his master, and doing his bidding. It is in this respect that the one description of "servant" "corresponds" ["answers"] to the other. And hence some persons have been led to apply all that is said in Scripture respecting Masters and *Servants*, to these times, and this Country: forgetting that the Analogy is not *complete*, and extends no further than the point above-mentioned. For the ancient "servants" (except when expressly spoken of as *hired*-servants) were *Slaves;* a part of the Master's *possessions.*

Connexion of time or place, &c.

4thly. Several things may be called by the same name (though they have no connexion of resemblance or analogy) from being *connected by vicinity of time or place;* under which head will come the connexion of *cause and effect*, or of *part and whole, &c.;* and the transference of words in this way from the primary to a secondary meaning, is what Grammarians call Metonymy. Thus, a *door* signifies both an opening in the wall (more strictly called the *door-way*) and a board which closes it; which are things neither similar nor analogous. When I say, "the rose *smells* sweet;" and "I *smell* the rose;" the word "smell" has two meanings: in the latter sentence, I am speaking of a certain *sensation* in my own mind; in the former, of a certain *quality* in the flower, which produces that sensation, but which of course cannot in the least resemble it; and here the word *smell* is applied with equal propriety to both. On this ambiguity have been founded the striking paradoxes of those who have maintained that there is no heat in fire, no cold in ice, *&c.* The *sensations* of heat, cold, *&c.* can of course only belong to a Sentient Being. Thus again the word "certainty," denotes either, primarily, the state of our own *mind* when we are free from doubt, or secondarily, the character of the *event* about which we feel certain. [See Appendix, No. I.] Thus, we speak of Homer, for "the works of Homer;" and this is a secondary or transferred meaning: and so it is when we say, "a good shot," for a good marksman: but the word "*shot*" has two other meanings, which are both equally proper; *viz. the thing put into a gun* in order to be discharged from it, and the *act* of discharging it.

Thus, "*learning*" signifies either the act of acquiring knowledge, or the knowledge itself; *e.g.* "he neglects his learning;" "Johnson was a man of learning." "*Possession*" is ambiguous in the same manner; and a multitude of others. A remarkable and most important instance is the ambiguity of such words as "*same,*" "*one,* &c. (See the Articles on those words in Appendix, and also Book IV. Ch. v. § 1 & 2.)

Much confusion often arises from ambiguity of this kind, when unperceived; nor is there any point in which the copiousness and consequent precision of the Greek language, is more to be admired than in its distinct terms for expressing an act, and the result of that act; *e.g.* *πραξις*, "the doing of anything;" *πραγμα,* the "thing done;" so, δοσις and δωρον—ληψις and λημμα, *&c.*

It will very often happen, that two of the meanings of a word will have no connexion with one another, but will each have some connexion with the third. Thus, "martyr" originally signified a *witness;* thence it was applied to those who *suffered* in bearing testimony to Christianity; and thence again it is often applied to "sufferers" in general: the first and third significations are not the least connected. Thus "*post*" signifies originally a pillar, *(postum,* from *pono)* then, a distance marked out by posts; and then, the carriages, messengers, *&c.* that travelled over this distance. Thus "Clerk," originally one in Holy Orders, came to be used as it is at present, from the "Clergy" having been, during the dark Ages, almost the only persons who could read.

It would puzzle any one, proceeding on mere conjecture, to make out how the word "premises" should have come to signify "a building."

Ambiguities of this kind belong practically to the first head: there being no *perceived* connexion between the different senses.

Elliptical language.

Another source of practical ambiguity (as has been just observed) "is, that, in respect of any subject concerning which the generality of men are accustomed to speak much and familiarly, in their conversation relative to that, they usually introduce ELLIPTICAL expressions; very clearly understood in the outset, but whose elliptical character comes, in time, to be so far lost sight of, that confusion of language, and thence, of thought, is sometimes the result. Thus, the expression of a person's possessing a fortune of 10,000*l.* is an elliptical phrase: meaning, at full length, that all his property if sold would exchange for that sum of money. And in ninety-nine instances out of a hundred, no error or confusion of thought arises from this language; but there is no doubt that it mainly contributed to introduce and foster the notion that Wealth consists especially of gold and silver (these being used to *measure* and *express* its amount); and that the sure way to enrich a country is to promote the importation, and prevent the export, of the precious metals; with all the other absurdities of what is commonly called 'the mercantile System.' So also we speak commonly of 'the *example* of such a one's punishment serving to *deter* others from crime.' And usually, no misapprehension results from this, which is, in truth, an *elliptical* expression. But sometimes sophistical reasoners take advantage of it, and men who are not clear-headed are led into confusion of thought. Strictly speaking, what deters a man from crime in such cases as those alluded to, is, the *apprehension* of *himself* suffering punishment. *That apprehension* may be excited by the *example* of another's being punished; or it may be excited *without* that example, if punishment be denounced, and there is good reason to expect that the threat will not be an empty one. And on the other hand, the example of others' suffering punishment does not deter any one, if it *fail* to excite this apprehension for himself; if for instance he consider himself as an *exempt* person, as is the case with a despot in barbarian countries, or with a madman who expects to be acquitted on the plea of insanity.

"Again, when a man complains of being 'out of *work*'—is 'looking out for employment,'—and hopes for subsistence by labour, this is elliptical language; well enough understood in general. We know that what man lives on, is food; and that he who is said to be looking out for work, is in want of food and other necessaries, which he hopes to procure in exchange for his labour, and has no hope of obtaining without it. But there is no doubt that this elliptical language has contributed to lead those who were not attentive to the character of the expression, to regard every thing as beneficial to the labouring classes which *furnishes employment*, *i.e.* gives trouble; even though no consequent increase should take place in the Country, of the food and other commodities destined for their support."* A snow-drift which obstructs a road, and a vein of valuable ore, may conceivably each furnish employment for an equal number of labourers.

The remedy for ambiguity is a *Definition* of the Term which is suspected of being used in two senses; *viz.* a *Nominal*, not necessarily a *Real* Definition: as was remarked in Book II. Chap. v.

Definition when most needed.

It is important to observe that the very circumstance which in any case "makes a definition the *more* necessary, is apt to lead to the *omission* of it: for when any terms are

* Pol. Econ. Lect. IX.

employed that are *not* familiarly introduced into ordinary discourse, such as 'parallelogram,' or 'sphere,' or 'tangent,' 'pencil of rays,' or 'refraction,'—'oxygen,' or 'alkali,'—the learner is ready to inquire, and the writer to anticipate the inquiry, what is meant by this or that term? And though in such cases it is undoubtedly a correct procedure to answer this inquiry by a definition, yet of the two cases, a definition is even more necessary in the other, where it is not so likely to be called for;—where the word, not being new to the student, but familiar to his ear, from its employment in every-day discourse, is liable to the ambiguity which is almost always the result. For in respect of words that sound something new and strange, though it is, as I have said, much better to define them in the outset, yet even without this, the student would gradually collect their meaning pretty correctly, as he proceeded in his study of any treatise; from having nothing to mislead him,—nothing from which to form his notions at all, except the manner in which the terms were employed in the work itself that is before him. And the very desire he had felt of a definition would lead him in this way to form one, and generally a sufficiently correct one, for himself.

"It is otherwise with terms to which we are familiarly accustomed. Of these, the student does not usually crave definitions, from supposing, for that reason, that he understands them well enough: though perhaps (without suspecting it) he has in reality been accustomed to hear them employed in various senses, and to attach but a vague and inaccurate notion to them. If you speak to an uninstructed hearer, of anything that is *spherical*, or *circular*, or *cylindrical*, he will probably beg for an explanation of your meaning; but if you tell him of anything that is *round*, it will not strike him that any explanation is needed: though he has been accustomed to employ the word, indiscriminately, in *all* the senses denoted by the other three."*

* Pol. Econ. Lect. IX.

Definitions, how far to be exacted.

But here it may be proper to remark,* that for the avoiding of Fallacy, or of Verbal-controversy, it is only requisite that the term should be employed uniformly in the same sense *as far as the existing question is concerned.* Thus, two persons might, in discussing the question whether Augustus was a GREAT man, have some such difference in their acceptation of the epithet "great," as would be non-essential to that question; *e.g.* one of them might understand by it nothing more than eminent intellectual and moral *qualities;* while the other might conceive it to imply the performance of splendid *actions:* this abstract difference of meaning would not produce any disagreement in the existing question, because both those circumstances are united in the case of Augustus; but if one (and not the other) of the parties understood the epithet "great" to imply pure patriotism,—GENEROSITY of character, *&c.*, then there *would* be a disagreement as to the application of the Term, even between those who might think alike of Augustus's character, as wanting in those qualities.† Definition, the specific for ambiguity, is to be employed, and demanded, with a view to this principle; it is sufficient on each occasion to define a Term *as far as regards the question in hand.*

If, for example, we were remonstrating with any one for quitting the church of which he was a member, wantonly, and not from strong and deliberate conscientious conviction, but from motives of taste or fancy, and he were to reply by asking, how do you *define* a Church? the demand would be quite irrelevant, unless he meant to deny that the Community he quits *is* a Church. But if we were to insist on designating any one religious-community on earth to which we might belong, as *the* universal or Catholic Church,—in demanding from all Christians submission to its ordinances

* See Book II. Ch. v. § 6.

† See Book iv. Ch. 4. § 1.

and decisions, and denouncing all who should not belong to it, as being out of the pale of Christ's *Church*, then indeed we might fairly be called on to give a definition, and one which should be consistent with facts.*

§ 11.

Of those cases where the ambiguity arises *from the context*, there are several species; some of which Logicians have enumerated, but have neglected to refer them, in the first place, to one common class (*viz.* the one under which they are here placed;) and have even arranged some under the head of Fallacies "*in dictione*," and others under that of "*extra dictionem*."

Fallacy of Division and Composition.

We may consider, as the first of these species, the Fallacy of "Division" and that of "Composition," taken together; since in each of these the Middle-term is used in one Premiss *collectively*, in the other, *distributively:* if the former of these is the major Premiss, and the latter, the minor, this is called the "Fallacy of Division;" the Term which is first taken collectively being afterwards divided; and *vice versâ*. The ordinary examples are such as these; "All the angles of a triangle are equal to two right angles: A B C is an angle of a triangle; therefore A B C is equal to two right angles." "Five is one number; three and two are five: therefore three and two are one number;" or, "three and two are two numbers, five is three and two, therefore five is two numbers:" it is manifest that the Middle-term, three and two (in this last example) is ambiguous, signifying, in the major Premiss, "taken distinctly;" in the minor, "taken together:" and so of the rest.

To this head may be referred the common Fallacy of

* See Appendix, Article "Truth."

over-rating, where each premiss of an argument is only *probable*, the probability of the conclusion; which, in that case, is less than that of the *less* probable of the premises.* For, suppose the probability of one of these to be $\frac{6}{10}$, and of the other $\frac{7}{10}$ (each *more* likely than not) the probability of the conclusion will be only $\frac{42}{100}$ or a little more than $\frac{2}{5}$; which is *less* than an even chance. This Fallacy may be most easily stated as a conditional; a form in which any Fallacy of ambiguous middle may easily be exhibited. *E. G.* "If it is more likely than not, that these premises are true: (*i. e.* that they are both true) it is more likely than not, that the conclusion is true: but it is more likely than not that the premises are true: (*i. e.* that *each* of them is so) therefore it is more likely than not that the conclusion is true." Here, a term in the antecedent, *viz.*—"that the premises are more likely than not to be true"—is taken *jointly* in the Major, and *dividedly* in the Minor.

To the same class we may refer the Fallacy by which men have sometimes been led to admit, or pretend to admit, the doctrine of Necessity; *e.g.* "he who necessarily goes or stays (*i. e.* in reality, 'who *necessarily goes*, or who *neces-*

* See below, § 14. Some persons profess contempt for all such calculations, on the ground that we cannot be quite sure of the *exact degree* of probability of each premiss. And this is true; but this *unavoidable* uncertainty is no reason why we should not guard against an *additional* source of uncertainty which *can* be avoided. It is some advantage to have no *more* doubt as to the degree of probability of the Conclusion, than we have respecting that of the premises.

And in fact there are Offices, kept by persons whose trade it is, in which calculations of this nature are made, in the purchase of *contingent reversions*, depending, sometimes, on a great variety of risks, which can only be conjecturally estimated; and in Insurances, not only against ordinary risks (the calculations of which are to be drawn from Statistical-tables) but also against every variety and degree of *extraordinary* risk; the *exact* amount of which, no one can confidently pronounce upon. But the calculations are based on the best estimate that can be formed.

sarily stays') is not a free agent; you must necessarily go or stay (*i. e.* 'you must necessarily *take the alternative'*), therefore you are not a free agent." Such also is the Fallacy which probably operates on most adventurers in lotteries; *e.g.* "the gaining of a high prize is no uncommon occurrence; and what is no uncommon occurrence may reasonably be expected: therefore the gaining of a high prize may reasonably be expected;" the Conclusion, when applied to the individual (as in practice it is), must be understood in the sense of "reasonably expected *by a certain individual;*" therefore for the Major-Premiss to be true, the middle-Term must be understood to mean, "no uncommon occurrence to some one *particular* person;" whereas for the Minor (which has been placed first) to be true, you must understand it of "no uncommon occurrence to *some one or other;*" and thus you will have the Fallacy of Composition.

There is no Fallacy more common, or more likely to deceive, than the one now before us. The form in which it is most usually employed, is to establish some truth, *separately*, concerning *each single* member of a certain class, and thence to infer the same of the *whole collectively.* Thus, some infidels have laboured to prove concerning *some one* of our Lord's miracles, that it might have been the result of an accidental conjuncture of natural circumstances; next, they endeavour to prove the same concerning *another;* and so on; and thence infer that *all* of them occurring as a series might have been so. They might argue in like manner, that because it is not very improbable one may throw sixes in any one out of a hundred throws, therefore it is no more improbable that one may throw sixes a hundred times running.

Thaumatrope-fallacy.

It will often happen that when two objects are *incompatible,* though either of them, *separately,* may be attained, the incompatibility is disguised by a rapid and frequent transition from the one to the other alternately. *E. G.* You may prove that 100*l.* would accomplish *this* object; and then, that it would accomplish *that:* and then, you recur to the former; and back again: till at length a notion is generated of the possibility of accomplishing *both* by this 100*l.* "Two distinct objects may, by being dexterously presented, again and again in quick succession, to the mind of a cursory reader, be so associated together *in his thoughts,* as to be conceived capable, when in fact they are not, of being *actually* combined in practice. The fallacious belief thus induced bears a striking resemblance to the optical illusion effected by that ingenious and philosophical toy called the Thaumatrope; in which two objects painted on opposite sides of a card,—for instance a man, and a horse,—a bird, and a cage,—are, by a quick rotatory motion, made to impress the eye in combination, so as to form one picture, of the man on the horse's back, the bird in the cage, &c. As soon as the card is allowed to remain at rest, the figures, of course, appear as they really are, separate and on opposite sides. A mental illusion closely analogous to this, is produced, when by a rapid and repeated transition from one subject to another alternately, the mind is deluded into an idea of the actual combination of things that are really incompatible. The chief part of the defence which various writers have advanced in favour of the system of *Penal-Colonies,* consists, in truth, of a sort of intellectual Thaumatrope. The *prosperity* of the *Colony,* and the *repression of crime,* are, by a sort of rapid whirl, presented to the mind as combined in one picture. A very moderate degree of calm and fixed attention soon shows that the two objects are painted on opposite sides of the card."*

Ambiguity of the word "All."

The Fallacy of Division may often be considered as turning on the ambiguity of the word "all;" which may easily be dispelled by substituting for it the word "each" or

* Remarks on Transportation, pp. 25, 26.

"every," where that is its signification; *e.g.* "all these trees make a thick shade," is ambiguous; meaning, either, "every one of them," or "all together."

This is a Fallacy with which men are extremely apt to deceive *themselves:* for when a multitude of particulars are presented to the mind, many are too weak or too indolent to take a comprehensive view of them; but confine their attention to each single point, by turns; and then decide, infer, and act, accordingly; *e.g.* the imprudent spendthrift, finding that he is able to afford this, *or* that, *or* the other expense, forgets that *all of them together* will ruin him.

To the same head may be reduced that fallacious reasoning by which men vindicate themselves to their own conscience and to others, for the neglect of those *undefined* duties, which though indispensable, and therefore not left to our choice *whether* we will practise them or not, are left to our discretion as to the *mode*, and the particular occasions, of practising them; *e.g.* "I am not bound to contribute to this charity in particular; nor to that; nor to the other:" the *practical* conclusion which they draw, is, that *all* charity may be dispensed with.

As men are apt to forget that any two circumstances (not naturally connected) are more rarely to be met with combined than separate, though they be not at all incompatible; so also they are apt to imagine, from finding that they *are* rarely combined, that there *is* an incompatibility; *e.g.* if the chances are ten to one against a man's possessing strong reasoning powers, and ten to one against exquisite taste, the chances against the combination of the two (supposing them neither connected nor opposed) will be a hundred to one. Many, therefore, from finding them so rarely united, will infer that they are in some measure incompatible; which Fallacy may easily be exposed in the form of Undistributed middle: "qualities unfriendly to each other are rarely combined; excellence in the reasoning powers, and in taste, are rarely combined; therefore they are qualities unfriendly to each other."

§ 12.

Fallacia accidentis.

The other kind of ambiguity arising from the context, and which is the last case of Ambiguous middle that I shall notice, is the "*fallacia accidentis;*" together with its converse, "*fallacia a dicto secundum quid ad dictum simpliciter;*" in each of which the Middle-Term is used, in one Premiss to signify something considered simply, in itself, and as to its essence; and in the other Premiss, so as to imply that its Accidents are taken into account with it: as in the well-known example, "what is bought in the market is eaten; raw meat is bought in the market; therefore raw meat is eaten." Here the Middle has understood in conjunction with it, in the Major-Premiss, "*as to its substance merely:*" in the Minor, "*as to its condition and circumstances.*"

To this head, perhaps, as well as to any, may be referred the Fallacies which are frequently founded on the occasional, partial, and temporary variations in the acceptation of some Term, arising from circumstances of person, time, and place, which will occasion something to be understood in conjunction with it beyond its strict literal signification. *E. G.* The word "loyalty," which properly denotes attachment to *lawful* government,—whether of a king, president, senate, *&c.*, according to the respective institutions of each nation,—has often been used to signify exclusively, attachment to *regal* authority; and that, even when carried *beyond* the boundaries of *law*. So, "reformer" has sometimes been limited to the protestant reformers of *religion;* sometimes, to the advocates of some particular *parliamentary* reform, *&c.* And whenever any phrase of this kind has become a kind of watch-word or gathering-cry of a party, the employment of it would commonly imply certain sentiments not literally expressed by the words. To assume therefore that one is friendly or unfriendly to "Loyalty" or to "Reform" in one sense, because he has declared himself friendly or unfriendly to it in another sense, when implying and connected with such and such other sentiments, is a Fallacy, such as may fairly be referred to the present head.

§ 13.

On the non-logical (or material) Fallacies: and first, of "begging the question;" *Petitio Principii.*

Begging the question. The indistinct and unphilosophical account which has been given by Logical writers of the Fallacy of "*non causa,*" and that of "*petitio principii,*" makes it very difficult to ascertain wherein they conceived them to differ, and what, according to them, is the nature of each. Without therefore professing to conform exactly to their meaning, and with a view to distinctness only, which is the main point, let us confine the name "*petitio principii*" to those cases in which the Premiss either appears manifestly to be the same as the Conclusion, or is actually proved from the Conclusion, or is such as would naturally and properly so be proved; *i. e.* such as the persons you are addressing* are not likely to know, or to admit, except as inferred from an admission of the Conclusion; as *e. g.* if any one should infer the actual occurrence of the eclipses recorded in the Chinese annals, from an assumption of the authenticity of those annals. And to the other class may be referred all other cases, in which the Premiss (whether the expressed or the suppressed one) is either proved false, or has no sufficient claim to be received as true.

* For it should be remembered that of two propositions, the one may be the more evident to some, and the other, to others.

Let it however be observed, that in such cases (apparently) as this, we must not too hastily pronounce the argument fallacious; for it may be perfectly fair at the *commencement* of an argument to assume a Premiss that is not more evident than the Conclusion, or is even ever so parodoxical, provided you proceed to prove fairly that Premiss; and in like manner it is both usual and fair to *begin* by deducing your Conclusion from a Premiss exactly equivalent to it; which is merely throwing the proposition in question into the form in which it will be most conveniently proved.

Arguing in a Circle.

Arguing in a Circle, however, must necessarily be unfair; though it frequently is practised undesignedly; *e.g.* some Mechanicians attempt to prove, (what they ought to have laid down as a probable but doubtful hypothesis,) that every particle of matter gravitates equally; "why?" because those bodies which contain more particles ever gravitate more strongly, *i.e.* are heavier: "but (it may be urged) those which are heaviest are not always more bulky;" "no, but still they contain more particles, though more closely condensed;" "how do you know that?" "because they are heavier;" "how does that prove it?" "because all particles of matter gravitating equally, that mass which is specifically the heavier must needs have the more of them in the same space."

Of course the *narrower* the Circle, the less likely it is to escape the detection, either of the reasoner himself, (for men often deceive *themselves* in this way) or of his hearers. When there is a long circuit of many intervening propositions before you come back to the original Conclusion, it will often not be perceived that the arguments really do proceed in a "Circle:" just as when any one is advancing in a *straight line* (as we are accustomed to call it) along a plain on this Earth's surface, it escapes our notice that we are really moving along the *circumference of a Circle,* (since the earth is a globe) and that if we could go on without interruption in the same line, we should at length arrive at the very spot we set out from. But this we readily perceive, when we are walking round a small hill.

For instance, if any one argues that you ought to submit to the guidance of himself, or his leader, or his party, &c. because these maintain what is right; and then argues that what is so maintained is right, because it is maintained by persons whom you ought to submit to; and that these are, himself and his party; or again, if any one maintains that so and so must be a thing morally wrong, because it is prohibited in the *moral portion* of the Mosaic-law, and then, that the prohibition of it does form a part of the *moral* (not the ceremonial, or the civil) portion of that Law, *because* it is a thing *morally wrong*,—either of these would be too narrow a Circle to escape detection, unless several intermediate steps were interposed. And if the *form of expression* of each proposition be *varied* every time it recurs,—the sense of it remaining the same,—this will greatly aid the deception.

Of course, the way to expose the Fallacy, is to reverse this procedure: to narrow the Circle, by cutting off the intermediate steps; and to exhibit the same proposition,—when it comes round the second time,—in the same words.

Obliquity of expression. Obliquity and disguise being of course most important to the success of the *petitio principii* as well as of other Fallacies, the Sophist will in general either have recourse to the "Circle," or else not venture to *state* distinctly his assumption of the point in question, but will rather assert some other proposition which *implies* it;* thus keeping out of sight (as a dexterous thief does stolen goods) the point in question, at the very moment when he is taking it for granted. Hence the frequent

* Gibbon affords the most remarkable instances of this kind of style. That which he really means to speak of, is hardly ever made the Subject of his Proposition. His way of writing reminds one of those persons who never dare look you full in the face.

union of this Fallacy with "*ignoratio elenchi*:" [vide § 15.] The English language is perhaps the more suitable for the Fallacy of *petitio principii*, from its being formed from two distinct languages, and thus abounding in synonymous expressions, which have no resemblance in sound, and no connexion in etymology; so that a Sophist may bring forward a proposition expressed in words of Saxon origin, and give as a reason for it, the very same proposition stated in words of Norman origin; *e. g.* "to allow every man an unbounded freedom of speech must always be, on the whole, advantageous to the State; for it is highly conducive to the interests of the Community, that each individual should enjoy a liberty perfectly unlimited, of expressing his sentiments."

§ 14.

Undue assumption.

The next head is, the falsity, or, at least, undue assumption, of a Premiss that is not equivalent to, or dependent on, the Conclusion; which, as has been before said, seems to correspond nearly with the meaning of Logicians, when they speak of "*non causa pro causa*." This name indeed would seem to imply a much narrower class: there being one species of arguments which are *from cause to effect;* in which, of course, two things are necessary; 1st, the *sufficiency* of the cause; 2d, its establishment; these are the two Premises; if therefore the *former* be unduly assumed, we are arguing from that which is *not* a sufficient cause as if it *were* so: *e. g.* as if one should contend from such a man's having been unjust or cruel, that he will certainly be visited with some heavy temporal judgment, and come to an untimely end. In this instance the Sophist, from having assumed, in the Premiss, the (granted) existence of a pretended cause, infers, in the Conclusion, the existence of the pretended effect, which we have supposed to be the Question. Or *vice versâ*, the pretended effect may be employed to establish the cause; *e.g.* inferring sinfulness from temporal calamity. But when *both* the pretended cause and effect are granted, *i. e.* granted to *exist*, then the Sophist will infer something from their pretended *connexion; i. e.* he will assume as a Premiss, that "of these two admitted facts, the one is the cause of the other:" as Whitfield attributed his being overtaken by a hail-storm to his having not preached at the last town; or as the opponents of the Reformation assumed that it was the cause of the troubles which took place at that period, and thence inferred that it was an evil.

Sign put for Cause.

Many are the cases in which a *Sign* (see *Rhet.* Part I.) from which one might fairly infer a certain phenomenon, is mistaken for the *Cause* of it: (as if one should suppose the falling of the mercury to be a cause of rain; of which it certainly is an indication) whereas the fact will often be the very reverse. *E. G.* a great deal of *money* in a country is a pretty sure proof of its wealth; and thence has been often regarded as the cause of it; whereas in truth it is an effect. The same, with a numerous and increasing *population.* Again, The *labour* bestowed on any commodity has often been represented as the cause of its value; though every one would call a fine pearl an article of value, even though he should meet with it accidentally in eating an oyster. Pearls are indeed generally obtained by laborious diving: but they do not fetch a high price from that cause; but on the contrary, men dive for them *because* they fetch a high price.* So also exposure to want and hardship in youth, has been regarded as a cause of the hardy constitution of those men and brutes which have been brought up in barren countries of uncongenial climate. Yet the most experienced cattle-breeders know that animals are, *cæteris paribus,* the more hardy for having been well fed and sheltered in youth; but early hardships, by destroying all the tender, ensure the hardiness of the survivors; which is the cause, not the effect,

* Pol. Econ. Lect. IX. p. 253.

of their having lived through such a training. So, loading a gun-barrel to the muzzle, and firing it, does not *give* it strength; though it *proves*, if it escape, that it *was* strong.

Appeal to supposed experience.

In like manner, nothing is more common than to hear a person state confidently, as from his own experience, that such and such a patient *was cured* by this or that medicine: whereas all that he absolutely *knows*, is that he took the medicine, and that he recovered.

Similar is the procedure of many who are no *theorists* forsooth, but have found by *experience* that the diffusion of education disqualifies the lower classes for humble toil. They have perhaps experienced really a deterioration in this last respect; and having a dislike to education, they shut their eyes to the increase of pauperism; *i. e.* of the habit of depending on parish-pay, rather than on independent exertions; which, to any unprejudiced eye would seem the most natural mode of explaining the relaxation of those exertions. But such men require us, on the ground that they are *practical* men, to adopt the results of their experience; *i. e.* to acquiesce in their crude guesses as to cause and effect, (like that of the rustic who made Tenterden-steeple the cause of Goodwin Sands,) precisely because they are *not* accustomed to reason.

Hurtful changes attributed to harmless ones.

I believe we may refer to the same head the apprehensions so often entertained, that a *change*, however small, and however in itself harmless, is necessarily a dangerous thing, as tending to *produce* extensive and hurtful innovations. Many instances may be found of small alterations being *followed* by great and mischievous ones;* but I doubt whether all history can furnish an instance of the greater innovation having been, properly speaking, *caused* by the lesser. Of course the first change will always *precede* the

* "Post hoc; ergo, propter hoc."

second; and many mischievous innovations *have* taken place; but these may all I think be referred to a mistaken effort to obtain some good, or get rid of some evil; not to the love of innovation for its own sake. The mass of mankind are, in the serious concerns of life, wedded to what is established and customary; and when they make rash changes, this may often be explained by the too long *postponement* of the requisite changes; which allows (as in the case of the Reformation) evils to reach an intolerable height, before any remedy is thought of. And even then, the remedy is often so violently resisted by many, as to drive others into dangerous extremes. And when this occurs, we are triumphantly told that experience shows what mischievous excesses are *caused* by once beginning to innovate. "I told you that if once you began to repair your house, you would have to pull it all down." "Yes; but you told me wrong; for if I had begun sooner, the replacing of a few tiles might have sufficed. The mischief was, not in taking down the first stone, but in letting it stand too long."

Cause and reason confounded together.

Such an argument as any of these might strictly be called "*non causa pro causa;*" but it is not probable that the Logical writers intended any such limitation (which indeed would be wholly unnecessary and impertinent,) but rather that they were confounding together *cause* and *reason;* the sequence of *Conclusion* from *Premises* being perpetually mistaken for that of *effect* from physical *cause.** It may be better, therefore, to drop the name which tends to perpetuate this confusion, and simply to state (when such is the case) that the premiss is "unduly assumed;" *i.e.* without being either self-evident, or satisfactorily proved.

The contrivances by which men may deceive themselves or others, in assuming Premises unduly, *so that that undue*

* See Appendix, No. I. article *Reason.*

assumption shall not be perceived, (for it is in *this* the *Fallacy* consists) are of course infinite. Sometimes (as was before observed) the *doubtful Premiss* is *suppressed,* as if it were too evident to need being proved, or even stated, and as if the whole question turned on the establishment of the other premiss. Thus Horne Tooke proves, by an immense induction, that all particles were originally nouns or verbs; and thence concludes, that in reality they are so still, and that the ordinary division of the parts of speech is absurd; keeping out of sight, as self-evident, the other premiss, which is absolutely false; *viz.* that the meaning and force of a word, now, and for ever, must be that which it, or its root, originally bore.

Indirect assumption.

Sometimes men are shamed into admitting an unfounded assertion, by being confidently told, that it is so evident, that it would argue great weakness to doubt it. In general, however, the more skilful Sophist will avoid a *direct assertion* of what he means unduly to assume; because that might direct the reader's attention to the consideration of the question whether it be *true* or not; since that which is indisputable does not so often need to be asserted. It succeeds better, therefore, to *allude* to the proposition, as something *curious* and remarkable; just as the Royal Society were imposed on by being asked to *account for* the fact that a vessel of water received no addition to its weight by a live fish put into it; while they were seeking for the *cause,* they forgot to ascertain the *fact;* and thus admitted without suspicion a mere fiction. Thus an eminent Scotch writer,* instead of *asserting* that the "advocates of Logic have been worsted and driven from the field in every controversy," (an assertion which, if made, would have been the more readily ascertained to be perfectly groundless,) merely *observes,* that "it is a circumstance not a little *remarkable.*"

* Dugald Stewart.

Again, any one who is decrying all appeal to *evidence* in behalf of Christianity, (see Appendix iii. Note) will hardly venture to *assert plainly* that such was the practice of the Apostles, and that they called on men to believe what they preached, without any reason for believing. *That* would present too glaring a contrast to the truth. He will succeed better by merely dwelling on the earnest demand of "faith" made by the Apostles; trusting that the inadvertent reader will forget that the *basis* on which this demand was made to rest, was, the evidence of miracles and prophecies; and will thus be led to infer that we are to imitate the Apostles by a procedure which is in fact the opposite of theirs.

Fallacy of References.

One of the many contrivances employed for this purpose, is what may be called the "Fallacy of *references*;" which is particularly common in popular theological works. It is of course a circumstance which adds great weight to any assertion, that it shall seem to be supported by many passages of Scripture, or of the Fathers and other ancient writers, whose works are not in many people's hands. Now when a writer can find few or none of these, that distinctly and decidedly favour his opinion, he may at least find many which may be conceived capable of being so understood, or which, in some way or other, remotely relate to the subject; but if these texts were inserted at length, it would be at once perceived how little they bear on the question; the usual artifice therefore is, to give merely *references* to them; trusting that nineteen out of twenty readers will never take the trouble of turning to the passages, but, taking for granted that they afford, each, some degree of confirmation to what is maintained, will be overawed by seeing every assertion supported, as they suppose, by five or six Scripture-texts,—as many from the Fathers, *&c.*

Great force is often added to the employment in a declamatory work, of the fallacy now before us, by bitterly *reproaching* or *deriding* an opponent, as denying some sacred truth, or some evident axiom; assuming, that is, that he denies the *true* premiss, and keeping out of sight the one on which the question really turns. *E.G.* a declaimer who is maintaining some doctrine as being taught in Scripture, may impute to his opponents a contempt for the authority of Scripture, and reproach them for impiety; when the question really is, whether the doctrine be scriptural or not.

Combination of this Fallacy with the following.

Frequently the Fallacy of *irrelevant-conclusion* [*ignoratio elenchi*] is called in to the aid of this; *i.e.* the Premiss is assumed on the ground of another proposition, *somewhat like it,* having been proved. Thus, in arguing by example, *&c.* the *parallelism* of two cases is often assumed from their being in *some respects* alike, though perhaps they differ in the very point which is *essential* to the argument. *E.G.* From the circumstance that some men of humble station, who have been well educated, are apt to think themselves above low drudgery, it is argued, that universal education of the lower orders would beget general idleness: this argument rests, of course, on the assumption of *parallelism* in the two cases, *viz.* the past and the future; whereas there is a circumstance that is absolutely essential, in which they differ; for when education is *universal,* it must cease to be a *distinction;* which is probably the very circumstance that renders men too proud for their work.

Again, parallels have been drawn by Hume, (in his Essay on Miracles) and by Christian writers, between the miracles recorded in the New Testament, and those in the Legends of pretended Saints; which last were received just as counterfeit coin is, from its *resemblance* to genuine.

This very same Fallacy is often resorted to on the opposite side: an attempt is made to invalidate some argument from Example, by pointing out *a difference* between the two cases: though they agree in every thing that is essential to the question.

Calculation of probabilities.

It should be added that we may often be deceived, not only by admitting a premiss which is absolutely unsupported, but also, by attributing to one which really is probable, a *greater* degree of probability than rightly belongs to it. And this effect will often be produced by our omitting to calculate the probability in each successive step of a long chain of argument, and being, in each, (see § 11,) deceived by the fallacy of Division. Each premiss successively introduced, may have, as was above explained, an excess of chances in its favour, and yet the ultimate conclusion may have a great preponderance against it; *e.g.* "All Y is (probably) X: all Z is (probably) Y: therefore Z is (probably) X:" now suppose the truth of the major premiss to be more probable than not; in other words, that the chances for it are more than $\frac{1}{2}$; say $\frac{4}{7}$; and for the truth of the minor, let the chances be greater still; say $\frac{2}{3}$: then by multiplying together the numerators, and also the denominators of these two fractions, $\frac{4}{7} \times \frac{2}{3}$, we obtain $\frac{8}{21}$, as indicating the degree of probability of the conclusion; which is less than $\frac{1}{2}$; *i.e.* the conclusion is less likely to be true than not. *E. G.* "The reports this author heard are (probably) true; this (something which he records) is a report which (probably) he heard; therefore it is true;" suppose, first, The *majority* of the reports he heard,—as 4 out of 7, (or 12 of 21,)—to be true; and, next, That he *generally*,—as twice in three times,—(or 8 in 12,)—repeats faithfully what he heard; it follows that of 21 of his reports, only 8 are true.

Of course, the results are proportionably striking when there is a long series of arguments of this description.

And yet weak and thoughtless reasoners are often influenced by hearing a great deal urged,—a *great number of probabilities* brought forward,—in support of some conclusion; *i.e.* a long chain, of which each successive link is weaker than the foregoing; instead of (what they mistake it for) a cumulation of arguments, each, *separately*, proving the certainty or probability, of the same conclusion.*

Lastly, it may be here remarked, conformably with what has been formerly said, that it will often be left to your

* The converse fallacy is treated of below in § 18.

When there really are several distinct and independent arguments, not incompatible, and not connected, each separately proving the probability of the same conclusion, we compute, from our estimate of the degree of probability of each, the joint [*cumulative*] force of them, by the same sort of calculation as the above, only *reversed:* viz. as, in the case of two probable premises, the conclusion is not established except on the supposition of their being *both* true, so, in the case of two (and the like holds good with any number) distinct and independent indications of the truth of some proposition, unless *both* of them *fail*, the proposition must be true: we therefore multiply together the fractions indicating the probability of *failure* of each,—the chances *against* it;—and the result being the total chances against the establishment of the conclusion by these arguments, this fraction being deducted from unity, the remainder gives the probability *for* it. *E. G.* a certain book is conjectured to be by such and such an author, partly, 1st. from its resemblance in style to his known works, partly (2dly) from its being attributed to him by some one likely to be pretty well-informed: let the probability of the Conclusion, as deduced from one of these arguments by itself, be supposed $\frac{2}{5}$, and, in the other case $\frac{3}{7}$; then the *opposite* probabilities will be, respectively, $\frac{3}{5}$ and $\frac{4}{7}$; which multiplied together give $\frac{12}{35}$, as the probability *against* the Conclusion; *i.e.* the chance that the work may *not* be his, notwithstanding those reasons for believing that it is: and consequently the probability in *favour* of that Conclusion will be $\frac{23}{35}$; or nearly $\frac{2}{3}$.

Observe however that, in some cases, a perfectly distinct argument arises from the *combination* of certain circumstances, which have, each separately, no force at all, or very little, towards establishing a conclusion which yet may be inferred, perhaps with a moral certainty, from that combination, when those circumstances are such that the chances are very great against their *accidental* concurrence. *E. G.* when two or more persons, undeserving of credit, coincide (where collusion would be impossible) in a full and circumstantial detail of some transaction. (See Rhet. Part. I. Ch. ii. § 4.)

choice whether to refer this or that fallacious argument to the present head, or that of Ambiguous-Middle; "*if* the middle term is here used in *this* sense, there is an *ambiguity; if* in *that* sense, the proposition is *false.*"

§ 15.

Irrelevant Conclusion. The last kind of Fallacy to be noticed is that of Irrelevant - Conclusion, commonly called *ignoratio elenchi.*

Various kinds of propositions are, according to the occasion, substituted for the one of which proof is required. Sometimes the Particular for the Universal; sometimes a proposition with different Terms: and various are the contrivances employed to effect and to conceal this substitution, and to make the Conclusion which the Sophist has drawn, answer, practically, the same purpose as the one he ought to have established. I say, "practically the same purpose," because it will very often happen that some *emotion* will be excited—some sentiment impressed on the mind—(by a dexterous employment of this Fallacy) such as shall bring men into the *disposition* requisite for your purpose, though they may not have assented to, or even stated distinctly in their own minds, the *proposition* which it was your business to establish.* Thus if a Sophist has to defend one who has been guilty of some *serious* offence, which he wishes to extenuate, though he is unable distinctly to prove that it is not such, yet if he can succeed in *making the audience laugh* at some casual matter, he has gained practically the same point.

So also if any one has pointed out the extenuating circumstances in some particular case of offence, so as to show that it differs widely from the generality of the same class,

* See Rhetoric, Part II.

the Sophist, if he find himself unable to disprove these circumstances, may do away the force of them, by simply *referring the action to that very class,* which no one can deny that it belongs to, and the very name of which will excite a feeling of disgust sufficient to counteract the extenuation; *e.g.* let it be a case of peculation; and that many *mitigating* circumstances have been brought forward which cannot be denied; the sophistical opponent will reply, "Well, but after all, the man is a *rogue,* and there is an end of it;" now in reality this was (by hypothesis) never the question; and the mere assertion of what was never denied, *ought* not, in fairness, to be regarded as decisive; but practically, the odiousness of the word, arising in great measure from the *association of those very circumstances* which belong to *most of the class,* but which we have supposed to be *absent* in *this particular* instance, excites precisely that *feeling of disgust,* which in effect destroys the force of the defence. In like manner we may refer to this head, all cases of improper appeals to the passions, and every thing else which is mentioned by Aristotle as extraneous to the matter in hand (ἔξω τοῦ πράγματος.)

In all these cases, as has been before observed, if the fallacy we are now treating of be employed for the apparent establishment, not of the *ultimate* Conclusion, but (as it very commonly happens) of a *Premiss,* (*i. e.* if the Premiss required be assumed on the ground that some proposition resembling it has been proved) then there will be a combination of this Fallacy with the last mentioned.

Combination of this Fallacy with the foregoing.

For instance, instead of proving that "this Prisoner has committed an atrocious fraud," you prove that "the fraud he is accused of is atrocious:" instead of proving (as in the well-known tale of Cyrus and the two coats) that "the taller boy had a right to force the other boy to exchange coats with him," you prove that "the exchange would have been advantageous to both:" instead of proving that "a man has not a right to educate his children or to dispose of his property, in the way *he thinks best*," you show that the way in which he educates his children, or disposes of his property is not *really the best:* instead of proving that "the poor ought to be relieved in this way rather than in that," you prove that "the poor *ought to be relieved:*" instead of proving that "an irrational-agent—whether a brute or a madman—can never be deterred from any act by apprehension of punishment," (as for instance, a dog, from sheep-biting, by fear of being beaten) you prove that "the beating of one dog does not operate as an *example* to *other* dogs," &c. and then you proceed to assume as premises, conclusions different from what have really been established.

A good instance of the employment and exposure of this Fallacy occurs in Thucydides, in the speeches of Cleon and Diodotus concerning the Mitylenæans: the former (over and above his appeal to the angry passions of his audience) urges the *justice* of putting the revolters to death; which, as the latter remarked, was nothing to the purpose, since the Athenians were not sitting in *judgment*, but in *deliberation;* of which the proper end is *expediency*. And to prove that they had a right to put them to death, did not prove this to be an *advisable* step.

This fallacy used in refutation.

It is evident, that *ignoratio elenchi* may be employed as well for the apparent *refutation* of your opponent's proposition, as for the apparent establishment of your own; for it is substantially the same thing, to *prove* what was not denied, or to *disprove* what was not asserted. The latter practice is not less common; and it is more offensive, because it frequently amounts to a personal affront, in attributing to a person opinions, *&c.* which he perhaps holds in abhorrence. Thus, when in a discussion one party vindicates, on the ground of general expediency, a particular instance of resistance to Government in a case of intolerable oppression, the opponent may gravely maintain, that "we ought not to do evil that good may come:" a proposition which of course had never been denied; the point in dispute being "whether resistance in this particular case *were* doing evil or not." Or again, by way of disproving the assertion of the "*right* of private-judgment in religion," one may hear a grave argument to prove that "it is impossible every one can be *right in his judgment*." In these examples, it is to be remarked, (as well as in some given just above,) that the Fallacy of *petitio principii* is combined with that of *ignoratio elenchi;* which is a very common and often successful practice; *viz.* the Sophist proves, or disproves, not the proposition which is really in question, but one which is so dependent on it as to proceed on the supposition that it is already decided, and can admit of no doubt; by this means his "assumption of the point in question" is so indirect and oblique, that it may easily escape notice; and he thus establishes, practically, his Conclusion, at the very moment he is withdrawing your attention from it to another question. *E. G.* An advocate will prove, and dwell on the high *criminality* of a certain act, and the propriety of severely punishing it; assuming (instead of proving) the *commission*.

Argumentum ad hominem, &c.

There are certain kinds of argument recounted and named by Logical writers, which we should by no means universally call Fallacies; but which *when unfairly* used, and *so far as they are* fallacious, may very well be referred to the present head; such as the "*argumentum ad hominem,*" ["or personal argument,"] "*argumentum ad verecundiam,*" "*argumentum ad populum,*" *&c.* all of them regarded as contradistinguished from "*argumentum ad rem;*" or, according to others (meaning probably the very same thing) "*ad judicium.*" These have all been described in the lax and popular language before alluded to, but not scientifically: the "*argumentum ad hominem,*" they say, "is addressed to the peculiar circumstances, character, avowed opinions, or past conduct of the individual, and therefore has a reference to him only, and does not bear directly and absolutely on the real question, as the '*argumentum ad rem*' does:": in like manner, the "*argumentum ad verecundiam*" is described as an appeal to our reverence for some respected authority, some venerable institution, *&c.* and the "*argumentum ad populum,*" as an appeal to the prejudices, passions, *&c.* of the multitude; and so of the rest. Along with these is usually enumerated "*argumentum ad ignorantiam,*" which is here omitted, as being evidently nothing more than the employment of *some* kind of Fallacy, in the widest sense of that word, towards such as are likely to be deceived by it.

Technical analysis of personal argument, &c.

It appears then (to speak rather more technically) that in the "*argumentum ad hominem*" the conclusion which actually is established, is not the *absolute* and *general* one in question, but *relative* and particular; *viz.* not that "such and such is the fact," but that "*this man* is bound to admit it, in conformity to his principles of Reasoning, or in consistency with his own conduct, situation," *&c.**

* The "argumentum ad hominem" will often have the effect of shifting the *burden of proof*, not unjustly, to the adversary. (See *Rhet.* Part I. chap. iii. § 2.) A common instance is the defence, certainly the readiest and most concise, frequently urged by the Sportsman, when accused of barbarity in sacrificing unoffending hares or trout to his amusement: he replies, as he may safely do, to most of his assailants, "why do you feed on the flesh of the harmless sheep and ox?" and that this answer presses hard, is manifested by its being usually opposed by a *palpable falsehood; viz.* that the animals which are killed for food are sacrificed to our *necessities;* though not only men *can*, but a large proportion (probably a great majority) of the human race actually *do*, subsist in health and vigour without flesh-diet; and the earth would support a much greater human population were such a practice universal.

When shamed out of this argument they sometimes urge that the brute creation would overrun the earth, if we did not kill them for food; an argument, which, if it were valid at all, would not justify their feeding on *fish;* though, if fairly followed up, it *would* justify Swift's proposal for keeping down the excessive population of Ireland. The true reason, *viz.* that they

Such a conclusion it is often both allowable and necessary to establish, in order to silence those who will not yield to fair general argument; or to convince those whose weakness and prejudices would not allow them to assign to it its due weight. It is thus that our Lord on many occasions silences the cavils of the Jews; as in the vindication of healing on the Sabbath, which is paralleled by the authorized practice of drawing out a beast that has fallen into a pit. All this, as we have said, is perfectly fair, provided it be done plainly, and *avowedly;* but if you attempt to *substitute* this partial and relative Conclusion for a more general one—if you triumph as having established your proposition absolutely and universally, from having established it, in reality, only as far as it relates to your opponent, then you are guilty of a Fallacy of the kind which we are now treating of: your Conclusion is not in reality that which was, by your own account, proposed to be proved. The fallaciousness depends upon the *deceit,* or attempt to deceive. The same observations will *apply* to "*argumentum ad verecundiam,*" and the rest.

Ambiguous terms employed in this Fallacy.

It is very common to employ an ambiguous Term for the purpose of introducing the Fallacy of irrelevant conclusion: *i. e.* when you cannot prove your proposition in the sense in which it was maintained, to prove it in some other sense; *e. g.* those who contend against the efficacy of *faith,* usually employ that word in their arguments in the sense of mere *belief,* unaccompanied with any moral or practical result, but considered as a mere intellectual process; and when they have thus proved their conclusion, they oppose it to one in which the word is used in a widely different sense.*

eat flesh for the gratification of the palate, and have a taste for the pleasures of the table, though not for the sports of the field, is one which they do not like to assign.

* "When the occasion or object in question is not such as calls for, or as is likely to excite in those particular readers or hearers, the emotions required, it is a common Rhetorical artifice to turn their attention to some object which

§ 16.

Shifting ground.

The Fallacy of "irrelevant-conclusion" [*ignoratio elenchi*] is nowhere more common than in protracted controversy, when one of the parties, after having attempted in vain to maintain his position, *shifts his ground* as covertly as possible to another, instead of honestly giving up the point. An instance occurs in an attack made on the system pursued at one of our Universities. The objectors, finding themselves unable to maintain their charge of the *present* neglect (*viz.* in the year 1810) of Mathematics in that place, (to which neglect they attributed the "late *general decline*" in those studies) shifted their ground, and contended that that University "was never famous for Mathematicians:" which not only does not establish, but absolutely overthrows, their own original assertion; for if it *never* succeeded in those pursuits, it could not have caused their late *decline*.

A practice of this nature is common in oral controversy especially; *viz.* that of combating *both* your opponent's

will call forth these feelings; and when they are too much excited to be capable of judging calmly, it will not be difficult to turn their Passions, once roused, in the direction required, and to make them view the case before them in a very different light. When the metal is heated it may easily be moulded into the desired form. Thus vehement indignation against some *crime*, may be directed against a *person* who has not been proved guilty of it; and vague declamations against corruption, oppression, *&c.* or against the mischiefs of anarchy; with high-flown panegyrics on liberty, rights of man, *&c.* or on social-order, justice, the constitution, law, religion, *&c.* will gradually lead the hearers to take for granted, without proof, that the measure proposed will lead to these evils, or to these advantages; and it will in consequence become the object of groundless abhorrence or admiration. For the very utterance of such words as have a multitude of what may be called *stimulating* ideas associated with them, will operate like a charm on the minds, especially of the ignorant and unthinking, and raise such a tumult of feeling, as will effectually blind their judgment; so that a string of vague abuse or panegyric will often have the effect of a train of sound Argument."—*Rhetoric*, Part II. Chap. ii. § 6.

Fallacy of combating the two Premises alternately.

Premises *alternately*, and shifting the attack from the one to the other, without waiting to have either of them decided upon before you quit it. "*And besides,*" is an expression one may often hear from a disputant who is proceeding to a fresh argument, when he cannot establish, and yet will not abandon, his first.

It has been remarked above, that one class of the propositions that may be, in this Fallacy, substituted for the one required, is the *particular* for the *universal:* similar to this, is the substitution of a conditional with a *universal* antecedent, for one with a *particular* antecedent; which will usually be the harder to prove: *e.g.* you are called on, suppose, to prove that "if *any* (*i. e.* some) private interests are hurt by a proposed measure, it is inexpedient;" and you pretend to have done so by showing that "if *all* private interests are hurt by it, it must be inexpedient." Nearly akin to this is the very common case of proving something to be *possible* when it ought to have been proved highly *probable;* or *probable,* when it ought to have been proved *necessary;* or, which comes to the very same, proving it to be *not necessary,* when it should have been proved *not probable;* or *improbable,* when it should have been proved *impossible.* Aristotle (*in Rhet.* Book II.) complains of this last branch of the Fallacy, as giving an undue advantage to the respondent; many a guilty person owes his acquittal to this; the jury considering that the evidence brought does not demonstrate the complete impossibility of his being innocent; though perhaps the chances are innumerable against it.

§ 17.

Fallacy of Objections.

Similar to this case is that which may be called the *Fallacy of objections: i. e.* showing that *there are* objections against some plan, theory, or system, and thence inferring that it should be rejected; when that which *ought* to have been proved is, that there are *more*, or *stronger* objections, against the receiving than the rejecting of it. This is the main, and almost universal Fallacy of anti-christians; and is that of which a young Christian should be first and principally warned.* They find numerous "objections" against various parts of Scripture; to some of which no satisfactory answer can be given; and the incautious hearer is apt, while his attention is fixed on these, to forget that there are infinitely more, and stronger objections against the supposition that the Christian Religion is of *human* origin; and that where we cannot answer all objections, we are bound in reason and in candour to adopt the hypothesis which labours under the least. That the case is as I have stated, I am authorized to assume, from this circumstance; that *no complete and consistent account has ever been given of the manner in which the Christian Religion, supposing it a human contrivance, could have arisen and prevailed* as it did. And yet this may obviously be demanded with the utmost fairness, of those who deny its divine origin. The Religion exists: that is the phenomenon; those who will not allow it to have come from God, are bound to solve the phenomenon on some other hypothesis less open to objections. They are not indeed called on to prove that it *actually did* arise in this or that way; but to suggest (consistently with acknowledged facts) some probable way in which it *may* have arisen, reconcileable with all the circumstances of the case. That infidels have never done this, though they have had 1800 years to try, amounts to a confession that no such hypothesis can be devised, which will not be open to greater objections than lie against Christianity.†

* See note at the end of Appendix, No. III.

† In an "Essay on the *Omissions* of our Sacred Writers," I have pointed out some circumstances which no one has ever attempted to account for on any supposition of their being other than, not only *true* witnesses, but supernaturally *inspired*.

Reforms are open to objections.

The Fallacy of Objections is also the stronghold of bigoted anti-innovators, who oppose all reforms and alterations indiscriminately; for there never was, or will be, any plan executed or proposed, against which strong and even unanswerable objections may not be urged; so that unless the opposite objections be set in the balance on the other side, we can never advance a step. *E. G.* The defenders of the Transportation-system,—a system which, as an eminent writer has observed, was "begun in defiance of all Reason, and persevered in, in defiance of all Experience"—are accustomed to ask "what kind of Secondary-punishment would you substitute?" and if any one is suggested, they adduce the objections, and difficulties, real and apparent, to which it is exposed; if another is proposed, they proceed in the same manner; and so on, without end. For of all the other plans of Secondary-punishment that have ever been tried, or imagined, the *best* must be open to *some* objections, though the very *worst* is much *less* objectionable than Transportation.* "There are objections," said Dr. Johnson, "against a *plenum*, and objections against a *vacuum;* but one of them must be true."

The very same Fallacy indeed is employed (as has been said) on the other side, by those who are for overthrowing whatever is established as soon as they can prove an objection against it; without considering whether more and weightier objections may not lie against their own schemes; but their opponents have this decided advantage over them, that they can urge with great plausibility, "we do not call upon you to *reject* at once whatever is objected to, but merely to *suspend your judgment,* and not come to a decision as long as there are reasons on both sides:" now since there always *will be* reasons on both sides, this *non*-decision is practically the very same thing as a *decision in favour of the*

* See Letters to Earl Grey on Transportation.

existing state of things. "Not to resolve, is to resolve."* The *delay* of trial becomes equivalent to an *acquittal*.†

§ 18.

Fallacy of proving a part of the question.

Another form of *ignoratio elenchi*, which is also rather the more serviceable on the side of the respondent, is, to prove or disprove *some part* of that which is required, and dwell on *that*, suppressing all the rest.

Thus, if a University is charged with cultivating *only* the mere elements of Mathematics, and in reply a list of the books studied there is produced, should even *any one* of those books be *not elementary*, the charge is in fairness refuted; but the Sophist may then earnestly contend that *some* of those books *are* elementary; and thus keep out of sight the real question, *viz.* whether they are *all* so.‡

So also, one may maintain (with perfect truth) that *mere* intellectual ability—the reasoning powers *alone*—are insufficient for the attainment of truth in religious questions; (see Appendix III. note) and may thence proceed to assume (as if it were the same proposition) that *all* employment of reasoning—all intellectual cultivation—are perfectly useless on such questions, and are to be discarded as foreign from the subject.

Art of framing a Reply.

This is the great art of the *answerer* of a book; suppose the main positions in any work to be irrefragable, it will be strange if some illustration of them, or some subordinate part, in short, will not admit of a plausible objection; the opponent then joins

* Bacon.

† How happy it is for mankind that in many of the most momentous concerns of life their decision is generally formed *for* them by external circumstances; which thus saves them not only from the perplexity of doubt and the danger of delay, but also from the pain of regret; since we acquiesce much more cheerfully in that which is unavoidable.

‡ "*Reply to calumnies of Edinb.* Review *against* Oxford," *1810.*

issue on one of these incidental questions, and comes forward with "a Reply" to such and such a work. And such a "Reply" is still easier and more plausible, when it happens—as it often will—that a real and satisfactory refutation can be found of some one, or more, of several arguments, each, singly, proving completely the same conclusion; (as many a theorem of Euclid admits of several different demonstrations) or an answer to one or more of several objections, each, separately, decisive against a certain scheme or theory; though it is evident on reflection, that if the rest, or any one of them, remain unrefuted and unanswerable, the conclusion is established, and stands as firm as if the answerer had urged nothing.

He who thus replies to the arguments urged, is in the condition of a commander defending all the practicable breaches in a fortification, *except one.* This kind of partial "reply" is properly available only in a case where each of the arguments does not go to establish the *certainty*, but only the *probability*, of the conclusion. *Then* indeed, the conclusion resting not wholly on the force of any *one* of the arguments, but on the *combination* of them, is proportionably weakened by the refutation of any of them. The fallacy I am now speaking of consists in the confounding of the preceding case either with this latter, or with the case formerly noticed [§ 14] of a *chain* of arguments, each proving, not, the *same* conclusion, but a premiss of the succeeding.

Danger of maintaining too much.

Hence the danger of ever advancing more than can be well maintained, since the refutation of *that* will often quash the whole. The Quakers would perhaps before now have succeeded in doing away our superfluous and irreverent oaths, if they had not, besides many valid and strong arguments, adduced so many that are weak and easily refuted. Thus also, a guilty person may often escape by having too much laid to his charge; so he may also, by having too much evidence against him, *i. e.* some that is not in itself satisfactory. Accordingly, a prisoner may sometimes obtain acquittal by showing that one of the witnesses against him is an infamous informer and spy; though perhaps if that part of the evidence had been omitted, the rest would have been sufficient for conviction.

Cases of this nature might very well be referred also to the Fallacy formerly mentioned, of inferring the Falsity of the Conclusion from the Falsity of a Premiss; which indeed is very closely allied to the present Fallacy: the real question is, "whether or not this Conclusion *ought to be admitted*;" the Sophist confines himself to the question, "whether or not it is *established by this particular argument*;" leaving it to be inferred by the audience, if he has carried his point as to the latter question, that the former is thereby decided; which is then, and then only, a correct inference, when there is good reason for believing that other and better arguments would have been adduced, if there had been any. (See above, at the end of § 6.)

§ 19.

Suppressed Conclusion.

It will readily be perceived that nothing is less conducive to the success of the Fallacy in question, than to state clearly, in the outset, either the proposition you are about to prove, or that which you ought to prove. It answers best to *begin* with the *Premises*, and to introduce a pretty long chain of argument before you arrive at the Conclusion. The careless hearer takes for granted, at the beginning, that this chain will lead to the Conclusion required; and by the time you are come to the end, he is ready to take for granted that the Conclusion which you draw *is* the one required; his idea of the question having gradually become indistinct. This Fallacy is greatly aided by the common practice of suppressing the Conclusion and leaving it to be supplied by the hearer;

who is of course less likely to perceive whether it be really that "which was to be proved," than if it were distinctly stated. The practice therefore is at best suspicious; and it is better in general to avoid it, and to give and require a distinct statement of the Conclusion intended.

The Fallacy now before us is, perhaps, the most common form of that confusion of thought to which those are liable who have been irregularly and unskilfully educated;—who have collected perhaps a considerable amount of knowledge, without arrangement, and without cultivation of logical habits;—who have learned (as I have heard it expressed) a good many *answers* without the *questions*. Most of the erroneous views in Morals, and in other subjects, which prevail among such persons, may be exhibited in the form of "Fallacies of Irrelevant-conclusion."* *E. G.* The well-known wrong decision respecting the two boys and their coats, for which Cyrus was punished by his preceptor, was a mistake of the real question: which was, not, "which coat *fitted* each boy the best," but "who had the *right* to dispose of them." And similar cases to this occur every day. An exact parallel is to be found in the questions relative to the imposition of restrictions or other penalties on those of a different creed from our own. They are usually argued as if the point to be decided were "which

* "The fallacy consists in confounding together the unbroken Apostolical succession of a *christian Ministry, generally*, and the same succession in an unbroken line, of *this or that individual Minister.* * * * * * * If each man's christian hope is made to rest on his receiving the christian Ordinances at the hands of a Minister to whom the sacramental virtue" [of ordination] "that gives efficacy to those ordinances, has been transmitted in unbroken succession from hand to hand, everything must depend on *that particular* Minister; and *his* claim is by no means established from our merely establishing the uninterrupted existence of *such a class of men as christian Ministers.* You teach me,—a man might say,—that my salvation depends on the possession by *you*—the *particular* Pastor under whom I am placed—of a certain qualification; and when I ask for the proof that you possess it, you prove to me that it is possessed *generally*, by a *certain class* of persons of whom you are one, and probably by a large majority of them!"—*On the Kingdom of Christ*, Essay II. § 30.

religion is the better," or, "whether the differences between them are important;" instead of being, "whether one man has a right to compel others to profess his religion," or, "whether the professors of the true Faith have a right to monopolize secular power and civil privileges." Or again (to put the same principles into another form) the questions "whether it be allowable for a Christian to fight in defending himself from oppression and outrage,"* and "whether a Christian magistrate may employ physical coercion and inflict secular punishment on evil-doers,"—these, are perpetually confounded with the questions "whether Christians are allowed to fight AS SUCH; *i. e.* to fight *for* their Religion, against those who corrupt or reject the Faith;" and, "whether a Christian magistrate may employ *coercion on behalf of* Christianity, and inflict *punishment on Heretics* as evil-doers."†

Again, such propositions as the following, one may often hear, sophistically or negligently, confounded together: "The Apostles *held religious assemblies* on the first day of the week," with "They *transferred the Sabbath* from the seventh day to the first:"‡ "A Jew, Mahometan, or Roman Catholic, is not the *most eligible person* to hold Office in a Protestant-christian country," with "Such persons ought not to be *legally eligible*:" "The Apostles *established* such and such a form of government in the Churches they founded," with "They designed this form to be binding on all Christians as *an Ordinance for ever*," &c.§

§ 20.

Jests. Before we dismiss the subject of Fallacies, it may not be improper to mention the just and ingenious remark, that *Jests* are mock-Fallacies; *i. e.*

* See Essay 1st, on the Kingdom of Christ.

† See Essays on the Dangers, &c. Notes E. and F.

‡ See Thoughts on the Sabbath.

§ See Kingdom of Christ, Essay II. § 9.

Fallacies so palpable as not to be likely to deceive any one, but yet bearing just that resemblance of Argument which is calculated to amuse by the contrast; in the same manner that a parody does, by the contrast of its levity with the serious production which it imitates. There is indeed something laughable even in Fallacies which are intended for serious conviction, when they are thoroughly exposed.*

There are several different kinds of joke and raillery, which will be found to correspond with the different kinds of Fallacy. The Pun (to take the simplest and most obvious case) is evidently, in most instances, a mock-argument founded on a palpable equivocation of the Middle-Term: and others in like manner will be found to correspond to the respective Fallacies, and to be *imitations* of serious argument.

It is probable indeed that all jests, sports, or games (παιδιαὶ) properly so called, will be found, on examination, to be *imitative* of serious transactions; as of War, or Commerce.† But to enter fully into this subject would be unsuitable to the present occasion.

I shall subjoin some general remarks on the legitimate province of Reasoning, and on its connexion with Inductive philosophy, and with Rhetoric; on which points much misapprehension has prevailed, tending to throw obscurity over the design and use of the Science under consideration.

A treatise on what are called the "laws of evidence"—the different *kinds*, strictly speaking, of arguments—and the occasions for which they are respectively suited, &c., which is what some would expect in a Logical Work, will be found in the 1st part of the "Elements of Rhetoric."

* See Wallis's Logic, and also Rhetoric, Part I. Ch. iii. § 7, p. 131.

† See some excellent remarks on "Imitation," in Dr. A. Smith's posthumous Essays.

BOOK IV.

DISSERTATION ON THE PROVINCE OF REASONING.

Logic being concerned with the theory of Reasoning, it is evidently necessary, in order to take a correct view of this Science, that all misapprehensions should be removed relative to the occasions on which the Reasoning-process is employed,—the purposes it has in view,—and the limits within which it is confined.

Simple and obvious as such questions may appear to those who have not thought much on the subject, they will appear on further consideration to be involved in much perplexity and obscurity, from the vague and inaccurate language of many popular writers. To the confused and incorrect notions that prevail respecting the Reasoning-process may be traced most of the common mistakes respecting the Science of Logic, and much of the unsound and unphilosophical argumentation which is so often to be met with in the works of ingenious writers.

These errors have been incidentally adverted to in the foregoing part of this work; but it may be desirable, before we dismiss the subject, to offer on these points some further remarks, which could not have been there introduced without too great an interruption to the development of the system. Little or nothing indeed remains to be said that is not *implied* in the principles which have been already laid down; but the results and applications of those principles are liable in many instances to be overlooked, if not distinctly pointed out. These supplementary observations will neither require, nor admit of, so systematic an arrangement as has hitherto been aimed at; since they will be such as are suggested principally by the objections and mistakes of those who have misunderstood, partially or entirely, the nature of the Logical system.

Let it be observed, however, that as I am not writing a review or commentary on any logical works, but an introduction to the science, I shall not deem it necessary to point out in all cases the agreement or disagreement between other writers and myself, in respect of the views maintained, or the terms employed, by each.

CHAP. I.—*Of Induction.*

§ 1.

Mistake of opposing Induction to Syllogism.

MUCH has been said by some writers of the superiority of the Inductive to the Syllogistic method of seeking truth; as if the two stood opposed to each other; and of the advantage of substituting the Organon of Bacon for that of Aristotle, *&c.* which indicates a total misconception of the nature of both. There is, however, the more excuse for the confusion of thought which prevails on this subject, because eminent Logical writers have treated, or at least have appeared to treat, of Induction as a kind of Argument distinct from the Syllogism; which if it were, it certainly might be contrasted with the Syllogism: or rather, the whole Syllogistic theory would fall to the ground, since one of the very first principles it establishes, is that *all* Reasoning, on whatever subject, is one and the same process, which may be clearly exhibited in the form of Syllogisms. It is hardly to be supposed, therefore, that this was the deliberate meaning of those writers; though it must be admitted that they have countenanced the error in question, by their inaccurate expressions.

Two senses of the word Induction.

This inaccuracy seems chiefly to have arisen from a vagueness in the use of the word Induction; which is sometimes employed to designate the process of *investigation* and of collecting facts; sometimes, the deducing of an inference *from* those facts. The former of these processes (*viz.* that of observation and experiment) is undoubtedly *distinct* from that which takes place in the Syllogism; but then it is not a process of *argumentation;* the latter again *is* an argumentative process; but then it is, like all other arguments, capable of being Syllogistically expressed. And hence Induction has come to be regarded as a *distinct* kind of *argument* from the Syllogism. This Fallacy cannot be more concisely or clearly stated, than in the technical form with which we may now presume our readers to be familiar.

> "Induction is distinct from Syllogism:
> Induction is a process of Reasoning;" therefore
> "There is a process of Reasoning distinct from Syllogism."

Here "Induction," which is the Middle-Term, is used in different senses in the two Premises.

Induction, so far forth as it is an *argument,* may, of course, be stated Syllogistically: but so far forth as it is a *process of inquiry* with a view to obtain the Premises of that argument, it is, of course, out of the province of Logic: and the latter is the original and strict sense of the word. Induction means properly, not the inferring of the conclusion, but the *bringing in,* one by one, of instances, bearing on the point in question, till a sufficient number has been collected. The ambiguity therefore, above alluded to, and which has led to much confusion, would be best avoided by saying that we do not, strictly speaking, reason *by* Induction, but reason *from* Induction: *i. e.* *from* our observations on one, or on several Individuals, (ἐκ τῶν καθ' ἕκαστον) we draw a conclusion respecting the Class (τὸ κάθολου) they come under: or, in like manner, from several Species, to the Genus which comprehends them:—in logical language, what we have predicated of certain *singular*-terms, we proceed to predicate of a *common*-term which comprehends them;—or proceed in the same manner from Species to Genus. *E.G.* "The Earth moves round the Sun in an elliptical orbit; so does Mercury; and Venus; and Mars, *&c.*: therefore a *Planet* (the common-term comprehending these singulars) moves round," *&c.* "Philip was reckless of human life; so was Alexander; and J. Cæsar; and Augustus, *&c.*: therefore this is the general character of a *Conqueror*."

Proper sense of Induction.

Now it appears as if the most obvious and simplest way of filling up such enthymemes as these, expressed as they are, would be, in the *third* figure; having of course a *particular* Conclusion:

" Earth, Mercury, Venus, *&c.* move, *&c.*
Mi. These are planets; therefore
Some planets move, *&c.*"

Inductive Argument expressed in a Syllogism,

But when we argue from Induction we generally mean to infer more than a particular conclusion; and accordingly most logical writers present to us the argument in the form of a syllogism in *Barbara;* inserting, of course, a different minor premiss from the foregoing, *viz.*: the simple converse of it. And if I am allowed to assume, not merely that "Mercury, Venus, and whatever others I may have named, are Planets," but

in the first figure.

also, that "All Planets are these,"—that these are the *whole* of the individuals comprehended under the Term Planet,—I am, no doubt, authorized to draw a universal conclusion. But such an assumption would, in a very great majority of cases where Induction is employed, amount to a palpable falsehood, if understood literally. For it is but seldom that we find an instance of what Logicians call a "perfect-induction;" *viz.* where there is a complete enumeration of all the individuals, respecting which we assert collectively what we had before asserted separately; as "John is in England; and so is Thomas; and so is William; and all the sons of such a one are John, Thomas, and William; therefore all his sons are in England." Such cases, I say, seldom occur; and still more rarely can such an Induction (which Bacon characterizes as "res puerilis" *)—since it does not lead the mind from what is better-known to what is less-known —serve any important purpose.

Perfect-Induction.

But in such Inductions as are commonly employed, the assumption of such a minor-premiss as in the above-example, would be, as I have said, strictly speaking, a false assumption. And accordingly those logicians who state an argument from Induction in the above form, mean, I apprehend, that it is to be understood with a certain latitude; *i. e.* that, in such propositions as "all planets are Mercury, Venus, *&c.*" or "all Conquerors are Philip, Alexander, and Cæsar," they mean, (by a kind of logical fiction) to denote that "all Conquerors are *adequately represented* by Philip, Alexander, *&c.*"—that these individual persons or cases are a sufficient *sample,* in respect of the matter in question, of the Class they belong to.

* It may very well happen too, that (as in the example above) a certain circumstance may, in fact, belong to each individual of a certain class, and yet may have no connexion, except accidentally, with the *Class itself, as such;* i. e. with the *description* of it, and that which *constitutes* it a Class. (See Appen. II. Ex. 118.)

The Major premiss suppressed.

I think it clearer, therefore, to state simply and precisely what it is that we do mean to assert. And in doing this, we shall find that the expressed premiss of the enthymeme,—*viz.:* that which contains the statement respecting the individuals—is the *Minor;* and that it is the Major that is suppressed, as being in all cases substantially the same: *viz.* that *what belongs to the individual or individuals we have examined, belongs* (certainly, or probably, as the case may be) *to the whole class under which they come. E. G.* From finding on examination of several sheep, that they each ruminate, we conclude that the same is the case with the *whole Species* of sheep: and from finding on examination of the sheep, ox, deer, and other animals deficient in upper cutting-teeth, that they each ruminate, we conclude (with more or less certainty) that quadrupeds thus deficient are ruminants: the hearer readily supplying, in sense, the suppressed major premiss; *viz.* that "what belongs to the individual sheep we have examined, is likely to belong to the whole species;" *&c.*

Whether that which is properly called Induction (*viz.* the inquiry respecting the several individuals or species) be sufficiently ample, *i. e.* takes in a sufficient number of individual, or of specific cases,—whether the character of those cases has been correctly ascertained—and how far the individuals we have examined are *likely to resemble,* in this or that circumstance, *the rest* of the class, *&c. &c.,* are points that require indeed great judgment and caution; but this judgment and caution are not to be aided by Logic; because they are, in reality, employed in deciding whether or not it is fair and allowable to *lay down your Premises; i. e.* whether you are authorized or not, to assert, that "what is true of the individuals you have examined, is true of the whole class:" and that this or that *is* true of those individuals. Now, the rules of Logic have nothing to do with the truth or falsity of the Premises; except, of course, when they are the conclusions of former arguments; but merely teach us to decide, not, whether the Premises are *fairly laid down*, but whether the Conclusion *follows fairly from* the Premises or not.

Necessity of assuming a Major-Premiss.

It has however been urged that what are described as the Major-premises in drawing inferences from Inductions, are resolvable ultimately into an assertion of the "Uniformity of the laws of Nature," or some equivalent proposition; and that this is, itself, obtained by *Induction;* whence it is concluded that there must be at least *one* Induction—and that, the one on which all others depend—incapable of being exhibited in a Syllogistic form.

But it is evident, and is universally admitted, that in *every* case where an inference is drawn from Induction (unless that name is to be given to a mere random guess without any grounds at all) we must form a judgment that the instance or instances adduced are "*sufficient* to authorize the Conclusion;"—that it is "*allowable*" to take these instances as a sample warranting an inference respecting the whole Class. Now the expression of this judgment in words, is *the very Major-premiss* alluded to. To acknowledge this, therefore, is to acknowledge that all reasoning from Induction *without exception* does admit of being exhibited in a syllogistic form; and consequently that to speak of one Induction that does *not* admit of it, is a contradiction.

Whether the belief in the constancy of Nature's laws,—a belief of which no one can divest himself—be intuitive and a part of the constitution of the human mind, as some eminent metaphysicians hold, or acquired, and in what way acquired, is a question foreign to our present purpose. For *that*, it is sufficient to have pointed out that the necessity of assuming a universal Major-premiss, expressed or understood, in order to draw any legitimate inference from Induction, is virtually acknowledged even by those who endeavour to dispute it.

§ 2.

Assumption of Premises in Induction.

Whether then the Premiss may fairly be assumed, or not, is a point which cannot be decided without a competent knowledge of the *nature of the subject*. *E. G.* in most branches of Natural Philosophy, in which the circumstances that in any case affect the result, are usually far more clearly ascertained than in human affairs, a *single instance* is usually accounted a sufficient Induction; *e. g.* having once ascertained that an individual magnet will attract iron, we are authorized to conclude that this property is universal. In Meteorology, however, and some other branches of Natural-philosophy, in which less advancement has been made, a much more copious Induction would be required. And in respect of the affairs of human life, an inference from a single instance would hardly ever be deemed allowable.

But it is worth remarking, that in all cases alike, of reasoning from Induction, the greater or less degree of confidence we feel is always proportioned to the belief of our having more or less completely *ascertained all the circumstances* that bear upon the question. All men practically acknowledge this to hold good in all cases alike, physical or moral, by invariably attributing any *failure* in their anticipations in any case, to some ignorance or miscalculation respecting some circumstances connected with the case. (See Append. I. Art. "Impossible.")

In some subjects, however, there will usually be more of these circumstances difficult to be accurately ascertained, than in others; and the degree of certainty belonging to the Major-premiss, will vary accordingly. But universally, the *degree of evidence* for any proposition we set out with as a Premiss (whether the expressed or the suppressed one) is not to be learned from mere Logic, nor indeed from *any one distinct* Science; but is the province of whatever Science furnishes the subject-matter of your argument. None but a Politician can judge rightly of the degree of evidence of a proposition in Politics; a Naturalist, in Natural History, *&c.*

Investigation. *E. G.* from examination of many horned animals, as sheep, cows, *&c.*, a Naturalist finds that they have cloven feet; now his *skill as a Naturalist* is to be shown in judging whether these animals are likely to resemble in the form of their feet all other horned animals; and it is the exercise of this judgment, together with the examination of individuals, that constitutes what is usually meant by the *Inductive process;* which is that by which we gain, what are properly, *new truths;* and which is not connected with Logic; being not what is strictly called *Reasoning,* but *Investigation.* But when this major Premiss is granted him, and is combined with the minor, *viz.* that the animals he has examined have cloven feet, then he *draws the Conclusion logically; viz.* that "the feet of all horned animals are cloven."* Again, if from several times meeting with ill-luck on a Friday, any one concluded that Friday, universally, is an unlucky day, one would object to his *Induction;* and yet it would not be, as an *argument, illogical;* since the Conclusion *follows* fairly, *if* you *grant* his implied Premiss; *viz.* that the events which happened on those particular Fridays are such as must happen, or are especially likely to happen, on all Fridays: but we should object to his *laying down this* Premiss; and therefore should justly say that his *Induction* is faulty, though his *argument* is correct.

The more doubtful Premiss suppressed in Induction. And here it may be remarked, that the ordinary rule for fair argument, *viz.* that in an Enthymeme the suppressed Premiss should be always the one of whose truth *least doubt* can exist, is not observed in Induction: for the Premiss which is usually the more doubt-

* I have selected an Instance in which Induction is the *only* ground we have to rest on; no reason, that I know of, having ever been assigned that could have led us to conjecture this curious fact *à priori.*

ful of the two, is, in this case, the *major*; it being in many cases not quite certain that the individuals, respecting which some point has been ascertained, are to be fairly regarded as a sample of the whole class: and yet the major-Premiss is seldom expressed; for the reason just given, that it is easily understood; as being (*mutatis mutandis*) the *same* in every Induction.

What has been said of Induction will equally apply to Example; which differs from it only in having a *singular*, instead of a general, conclusion; and that, from a *single* case. *E. G.* in one of the instances above, if the conclusion had been drawn, not respecting conquerors in general, but respecting *this or that* conqueror, that he was not likely to be careful of human life, *each* of the cases adduced to prove this would have been called an Example. (See *Elements of Rhetoric*, Part I. ch. ii. § 6.)

Some have maintained that in employing an Example we proceed at once from one individual case to another, without the intervention of any universal premiss. But whether we are fairly *authorized* or not to draw an inference from any example, must depend on what is called the PARALLELISM of the two cases; *i. e.* their being likely to agree in respect of the point in question: and the assertion, in words, of this parallelism, is a *universal proposition*. He who has in his mind this proposition, has virtually asserted such a major-premiss as I have been speaking of: and he who has it not, if he should be right in the inference itself that he draws, is, confessedly, right only by chance.

Chap. II.—*On the Discovery of Truth.*

§ 1.

Whether it is by a process of Reasoning that New Truths are brought to light, is a question which seems to be decided in the negative by what has been already said; though many eminent writers seem to have taken for granted the affirmative. It is, perhaps, in a great measure, a dispute concerning the use of words; but it is not, for that reason, either uninteresting or unimportant; since an inaccurate use of language may often, in matters of Science, lead to confusion of thought, and to erroneous conclusions. And, in the present instance, much of the undeserved contempt which has been bestowed on the Logical system may be traced to this source. For when any one has laid down, that "Reasoning is important in the discovery of Truth," and that "Logic is of no service in the discovery of Truth," (each of which propositions is true in a certain sense of the terms employed, but not in the *same* sense) he is naturally led to conclude, that there are processes of Reasoning to which the Syllogistic theory does not apply; and, of course, to misconceive altogether the nature of the Science.

Different uses of the words "discovery" and "new" as applied to truths.

In maintaining the negative side of the above question, three things are to be premised: first, that it is not contended that discoveries of any kind of Truth beyond what actually falls under the senses, can be made (or at least are usually made) *without* Reasoning; only, that Reasoning is not the *whole* of the process, nor the whole of that which is important therein; secondly, that Reasoning shall be taken in the sense, not of *every* exercise of the Reason, but of *Argumentation*, in which we have all along used it, and in which it has been defined by all the Logical writers, *viz.* "from certain granted propositions to infer another proposition as the consequence of them:" thirdly, that by a "New Truth," be understood, something neither expressly nor virtually asserted before,—not implied [involved] in anything already known.

To prove, then, this point demonstratively, becomes, on these data, perfectly easy; for since all Reasoning (in the sense above defined) may be resolved into Syllogisms; and since even the objectors to Logic make it a subject of complaint, that in a Syllogism the Premises do virtually assert the Conclusion, it follows at once that no New Truth (as above defined) can be elicited by any process of Reasoning.

It is on this ground, indeed, that the justly-celebrated author of the *Philosophy of Rhetoric*, and many others, have objected to the Syllogism altogether, as necessarily involving a *petitio principii;* an objection which, of course, he would not have been disposed to bring forward, had he perceived that, whether well or ill-founded, *it lies against all arguments whatever.* Had he been aware that a Syllogism is no distinct kind of argument otherwise than in form, but is, in fact, *any* argument whatever,* stated regularly and at full length, he would have obtained a more correct view of the object of all Reasoning; which is merely to expand and unfold the assertions wrapt up, as it were, and implied in those with which we set out, and to bring a person to perceive and acknowledge the full force of that which he has admitted;—to contemplate it in various points of view;—to admit in one shape what he has already admitted in another,—and to give up and disallow whatever is inconsistent with it.

Development of the meaning of a term.

Nor is it always a very easy task to bring before the mind the several bearings,—the various applications,—of even any one proposition. A common Term comprehends an indefinite—sometimes a very great—number of individuals,

* Which Dugald Stewart admits, though he adopts Campbell's objection.

and often of Classes; and these, often, in some respects, widely differing from each other: and no one can be, on each occasion of his employing such a Term, attending to and fixing his mind on each of the Individuals, or even of the Species, so comprehended. It is to be remembered, too, that both Division and Generalization are in a great degree arbitrary; *i. e.* that we may both divide the same genus on several different principles, and may refer the same individuals or species to several different classes, according to the nature of the discourse and drift of the argument; each of which classes will furnish a distinct Middle-Term for an argument, according to the question. *E. G.* If we wished to prove that "a horse feels," (to adopt an ill-chosen example from the above writer,) we might refer it to the genus "animal;" to prove that "it has only a single stomach," to the genus of "non-ruminants;" to prove that it is "likely to degenerate in a very cold climate," we should class it with "original productions of a hot climate," *&c. &c.* Now, each of these, and numberless others to which the same thing might be referred, are implied by the very term, "horse;" yet it cannot be expected that they can all be at once present to the mind whenever that term is uttered. Much less, when, instead of such a Term as that, we are employing Terms of a very abstract and, perhaps, complex signification,* as "government, justice," *&c.*

When then we say "Every Y is Z, and X is Y," there may be an indefinite, and perhaps a great number of other terms of which "Z" might be affirmed; but we fix our minds on one, *viz.* "Y;" of which again an indefinite number of other predicates besides "Z" might be affirmed; and then again out of an indefinite number of things of which "Y" might be affirmed, we fix on "X;" thus bringing before the mind,—where it is needful to express both premises,—what must in every case be assumed,—whether

* On this point there are some valuable remarks in the *Philosophy of Rhetoric* itself, Book IV. Chap. vii.

stated in words, or understood—in order to draw the Conclusion. And usually this process has to be repeated for the proof of one or both of the premises; and perhaps again, for the premises by which *they* are proved; *&c.*

But one cause which has led the above-mentioned writers into their error, is, their selecting examples (such as, it must be owned, are abundant in Logical treatises) in which the Conclusion is merely a portion of what one of the Premises by itself has already implied in the very *signification* of the term that is taken as its Subject, so plainly as to be present to the mind of every one who utters it: as, in the above example, the very term "horse" implies ["connotes"] "animal" to every one who utters those words and understands their meaning.* And hence it is that some writers not destitute of intelligence have been led to imagine that in Reasoning we draw a Conclusion from a single Premiss.

Evil consequence of selecting trifling examples.

But suppose, instead of such an example as Campbell, &c. fix on, we take that of the inference drawn by some Naturalist respecting a fossil-animal, which he concludes to be a "ruminant" from its having horns on the skull. The labourers perhaps who dug up the remains, may be ignorant that "all horned animals are ruminant;" and a naturalist again who is not on the spot, and has heard but an imperfect account of the skeleton, may be ignorant that "this animal was horned." Now neither of these parties could arrive at the conclusion that "it was a ruminant." But when the two premises are *combined*, they do, *jointly* imply and *virtually assert* the conclusion; though, separately, neither of them does so.

Syllogism represented as a snare.

And hence a Syllogism has been represented (even by those who acknowledge that all sound Reasoning may be exhibited in that form) as a contrivance for ensnaring men in a

* See Book II. Chap. v. § 1.

trap from which they cannot afterwards escape. But a man *can* escape admitting the *truth* of a conclusion: he may perceive its falsity; and may thus be taught the falsity of one of the Premises. But in a case where *neither* of these alternatives is necessary—where, after admitting the whole of what is assumed to be certain or probable, you are left free to admit or deny what is inferred, and have no more knowledge of its certainty or of its probability than you had before,—*this*, every one would perceive to be no real, but only an *apparent* argument.

But, as I have said, the flat truisms commonly given as examples by logical writers, have led those who have not carefully analysed the reasoning-process generally, into the notion that a Syllogism is necessarily of that trifling character. He who has asserted that the two items of a certain account are 3 and 2, has virtually asserted that the sum-total is 5: and of *this* few would need even to be *reminded:* but it is equally certain that he who has stated the items when they amount to some hundreds, has virtually asserted that the sum-total is so and so; and yet the readiest accountant requires, in this case, some time to bring these items together before his mind.

A Subject concerning which something is to be proved, is referred, as has been above remarked, to this or to that Class, according to what it is that is to be proved.

Categories. The Categories* or Predicaments, which Aristotle and other Logical writers have

* The Categories enumerated by Aristotle, are *οὐσία, πόσον, ποῖον, πρόστι, ποῦ, πότε, κεῖσθαι, ἔχειν, ποιεῖν, πάσχειν*; which are usually rendered, as adequately as, perhaps, they can be in our language, Substance, Quantity, Quality, Relation, Place, Time, Situation, Possession, Action, Suffering. The Catalogue (which certainly is but a very crude one) has been by some writers enlarged, as it is evident may easily be done by subdividing some of the heads; and by others curtailed, as it is no less evident that all may ultimately be referred to the two heads of *Substance*, and *Attribute*, or (in the language of some Logicians) *Accident*.

treated of, being certain general-heads or *summa genera*, to one or more of which every Term may be referred, serve the purpose of marking out certain tracks, as it were, which are to be pursued in searching for middle Terms, in each argument respectively; it being essential that we should generalize on a right principle, with a view to the question before us; or, in other words, that we should abstract that portion of any object presented to the mind, which is important to the argument in hand. There are expressions in common use which have a reference to this caution: such as, "this is a question, not as to the nature of the object, but the *magnitude* of it:" "this is a question of *time*, or of *place*," *&c.*, *i. e.* "the subject must be referred to this or to that Category."

With respect to the meaning of the Terms in question, "Discovery," and "New Truth;" it matters not whether we confine ourselves to the narrowest sense, or admit the widest, provided we do but *distinguish*. There certainly *are* two kinds of "New Truth" and of "Discovery," if we take those words in the widest sense in which they are ever used. First, such Truths as were, before they were discovered, *absolutely* unknown, being not implied by anything we previously knew, though we might perhaps suspect them as probable. Such are all *matters of fact* strictly so called, when first made known to one who had not any such previous knowledge, as would enable him to ascertain them *à priori; i. e.* by Reasoning; as if we inform a man that we have a colony in New-South-Wales; or that the Earth is at such a distance from the sun; or that platina is heavier than gold. The communication of this kind of knowledge is most usually, and most strictly, called *information*. We gain it from *observation*, and from *testimony*. No *mere internal workings* of our own minds (except when the mind itself is the very object to be observed), or *mere* discussions in words, will make a fact known to us;

Two kinds of Discovery.

Information.

though there is great room for sagacity *in judging what testimony to admit*, and in the forming of *conjectures* that may *lead* to *profitable observation*, and to experiments with a view to it.

Instruction. The other class of Discoveries is of a very different nature. That which may be elicited by Reasoning, and consequently is implied in that which we already know, we assent to on that ground, and not from observation or testimony. To take a Geometrical truth upon *trust*, or to attempt to ascertain it by *observation*, would betray a total ignorance of the nature of the Science. In the longest demonstration, the Mathematical teacher seems only to lead us to make use of our own stores, and point out to us how much we had already admitted; and, in the case of many Ethical propositions, we assent at first hearing, though perhaps we had never heard or thought of the proposition before. So also do we readily *assent* to the *testimony* of a respectable man who tells us that our troops have gained a victory; but how different is the nature of the assent in the two cases. In the latter we are disposed to *thank* the man for his information, as being such as no wisdom or learning would have enabled us to ascertain; in the former, we usually exclaim "*very true!*" "that is a valuable and just remark; that never *struck* me before!" implying at once our practical ignorance of it, and also our consciousness that we possess, in what we already know, the means to ascertain the truth of it; that we have a right, in short, to bear *our testimony* to its truth.

To all practical purposes, indeed, a Truth of this description may be as completely unknown to a man as the other; but as soon as it is set before him, and the argument by which it is connected with his previous notions is made clear to him, he *recognizes* it as something conformable to, and contained in, his former belief.

Plato's theory. It is not improbable that Plato's doctrine of Reminiscence arose from a hasty extension of what he had observed in this class, to all acquisition of knowledge whatever. His Theory of ideas served to confound together *matters of fact* respecting the nature of things, (which may be perfectly new to us) with propositions *relating to our own notions*, and modes of thought; (or to speak, perhaps, more correctly, our own arbitrary Signs) which propositions must be contained and implied in those very complex notions themselves; and whose truth is a conformity, not to the nature of things, but to our own hypothesis. Such are all propositions in pure Mathematics, and many in Ethics, *viz.* those which involve no assertion as to real matters of fact. It has been rightly remarked,* that Mathematical propositions are not properly true or false, in the same sense as any proposition respecting real fact is so called. And hence, the truth (such as it is) of such propositions is necessary and eternal; since it amounts only to a *conformity* with *the hypothesis* we set out with. The proposition, that "the belief in a future state, combined with a complete devotion to the present life, is not consistent with the character of prudence," would be not at all the less true if a future state were a chimera, and prudence a quality which was nowhere met with; nor would the truth of the Mathematician's conclusion be shaken, that "circles are to each other as the squares of their diameters," should it be found that there never had been a circle, or a square, conformable to the definition, in *rerum naturæ*.

And accordingly an able man, may, by patient Reasoning, attain any amount of mathematical truths; because these are all implied in the Definitions. But no degree of labour and ability, would give him the knowledge, by "*Reasoning*" *alone*, of what has taken place in some foreign country; nor would enable him to know, if he had never seen, or heard of, the experiments, what would become of a spoonful of salt, or a spoonful of chalk, if put into water,

* Dugald Stewart's Philosophy, Vol. II.

or what would be the appearance of a ray of light when passed through a prism.

Facts, not demonstrable.

Hence the futility of the attempt of Clarke, and others, to *demonstrate* (in the mathematical sense) the existence of a Deity. This can only be (apparently) done by covertly assuming in the Premises the very point to be proved. No *matter of fact* can be mathematically demonstrated; though it may be proved in such a manner as to leave no doubt on the mind. *E.G.* I have no more doubt that I met such and such a man, in this or that place, yesterday, than that the angles of a triangle are equal to two right angles: but the *kind* of certainty I have of these two truths is widely different; to say, that I did *not* meet the man, would be false indeed, but it would not be anything *inconceivable, self-contradictory,* and *absurd;* but it would be so, to deny the equality of the angles of a triangle to two right angles.

Information and instruction, distinct.

It is of the utmost importance to distinguish these two kinds of Discovery of Truth. In relation to the former, as I have said, the word "*information*" is most strictly applied; the communication of the latter is more properly called "*instruction*." I speak of the *usual* practice; for it would be going too far to pretend that writers are uniform and consistent in the use of these, or of any other term. We say that the Historian gives us *information* respecting past times; the Traveller, respecting foreign countries: on the other hand, the Mathematician gives *instruction* in the principles of his Science; the Moralist *instructs* us in our duties, &c. However, let the words be used as they may, the things are evidently different, and ought to be distinguished. It is a question comparatively unimportant, whether the term "Discovery" shall or shall not be extended to the eliciting of those Truths, which, being implied in our previous knowledge, may be established by mere strict Reasoning.

Similar verbal questions, indeed, might be raised respecting many other cases: *e. g.* one has forgotten (*i. e.* cannot *recollect*) the name of some person or place; perhaps we even try to think of it, but in vain; at last some one reminds us, and we instantly *recognize* it as the one we wanted to recollect: it may be asked, was this in our mind, or not? The answer is, that in one sense it was, and in another sense, it was not. Or, again, suppose there is a vein of metal on a man's estate, which he does not know of; is it part of his possessions or not? and when he finds it out and works it, does he then *acquire* a *new* possession or not? Certainly not, in the same sense as if he has a fresh estate bequeathed to him, which he had formerly no *right* to; but to all practical purposes it *is* a new possession. This case, indeed, may serve as an illustration of the one we have been considering; and in all these cases, if the real distinction be understood, the verbal question will not be of much consequence.

To use one more illustration. Reasoning has been aptly compared to the piling together blocks of stone; on each of which, as on a pedestal, a man can raise himself a small, and but a small height above the plain; but which, when skilfully built up, will form a flight of steps, which will raise him to a great elevation. Now (to pursue this analogy) when the materials are all ready to the builder's hand, the blocks ready dug and brought, his work resembles one of the two kinds of Discovery just mentioned, *viz.* that to which we have assigned the name of *instruction:* but if his materials are to be entirely, or in part, provided by himself,—if he himself is forced to dig fresh blocks from the quarry,—this corresponds to the other kind of Discovery.*

* "The fundamental differences between these two great branches of human knowledge, as well as their consequences, cannot perhaps be more strikingly illustrated than in the following familiar exposition by a celebrated writer. 'A clever man,' says Sir J. Herschel, 'shut up alone and allowed all unlimited time, might reason out for himself all the truths of mathematics,

§ 2.

Physical Discoveries. I have hitherto spoken of the employment of Argument in the establishment of those hypothetical Truths (as they may be called) which relate only to our own abstract notions. It is not, however, meant to be insinuated that there is no room for Reasoning in the establishment of a matter of fact: but the other class of Truths have first been treated of, because, in discussing subjects of that kind, the process of Reasoning is always the *principal*, and often the *only* thing to be attended to, if we are but certain and clear as to the meaning of the terms; whereas, when assertions respecting *real existence* are introduced, we have the additional and more important business of ascertaining and keeping in mind the *degree* of *evidence* for those facts; since, otherwise, our Conclusions could not be relied on, however accurate our Reasoning. But, undoubtedly, we may by Reasoning arrive at knowledge concerning matters of fact, *if* we have *facts to set out with as data;* only that it will very often happen that, "from certain facts," as Campbell remarks, "we draw only probable Conclusions;" because the other Premiss introduced (which he overlooked) is only probable. And the maxim of Mechanics holds good in arguments; that "nothing is stronger than its *weakest* part."

by proceeding from those simple notions of space and number of which he cannot divest himself without ceasing to think; but he would never tell by any effort of reasoning what would become of a lump of sugar, if immersed in water, or what impression would be produced on his eye by mixing the colours yellow and blue,' results which can be learnt only from experience.

"Thus then the extremes of human knowledge may be considered as founded on the one hand purely upon reason, and on the other purely upon sense. Now, a very large portion of our knowledge, and what in fact may be considered as the most important part of it, lies between these two extremes, and results from a union or mixture of them, that is to say, consists of the application of rational principles to the phenomena presented by the objects of nature."—*Prout's Bridgewater Treatise*, p. 2.

He observed that in such an instance, for example, as the one lately given, we infer from the *certainty* that such and such tyrannies have been short-lived, the *probability* that others will be so; and he did not consider that there is an understood Premiss which is essential to the argument; (*viz.* that "all tyrannies will resemble those we have already observed") which being only of a probable character, must attach the same degree of uncertainty to the Conclusion. And the doubtfulness is *multiplied,* if *both* Premises are uncertain. For since it is only on the supposition of *both* Premises being true, that we can calculate on the truth of the Conclusion, we must state in fractional numbers the chances of each Premiss being true, and then multiply these together, to judge of the degree of evidence of the Conclusion.*

An *individual* fact is not unfrequently elicited by skilfully combining, and reasoning from, those already known; of which many curious cases occur in the detection of criminals by officers of justice, and by Barristers, who acquire by practice such dexterity in that particular department, as to draw sometimes the right conclusion from data, which might be in the possession of others, without being applied to the same use. But in all cases of the inferring of a *general* law from Induction, that conclusion (as has been formerly remarked) is *ultimately* established by Reasoning. *E. G.* Bakewell, the celebrated cattle-breeder, observed, in a great number of individual beasts, a tendency to fatten readily; and in a great number of others, the absence of this constitution: in every individual of the former description, he *observed* a certain peculiar *make,* though they differed widely in size, colour, *&c.* Those of the latter description differed no less in various points, but agreed in being of a different make

General laws established by reasoning from Induction.

* See Book III. § 14.

from the others: these facts were his data; from which, combining them with the general principle, that Nature is steady and uniform in her proceedings, he *logically* drew the conclusion that beasts of the specified make have universally a peculiar tendency to fattening. But then his principal merit consisted in *making* the observations, and in so *combining* them as to *abstract* from each of a multitude of cases, differing widely in many respects, the circumstances in which they all agreed; and also in conjecturing skilfully how far those circumstances were likely to be found in the whole class. The making of such observations, and still more the combination, abstraction, and judgment employed,* are what men commonly mean (as was above observed) when they speak of *Induction;* and these operations are certainly distinct from Reasoning.† The same observations will apply to numberless other cases; as, for instance, to the Discovery of the law of "*vis inertiæ*," and the other principles of Natural Philosophy.

It may be remarked here, that even the most extensive observations of facts will often be worse than useless to those who are deficient in the power of discriminating and selecting. Their knowledge, whether much or little, is like food to a body whose digestive system is so much impaired as to be incapable of separating the nutritious portions. To attempt to remedy the defect of minds thus constituted "by imparting to them additional knowledge,—to confer the advantage of wider experience on those who have not the power of profiting by experience,—is to attempt enlarging the prospect of a short-sighted man by bringing him to the top of a hill."‡

But to what class, it may be asked, should be referred the Discoveries we have been speaking of? All would agree in calling them, when first ascertained, "New Truths,"

* See Polit. Econ. Lect. IX. p. 229—239.

† See Book I. § 1. *Note.*

‡ Polit. Econ. Lect. IX. p. 236.

in the strictest sense of the word; which would seem to imply their belonging to the class which may be called by way of distinction, "*Physical Discoveries:*" and yet their being ultimately established by Reasoning, would seem, according to the foregoing rule, to refer them to the other class, *viz.* what may be called "*Logical Discoveries;*" since whatever is established by Reasoning must have been contained and virtually asserted in the Premises. In answer to this, I would say, that they certainly do belong to the latter class, *relatively* to a person who is *in possession of the data:* but to him who is *not,* they are New Truths of the other class. For it is to be remembered, that the words "Discovery" and "New Truths" are necessarily *relative.* There may be a proposition which is to one person completely *known;* to another (*viz.* one to whom it has never *occurred,* though he is in possession of all the data from which it may be *proved*) it will be (when he comes to perceive it, by a process of *instruction*) what we have called a *Logical Discovery:* to a third (*viz.* one who is ignorant of these data) it will be absolutely *unknown,* and will have been, when made known to him, a perfectly and properly New Truth,—a piece of information,—a *Physical Discovery,* as we have called it.* To the Philosopher, therefore, who arrives at the Discovery by reasoning from his observations, and from established principles combined with them, the Discovery is of the former class; to the multitude, probably

Logical Discoveries.

* It may be worth while in this place to define what is properly to be called *Knowledge:* it implies three things; 1st, firm *belief,* 2dly, of what is *true,* 3dly, on sufficient *grounds.* If any one, *e.g.* is in *doubt* respecting one of Euclid's demonstrations, he cannot be said to *know* the proposition proved by it; if, again, he is fully *convinced* of anything that is not *true,* he is mistaken in supposing himself to know it; lastly, if two persons are each *fully confident,* one that the moon is inhabited, and the other that it is not, (though one of these opinions must be *true*) neither of them could properly be said to *know* the truth, since he cannot have sufficient *proof* of it.

of the latter; as *they* will have been most likely not possessed of all his data.

§ 3.

Character of scientific truths.

It follows from what has been said, that in pure Mathematics, and in such Ethical propositions as we were lately speaking of, we do not allow the possibility of *any* but a Logical Discovery: *i.e.* no proposition of that class can be true, which was not implied in the Definitions and Axioms we set out with, which are the first principles. For since the propositions do not profess to state any fact, the only truth they *can* possess, *consists* in conformity to the original principles. To one, therefore, who *knows* these principles, such propositions are Truths already implied; since they may be developed to him by Reasoning, if he is not defective in the discursive faculty; and again, to one who does *not* understand those principles (*i.e.* is not master of the Definitions) such propositions are, so far unmeaning. On the other hand, propositions relating to matters of fact, *may be*, indeed, implied in what he already knew; (as he who knows the climate of the Alps, the Andes, *&c. &c.* has virtually admitted the general fact, that "the tops of mountains are comparatively cold") but as these possess an absolute and physical Truth, they *may* also be absolutely "new," their Truth not being *implied in the mere terms of the propositions.* The truth or falsity of any proposition concerning a triangle, is implied by the meaning of that and of the other Geometrical terms; whereas, though one may *understand* (in the ordinary sense of that word) the full meaning of the terms "planet," and "inhabited," and of all the other terms in the language, he cannot thence derive any certainty that the planets are, or are not, inhabited.

As I have elsewhere observed, "Every branch of study, which can at all claim the character of a science (in the widest acceptation,) requires two things: 1. A correct *ascertainment of the data* from which we are to reason; and, 2. Correctness in the process of *deducing conclusions* from them. But these two processes, though both are in every case indispensable, are, in different cases, extremely different in their relative difficulty and amount;—in the space, if I may so speak, which they occupy in each branch of study. In pure Mathematics, for instance, we set out from arbitrary Definitions, and Postulates, readily comprehended, which are the principles from which, by the help of Axioms hardly needing even to be stated, our reasonings proceed. No facts whatever require to be ascertained; no process of induction to be carried on; the reasoning-process is nearly every thing. In Geology, (to take an instance of an opposite kind) the most extensive information is requisite; and though sound reasoning is called for in making use of the knowledge acquired, it is well known what erroneous systems have been devised, by powerful reasoners, who have satisfied themselves too soon with observations not sufficiently accurate and extensive.

"Various branches of Natural-philosophy occupy, in this respect, various intermediate places. The two processes which I have endeavoured to describe, under the titles of 'Physical investigation' and 'Logical investigation,' will, in different cases, differ very much in their relative importance and difficulty. The science of Optics, for instance, furnishes an example of one approaching very near to pure mathematics; since, though the foundation of it consists in facts ascertained by experiment, these are fewer and more easily ascertained than those pertaining to other branches of Natural-philosophy. A very small number of principles, comprehensible even without being verified by the senses, being assumed, the deductions from them are so extensive, that, as is well known, a blind mathematician, who had no remembrance of seeing, gave an approved course of lectures on the subject. In the *application*, however, of this science to the explanation of many of the curious natural phenomena that occur, a most extensive and exact knowledge of facts is called for.

"In the case of Political-Economy, that the facts on which the science is founded are few, and simple, and within the range of every one's observation, would, I think, never have been doubted, but for the error of confounding together the theoretical and the practical branches of it;—the *science* of what is properly called Political-Economy,—and the practical *employment* of it. The theory supplies principles, which we may afterwards apply practically to an indefinite number of various cases; and in order to make this application correctly, of course an accurate knowledge of the circumstances of each case is indispensable. But it should be remembered that the same may be said even with respect to Geometry. As soon as we come to the practical branch of it, and apply it in actual measurements, a minute attention to facts is requisite for an accurate result. And in each practical question in Political-Economy that may arise, we must be prepared to ascertain, and allow for, various disturbing causes, which may more or less modify the results obtained from our general principles; just as, in Mechanics, when we come to practice, we must take into account the thickness, and weight, and the degrees of flexibility, of ropes and levers.

"The facts then which it may be necessary to ascertain for the practical decision of any *single* case that may arise, are, of course, in Political-Economy (as in respect of the *application* of the principles of *any* science), indefinite in number, and sometimes difficult to collect; the facts on which the general principles of the science are *founded*, come within the range of every one's experience." *

* Polit. Econ. Lect. IX. p. 225.

§ 4.

Ambiguity of the word Reasoning.

When it is asked, then, whether such great Discoveries, as have been made in Natural Philosophy, were accomplished, or can be accomplished, by *Reasoning?* the inquirer should be reminded, that the question is ambiguous. It may be answered in the affirmative, if by "Reasoning" is meant to be included the *assumption of Premises.* To the right performance of *that* work, is requisite, not only, in many cases, the ascertainment of facts, and of the degree of evidence for doubtful propositions, (in which, observation and experiment will often be indispensable,) but also a skilful *selection* and *combination* of known facts and principles; such as implies, amongst other things, the exercise of that powerful *abstraction* which seizes the common circumstances—the point of agreement—in a number of, otherwise, dissimilar individuals; and it is in this that the greatest genius is shown. But if "Reasoning" be understood in the limited sense in which it is usually defined, then we must answer in the negative; and reply that such Discoveries are made by means of Reasoning *combined* with other operations.

In the process I have been speaking of, there *is* much Reasoning throughout; and thence the whole has been carelessly called a "process of Reasoning."

It is not, indeed, any just ground of complaint that the word Reasoning is *used in two senses;* but that the two senses are perpetually *confounded together:* and hence it is that some Logical writers fancied that Reasoning (*viz.* that which Logic treats of) was the method of discovering Truth; and that so many other writers have accordingly complained of Logic for not accomplishing that end; urging that "Syllogism" (*i. e.* Reasoning; though they overlooked the coincidence) never established any thing that is, strictly speaking, *unknown* to him who has granted the Premises: and proposing the introduction of a certain "rational Logic" to accomplish this purpose; *i.e.* to direct the mind in the process of investigation. Supposing that some such system could be devised—that it could even be brought into a scientific form, (which he must be more sanguine than scientific who expects,)—that it were of the greatest conceivable utility,—and that it should be allowed to bear the name of "Logic" (since it would not be worth while to contend about a name) still it would not, as these writers seem to suppose, have the same object proposed with the Aristotelian Logic; or be in any respect a rival to that system. A *plough* may be a much more ingenious and valuable instrument than a *flail;* but it never can be substituted for it.

New truths may be such in a different sense to different persons.

Those Discoveries of general laws of Nature, &c. of which we have been speaking, being of that character which we have described by the name of "Logical Discoveries," *to him who is in possession of all the Premises from which they are deduced;* but being, *to the multitude* (who are unacquainted with many of those Premises) strictly "New Truths," hence it is, that men in general give to the *general* facts, and to them, most peculiarly, the name of *Discoveries;* for to *themselves* they *are* such, in the strictest sense; the Premises from which they were inferred being not only originally unknown to them, but frequently *remaining unknown to the very last. E. G.* the general conclusion concerning cattle, which Bakewell made known, is what most Agriculturists (and many others also) are acquainted with; but the Premises he set out with, *viz.* the facts respecting this, that, and the other, individual ox, (the ascertainment of which facts was his first *Discovery,*) these are what few know, or care to know, with any exact particularity.

And it may be added, that these discoveries of particular

Observation and experiment.

facts, which are the *immediate* result of *observation*, are, in themselves, uninteresting and insignificant, *till* they are combined so as to lead to a grand general result. Those who on each occasion watched the motions, and registered the times of occultation, of Jupiter's satellites, little thought, perhaps, themselves, what important results they were preparing the way for.* So that there is an additional cause which has confined the term Discovery to these grand general conclusions; and, as was just observed, they are, to the generality of men, perfectly New Truths in the strictest sense of the word; not being implied in any previous knowledge *they* possessed. Very often it will happen, indeed, that the conclusion thus drawn will amount only to a *probable conjecture;* which conjecture will dictate to the inquirer such an *experiment*, or course of experiments, as will fully establish the fact. Thus Sir H. Davy, from finding that the flame of hydrogen gas was not communicated through a long slender tube, conjectured that a shorter but still slenderer tube would answer the same purpose; this led him to try the experiments, in which, by continually shortening the tube, and at the same time lessening its bore, he arrived at last at the wire-gauze of his safety-lamp.

It is to be observed also, that whatever *credit* is conveyed by the word "Discovery," to him who is regarded as the author of it, is well deserved by those who skilfully select and combine known Truths (*especially* such as have been *long* and *generally known*) so as to elicit important, and hitherto unthought-of, conclusions. Theirs is the master-mind: — ἀρχιτεκτονικὴ φρόνησις: whereas men of very inferior powers may sometimes, by immediate observation, discover perfectly new facts, empirically; and thus be of

* Hence, Bacon urges us to pursue *Truth*, without always requiring to perceive its practical application.

service in furnishing materials to the others; to whom they stand in the same relation (to recur to a former illustration) as the brickmaker or stonequarrier to the architect. It is peculiarly creditable to Adam Smith, and to Malthus, that the data from which they drew such important Conclusions had been in every one's hands for centuries.

As for Mathematical Discoveries, they (as we have before said) must *always* be of the description to which we have given the name of "Logical Discoveries;" since to him who properly comprehends the meaning of the Mathematical terms, (and to no other are the Truths themselves, properly speaking, intelligible) those results are implied in his previous knowledge, since they are logically deducible therefrom. It is not, however, meant to be implied, that Mathematical Discoveries are effected by pure Reasoning, and by that *singly*. For though there is not here, as in Physics, any exercise of judgment as to the degree of evidence of the Premises, nor any experiments and observations, yet there is the same call for skill in the *selection* and *combination* of the Premises in such a manner as shall be best calculated to lead to a new,—that is, *unperceived* and *unthought-of*—Conclusion.

In *following*, indeed, and *taking in* a demonstration, nothing is called for but pure Reasoning; but *the assumption of Premises is not a part* of Reasoning, in the strict and technical sense of that term. Accordingly, there are many who can *follow* a Mathematical demonstration, or any other train of argument, who would not succeed well in *framing* one of their own.*

§ 5.

Operations connected with Reasoning.

For both kinds of Discovery then, the Logical, as well as the Physical, certain operations are requisite, beyond those which can fairly be comprehended under the strict sense of the

* Hence, the Student must not confine himself to this passive kind of employment, if he will truly become a Mathematician.

word "Reasoning." In the Logical, is required a skilful *selection* and *combination of known Truths:* in the Physical, we must employ, in *addition* (generally speaking) to that process, *observation* and *experiment.* It will generally happen, that in the study of nature, and, universally, in all that relates to matters of fact, *both* kinds of investigation will be united: *i. e.* some of the facts or principles you *reason from* as Premises, must be ascertained by *observation;* or, as in the case of the safety-lamp, the ultimate *Conclusion* will need *confirmation* from experience; so that both Physical and Logical Discovery will take place in the course of the same process. We need not, therefore, wonder, that the two are so perpetually confounded. In Mathematics, on the other hand, and in great part of the discussions relating to Ethics and Jurisprudence, there being no room for any Physical Discovery whatever, we have only to make *a skilful use* of the propositions in our possession, to arrive at every attainable result.

The investigation, however, of the latter class of subjects differs in *other* points also from that of the former. For, setting aside the circumstance of our having, in these, no question as to *facts,*—no room for observation,—there is also a considerable difference in what may be called, in both instances, the process of *Logical investigation;* the *Premises* on which we proceed being of so different a nature in the two cases.

Mathematical and other Reasoning.

To take the example of Mathematics, the Definitions, which are the principles of our Reasoning, are very *few,* and the Axioms still fewer; and both are, for the most part, *laid down* and *placed before the student in the outset;* the introduction of a new Definition or Axiom, being of comparatively rare occurrence, at wide intervals, and with a *formal* statement; besides which, there is no room for *doubt* concerning either. On the other hand, in all Reasonings which regard matters of fact, we introduce, almost at *every step*, fresh and fresh propositions (to a very great number) which had not been elicited in the course of our Reasoning, but are taken for granted; *viz.* facts, and Laws of Nature, which are here the principles of our Reasoning, and *maxims*, or "elements of belief," which answer to the axioms in Mathematics. If, at the opening of a Treatise, for example, on Chemistry, on Agriculture, on Political-Economy, *&c.* the author should make, as in Mathematics, a formal statement of all the propositions he intended to assume as granted, throughout the whole work, both he and his readers would be astonished at the number; and, of these, many would be only probable, and there would be much room for doubt as to the *degree* of probability, and for judgment in ascertaining that degree.

Moreover, Mathematical axioms are always employed precisely *in the same simple form; e. g.* the axiom that "the things equal to the same are equal to one another," is cited, whenever there is need, in those very words; whereas the maxims employed in the other class of subjects, admit of, and require, continual modifications in the application of them. *E. G.* "the stability of the laws of Nature," which is our constant assumption in inquiries relating to Natural Philosophy, appears in many different shapes, and in some of them does not possess the same complete certainty as in others; *e. g.* when, from having always observed a certain sheep ruminating, we infer, that this individual sheep will continue to ruminate, we assume that "the property which has hitherto belonged to this sheep will remain unchanged;" when we infer the same property of all sheep, we assume that "the property which belongs to this individual belongs to the whole species:" if, on comparing sheep with some other kinds of horned animals,* and finding that all agree in ruminating, we infer

* *Viz.* having horns *on the skull.* What are called the horns of the Rhinoceros are quite different in origin, and in structure, as well as in situation, from what are properly called horns.

that "all horned animals ruminate," we assume that "the whole of a genus or class are likely to agree in any point wherein many species of that genus agree:" or in other words, "that if one of two properties, *&c.* has *often* been found accompanied by another, and never without it, the former will be *universally* accompanied by the latter:" now all these are merely different forms of the maxim, that "nature is uniform in her operations," which, it is evident, varies in expression in almost every different case where it is applied, and the application of which admits of every degree of evidence, from perfect moral certainty, to mere conjecture.*

The same may be said of an infinite number of principles and maxims appropriated to, and employed in, each particular branch of study. Hence, all such reasonings are, in comparison of Mathematics, very complex; requiring so much *more* than that does, beyond the process of merely deducing the conclusion logically from the premises: so that it is no wonder that the longest Mathematical demonstration should be so much more easily constructed and understood, than a much shorter train of just reasoning concerning real facts. The former has been aptly compared to a long and steep, but even and regular, flight of steps, which tries the breath, and the strength, and the perseverance only; while the latter resembles a short, but rugged and uneven, ascent up a precipice, which requires a quick eye, agile limbs, and a firm step; and in which we have to tread now on this side, now on that—ever considering, as we proceed, whether this or that projection will afford room for our foot, or whether some loose stone may not slide from under us. There are probably as many steps of pure reasoning in one of the longer of Euclid's demonstrations, as in the whole of an argumentative treatise on some other subject, occupying perhaps a considerable volume.

* See Append. Art. "Impossible."

Mathematics useful as an introductory praxis of Reasoning.

It may be observed here that Mathematical Reasoning, as it calls for no exercise of judgment respecting probabilities, is the best kind of introductory exercise; and, from the same cause, is apt, when too exclusively pursued, to make men incorrect moral-reasoners.

As for those Ethical and Legal Reasonings which were lately mentioned as in some respects resembling those of Mathematics, (*viz.* such as keep clear of all assertions respecting facts) they have this difference; that not only men are not so completely *agreed* respecting the maxims and principles of Ethics and Law, but the meaning also of each Term cannot be absolutely, and for ever, fixed by an arbitrary definition; on the contrary, a great part of our labour consists in distinguishing accurately the various senses in which men employ each Term,—ascertaining which is the most proper,—and taking care to avoid confounding them together.*

Fallacious disparagement of reasoning.

It may be worth while to add in this place that as a candid disposition,—a hearty desire to judge fairly, and to attain truth,—are evidently necessary with a view to give fair play to the reasoning-powers, in subjects where we are liable to a bias from interest or feelings, so, a fallacious perversion of this maxim finds a place in the minds of some persons: who accordingly speak disparagingly of *all* exercise of the reasoning-faculty in moral and religious subjects; declaiming on the insufficiency of *mere* intellectual power for the attainment of truth in such matters,—on the necessity of appealing to the heart rather than to the head, &c.† and then leading their readers or themselves to the Conclusion that the less we *reason* on such subjects the safer we are.

* See Appendix on Ambiguous Terms.

† See Appendix III.

Proper office of candour.

But the proper office of candour is to *prepare* the mind not for the *rejection* of all evidence, but for the right *reception* of evidence;—not, to be a *substitute* for reasons, but to enable us *fairly to weigh* the reasons on both sides. Such persons as I am alluding to are in fact saying that since just weights *alone*, without a just balance, will avail nothing, therefore we have only to take care of the scales, and let the weights take care of themselves.

This kind of tone is of course most especially to be found in such writers as consider it expedient to inculcate on the mass of mankind what—there is reason to suspect—they do not themselves fully believe, and which they apprehend is the more likely to be rejected the more it is investigated.*

CHAP. III.—*Of Inference and Proof.*

§ 1.

SINCE it appears, from what has been said, that universally a man must possess something else besides the Reasoning-faculty, in order *to apply* that faculty properly to his own purpose, whatever that purpose may be; it may be inquired whether some theory could not be made out, respecting those "*other operations*" and "intellectual processes, distinct from Reasoning, which it is necessary for us sometimes to employ in the investigation of truth;"† and whether rules could not be laid down for conducting them.

Different applications of Reasoning.

Something has, indeed, been done in this way by more than one writer; and more might probably be accomplished by one who should fully comprehend and carefully bear in mind

* See Powell's "Tradition unveiled."

† D. Stewart.

the principles of Logic, properly so called; but it would hardly be possible to build up anything like a regular *Science* respecting these matters, such as Logic is with respect to the theory of Reasoning. It may be useful, however, to observe, that these "*other operations*" of which we have been speaking, and which are preparatory to the exercise of Reasoning, are of *two kinds,* according to the nature of the end proposed; for Reasoning comprehends *Inferring* and *Proving;* which are not two different things, but the same thing regarded in *two different points of view:* like the road from London to York, and the road from York to London. He who infers,* proves; and he who proves, infers; but the word "infer" fixes the mind *first* on the Premiss and then on the *Conclusion;* the word "prove," on the contrary, leads the mind *from* the Conclusion to the Premiss. Hence, the substantives derived from these words respectively, are often used to express that which, on each occasion, is *last* in the mind; *Inference* being often used to signify the *Conclusion (i. e. Proposition inferred),* and *Proof,* the *Premiss.* We say, also, "How do you *prove* that?" and "What do you *infer from* that?" which sentences would not be so properly expressed if we were to transpose those verbs. One might, therefore, define *Proving,* "the assigning of a reason [or argument] for the support of a *given* proposition:" and *Inferring,* "the deduction of a Conclusion from *given* Premises." In the one case our *Conclusion* is *given (i. e.* set before us as the Question) and we have to *seek* for *arguments;* in the other, our Premises are *given,* and we have to *seek* for a Conclusion: *i.e.* to put together our own propositions, and try *what* will follow from them; or, to speak more Logically, in the one case, we seek *to refer the Subject of which we would predicate something, to a class*†

* I mean, of course, when the word is understood to imply *correct* Inference.

† Observe, that "Class" is used, here and elsewhere, for either an actual, or what may be called a potential Class: see Book i. § 3.

to which that Predicate will (affirmatively or negatively) *apply;* in the other, we seek *to find comprehended, in the Subject of which we have predicated something, some other term* to which that Predicate had not been before applied.* *Each of these is a definition of Reasoning.*

§ 2.

Investigator and Advocate.

To *infer*, then, is the business of the *Philosopher;* to *prove*, of the *Advocate;* the former, from the great mass of known and admitted truths, wishes to elicit *any* valuable additional truth whatever, that has been hitherto unperceived; and perhaps, without knowing, with certainty, what will be the terms of his Conclusion. Thus the Mathematician, *e.g.* seeks to ascertain *what* is the ratio of circles to each other, or *what* is the line whose square will be equal to a given circle. The Advocate, on the other hand, has a Proposition put before him, which he is to maintain as well as he can. His business, therefore, is to *find middle-terms* (which is the *inventio* of Cicero); the Philosopher's to combine and select known facts or principles, suitably, for gaining from them Conclusions which, though implied in the Premises, were before unperceived: in other words, for making "Logical Discoveries."

Questions concerning Predicate, and concerning Copula.

It may be added that all questions may be considered as falling under two classes; *viz.* "*What* shall be *predicated* of a certain Subject;" and, "*Which Copula*, affirmative or negative, shall connect a certain Subject and Predicate." We inquire, in short, either 1st. "What is A?" or, 2d, "Is A, B, or is it not?" The former class of questions belongs to the Philosopher; the latter to the Advocate. (See *Rhet.* Appendix G. p. 387.)

* "Proving" may be compared to the act of *putting away* any article into the proper receptacle of goods of that description; "inferring," to that of *bringing out* the article when needed.

The distinction between these two classes of questions is perhaps best illustrated by reference to some case in which our decision of *each* of the questions involved in some assertion, is controverted, by different parties. *E.G.* Paul says, that the apostles preached "Christ crucified; to the Jews a stumbling-block, and to the Greeks, foolishness:" that Jesus, who had suffered an ignominious death, was the Messiah, the Saviour of the World, was a doctrine opposed both by Jews and Gentiles: though on different grounds, according to their respective prejudices: the Jews who "required a Sign" (*i.e.* the coming of the Messiah in the clouds to establish a splendid temporal kingdom) were "offended"—"scandalized"—at the doctrine of a *suffering* Messiah: the Greeks who "sought after philosophical Wisdom" (*i.e.* the mode of *themselves* exalting their own nature, without any divine aid) ridiculed the idea of a Heavenly Saviour altogether; which the Jews admitted. In logical language, the Gentiles could not comprehend the Predicate; the Jews, denied the Copula.

Charges of paradox and nonsense.

It may be added, that in modern phraseology, the operations of corresponding prejudices are denoted, respectively, by the words "paradox" (a "stumbling-block") and "nonsense;" ("foolishness") which are often used, the one, by him who has been accustomed to hold an *opposite* opinion to what is asserted, the other, by him who has formed *no* opinion on the subject. The writer who proves an *unwelcome* truth, is censured as paradoxical; he who brings to light truths *unknown* or *unthought-of,* as nonsensical.

§ 3.

Different habits of mind connected with these processes.

Such are the respective preparatory processes in these two branches of study, the philosophical, and the rhetorical. They are widely different; they arise from, and generate, very different habits of mind; and require a very different kind of training and precept. It is evident that the business of the Advocate and that of the Judge, are, in this point, opposed; the one being, to find arguments for the support of his client's cause; the other, to ascertain the truth. And hence it is, that those who have excelled the most in the former department, sometimes manifest a deficiency in the latter, though the *subject matter*, in which they are conversant, remains the same. The Pleader, or Controversialist, or, in short, the Rhetorician in general, who is, in his own province, the most skilful, may be but ill-fitted for philosophical-investigation, even where there is no *observation* wanted:—when the facts are all *ready ascertained* for him. And again, the ablest Philosopher may make an indifferent disputant; especially, since the arguments which have led *him* to the conclusion, and have, with him, the most weight, may not, perhaps, be the most powerful in controversy.

The commoner fault, however, by far, is to forget the Philosopher or Theologian, and to assume the Advocate, improperly. It is therefore of great use to dwell on the distinction between these two branches. As for the bare process of Reasoning, *that* is the same in both cases; but the preparatory processes which are requisite, *in order to employ* Reasoning profitably, these, we see, branch off into two distinct channels. In each of these, undoubtedly, useful rules may be laid down; but they should not be confounded together. Bacon has chosen the department of Philosophy; giving rules in his *Organon*, not only for the conduct of experiments to ascertain new facts, but also for the selection and combination of known facts and principles, with a view of obtaining valuable *Inferences;* and it is probable that a system of such rules is what some writers mean (if they have any distinct meaning) by their proposed "Logic."

Philosophical Inquiry.

Rhetorical Inquiry.

In the other department, precepts have been given by Aristotle and other Rhetorical writers, as a part of their plan.* How far these precepts are to be considered as belonging to the present system,—whether "Method" is to be regarded as a *part* of *Logic,*—whether the *Matter* of Logic (*i. e.* genera maxims, axioms, or common-places) is to be included in the system,—whether Bacon's is properly to be reckoned a kind of Logic; all these are merely verbal questions, relating to the extension, not of the *Science,* but of the *name.* The bare process of Reasoning, *i. e.* deducing a Conclusion from Premises, must ever remain a distinct operation from the *assumption* of Premises; however useful the rules may be that have been given, or may be given, for conducting this latter process, and others connected with it; and however properly such rules may be subjoined to the precepts of that system to which the name of Logic is applied in the narrowest sense. Such rules as I now allude to may be of eminent service; but they must always be, as I have before observed, comparatively vague and general, and incapable of being built up into a regular demonstrative theory like that of the Syllogism; to which theory they bear much the same relation as the principles and rules of Poetical and Rhetorical criticism to those of Grammar; or those of practical Mechanics, to strict Geometry. I find no fault with the extension of a Term; but I would suggest a caution against confounding together, by means of a common name, things essentially different; and above all I would deprecate the sophistry of striving to depreciate what is called "the school-Logic," by perpetually *contrasting* it with systems with which it has nothing in common but the *name,* and whose object is essentially different.

* I have attempted the same in Part I. of Elements of Rhetoric; although, (through some inadvertency) I have found myself mentioned along with some other writers, as having declared that the thing is *impossible.* If I ever *had* made such an assertion, I should probably have been the first person that ever undertook to accomplish an *acknowledged* impossibility.

§ 4.

Aristotle's Organon and Bacon's.

It is remarkable that writers, whose expressions tend to confound together, by means of a common name, two branches of study which have nothing else in common (as if they were two different plans for attaining *one and the same* object,) have themselves complained of one of the effects of this confusion, *viz.* the introduction, early in the career of Academical Education, of a course of *Logic;* under which name, they observe, "men now* universally comprehend the works of Locke, Bacon, *&c.*" which, (as is justly remarked) are unfit for beginners. Now this would not have happened, if men had always kept in mind the meaning or meanings of each name they used.

And it may be added, that, however justly the word Logic may be thus extended, we have no ground for applying to the Aristotelian Logic the remarks above quoted respecting the Baconian; which the ambiguity of the word, if not carefully kept in view, might lead us to do. Grant that Bacon's work is a part of Logic; it no more follows, from the unfitness of *that* for *learners*, that the Elements of the Theory of Reasoning should be withheld from them, than it follows that the elements of Euclid, and common Arithmetic, are unfit for boys, because *Newton's Principia*, which also bears the title of *Mathematical*, is above their grasp. Of two branches of study which bear the same name, or even of two parts of the same branch, the one may be suitable to the commencement, the other to the close of the Academical career.

At whatever period of that career it may be proper to introduce the study of such as are usually called Metaphysical writers, it may be safely asserted, that those who have had the most experience in the business of giving

* *i. e.* In the Scotch universities.

instruction in Logic properly so called, as well as in other branches of knowledge, prefer and generally pursue the plan of letting their pupils *enter* on that study, next in order after the elements of Mathematics.

Chap. IV.—*Of Verbal and Real Questions.*

§ 1.

The ingenious author of the *Philosophy of Rhetoric,* and other writers, having maintained, or rather assumed, that Logic is applicable to Verbal controversy alone, there may be an advantage (though it has been my aim throughout to show the application of it to all Reasoning) in pointing out the difference between Verbal and Real Questions, and the probable origin of Campbell's mistake. For to trace any error to its source, will often throw more light on the subject in hand than can be obtained if we rest satisfied with merely detecting and refuting it.

Difference between a verbal and a real question.

Every Question that can arise, is in fact a Question whether a certain Predicate is or is not applicable to a certain Subject, or, *what* Predicate is applicable;* and whatever other account may be given by any writer, of the nature of any matter of doubt or debate, will be found ultimately to resolve itself into this. But sometimes the Question turns on the meaning and extent of the *terms* employed; sometimes, on the *things* signified by them. If it be made to appear, therefore, that the opposite sides of a certain Question may be held by persons not differing in their *opinion of the matter* in hand, then, that Question may be pronounced Verbal; as depending on the different senses in which they respectively employ the *terms.* If,

* See Chap. iii. § 2.

on the contrary, it appears that they employ the Terms in the same sense, but still differ as to the application of one of them to the other, then it may be pronounced that the Question is Real;—that they differ as to the opinions they hold of the *things* in Question.

If, for instance, (to recur to an example formerly given, Book III. § 10.) two persons contend whether Augustus deserved to be called a "great man," then, if it appeared that the one included, under the term "great," disinterested *patriotism*, and *on that ground* excluded Augustus from the class, as wanting in that quality; and that the other also gave him no credit for that quality, but understood no more by the term "great," than high intellectual qualities, energy of character, and brilliant actions, it would follow that the parties did not differ in opinion except as to the use of a Term, and that the Question was Verbal.

If, again, it appeared that the one *did* give Augustus credit for such patriotism as the other denied him, both of them including that idea in the term great, then, the Question would be Real. Either kind of Question, it is plain, is to be argued according to Logical principles; but the *middle-terms employed would be different;* and for this reason, among others, it is important to distinguish Verbal from Real controversy. In the former case, *e. g.* it might be urged (with truth) that the common use of the expression "great *and* good" proves that the idea of good is not implied in the ordinary sense of the word great; an argument which could have, of course, no place in deciding the other Question.*

§ 2.

Verbal Questions mistaken for Real.

It is by no means to be supposed that all Verbal Questions are trifling and frivolous. It is often of the highest importance to settle correctly the meaning of a word, either

* See Book III. the latter part of § 10.

according to ordinary use, or according to the meaning of any particular writer or class of men. But when Verbal Questions are *mistaken* for Real, much confusion of thought and unprofitable wrangling,—what is usually designated as *Logomachy*—will be generally the result. Nor is it always so easy and simple a task, as might at first sight appear, to distinguish them from each other. For, several objects to which one common name is applied, will often have many points of difference; and yet that name may perhaps be applied to them all [univocally] in the same sense, and may be fairly regarded as the Genus they come under, if it appear that they all agree in what is designated by that name, and that the differences between them are in points not essential to the character of that genus. A cow and a horse differ in many respects, but agree in all that is implied by the term "quadruped," which is therefore applicable to both in the same sense.* So also the houses of the ancients differed in many respects from ours, and their ships still more; yet no one would contend that the terms "house" and "ship," as applied to both, are ambiguous, or that οἶκος might not fairly be rendered *house*, and ναῦς *ship*; because the essential characteristic of a house is, not its being of this or that form or materials, but its being a dwelling for men; these therefore would be called *two different kinds* of houses; and consequently the term "house" would be applied to each, without any equivocation, [univocally] in the same sense: and so in the other instances.

Logomachy.

* Yet the charge of equivocation is sometimes unjustly brought against a writer in consequence of a gratuitous assumption of our own. An Eastern writer, *e.g.* may be speaking of "beast of burden;" and the reader may chance to have the idea occur to his mind of Horses and Mules; he thence takes for granted that these were meant; and if it afterwards come out that it was Camels, he perhaps complains of the writer for misleading him by not expressly mentioning the Species; saying, "I could not know that he meant Camels." He did *not* mean Camels, in particular; he meant, as he said, "beasts of burden:" and Camels are such, as well as Horses and Mules. He is not accountable for your suppositions.

On the other hand, two or more things may bear the same name, and may also have a resemblance in many points, nay, and may from that resemblance have come to bear the same name, and yet if the circumstance which is essential to each be wanting in the other, the term may be pronounced ambiguous. *E. G.* The word " Plantain" is the name of a common herb in Europe, and of an Indian fruit-tree: both are *vegetables;* yet the term is ambiguous, because it does not denote them *so far forth as they agree.*

Again, the word " Priest" is applied to the Ministers of the Jewish and of the Pagan religions, and also to those of the Christian; and doubtless the term has been so transferred in consequence of their being both *ministers* (in some sort) of religion.* Nor would every difference that might be found between the Priests of different religions constitute the term ambiguous, provided such differences were non-essential to the idea suggested by the word Priest; as *e.g.* the Jewish Priest served the true God, and the Pagan, false Gods: this is a most important difference, but does not constitute the term ambiguous, because neither of these circumstances is implied and suggested by the term Ἱερεὺς; which accordingly was applied both to Jewish and Pagan Priests. But the term Ἱερεὺς does seem to have implied the office of offering *sacrifice*,—atoning for the sins of the people,—and acting as mediator between Man and the object of his worship. And accordingly that term is never applied to any one under the Christian system, except to the ONE great Mediator. The Christian ministers not having that office which was implied as essential in the term Ἱερεὺς, [sacerdos] were never called by that name, but by that of πρεσβύτερος.† It may be concluded, therefore, that the term Priest is ambiguous, as corresponding to the terms

* See Discourse on " the Christian Priesthood," appended to the Bampton Lectures.

† From which our word Priest is derived, but which (it is remarkable) is never translated " Priest" in our version of the Scriptures, but " Elder."

Ἱερεὺς and πρεσβύτερος respectively, notwithstanding that there are points in which these two agree. These therefore should be reckoned, not two different *kinds* of Priests, but Priests in two different *senses;* since (to adopt the phraseology of Aristotle) the definition of them, so far forth as they are Priests, would be different.

Real Questions mistaken for Verbal.

A "real" question again is liable to be mistaken for a "verbal," when different persons who are in fact using a term in the same sense, are supposed to be using it in different senses; sometimes, from its being erroneously taken for granted that what *commonly belongs* to the *thing* spoken of must be implied in the *common acceptation* of the *name* of that thing:—as *e. g.* if any one should conclude, from the *ordinary* kinds of wood being lighter than water, that the *ordinary sense* of the term "wood" implies floating in water: sometimes again, from its being rashly inferred from two persons having a difference of opinion respecting some *thing*, that they each denote that opinion in their use respectively, of the *term* which expresses that thing: as *e. g.* if two persons differing in opinion as to the question of episcopacy, should be considered as differing in their use of the word "Episcopalian," and implying by it, the one a *right* and the other a *wrong* form of Church-government; whereas the word itself does not express or imply [connote] either the one or the other, but simply "an adherent to an episcopal form of government." They both mean the same thing; their difference of opinion being, whether that thing be right or wrong.

Different applications of a term do not imply ambiguity.

And most especially is ambiguity likely to be erroneously attributed to some term, when different persons who employ it in reality in the *same sense,* are accustomed to *apply* it differently, according to circumstances, and thus to *associate* it habitually in their minds with different things. *E. G.* "Patriotism" is *applied* by each in reference to *his own* country; but the word itself has the same signification with each; just as the word "Father;" though it is likely to recall to the mind of each a different individual. So also the term "true-believer," which is applied by Mahometans to a believer in the Koran, would be considered by Christians as more applicable to a believer in the Gospel; but it would not be correct to say that "the one party *means* by this term, so and so, and the other, something different:" for they do not attach *different senses to the word* "true," or to the word "believe;" they differ only in their persuasions of what *is* true, and *ought* to be believed.

I have noticed some instances of the above kinds of mistake in the Appendix to the third Series of Essays; and also in the Introduction to "Political Economy," from which I will here cite a passage.

"In speaking of exchanges, I did not mean to limit myself to *voluntary* exchanges;—those in which the whole transaction takes place with the full consent of both parties to all the terms of it. Most exchanges, indeed, are of this character; but the case of taxation,—the revenue levied from the subject in return for the protection afforded by the sovereign, constitutes a remarkable exception; the payment being compulsory, and not adjusted by agreement with the payer. Still, whether in any case it be *fairly* and reasonably adjusted, or the contrary, it is not the less an exchange. And it is worth remarking, that it is just so far forth as it is an exchange,—so far forth as protection, whether adequate or not, is afforded in exchange for this payment, that the payment itself comes under the cognizance of this science. There is nothing else that distinguishes *taxation* from *avowed robbery*.

"Though the generality of exchanges are voluntary, this circumstance is not essential to an exchange: since otherwise the very expression 'voluntary exchange,' would be tautological and improper. But it is a common logical error to suppose that what *usually* belongs to the *thing*, is implied by the *usual* sense of the *word*. Although most noblemen possess large estates, the word 'nobleman' does not imply the possession of a large estate. Although most birds can fly, the ordinary use of the term 'bird' does not imply this; since the penguin and the ostrich are always admitted to be birds. And though, in a great majority of cases, wealth is acquired by labour, the ordinary use of the word 'wealth' does not include this circumstance, since every one would call a pearl an article of wealth, even though a man should chance to meet with it in eating an oyster."

It is evidently of much importance to keep in mind the above distinctions, in order to avoid, on the one hand, stigmatizing, as Verbal controversies, what in reality are not such, merely because the Question turns (as *every* question must) on the applicability of a certain Predicate to a certain Subject; or, on the other hand, falling into the opposite error of mistaking words for things, and judging of men's agreement or disagreement in opinion in every case, merely from their agreement or disagreement in the terms employed.

Chap. V.—*Of Realism.*

§ 1.

Nothing has a greater tendency to lead to the mistake just noticed, and thus to produce *undetected* Verbal Questions and fruitless Logomachy, than the prevalence of the notion of the Realists,* that Genus and Species are some

* It is well known what a furious controversy long existed in all the universities of Europe between the sects of the Realists and the Nominalists; the heat of which was allayed by the Reformation, which withdrew men's attention to a more important question.

real THINGS, existing independently of our conceptions and expressions; and that, as in the case of Singular-terms there is some real individual corresponding to each, so, in Common-terms also, there is some Thing corresponding to each; which is the object of our thoughts when we employ any such term.*

Technical sense of Species when applied to organized Beings.

There is one circumstance which ought to be noticed, as having probably contributed not a little to foster this error: I mean, the peculiar technical sense of the word "Species" when applied to *organized Beings.*

It has been laid down in the course of this work, that when several individuals are observed to resemble each other in some point, a common name may be assigned to them indicating [implying, or "connoting"†] that point,—applying to all or any of them so far forth as respects that common attribute,—and distinguishing them from all others; as, *e. g.* the several individual buildings, which, however different in other respects, agree in being constructed for men's dwelling, are called by the common name of "House:" and it was added, that as we select at pleasure the circumstance that we chuse to abstract, we may thus refer the same Individual to any one of several different Species, and again, the same Species, to one Genus or to another, according as it suits our purpose; whence it seems

* A doctrine commonly, but falsely attributed to Aristotle, who expressly contradicts it. He calls individuals "primary substances" (*πρῶται οὐσιαι*); Genus and Species "secondary," as not denoting (*τόδε τι*) a "really-existing thing." *Πᾶσα δὲ οὐσία δοκεῖ τόδε τι σημαίνειν. Ἐπὶ μὲν οὖν τῶν πρώτων οὐσιῶν ἀναμφισβήτητον καὶ ἀληθές ἐστιν, ὅτι τόδε τι σημαίνει· ἄτομον γὰρ καὶ ἓν ἀριθμῷ τὸ δηλούμενον ἐστιν. Ἐπὶ δὲ τῶν δευτέρων οὐσιῶν,* ΦΑΙΝΕΤΑΙ *μὲν ὁμοίως τῷ σχήματι τῆς προσηγορίας τόδε τι σημαίνειν, ὅταν εἴπῃ, ἄνθρωπος, ἢ ζῶον·* ΟΥ ΜΗΝ ΓΕ ΑΛΗΘΕΣ· *ἀλλὰ μᾶλλον* ΠΟΙΟΝ ΤΙ *σημαίνει· κ. τ. λ.* Aristotle, *Categ.* § 3. See Appendix, Art. "Same." There is however a continual danger of sliding into Realism *inadvertently*, unless one is continually on the watch against it: of which Aristotle as well as many other writers not deliberately holding the doctrine, furnish instances.

† See Book II. Chap. v. § 1.

plainly to follow that Genus and Species are no *real things* existing independent of our thoughts, but are creatures of our own minds.

Yet in the case of Species of *organized* Beings, it seems at first sight as if this rule did not hold good; but that the Species to which each individual belongs, could not be in any degree *arbitrarily* fixed by us, but must be something real, unalterable, and independent of our thoughts. Cæsar or Socrates, for instance, it may be said, must belong—different as they may be—to the Species Man, and can belong to no other; and the like, with any individual Brute, or Plant: *e. g.* a horned and a hornless sheep every naturalist would regard as belonging to the same Species.

On the other hand, if any one utters such a proposition as "this apple-tree is a codlin;"—"this dog is a spaniel,"—"Argus was a mastiff," to what head of Predicables would such a Predicate be referred? Surely our logical principles would lead us to answer, that it is the *Species;* since it could hardly be called an Accident, and is manifestly no other Predicable. And yet every Naturalist would at once pronounce that Mastiff is no distinct Species, but only a *variety* of the Species Dog. This however does not satisfy our inquiry as to the head of Predicables to which it is to be referred. It should seem at first sight as if one needed, in the case of organized Beings, an additional head of Predicables to be called "Variety" or "Race."

Species distinguished by Naturalists from variety.

The solution of the difficulty is to be found in the consideration of the peculiar technical sense [or "second intention"] of the word "Species" when applied to *organized Beings:* in which case it is always applied (when we are speaking strictly, as naturalists) to such individuals as are supposed to be *descended from a common stock,* or which *might* have so descended; *viz.* which resemble one another (to use M. Cuvier's expression) as much as those of the same stock do. Now this being a point on which all (not merely Naturalists) are agreed, and since it is a *fact*, (whether an *ascertained* fact or not) that certain individuals are, or are not, thus connected, it follows, that every question whether a certain individual Animal or Plant belongs to a certain Species or not, is a question not of mere *arrangement*, but of *fact*. But in the case of questions respecting *Genus*, it is otherwise. If, *e. g.* two Naturalists differed, in the one placing (as Linnæus) all the Species of Bee under one *Genus*, which the other subdivided (as later writers have done) into several genera, it would be evident that there was no question of *fact* debated between them, and that it was only to be considered which was the more *convenient arrangement*. If, on the other hand, it were disputed whether the African and the Asiatic Elephant are distinct *Species*, or merely Varieties, it would be equally manifest that the question is one of fact; since both would allow that if they are descended (or might have descended) from the same stock, they are of the same Species; and if otherwise, of two: this is the fact, which they endeavour to ascertain, by such indications as are to be found.

Questions of fact and questions of arrangement.

For it is to be further observed, that this fact being one which can seldom be *directly* known, the consequence is, that the *marks* by which any Species of Animal or Plant is *known*, are not the very *Differentia* which *constitutes* that Species. Now, in the case of unorganized Beings, these two coincide; the marks by which a Diamond, *e. g.* is distinguished from other minerals, being the very Differentia that constitutes the Species Diamond, And the same is the case in the *Genera* even of organized Beings: the Linnæan Genus "felis," *e. g.* (when considered as a Species, *i. e.* as falling under some more comprehensive Class) is distinguished from others under the same Order, by those very marks which constitute its Differentia. But in the "Infimæ Species" (according to the view of a

Mark by which a Species is known not always the Differentia.

Naturalist) of plants and animals, this, as has been said, is not the case; since here the Differentia which constitutes each Species includes in it a circumstance which cannot often be directly ascertained (*viz.* the being sprung from the same stock), but which we conjecture, from certain circumstances of resemblance; so that the *marks* by which a Species is known, are not in truth the whole of the Differentia itself, but *indications* of the existence of that Differentia; *viz.* indications of descent from a common stock.

There are a few, and but a few, other Species to which the same observations will in a great degree apply: I mean in which the *Differentia* which *constitutes* the Species, and the *mark* by which the Species is *known*, are not the same: *e. g.* "Murder:" the Differentia of which is that it be committed "with malice aforethought;" this cannot be *directly* ascertained; and therefore we *distinguish* murder from any other homicide by circumstances of preparation, *&c.*, which are not in reality the Differentia, but *indications* of the Differentia; *i. e.* grounds for concluding that the malice did exist.

Hence it is that Species, in the case of organized Beings, and also in a few other cases, have the appearance of being some real things, independent of our thoughts and language. And hence, naturally enough, the same notions have been often extended to the *Genera* also, and to Species of *other things:* so that men have a notion that each individual of every description *truly* belongs to some one Species and no other: and each Species, in like manner, to some one Genus; whether we happen to be right or not in the ones to which we refer them.

Few, if any indeed, in the present day avow and maintain this doctrine: but those who are not especially on their guard, are perpetually sliding into it unawares.

Nothing so much conduces to the error of Realism as

the transferred and secondary use of the words "same,"* "one and the same," "identical," *&c.* when it is not clearly perceived and carefully borne in mind, that they *are* employed in a secondary sense, and *that*, more frequently even than in the primary.

Ambiguity of the words "same," "one," &c.

Suppose *e.g.* a thousand persons are thinking of the Sun: it is evident it is one and the same individual object on which all these minds are employed. So far all is clear. But suppose all these persons are thinking of a Triangle;—not any individual triangle, but Triangle in general;—and considering, perhaps, the equality of its angles to two right angles: it would seem as if, in this case also, their minds were all employed on "one and the same" object: and this object of their thoughts, it may be said, cannot be the *mere word* Triangle, but that which is *meant* by it: nor again, can it be everything that the word will apply to: for they are not thinking of *triangles*, but of *one* thing. Those who do not maintain that this "one thing" has an existence independent of the human mind, are in general content to tell us, by way of explanation, that the object of their thoughts is the abstract "idea" of a triangle;† an explanation which satisfies, or at least silences many; though it may be doubted whether they very clearly understand what sort of a thing an "idea" is; which may thus exist in a thousand different minds at once, and yet be "one and the same."

The fact is, that "unity" and "sameness" are in such cases employed, not in the primary sense, but, to denote perfect *similarity*. When we say that ten thousand different persons have all "one and the same" Idea in their minds, or, are all of "one and the same" Opinion, we

* See Appendix, No. I. Art. "Same."

† *Conceptualists* is a name sometimes applied to those who adopt this explanation (if it can be called an explanation); to which class Locke is referred.

mean no more than that they are all *thinking exactly alike.* When we say that they are all in the "same" posture, we mean that they are all *placed alike:* and so also they are said all to have the "same" disease, when they are all diseased alike.

Logomachy resulting from this ambiguity.

One instance of the confusion of thought and endless logomachy which may spring from inattention to this ambiguity of the words "same," *&c.*, is afforded by the controversy arising out of a sermon of Dr. King (Archbishop of Dublin), published about a century ago. He remarked (without expressing himself perhaps with so much guarded precision as the vehemence of his opponents rendered needful) that "the attributes of the Deity (*viz.* Wisdom, Justice, *&c.*) are not to be regarded as the *same* with those human qualities which bear the *same* names, but are called so by resemblance and analogy only." For this he was decried by Bishop Berkeley and a host of other objectors, down to the present time, as an Atheist, or little better. "If the divine attributes," they urged, "are not precisely the same in kind (though superior in degree) with the human qualities which bear the same name, we cannot *imitate* the Deity as the Scriptures require;—we cannot know on what principles we shall be judged:—we cannot be sure that God exists at all;" with a great deal more to the same purpose; all of which would have been perceived to be perfectly idle, had the authors but recollected to ascertain the meaning of the principal word employed.

Sameness consisting in resemblance and analogy.

For, 1st, when any two persons (or other objects) are said to have the "*same*" quality, accident, *&c.*, what we predicate of them is evidently a certain *resemblance*, and nothing else. One man *e.g.* does not feel *another's* sickness; but they are said to have the "same" disease, (not in the sense in which two men may be killed by the same cannon-ball, but) if they are precisely *similar* in respect of their ailments: and so also they are said to have the same complexion, if the hue and texture of their skins be alike. 2dly, Such qualities as are entirely *relative*, which consist in the relation borne by the subject to certain other things,—in these, it is manifest, the only *resemblance* that *can* exist, is, *resemblance of relations*, *i.e.* ANALOGY. Courage, *e.g.* consists in the relation in which one stands* towards dangers; Temperance or Intemperance,—towards bodily pleasures, *&c.* When it is said, therefore, of two courageous men, that they have both the *same* quality, the only meaning this expression *can* have, is, that they are, so far, completely *analogous* in their characters;—having similar ratios to certain similar objects. In short, as in all qualities, *sameness* can mean only strict *resemblance*, so, in those which are of a *relative* nature, *resemblance* can mean only *analogy*. Thus it appears, that what Dr. King has been so vehemently censured for asserting respecting the Deity, is literally true even with respect to men themselves; *viz.* that it is only by Analogy that two persons can be said to possess the same virtue, or other such quality. 3dly, But what he means, is, plainly, that this analogy is far less *exact and complete* in the case of a comparison between the Deity and his creatures than between one man and another; which surely no one would venture to deny. But the doctrine against which the attacks *have* been directed, is self-evident, the moment we consider the meaning of the term employed.†

In the Introduction and Notes to the last edition of Archbishop King's Discourse, I have considered the matters in debate more fully; but this slight notice of them has been introduced in this place, as closely connected with the present subject.

* Ἐν τῷ ἔχειν πῶς πρὸς, Arist.

† See Dr. Copleston's excellent Analysis and Defence of Archbishop King's principles, in the Notes to his "Four Discourses."

§ 2.

Origin of the ambiguity of "same," &c.

The origin of this secondary sense of the words, "same," "one," "identical," *&c.* (an attention to which would clear away an incalculable mass of confused Reasoning and Logomachy,) is easily to be traced to the use of Language and of other *signs*, for the purposes of reasoning and of mutual communication. If any one utters the "one single" word "triangle," and gives "one single" definition of it, each of the persons who hears him forms a certain notion in his own mind, *not differing* in any respect from that of each of the rest. They are said therefore to have all "one and the same" notion, because, resulting from, and corresponding with, (that which is, in the primary sense) "one and the same" expression; and there is said to be "one single" idea of every triangle (considered merely as a triangle) because one single *name* or *definition* is equally applicable to each. In like manner, all the coins struck by the same single die, are said to have "one and the same" impression, merely because the (numerically) "one" *description* which suits one of these coins will equally suit any other that is exactly like it. The expression accordingly which has only of late begun to prevail, "such and such things are *of the same description*," is perhaps the most philosophical that can be employed.

It is not intended to recommend the disuse of the words "same" "identical," *&c.* in this transferred sense; which, if it were desirable, would be utterly impracticable; but merely, a steady attention to the ambiguity thus introduced, and watchfulness against the errors thence arising. "It is with *words* as with *money*. Those who know the value of it best are not therefore the least liberal. We may *lend* readily and largely; and though this be done quietly and without ostentation, there is no harm in keeping an exact account in our private memorandum-book of the sums, the persons, and the occasions on which they were lent. It may be, we shall want them again for our own use; or they may be employed by the borrower for a wrong purpose; or they may have been so long in his possession that he begins to look upon them as his own. In either of which cases it is allowable, and even right, to call them in."*

The difficulties and perplexities which have involved the questions respecting *personal-identity*, among others, may be traced principally to the neglect of this caution. I mean that many writers have sought an explanation of the *primary* sense of identity (*viz.* personal) by looking to the *secondary*. Any grown man, *e.g.* is, in the primary sense the *same* person he was when a child: this sameness is, I conceive, a simple notion, which it is vain to attempt explaining by any other more simple; but when philosophers seek to gain a clearer notion of it by looking to the cases in which sameness is predicated in another sense, *viz. similarity*, such as exists between several individuals denoted by a common name, (as when we say that there are growing on Lebanon some of the *same* trees with which the Temple was built; meaning, cedars of that *species*) this is surely as idle as if we were to attempt explaining the primary sense, *e.g.* of "rage" as it exists in the human mind, by directing our attention to the "rage" of the sea. Whatever personal identity does consist in, it is plain that it has no necessary connexion with similarity; since every one would be ready to say, "When I WAS a child I thought as a child,—I spake as a child,—I understood as a child; but when I became a man, I put away childish things."

But a full consideration of this question would be unsuitable to the subject of the present work.

* "Logic Vindicated." Oxford, 1809.

APPENDIX.

APPENDIX.

No. I.

ON CERTAIN TERMS WHICH ARE PECULIARLY LIABLE TO BE USED AMBIGUOUSLY.

LIST OF WORDS EXPLAINED IN THE FOLLOWING APPENDIX.

It has appeared to me desirable to illustrate the importance of attending to the ambiguity of terms, by a greater number of instances than could have been conveniently either inserted in the context or introduced in a note, without too much interrupting the course of the dissertation on Fallacies.

I have purposely selected instances from *various* subjects, and some, from the most important; being convinced that the disregard and contempt with which logical studies are usually treated, may be traced, in part, to a notion, that the science is incapable of useful application to any matters of real importance, and is merely calculated to afford an exercise of ingenuity on insignificant truisms;—syllogisms to prove that a horse is an animal, and distinctions of the different senses of "canis" or of "gallus;"—a mistake which is likely to derive some countenance (however unfairly) from the *exclusive* employment of such trifling exemplifications.

The words and phrases which may be employed as ambiguous Middle-terms are of course innumerable: but it may be, in several respects, of service to the learner, to explain the ambiguity of a few of those most frequently occurring in the most important discussions, and whose double meaning has been the most frequently overlooked; and this, not by entering into an examination of *all* the senses in which each term is ever employed, but of those only which are the most liable to be confounded together.

It is worth observing, that the words whose ambiguity is the most frequently overlooked, and is productive of the greatest amount of confusion of thought and fallacy, are among the *commonest*, and are those of whose meaning the generality consider there is the least room to doubt.* It is indeed from those very circumstances that the danger arises; words in very common use are both the most liable, from the looseness of ordinary discourse, to slide from one sense into another, and also the least likely to have that ambiguity suspected. *Familiar acquaintance* is perpetually mistaken for *accurate knowledge*.†

It may be necessary here to remark, that inaccuracy not unfrequently occurs in the employment of the very phrase, "such an author uses such a word in this, or that sense,"

* See Book III. § 10. † See Pol. Econ. Lect. IX.

or "means so and so, by this word." We should not use these expressions (as some have inadvertently done) in reference, necessarily, to the notion which may exist, *in the author's* mind, of the *object* in question;—his belief or opinion respecting the thing he is speaking of;—for the notions *conveyed* to *others* by the *word*, may often (even according to the writer's own expectation) fall short of this. He may be convinced, *e.g.* that "the moon has no atmosphere," or that "the Spartans were brave;" but he cannot suppose that the terms "moon" or "Spartan" imply [connote] any such thing.* Nor again, should we regard the sense in which *they* understand him, as necessarily *his* sense, (though it is *theirs*) of the word employed; since they may *mistake* his meaning: but we must consider what sense it is likely he *expected* and intended to convey, to those to whom he addressed himself. And a judicious writer will always expect each word to be understood, as nearly as the context will allow, in the sense, or in one of the senses, which *use* has established; except so far as he may have given some different explanation. But there are many who, from various causes, frequently fail of conveying the sense they design. And it may be added, that there are, it is to be feared, some persons in these days who *design* to convey different senses by the same expression, to different men;—to the ordinary reader, and to the initiated;—reserving to themselves a back-door for evasion when charged with any false teaching, by pleading that they have been misunderstood "in consequence of the reader's not being aware of the *peculiar sense* in which they use words!"

It is but fair perhaps to add this warning to my readers; that one who takes pains to ascertain and explain the sense of the words employed in any discussion, whatever care he may use to show that what he is inquiring after, is, the *received* sense, is yet almost sure to be charged, by the inaccurate, and the sophistical, with attempting to intro-

* See Note to last Essay, 3d Series; and also Book IV. Ch. iv. § 2.

duce some *new* sense of the words in question, in order to serve a purpose.

i. ARGUMENT, in the strict logical sense, has been defined in the foregoing treatise; (Compendium, Book II. Ch. iii. § 1): in that sense it includes (as is there remarked) the Conclusion as well as the Premises: and thus it is, that we say a Syllogism consists of *three* propositions; *viz.* the Conclusion which is proved, as well as those by which it is proved. Argumentum is also used by many logical writers to denote the middle term.

But in ordinary discourse, Argument is very often used for the *Premises* alone, in contradistinction to the Conclusion; *e.g.* "the Conclusion which this Argument is intended to establish is so and so."

It is also sometimes employed to denote what is, strictly speaking, a *course or series* of such Arguments; when a certain Conclusion is established by Premises, which are themselves, in the same dissertation, proved by other propositions, and perhaps those again, by others; the whole of this dissertation is often called an *Argument* to prove the ultimate conclusion designed to be established; though in fact it is a *train* of Arguments. It is in this sense, *e.g.* that we speak of "Warburton's *Argument* to prove the divine legation of Moses," &c.

Sometimes also the word is used to denote what may be properly called a *Disputation;* i.e. *two* trains of argument, opposed to each other: as when we say that A and B had a long Argument on such and such a subject; and that A had the best of the Argument. Doubtless the use of the word in this sense has contributed to foster the notion entertained by many, that Logic is the "art of wrangling," that it makes men contentious, *&c.:* they have heard that it is employed about *Arguments;* and hastily conclude that it is confined to cases where there is *opposition and contest.*

It may be worth mentioning in this place, that the *various forms of stating* an Argument are sometimes spoken of as *different kinds* of Argument: as when we speak of a Categorical or Hypothetical Argument, or of one in the first or some other figure; though every logician knows that the same individual Argument may be stated in various figures, *&c.*

This, no doubt, has contributed to the error of those who speak of the Syllogism as a peculiar kind of Argument; and of "Syllogistic Reasoning," as a distinct mode of Reasoning, instead of being only a certain *form* of expressing *any* argument.

For an account of the *different kinds of argument*, properly so called, the reader is referred to the "Elements of Rhetoric."

ii. AUTHORITY.—This word is sometimes employed in its primary sense, when we refer to any one's example, testimony, or judgment: as when, *e.g.* we speak of correcting a reading in some book, on the Authority of an ancient MS.—giving a statement of some fact, on the Authority of such and such historians, *&c.*

In this sense the word answers pretty nearly to the Latin "Auctoritas." It is a claim to *deference.*

Sometimes again it is employed as equivalent to "Potestas," Power: as when we speak of the Authority of a Magistrate, *&c.* This is a claim to *obedience.* It is in the former sense that it is used in our 20th Article; which speaks of the Church having *power* to decree *rites and ceremonies*, and "*authority*" in controversies of *Faith.*

Many instances may be found in which writers have unconsciously slid from one sense of the word to another, so as to blend confusedly in their minds the two ideas. In no case perhaps has this more frequently happened than when we are speaking of the Authority of the Church: in which the ambiguity of the latter word (see the Article

Church) comes in aid of that of the former. The Authority (in the primary sense) of the Catholic, *i. e.* Universal Church, at any particular period, is often appealed to, in support of this or that doctrine or practice: and it is, justly, supposed that the opinion of the great mass of the Christian World affords a *presumption* (though only a presumption) in favour of the correctness of any interpretation of Scripture, or the expediency, at the time, of any ceremony, regulation, *&c.*

But it is to be observed that the "authority," in this sense, of any Church or other Community, is not that of the Body, *as such*, but of the *individuals* composing it. The presumption raised is to be measured by the numbers, knowledge, judgment, and honesty of those individuals, considered as individual persons, and not in their corporate capacity.

On the other hand, each *particular* Church has Authority in the other sense, *viz.* Power, over its own members, (as long as they choose to remain members) to enforce anything not contrary to God's word.* But the *Catholic or Universal* Church, not being one religious Community on earth, can have no "authority" in the sense of *Power;* since it is notorious there never was a time when the power of the Pope, of a Council, or of any other human Governors, over *all* Christians, was in fact admitted, whatever arguments may be urged to prove its claim to be admitted.

Authority again in the sense of Auctoritas (claim to *deference*) may have every degree of weight, from absolute infallibility, (such as, in religious matters, Christians attribute to the Scriptures) down to the faintest presumption. On the other hand, "authority" in the sense of "legitimate *power*" does not admit of *degrees.* One person may indeed possess a *greater extent* of power than another: but in each particular instance, he either has a rightful claim to obedience or he has none. See Hawkins on *Tradition.*

* See Essay on the Dangers to Christian Faith, &c. Note A.

Hinds's *History of the Early Progress of Christianity*, Vol. II. p. 99. Hinds on *Inspiration*. *Errors of Romanism*, Chap. iv. *Essay on the Omission of Creeds, &c. in the New Testament*. And *Essay II. on the Kingdom of Christ*.

CAN.—*See* "MAY," "MUST."

CAPABLE.—*See* "POSSIBLE," "IMPOSSIBLE," and "NECESSARY."

iii. CASE.—Sometimes Grammarians use this word to signify (which is its strict sense) a certain "variation in the writing and utterance of a Noun, denoting the relation in which it stands to some other part of the sentence;" sometimes to denote *that relation itself:* whether indicated by the termination, or by a preposition, or by its collocation; and there is hardly any writer on the subject who does not occasionally employ the term in each sense, without explaining the ambiguity. Much confusion and frivolous debate has hence resulted. Whoever would see a specimen of this, may find it in the Port Royal Greek Grammar; in which the Authors insist on giving the Greek language an *Ablative case*, with the same termination, however, as the Dative: (though, by the way, they had better have fixed on the *Genitive;* which oftener answers to the Latin Ablative) urging, and with great truth, that if a distinct termination be necessary to constitute a case, many Latin Nouns will be without an Ablative, some without a Genitive or without a Dative, and all Neuters without an Accusative. And they add, that since it is possible, in every instance, to render into Greek the Latin Ablative, consequently there must be an Ablative in Greek.* If they had known and recollected that in the language of

* It is in the same way that some of the Latin-grammarians have made one of the *Moods* into three; Subjunctive, Potential, and Optative.

Lapland, there are, as we are told, thirteen Cases, they would have hesitated to use an argument which would prove that there must therefore be thirteen Cases in Greek and Latin also! All this confusion might have been avoided, if it had but been observed that the word "Case" is used in two senses. See Book III. § 10. §§ 4.

CAUSE.—*See* "REASON," and "WHY."

iv. CERTAIN.—This is a word whose ambiguity, together with that of many others of kindred signification (as "may," "can," "must," "possible," *&c.*) has occasioned infinite perplexity in discussions on some of the most important subjects; such as the freedom of human actions, the divine foreknowledge, *&c.*

In its primary sense, it is applied (according to its etymology from *cerno*) to the state of a person's mind; denoting any one's full and complete conviction; and, generally, though not always, implying that there is sufficient *ground* for such conviction. It was thence easily transferred metonymically to the *truths or events*, respecting which this conviction is rationally entertained. And "Uncertain" (as well as the substantives and adverbs derived from these adjectives) follows the same rule. Thus we say, "it is certain that a battle has been fought:" "it is certain that the moon will be full on such a day:" "it is uncertain whether such a one is alive or dead:" "it is uncertain whether it will rain to-morrow:" meaning, in these and in all other cases, that *we* are certain or uncertain respectively; not indicating any difference in the character of the *events* themselves, except in reference to our knowledge respecting them; for the same thing may be, at the same time, both certain and uncertain, to different individuals; *e.g.* the life or death at a particular time, of any one, is certain to his friends on the spot; uncertain or contingent, to those at a distance.

From not attending to this circumstance, the words "uncertain" and "contingent" (which is employed nearly in the same sense as uncertain in its secondary meaning) have been considered by many writers* as denoting some quality in the things themselves; and have thus become involved in endless confusion. "Contingent" is indeed applied to events only, not to persons: but it denotes no quality in the events themselves; only, as has been said, the relation in which they stand to a person who has no complete knowledge respecting them. It is from overlooking this principle, obvious as it is when once distinctly stated, that Chance or Fortune has come to be regarded as a real *agent*, and to have been, by the ancients, personified as a Goddess, and represented by statues.

v. CHURCH is sometimes employed to signify *the* Church, *i. e.* the Universal or Catholic Church,—comprehending in it all Christians; who are "Members one of another," and who compose the Body, of which Christ is the Head; which, collectively taken, has no visible supreme Head or earthly governor, either individual, or council; and which is *one*, only in reference to its One invisible Governor and Paraclete, the Spirit of Christ, dwelling in it,—to the one common faith, and character, which ought to be found in all Christians,—and the com-

* Among others, Archbishop King, in his Discourse on Predestination, has fallen into this error; as is explained in the Notes and the Appendix to my edition of that work.

It may be requisite to mention in this place, that I have been represented as coinciding with him as to the point in question, in a note to Mr. Davison's work on Prophecy; through a mistake, which the author candidly acknowledged, and promised to rectify. His mistake arose from his having (as he himself informed me) spoken from conjecture only, without having read my publication. Unfortunately the error was allowed to remain uncorrected for several years after it had been pointed out: in fact, till the whole of the edition containing the mis-statement had been sold off.

mon principles on which all Christian societies should be constituted. See Hinds's *History of the Rise of Christianity,* and Bernard's *Church and Synagogue,* an abridged translation from Vitringa.

Sometimes again it is employed to signify *a* Church; *i. e.* any one Society, constituted on these general principles; having governors on earth, and existing as a Community possessing a certain power over its own members; in which sense we read of the "Seven Churches in Asia;"—of Paul's having "the care of all the Churches," *&c.* This ambiguity has often greatly favoured the cause of the Church of Rome; which being admitted by her opponents to be a Church, *i. e.* a branch, though an unsound and corrupt one, of the universal Church of Christ, is thence assumed to be *the* Church,—the Society in which all men are called upon to enrol themselves; a doctrine which, whether true or not, is at least not to be taken for granted as admitted universally. —*See the article* "TRUTH," and *Essay II. on the Kingdom of Christ.*

The Church is also not unfrequently used to denote the *Clergy,* in contradistinction to the Laity; as, when we speak of any one's being educated for the Church, meaning, "for the Ministry." Some would perhaps add that it is in this sense we speak of the *endowments* of the Church; since the immediate emolument of these is received by clergymen. But if it be considered that they receive it in the capacity of *public instructors* and spiritual Pastors, these endowments may fairly be regarded as belonging, in a certain sense, to the whole Body, for whose benefit they are, in this way, calculated; in the same manner as we consider, *e. g.* the endowment of a professorship in a university, as a benefaction, not to the professors alone, but to the university at large.

vi. ELECTION.—This is one of the terms which is often to all practical purposes ambiguous, when not employed, strictly speaking, in two different *senses*, but with different *applications*, according to that which is understood in conjunction with it. — *See* Book III. § 10. *See* also *Essays on some of the Difficulties, &c.* Essay III. "On Election."

vii. EXPECT.—This word is liable to an ambiguity, which may sometimes lead, in conjunction with other causes, to a practical bad effect. It is sometimes used in the sense of "anticipate"—"calculate on," *&c.* (ἐλπίζω) in short, "consider as *probable*;" sometimes for "require or demand as reasonable,"—"consider as right," (ἀξιῶ.)

Thus, I may fairly "expect" (ἀξιῶ) that one who has received kindness from me, should protect me in distress; yet I may have reason to expect (ἐλπίζειν) that he will not. "England expects every man to do his duty;" but it would be chimerical to expect, *i. e.* anticipate, a universal performance of duty. Hence, when men of great revenues, whether civil or ecclesiastical, live in the splendour and sensuality of Sardanapalus, they are apt to plead that this is *expected* of them; which may be perhaps sometimes true, in the sense that such conduct is anticipated as probable; not true, as implying that it is required or approved. Thus also, because it would be romantic to expect (*i. e.* calculate upon) in public men a primary attention to the public good, or in men in general an adherence to the rule of doing as you would be done by, many are apt to flatter themselves that they cannot reasonably be expected (*i. e.* fairly called upon) to act on such principles. What may reasonably be expected (in one sense of the word) must be, precisely the practice of the majority; since it is the majority of instances that constitutes *probability:* what may reasonably be expected (in the other sense) is something much beyond the practice of the generality; as long at least as it shall be true that "narrow is the way that leadeth unto life, and few there be that find it."

viii. EXPERIENCE.*—This word, in its strict sense, applies to what has occurred within a person's own knowledge. Experience, in this sense, of course, relates to the *past* alone. Thus it is that a man knows by Experience what sufferings he has undergone in some disease; or, what height the tide reached at a certain time and place.

More frequently the word is used to denote that Judgment which is derived from *Experience in the primary sense,* by reasoning from that, in combination with other data. Thus, a man may assert, on the ground of Experience, that he was cured of a disorder by such a medicine—that that medicine is, generally, beneficial in that disorder; that the tide may always be expected, under such circumstances, to rise to such a height. Strictly speaking, none of these can be known *by* Experience, but are conclusions derived *from* Experience. It is in this sense only that Experience can be applied to the *future,* or, which comes to the same thing, to any *general* fact; as *e. g.* when it is said that we know by Experience that water exposed to a certain temperature will freeze.

"Men are so formed as (often unconsciously) to reason, whether well or ill, on the phenomena they observe, and to mix up their inferences with their statements of those phenomena, so as in fact to theorize (however scantily and crudely) without knowing it. If you will be at the pains carefully to analyze the simplest descriptions you hear of any transaction or state of things, you will find, that the process which almost invariably takes place is, in logical language, this; that each individual has in his mind certain *major-premises* or principles, relative to the subject in question; that observation of what actually presents itself to the senses, supplies *minor-premises;* and that the statement given (and which is reported as a thing experienced)

* See Elements of Rhetoric, Book I.

consists in fact of the *conclusions* drawn from the combinations of those premises.

"Hence it is that several different men, who have all had equal, or even the very same, experience, *i. e.* have been witnesses or agents in the same transactions, will often be found to resemble so many different men looking at the same book: one perhaps, though he distinctly sees black marks on white paper, has never learned his letters; another can read, but is a stranger to the *language* in which the book is written; another has an *acquaintance* with the language, but understands it imperfectly; another is familiar with the *language*, but is a stranger to the *subject* of the book, and wants power, or previous instruction to enable him fully to take in the author's drift; while another again perfectly comprehends the whole.

"The object that strikes the eye is to all of those persons the same; the difference of the impressions produced on the mind of each is referable to the differences in their minds.

"And this explains the fact, that we find so much discrepancy in the results of what are called Experience and Common-sense, as contra-distinguished from theory. In former times men knew by experience, that the earth stands still, and the sun rises and sets. Common-sense taught them that there could be no antipodes, since men could not stand with their heads downwards, like flies on the ceiling. Experience taught the King of Bantam that water could not become solid. And (to come to the consideration of human affairs) the experience and common-sense of one of the most observant and intelligent of historians, Tacitus, convinced him, that for a mixed government to be so framed, as to combine the elements of Royalty, Aristocracy, and Democracy, must be next to impossible, and that if such a one could be framed, it must inevitably be very speedily dissolved."*

* Pol. Econ. Lect. III.

There are again two different *applications* of the word (*see* Book III. § 10), which, when not carefully distinguished, lead in practice to the same confusion as the employment of it in two senses; *viz.* we sometimes understand *our own* personal Experience; sometimes, *general* Experience. Hume has availed himself of this (practical) ambiguity, in his Essay on Miracles; in which he observes, that we have Experience of the frequent falsity of Testimony, but that the occurrence of a Miracle is contrary to our Experience, and is consequently what no testimony ought to be allowed to establish. Now had he explained *whose* Experience he meant, the argument would have come to nothing: if he means, the Experience of mankind universally, *i. e.* that a Miracle *has never* come under the Experience of *any one,* this is palpably begging the question: if he means the Experience of each individual who has never himself witnessed a Miracle, this would establish a rule (*viz.* that we are to believe nothing of which we have not ourselves experienced the like) which it would argue insanity to act upon. Not only was the King of Bantam justified (as Hume himself admits) in listening to no evidence for the existence of Ice, but *no one would be authorized on this principle to expect his own death.* His Experience informs him, directly, only that *others* have died. Every disease under which *he himself* may have laboured, his Experience must have told him *has not* terminated fatally; if he is to judge strictly of the future by the past, according to this rule, what should hinder him from expecting the like of all future diseases?

Some have never been struck with this consequence of Hume's principles; and some have even failed to perceive it when pointed out: but if the reader thinks it worth his while to consult the author, he will see that his principles, according to his own account of them, are such as I have stated.

Perhaps however he meant, if indeed he had any distinct

meaning, something intermediate between *universal,* and *individual* experience; *viz.* the Experience of the *generality,* as to what is common and of ordinary occurrence; in which sense the maxim will only amount to this, that false Testimony is a thing of common occurrence, and that Miracles are not. An obvious truth, indeed; but too general to authorize, of itself, a conclusion in any particular case. In any other individual question, as to the admissibility of evidence, it would be reckoned absurd to consider merely the *average chances* for the truth of *Testimony in the abstract,* without inquiring *what* the Testimony is, in the *particular instance* before us. As if, *e. g.* any one had maintained that no testimony could establish Columbus's account of the discovery of America, because it is more common for travellers to lie, than for new Continents to be discovered.* Such a procedure involves a manifest ignoratio elenchi; the two propositions brought forward as opposed, being by no means incompatible: Experience tells us that "a destructive hurricane is not a common occurrence;" certain persons tell us that "a destructive hurricane occurred in the West Indies, at such a time;" there is (as Dr. Campbell has pointed out) no *opposition* between these two assertions.

It is to be observed by the way, that there is yet an additional ambiguity in the *entire phrase* "contrary to experience;" in one sense, a miracle, or any other event, may be called *contrary* to the experience of any one who has never *witnessed* the like; as the freezing of water was to that of the King of Bantam; in another and stricter sense, that only is *contrary* to a man's experience, which he knows by experience not to be true; as if one should be told of an infallible remedy for some disorder, he having seen it administered without effect. No testimony can establish what is, *in this latter sense,* contrary to experience. We

* See "Historic Doubts relative to Napoleon Buonaparte."

need not wonder that ordinary minds should be bewildered by a sophistical employment of such a mass of ambiguities.

Such reasonings as these are accounted ingenious and profound, on account of the subject on which they are employed; if applied to the ordinary affairs of life, they would be deemed unworthy of serious notice.

The reader is not to suppose that the refutation of Hume's Essay on Miracles was my object in this Article. That might have been sufficiently accomplished, in the way of a "reductio ad absurdum," by mere reference to the case of the King of Bantam adduced by the author himself. But this celebrated Essay, though it has often perhaps contributed to the amusement of an anti-christian sophist at the expense of those unable to expose its fallacy, never probably made one convert. The author himself seems plainly to have meant it as a specimen of his ingenuity in arguing on a given hypothesis; for he disputes against miracles as contrary to the Course of Nature; whereas, according to him, there is no such thing as a Course of Nature; his scepticism extends to the whole external world;—to every thing, except the ideas or impressions on the mind of the individual; so that a miracle which is *believed*, has, in that circumstance alone, on his principles, as much reality as *any* thing *can* have.

But my object has been to point out, by the use of this example, the fallacies and blunders which may result from inattention to the ambiguity of the word Experience: and this cannot be done by a mere indirect argument; which *refutes* indeed, but does not *explain*, an error.

FALSEHOOD and FALSITY.—*See* "TRUTH."

ix. GOD.—The Greek and Latin words which we translate "God" having been applied by the Heathen to the highest objects of their *worship*, were, naturally, employed by Jews and Christians to denote the object of *their own* worship. But the Heathen were far from regarding any of these supposed Beings as eternal, or as the Maker and Governor of the Universe. They regarded them as the same kind of Beings with the Fairies, Demons, Nixes, Bogles, Genii, &c., which in various parts of the world are still feared, and in some places propitiated by offerings and other marks of reverence; and which in fact are the very *Gods* (though no longer called by that title) which our Pagan forefathers worshipped; and a superstitious dread of which survived the introduction of the belief in a supreme Creator. But Christians and also Mahometans (whose creed is a corrupted offset of Christianity) imply [connote] by the term "God" the supreme Author and Governor of the Universe: as is plain from this; that any one who should deny the existence of any such Being, would be universally considered as an *Atheist; i. e.* as maintaining that there is *no* "God." And he would be not the less reckoned an Atheist, even though he should believe (which is conceivable) that there do exist Beings superior in power to Man, such as Fairies, &c.

The Heathen therefore, for the most part, come under this description. They did not believe in *any God* in our *sense of the word.* And accordingly the Apostle Paul expressly designates them as Atheists, [" without God "] ἄθεοι.

The more any one studies the ancient Classical writers, the more in error he will be respecting their notions, if he is not attentive to the difference between the meanings they attached to certain terms and those which we, now, attach to corresponding terms. The present is one instance: and another is, "immortality of the soul." See Essay I. 1st Series.

x. GOSPEL.—This is instanced as one of the words which is practically ambiguous, from its different applications, even though not employed (as it sometimes is) in different senses.

Conformably to its etymological meaning of "Good-tidings," it is used to signify (and that especially and exclusively) the welcome intelligence of Salvation to man, as preached by our Lord and his followers. But it was afterwards transitively applied to each of the four histories of our Lord's life, published by those who are called the Evangelists. And the term is often used to express collectively the Gospel-*doctrines; i. e.* the instructions given men how to *avail* themselves of the offer of salvation: and *preaching* the Gospel, is accordingly often used to include not only the *proclaiming* of the *good tidings*, but the *teaching* of what is to be believed and done, in consequence.* This ambiguity is one source of some important theological errors: many supposing that Gospel truth is to be found exclusively, or chiefly in the *Gospels;* to the neglect of the other Sacred Writings.

Again, since Jesus is said to have preached the "Gospel," and the same is said of the Apostles, the conclusion is often hence drawn, that the discourses of our Lord and the Apostolic Epistles must exactly coincide; and that in case of any apparent difference, the former must be the standard, and the latter must be taken to bear no other sense than what is implied by the other; a notion which leads inevitably and immediately to the neglect of the Apostolic Epistles, when every thing they contain must be limited and modified into a complete coincidence with our Lord's Discourses. Whereas it is very conceivable, that though both might be in a certain sense "good tidings," yet, one may contain a much more full development of the Christian scheme than the other. Which is confirmed by the consideration, that the principal events on which the Religion is founded (the atoning sacrifice and resurrection of Christ) had not taken place, nor could be clearly declared by our Lord, when He preached, saying, "the Kingdom of Heaven is *at hand;*" not that it was actually *established;* as

* See Discourse I. appended to "Essays on the Dangers," &c. p. 204.

it was, when his Apostles were sent forth to preach to all nations. See *Essays on the Difficulties*, &c. Essay II.

HENCE.—*See* "REASON" and "WHY."

IDENTICAL.—*See* "ONE" and SAME."

xi. IMPOSSIBILITY.—According to the definition we may choose to give of this word, it may be said either that there are three Species of it, or that it may be used in three different senses. 1st. What may be called a *mathematical* impossibility, is that which involves an absurdity and self-contradiction; *e.g.* that two straight lines should enclose a space, is not only impossible but inconceivable, as it would be at variance with the definition of a straight line. And it should be observed, that inability to accomplish any thing which is, in this sense, impossible, implies no limitation of *power*, and is compatible, even with omnipotence, in the fullest sense of the word. If it be proposed, *e.g.* to construct a triangle having one of its sides equal to the other two, or to find two numbers having the same ratio to each other as the side of a square and its diameter, it is not from a defect of power that we are precluded from solving such a problem as these; since in fact the problem is in itself unmeaning and absurd: it is, in reality, *nothing*, that is required to be done.

It is important to observe respecting an Impossibility of this kind, that it is always susceptible *of demonstrative proof*. Not that every such Impossibility *has* actually been proved such: or that we can be certain it ever will be; but that it must be *in itself capable* of proof:—the materials of such proof—the data on which it may be founded,—being (whether discovered or not) within the range of our knowledge. This follows from the very character (as above described)* of such truths as the mathematical: mathema-

* Book IV. Ch. ii. § 1.

tical-*impossibilities* being of course included under that term. For, every such truth must be implied—however tedious and difficult may be the task of eliciting it—in the Definitions we set out with, and consequently in the Terms, which are the exact representatives of those Definitions. *E. G.* That any two sides of a Triangle are greater than the third—in other words that it is *impossible* to construct a triangle, one of whose sides shall be equal to the other two —is a matter of easy and early demonstration. The incommensurability of the Side and the Diameter of a square,—in other words the impossibility of finding two numbers having to one another the ratio of the Side to the Diameter, —is a truth which was probably believed some time before a demonstration of it was found: but it is no less implied in the definitions of "Straight line," "Square," &c. In the case of the Circle again, the ratio of the Diameter to the Circumference has been long sought by mathematicians; and no one has yet demonstrated, or perhaps ever will, either, what their ratio is, or, on the other hand, that they are incommensurable: but one or the other must be within the sphere of mathematical demonstration.

When therefore any one says that perhaps so and so *may be* an Impossibility in the mathematical sense, though we may never be able to prove it such,* he is to keep in mind that at least such proof is *within the scope of inquiry*, and that no increase of *knowledge*, in the sense of "Information respecting facts,"† can be needed to furnish materials for the demonstration. Every such Impossibility must be implied—though we may not perceive it, in the *terms* employed; in short, it must be properly a "*contradiction in terms.*"

2dly. What may be called a *Physical* Impossibility is something at variance with the existing Laws of Nature,

* See Bishop Copleston on Predestination.

† See Book IV. Ch. ii. § 1.

and which consequently no Being, subject to those Laws, (as we are) can surmount; but we can easily conceive a Being capable of bringing about what in the ordinary course of Nature is impossible. *E.G.* to multiply five loaves into food for a multitude, or to walk on the surface of the waves, are things physically impossible, but imply no contradiction; on the contrary, we cannot but suppose that the Being, if there be such an one, who created the Universe, is able to alter at will the properties of any of the substances it contains.*

And an occurrence of this character, we call *miraculous*. Not but that one person may perform without supernatural power what is, to another, physically impossible; as *e.g.* a *man* may lift a great weight, which it would be physically impossible for a *child* to raise; because it is contrary to the Laws of Nature that a muscle of *this* degree of strength should overcome a resistance which one of *that* degree is equal to. But if any one perform what is beyond his own natural powers, or the natural powers of Man universally, he has performed a miracle.

Much sophistry has been founded on the neglect of the distinction between these two senses. It has even been contended, that no evidence ought to induce a man of sense to admit that a miracle has taken place, on the ground that it is a thing impossible; in other words, that it *is a miracle;* for if it were *not* a thing impossible to man, there would be no miracle in the case: so that such an argument is palpably begging the question; but it has often probably been admitted from an indistinct notion being suggested of Impossibility in the first sense; in which sense (*viz.* that of self-contradiction) it is admitted that no evidence would justify belief.

3dly. *Moral* Impossibility signifies only that high degree

* See an able disquisition on Miracles, subjoined to the Life of Apollonius Tyanæus, in the *Encyclopædia Metropolitana.*

of improbability which leaves no room for doubt. In this sense we often call a thing impossible, which implies no contradiction, or any violation of the Laws of Nature, but which yet we are rationally convinced will never occur, merely from the multitude of chances against it; as, *e.g.* that unloaded dice should turn up the same faces one hundred times successively.* And in this sense, we cannot accurately draw the line, so as to determine at what point the improbability amounts to an Impossibility; and hence we often have occasion to speak of this or that as *almost* impossible, though not quite, *&c.* The other impossibilities do not admit of degrees of approach. That a certain throw should recur two or three times successively, we should not call very improbable; the improbability is increased at each successive step: but we cannot say exactly when it becomes impossible; though no one would scruple to call one hundred such recurrences impossible.

In the same sense we often call things impossible which are completely within the *power* of known agents to bring about, but which we are convinced they never *will* bring about. Thus, *e.g.* that all the civilized people in the world should with one accord forsake their habitations and wander about the world as savages, every one would call an impossibility; though it is plain they have the power to do so, and that it depends on their choice which they will do; and moreover that there even have been instances of some few persons doing so. In like manner, if we were told of a man's having disgracefully fled from his post, whom we knew to be possessed of the most undaunted courage, we should without scruple (and with good reason, supposing the idea formed of his character to be a just one) pronounce this an Impossibility; meaning, that there is sufficient ground for being fully convinced that the thing could never take place;

* And yet why should they not? since the chances are the very same against *any* given 100 throws. See Rhet. Part I. Ch. ii. § 4.

not from any idea of his not having *power* and liberty to fly if he would; for our certainty is built on the very circumstance of his being free to act as he will, together with his being of such a disposition as never to have the will to act disgracefully. If, again, a man were bound hand and foot, it would be, in the other sense, impossible for him to fly; *viz.* out of his *power*.

"Capable" has a corresponding ambiguity. *E.G.* We speak of this or that man being "capable" or "incapable" of a cowardly act, in a different sense from that in which we speak of him as "capable" or "incapable" of writing a fine poem.

The performance of anything that is *morally* impossible to a mere man, is to be reckoned a *miracle*, as much as if the impossibility were *physical*. *E.G.* It is morally impossible for poor Jewish fishermen to have framed such a scheme of ethical and religious doctrine as the Gospel exhibits. It is morally impossible for a man to foretel distant and improbable future events with the exactitude of many of the prophecies in Scripture.

Much of the confusion of thought which has pervaded, and has interminably protracted, the discussions respecting the long agitated question of human freedom, has arisen from inattention to the ambiguity which has been here noticed. If the Deity, it is said, "foresees exactly what I shall do on any occasion, it must be *impossible* for me to act otherwise;" and thence it is inferred that man's actions cannot be free. The middle-term employed in such an argument as this is "impossible," or "impossibility" employed in two senses. He to whom it is, in one sense, impossible, (*viz. physically*) to act otherwise than he does, (*i.e.* who has it not in his *power*) is not a free agent; correct foreknowledge implies impossibility (in another sense, *viz. moral* impossibility;—the absence of all room for *doubt*:) and the perplexity is aggravated by resorting, for the purpose of explanation, to such words as "may," "can," "possible," "must," *&c.*, all of which are affected by a corresponding ambiguity.*

It should be observed, that many things which are not usually termed "mathematically" necessary or impossible, will at once appear such, when stated, not *abstractedly*, but with all their actual circumstances: *e. g.* that "Brutus stabbed Cæsar," is a fact, the denial of which, though a falsehood, would not be regarded as self-contradictory (like the denial of the equality of two right angles;) because, *abstractedly*, we can conceive Brutus acting otherwise: but if we *insert the circumstances* (which of course really existed) of his having complete *power, liberty, and also a predominant will* to do so, then, the denial of the action amounts to a "mathematical" impossibility, or self-contradiction; for to act voluntarily against the dictates of a predominant will, implies an effect without a cause.

Of Future events, that Being, and no other, can have the same knowledge as of the past, who is acquainted with all the causes, remote or immediate, internal and external, on which each depends.

But every one is accustomed to anticipate future events, in human affairs, as well as in the material world, *in proportion* to his *knowledge of the several circumstances* connected with each; however different in amount that knowledge may be, in reference to different occurrences. And in both cases alike, we always attribute the *failure* of any anticipation to our *ignorance* or mistake respecting some of the circumstances. When *e. g.* we fully expect, from our supposed knowledge of some person's character, and of the circumstances he is placed in, that he will do something which, eventually, he does not do, we at once and without

* *See* Tucker's "Light of Nature," in the Chapters on Providence, on Free-will, and some others. I have endeavoured to condense and to simplify some of the most valuable parts of his reasonings in the Notes and Appendix to an edition of Archbishop King's Discourse on Predestination, published at the end of the Bampton Lectures.

hesitation conclude that we were *mistaken* either as to his character, or as to his situation, or as to our acquaintance with human nature, generally; and we are accustomed to adduce any such failure as a *proof* of such mistake; saying "it is plain you *were mistaken in your estimate* of that man's character; FOR he has done so and so:" and this, as unhesitatingly as we should attribute the non-occurrence of an eclipse we had predicted, not, to any change in the Laws of Nature, but to some error in our calculations.

xii. INDIFFERENCE, in its application in respect of the *Will* and of the *Judgment*, is subject to an ambiguity which some of my readers may perhaps think hardly worth noticing; the distinction between *unbiassed candour* and impartiality, on the one side, and *carelessness*, on the other, being so very obvious. But these two things nevertheless have been, from their bearing the same name, confounded together; or at least represented as inseparably connected. I have known a person maintain, with some plausibility, the inexpediency, with a view to the attainment of truth, of educating people, or appointing teachers to instruct them, in any particular systems or theories, of astronomy, medicine, religion, politics, *&c.*, on the ground, that a man must *wish* to believe, and to find good reasons for believing, the system in which he has been trained, and which he has been engaged in teaching; and this wish must prejudice his understanding in favour of it, and consequently render him an incompetent judge of truth.*

Now let any one consider whether such a doctrine as this could have been even plausibly stated, but for the ambiguity of the word Indifference, and others connected with it. For it would follow, from such a principle, that no physician is to be trusted, who has been instructed in a certain mode of treating any disorder, because he must wish to think the theory correct which he has learned: nay, no

* See Essay I. Second Series.

physician should be trusted who is not utterly indifferent whether his patient recovers or dies; since else, he must wish to find reasons for hoping favourably from the mode of treatment pursued. No plan for the benefit of the public, proposed by a *philanthropist*, should be listened to; since such a man cannot but wish it may be successful; *&c.*

No doubt the judgment is often biassed by the inclinations; but it is possible, and it should be our endeavour, to guard against this bias. If a scheme be proposed to any one for embarking his capital in some speculation which promises great wealth, he will doubtless wish to find that the expectations held out are well founded: but every one would call him very imprudent, if (as some do) he should suffer this wish to bias his judgment, and should believe, on insufficient grounds, the fair promises held out to him. But we should not think such imprudence an inevitable consequence of his desire to increase his property. His wishes, we should say, were both natural and wise; but since they could not render the event more probable, it was most unwise to allow them to influence his decision. In like manner, a good man will indeed wish to find the evidence of the Christian religion satisfactory; but a wise man does not for that reason take for granted that it *is* satisfactory; but weighs the evidence the more carefully on account of the importance of the question.

It is curious to observe how fully aware of the operation of this bias, and how utterly blind to it, the same persons will be, in opposite cases. Such writers, *e.g.* as I have just alluded to, disparage the judgment of those who have been accustomed to study and to teach the Christian religion, and who derive hope and satisfaction from it, on the ground that they must wish to find it true. And let it be admitted that their *authority* shall go for nothing; and that the question shall be tried entirely by the *reasons* adduced. But then, on the same principle, how strong must be the testimony of the multitudes who admit the truth of Christianity, though it is to them a source of uneasiness or of dismay;—who have not adopted any antinomian system to quiet their conscience while leading an unchristian life; but, when they hear of "righteousness, temperance, and judgment to come, tremble," and try to dismiss such thoughts till "a more convenient season." The case of these, who have every reason to wish Christianity untrue, is passed by, by the very same persons who are insisting on the influence of the opposite bias. According to the homely but expressive proverb, they are "deaf on one ear."

And it may be added, that it is utterly a mistake to suppose that the bias is always *in favour* of the conclusion wished for: it is often in the contrary direction. The proverbial expression of "too good news to be true," bears witness to the existence of this feeling. There is in some minds a tendency to unreasonable doubt in cases where their wishes are strong;—a morbid distrust of evidence which they are especially anxious to find conclusive; *e. g.* groundless fears for the health or safety of an ardently-beloved child, will frequently distress anxious parents.

Different temperaments (sometimes varying with the state of health of each individual) lead towards these opposite miscalculations,—the over-estimate or under-estimate of the reasons for a conclusion we earnestly wish to find true.

Our aim should be to guard against both extremes, and to decide according to the *evidence;* preserving the Indifference of the *Judgment,* even where the *Will* neither *can,* nor *should* be indifferent.

xiii. LAW is, etymologically, that which is "laid" down; and is used, in the most appropriate sense, to signify some general injunction, command, or regulation, addressed to certain Persons, who are called upon to conform to it. It is in this sense that we speak of "the Law of Moses," "the Law of the Land," *&c.*

It is also used in a transferred sense, to denote the statement of some *general fact*, the several individual instances of which exhibit a conformity to that statement, *analogous* to the conduct of persons in respect to a Law which they obey. It is in this sense that we speak of "the Laws of Nature:" when we say that "a seed in vegetating directs the radicle downwards and the plumule upwards, in compliance with a Law of Nature," we only mean that such is *universally the fact;* and so, in other cases.

It is evident therefore that, in this sense, the conformity of individual cases to the general rule is that which *constitutes* a Law of Nature. If water should henceforth never become solid, at any temperature, then the freezing of water would no longer be a Law of Nature: whereas in the other sense, a Law is not the more or the less a Law from the conformity or non-conformity of individuals to it: if an Act of our Legislature were to be disobeyed and utterly disregarded by every one, it would not on that account be the less a Law.

This distinction may appear so obvious when plainly stated, as hardly to need mention: yet writers of great note and ability have confounded these two senses together: I need only mention Hooker (in the opening of his great work) and Montesquieu: the latter of whom declaims on the much stricter observance in the Universe of the Laws of Nature, than in mankind, of the divine and human Laws laid down for their conduct: not considering that, in the former case, it is the observance that *constitutes* the Law.

xiv. MAY, and likewise MUST, and CAN, (as well as CANNOT) are each used in two senses, which are very often confounded together. They relate sometimes to *Power*, or *Liberty*, sometimes to *Contingency*.

When we say of one who has obtained a certain sum of money, "now he *may* purchase the field he was wishing for," we mean that it is in his *power;* it is plain that he *may*, in the same sense, hoard up the money, or spend it on something else; though perhaps we are convinced, from our knowledge of his character and situation, that he will not. When again we say, "it may rain to-morrow," or "the vessel may have arrived in port," the expression does not at all relate to power, but merely to contingency: *i. e.* we mean, that though we are not sure such an event will happen or has happened, we are not sure of the reverse.

When, again, we say, "this man, of so grateful a disposition, *must* have eagerly embraced such an opportunity of requiting his benefactor," or "one who approves of the slave trade *must* be very hard-hearted," we only mean to imply the absence of all *doubt* on these points. The very notions of gratitude and of hard-heartedness exclude the idea of *compulsion*, and of yielding to irresistible power. But when we say that "all men *must* die," or that "a man *must* go to prison who is dragged by force," we mean "whether they will or not"—that there is no *power* to resist. So also, if we say that a Being of perfect goodness "*cannot*" act wrong, we do not mean that it is out of his *power;* since that would imply no goodness of character; but that there is sufficient reason for feeling sure that He *will* not. It is in a very different sense that we say of a man fettered in a prison, that he "*cannot*" escape: meaning, that though he has the *will*, he wants the *ability*.

These words are commonly introduced, in questions connected with Fatalism and the Freedom of human actions, to explain the meaning of "necessary," "impossible," *&c.;* and having themselves a corresponding ambiguity, they only tend to increase the perplexity.*

> "——— Chaos umpire sits,
> And by deciding worse embroils the fray."

MUST.—*See* "MAY."

XV. NECESSARY.—This word is used as the contrary to "impossible" in all its senses, and is of course liable to a corresponding ambiguity. Thus it is "mathematically Necessary" that two sides of a triangle should be greater than the third; there is a "physical Necessity" for the fall of a stone; and a "moral Necessity" that Beings of such and such a character should act, when left perfectly free, in such and such a manner; *i.e.* we are sure they *will* act so; though of course it is in their power to act otherwise; else there would be no moral agency.* This ambiguity is employed sophistically to justify immoral conduct; since no one is *responsible* for anything done under "necessity,"—*i. e.* "physical necessity;" as when a man is dragged anywhere by external force, or falls down from being too weak to stand; and then the same excuse is fallaciously extended to "moral necessity" also.

There are likewise numberless different *applications* of the word "necessity" (as well as of those derived from it) in which there is a practical ambiguity, from the difference of the things *understood in conjunction* with it: *e.g.* food is "necessary;" *viz.*—to life; great wealth is "necessary"—to the gratification of a man of luxurious habits; the violation of moral duty is in many cases "necessary"—for the attainment of certain worldly objects; the renunciation of such objects, and subjugation of the desires, is "necessary"—to the attainment of the Gospel-promises, *&c.* And thus it is that "necessity" has come to be "the tyrant's plea;" for as no one is at all responsible for what is a matter of physical necessity,—what he has no power to avoid,—so, a degree of allowance is made for a man's doing what he *has* power to avoid, when it appears to be the less of two evils; as *e.g.* when a man who is famishing takes the first food he meets with, as "necessary" to support life, or throws over goods in a storm, when it is "necessary" in order to save the ship. But if the plea of necessity be admitted without inquiring *for what* the act

* See the article "Impossibility;" note.

in question is necessary, anything whatever may be thus vindicated; since no one commits any crime which is not, in his view, "necessary" to the attainment of some supposed advantage or gratification.

The confusion of thought is further increased by the employment on improper occasions of the phrase "*absolutely* necessary;" which, strictly speaking, denotes a case in which there is no possible alternative. It is necessary *for* a man's safety, that he should remain in a house which he cannot quit without incurring danger: it is *absolutely* (*or simply*) necessary that he should remain there, if he is closely imprisoned in it.

I have treated more fully on this fruitful source of sophistry in the Appendix (No. I.) to King's "Discourse on Predestination." In the course of it, I suggested (in the first edition) an etymology of the word, which I have reason to think is not correct; but it should be observed, that this makes no difference in the reasoning, which is not in any degree founded on that etymology; nor have I, as some have represented, attempted to introduce any new or unusual sense of the word, but have all along appealed to *common use*,—the only right standard,—and merely pointed out the senses in which each word *has actually* been employed. *See* the introduction to this Appendix.

xvi. OLD.—This word, in its strict and primary sense, denotes the *length* of time that any object has existed; and many are not aware that they are accustomed to use it in any other. It is, however, very frequently employed instead of "Ancient," to denote *distance* of time. The same transition seems to have taken place, in Latin. Horace says of Lucilius, who was one of the most *ancient* Roman authors, but who did not live to be *old*—

——— "quo fit ut omnis
Votiva pateat veluti descripta tabella
Vita *Senis*."

The present is a remarkable instance of the influence of an ambiguous word over the thoughts even of those who are not *ignorant* of the ambiguity, but are not carefully on the watch against its effects; the impressions and ideas associated by habit with the word when used in one sense, being always apt to obtrude themselves unawares when it is employed in another sense, and thus to affect our reasonings. *E. G.* "*Old* times,"—"the *Old* world," *&c.* are expressions in frequent use, and which, oftener than not, produce imperceptibly the associated impression of the superior wisdom resulting from experience, which, as a general rule, we attribute to Old *men.* Yet no one is really ignorant that the world is older now than ever it was; and that the instruction to be derived from observations on the past (which is the advantage that *Old persons* possess) must be greater, supposing other things equal, to every successive generation; and Bacon's remark to this purpose appears, as soon as distinctly stated, a mere truism: yet few, perhaps, that he made, are more important. There is always a tendency to appeal with the same kind of deference, to the authority of "Old times," as of aged men.

It should be kept in mind, however, that ancient *customs, institutions, &c.* when they *still exist,* may be literally called Old; and have this advantage attending them, that their effects may be estimated from long experience; whereas we cannot be sure, respecting any recently-established Law or System, whether it may not produce in time some effects which were not originally contemplated.*

xvii. ONE—is sometimes employed to denote strict and proper numerical Unity; sometimes, close Resemblance;—correspondence with one single description.—*See* "SAME."

————"Facies non omnibus UNA,
Nec diversa tamen; qualem decet esse sororum."—*Ov. Met.* b. ii.

* See however the Article reprinted from the London Review, in the first letter to Earl Grey on Secondary Punishments.

It is in the secondary or improper, not the primary and proper sense of this word, that men are exhorted to "be of one mind;" *i. e.* to agree in their faith,—pursuits,—mutual affections, *&c.* "The Church" [*viz.:* the Universal or Catholic Church] "is undoubtedly *one*, and so is the Human Race *one;* but not as a *Society*. It was from the first composed of distinct Societies; which were called one, because formed on common principles. *It is One Society* only when considered as to its future existence. The circumstance of its having one common Head, Christ, one Spirit, one Father, are points of unity, which no more make the Church One Society on earth, than the circumstance of all men having the same *Creator*, and being derived from the same Adam, renders the Human Race one Family."*

It is also in this sense that two guineas, *e.g.* struck from a wedge of uniform fineness, are said to be "of one and the same form and weight," and also "of one and the same substance." In this secondary or improper sense also, a child is said to be "of one and the same (bodily) substance with its mother;" or, simply "of the substance of its mother:" for these two pieces of money, and two human Beings, are *numerically* distinct.

It is evidently most important to keep steadily in view, and to explain on proper occasions, these different uses of the word; lest men should insensibly slide into error on the most important of all subjects, by applying, in the secondary sense, expressions which ought to be understood in the primary and proper.—(*See* "PERSON.") *Unity* is, as might have been expected, liable to corresponding ambiguities. *E. G.* Sometimes what the Apostles say concerning "Unity of Spirit"—of Faith—*&c.* is transferred to Unity of Church-Government.

* Encyclop. Metrop., p. 774.

xviii. PAY.—In the strict sense, a person is said to "pay," who transfers to another what was *once his* own: in another sense "pay" is used to denote the mere act of *handing over* what perhaps *never was* one's own. In this latter sense a gentleman's steward or housekeeper is said to pay the tradesmen their bills; in the other sense, it is the master who pays them.

It is in the secondary or improper sense that an executor is said to pay legacies,—a landowner or farmer to pay tithes, *&c.*, since the money these hand over to another *never was theirs*. *See* "EVIDENCE," (in vol. of Tracts,) p. 339.

xix. PERSON,* in its ordinary use at present, invariably implies a numerically distinct substance. Each man is one Person, and can be but one. It has also a peculiar theological sense, in which we speak of the "three Persons" of the blessed Trinity. It was probably thus employed by our Divines as a literal, or perhaps etymological, rendering of the Latin word "Persona." I am inclined to think, however, from the language of Wallis (the Mathematician and Logician) in the following extract, as well as from that of some other of our older writers, that the English word Person was formerly not so strictly confined as now, to the sense it bears in common conversation among us.

"That which makes these expressions" (*viz.* respecting the Trinity) "seem harsh to some of these men, is because they have used themselves to fansie that notion only of the word Person, according to which three men are accounted to be three persons, and these three persons to be three men. But he may consider that there is another notion of the word Person, and in common use too, wherein the same man may be said to sustain divers persons, and those

* Most of the following observations will apply to the word "Personality."

persons to be the same man: that is, the same man as sustaining divers capacities. As was said but now of Tully, *Tres Personas Unus sustineo; meam, adversarii, judicis.* And then it will seem no more harsh to say, The Three Persons, Father, Son, and Holy Ghost, are One God, than to say, God the Creatour, God the Redeemer, and God the Sanctifier, are one God . . . . . it is much the same thing whether of the two forms we use."—*Letters on the Trinity*, p. 63.

"The word Person *(persona)* is originally a Latin word, and does not properly signify a *Man;* (so that *another person* must needs imply *another man)* for then the word *Homo* would have served, and they needed not have taken in the word *Persona;* but rather, one *so circumstantiated.* And the *same Man*, if considered in other circumstances (considerably different) is reputed *another person.* And that this is the true notion of the word Person, appears by those noted phrases, *personam induere, personam deponere, personam agere*, and many the like, in approved Latin authours. Thus the same man may at once sustain the Person, of a *King* and a *Father*, if he be invested both with *regal* and *paternal* authority. Now because the King and the Father are for the most part not only different persons but different men also, (and the like in other cases) hence it comes to pass that *another Person* is sometimes supposed to imply *another man;* but not always, nor is that the proper sense of the word. It is Englished in our dictionaries by the *state, quality* or *condition whereby one man differs from another;* and so, as the condition alters, the Person alters, though the man be the same.

"The hinge of the controversy, is, that notion concerning the *three somewhats*, which the Fathers (who first used it) did intend to design by the name Person; so that we are not from the word *Person* to determine what was that *Notion;* but from that Notion which they would express, to determine in what sense the word Person is here used," *&c. &c.*—*Letter V. in Answer to the Arian's Vindication.**

What was precisely the notion which these Latin Fathers intended to convey, and how far it approached the classical signification of the word "Persona," it may not be easy to determine. But we must presume that they did not intend to employ it in what is, now, the ordinary sense of the word Person; both because "Persona" never, I believe, bore that sense in pure Latinity, and also because it is evident that, in that sense, "three divine Persons" would have been exactly equivalent to "three Gods;" a meaning which the orthodox always disavowed.

It is probable that they had nearly the same view with which the Greek theologians adopted the word Hypostasis; which seems calculated to express "that which stands under (*i.e.* is the Subject of) Attributes." They meant, it may be presumed, to guard against the suspicion of teaching, on the one hand, that there are three Gods, or three Parts of the one God; or, on the other hand, that Father, Son, and Holy Ghost are no more than three *names*,† all, of the same signification; and they employed accordingly a term which might serve to denote, that, (though divine Attributes

* Dr. Wallis's theological works, considering his general celebrity, are wonderfully little known. He seems to have been, in his day, one of the ablest Defenders of the Church's doctrine, against the Arians and Socinians of that period. Of course he incurred the censure, not only of them, but of all who, though not professedly Arian, gave such an exposition of their doctrine as amounts virtually to Tritheism. I beg to be understood however as not demanding an implicit deference for his, or for any other human authority, however eminent. We are taught to "call no man Master, on earth." But the reference to Dr. Wallis may serve both to show the use of the word in his days, and to correct the notion, should any have entertained it, that the views of the subject here taken are, in our Church, anything novel.

† It is possible that some may have used this expression in the very sense attached by others to the word "Person;" led, in a great degree, by the peculiar signification of "Name" in Scripture. For some very important remarks on that signification, *see* Hinds's History, and also a Sermon on the Name Emmanuel in the vol. I lately published.

belong to all and each of these, yet) there are Attributes of each, respectively, which are not so strictly applicable to either of the others, as such; as when, for instance, the Son is called especially the "Redeemer," and the Holy Spirit, the "Comforter or Paraclete,"* *&c.* The notion thus conveyed is indeed very *faint*, and *imperfect;* but is perhaps for that very reason, (considering what Man is, and what God is,) the less likely to lead to error. One may convey to a blind man a notion of seeing, correct as far as it goes, and instructive to him, though very imperfect: if he form a more full and *distinct* notion of it, his ideas will inevitably be *incorrect.*—*See* Essay VII. § 5, Second Series. †

It is perhaps to be regretted that our Divines, in rendering the Latin "Persona," used the word Person, whose ordinary sense, in the present day at least, differs in a most important point from the theological sense, and yet is not so remote from it as to preclude all mistake and perplexity. If "Hypostasis," or any other completely foreign term had been used instead, no idea at all would have been conveyed except that of the explanation given; and thus the danger at least of being misled by a word, would have been avoided. ‡

Our Reformers however did not introduce the word into their Catechism; though it has been (I must think, injudiciously) employed in some popular expositions of the

* English readers are not usually aware that the title of "Paraclete" is ever distinctly applied to Christ in Scripture, as it is in 1 John ii. 1, because it is there translated "advocate" instead of "comforter."

† It is worth observing, as a striking instance of the little reliance to be placed on *etymology* as a guide to the meaning of a word, that "Hypostasis," "Substantia," and "Understanding," so widely different in their sense, correspond in their etymology.

‡ I wish it to be observed, that it is the *ambiguity* of the word Person which renders it objectionable; not, its being nowhere employed in *Scripture* in the technical sense of theologians; for this circumstance is rather an advantage.—*See* Essay VI. (Second Series) § 4, note.

Catechism, without any explanation, or even allusion to its being used in a peculiar sense.

As it is, the danger of being not merely *not* understood but *mis*understood, should be guarded against most sedulously, by all who wish not only to keep clear of error, but to inculcate important truth; by seldom or never employing this ambiguous word without some explanation or caution. For if we employ, without any such care, terms which we must be sensible are likely to mislead, at least the unlearned and the unthinking, we cannot stand acquitted on the plea of not having directly inculcated error.

I am persuaded that much heresy, and some infidelity, may be traced in part to the neglect of this caution. It is not wonderful that some should be led to renounce a doctrine, which, through the ambiguity in question, may be represented to them as involving a self-contradiction, or as leading to Tritheism;—that others should insensibly slide into this very error;—or that many more (which I know to be no uncommon case) should, for fear of that error, deliberately, and on principle, keep the doctrine of the Trinity out of their thoughts, as a point of speculative belief, to which they have assented once for all, but which they find it dangerous to dwell on; though it is in fact the very Faith into which,* by our Lord's appointment, we are baptized.

Nor should those who do understand, or at least have once understood, the ambiguity in question, rest satisfied that they are thenceforward safe from all danger in that quarter. It should be remembered that the thoughts are habitually influenced, through the force of association, by the recurrence of the ordinary sense of any word to the mind of those who are not especially on their guard against it. *See* "Fallacies," § 5.

* εἰς τὸ ὄνομα, "*into* the Name;" not "*in* the Name." Matt. xxviii. 19.

The correctness of a *formal* and *deliberate Confession* of Faith, is not always, of itself, a sufficient safeguard against error in the *habitual impressions* on the mind. The Romanists flatter themselves that they are safe from Idolatry, because they distinctly acknowledge the truth, that "God only is to be *served;*" *viz.* with "Latria;" though they allow ADORATION, ("hyperdulia" and "dulia") to the Virgin and other Saints,—to Images,—and to Relics: to which it has been justly replied, that supposing this distinction correct in itself, it would be, in practice, nugatory; since the mass of the people must soon (as experience proves) lose sight of it entirely in their habitual devotions.

Nor again is the habitual acknowledgment of *One* God, of itself a sufficient safeguard; since, from the additional ambiguities of "One" and "Unity," (noticed in a preceding Article) we may gradually fall into the notion of a merely *figurative* Unity; such as unity of substance merely, (see a preceding Article)—Unity of purpose,—concert of action, *&c.* such as is often denoted by the phrase "one mind." *See* "SAME," in this Appendix, and "Dissertation," Book IV. Ch. v.

When however I speak of the necessity of *explanations*, the reader is requested to keep in mind, that I mean, not explanations of the *nature of the Deity*, but of our *own use of words.* On the one hand we must not content ourselves with merely saying that the whole subject is mysterious and must not be too nicely pried into; while we neglect to notice the distinction between divine revelations, and human explanations of them;—between inquiries into the mysteries of the divine nature, and into the mysteries arising from the ambiguities of language, and of a language too, adopted by uninspired men. For, whatever Scripture declares, the Christian is bound to receive implicitly, however unable to understand it: but to claim an uninquiring assent to expressions of man's framing, (however judiciously framed) without even an attempt to ascertain their meaning, is to fall into one of the worst errors of the Romanists.

On the other hand, to require explanations of what God is in Himself, is to attempt what is beyond the reach of the human faculties, and foreign from the apparent design of Scripture-revelation; which seems to be, chiefly, if not wholly, to declare to us, (at least to insist on among the essential articles of faith) with a view to our practical benefit, and to the influencing of our feelings and conduct, not so much the intrinsic nature of the Deity, as, what He is and does, relatively to us. Scripture teaches us (and our Church-Catechism directs our attention to these points) to "believe in God, who, as the Father, *hath made* us and all the world,—as the Son, *hath redeemed* us and all mankind, —as the Holy Ghost, *sanctifieth* us, and all the elect people of God."* And this distinction is, as I have said, pointed out in the very form of Baptism. Nothing indeed can be more decidedly *established* by Scripture,—nothing more *indistinctly explained* (except as far as relates to *us*) than the doctrine of the Trinity;† nor are we perhaps capable, with our present faculties, of comprehending it more fully.

In these matters, our inquiry,—at least our *first* inquiry,—should always be, what is *revealed:* nor, if any one refuses to adopt as an article of faith, this or that exposition, should he be understood as necessarily maintaining its *falsity*. For we are sure that there must be many truths relative to the Deity, which we have no means of ascertaining: nor does it follow that even every

* Hawkins's Manual, p. 12.

† Compare together, for instance, such passages as the following; for it is by *comparing* Scripture with Scripture, not by dwelling on *insulated* texts, that the Word of God is to be rightly understood: Luke i. 35, and John xiv. 9; John xiv. 16, 18, 26, Matt. xxviii. 19, 20; John xvi. 7, Coloss. ii. 9; Philip. i. 19, 1 Cor. vi. 19; Matt. x. 20, and John xiv. 23.

truth which *can* be ascertained, must be a part of the essential faith of a Christian.

And as it is wise to reserve for mature age, such instructions as are unsuitable to a puerile understanding, so, it seems the part of a like wisdom, to abstain, during this our state of childhood, from curious speculations on subjects in which even the ablest of human minds can but "see by means of a glass, darkly." On these, the Learned can have no advantage over others; though we are apt to forget that any mysterious point inscrutable to Man, as Man,—surpassing the utmost reach of human intellect,—must be such to the learned and to the ignorant, to the wise and to the simple, alike;—that in utter darkness, the strongest sight, and the weakest, are on a level. "Sir, in these matters," (said one of the most eminent of our Reformers, respecting another mysterious point,) "I am so fearful, that I dare speak no further, yea almost none otherwise, than as the Scripture doth as it were *lead me by the hand*."

And surely it is much better thus to *consult* Scripture, and take it for a *guide*, than to resort to it merely for *confirmations*, contained in detached texts, of the several parts of some System of Theology, which the student fixes on as reputed orthodox, and which is in fact made the guide which he permits to "lead him by the hand;" while passages culled out from various parts of the Sacred Writings in subserviency to such system, are formed into what may be called an *anagram* of Scripture: and then, by reference to this system as a standard, each doctrine or discourse is readily pronounced Orthodox, or Socinian, or Arian, or Sabellian, or Nestorian, *&c.*; and all this, on the ground that the theological scheme which the student has adopted, is supported by Scripture. The *materials* indeed are the stones of the Temple; but the *building* constructed with them is a fabric of human contrivance. If instead of this, too common, procedure, students would fairly search the Scriptures with a view not merely to *defend* their opinions, but to *form* them,—not merely for *arguments*, but for *truth*,—keeping human expositions to their own proper purposes [*See* Essay VI. First Series,] and not allowing these to become, practically, a standard,—if, in short, they were as honestly desirous to be *on the side of Scripture*, as they naturally are to have *Scripture on their side*, how much sounder, as well as more charitable, would their conclusions often be!

With presumptuous speculations, such as I have alluded to, many theologians, even of those who lived near, and indeed during, the Apostolical times, seem to have been alike chargeable, widely as they differed in respect of the particular explanations adopted by each:

> "Unus utrique
> Error; sed variis illudit partibus."

And it is important to remember,—what we are very liable to lose sight of—the circumstance, that, not only there arose grievous errors during the time of the Apostles, and consequently such were likely to exist in the times immediately following, but also that when these *inspired* guides were removed, there was no longer the same infallible authority to decide what *was* error. In the absence of such a guide, some errors might be received as orthodox, and some sound doctrines be condemned as heterodox.

The Gnostics* introduced a theory of Æons, or successive emanations from the divine "Pleroma" or Fulness; one of whom was Christ, and became incarnate in the man Jesus.† The Sabellians are reported to have described Christ as bearing the same relation to the Father, as the illuminating (φωτιστικὸν) quality does to the Sun; while the Holy Ghost corresponded to the warming quality

* Of these, and several other ancient heretics, we have no accounts but those of their *opponents*; which however we may presume to contain more or less of approximation to what was usually maintained.

† These heretics appear to have split into many different sects, teaching various modifications of the same absurdities.—See *Burton's Bampton Lectures*.

(θαλπὸν): or again, the Three as corresponding to the Body, Soul, and Spirit, of a man; or again, to Substance,—Thought or Reason,—and Will or Action. The Arians again represented the Son and the Holy Spirit, as created Beings, but with a certain imparted divinity. The Nestorians and Eutychians gave opposite, but equally fanciful and equally presumptuous explanations of the Incarnation, *&c. &c.*

Nor were those who were accounted orthodox, altogether exempt from the same fault of presumptuous speculation. "Who," says Chrysostom, "was he to whom God said, Let us make man? who but he . . . . . the Son of God?" And Epiphanius, on the same passage, says, "This is the language of God to his Word." Each of these writers, it may be observed, in representing *God* (under *that* title) as addressing Himself to the Son as to a distinct Being previously to the birth of Jesus on earth, approaches very closely to the Arian view. And Justin Martyr, in a similar tone, expressly speaks of God as "One, not in *number*, but in judgment or designs."* I will not say that such passages as these may not be so interpreted as to exclude every form of tritheism; but it is a dangerous thing, to use (and that, not in the heat of declamation, but in a professed *exposition*) language of such a nature that it is a mere chance whether it may not lead into the most unscriptural errors. If the early writers had not been habitually very incautious in this point, that could hardly have taken place which is recorded respecting the council held at Rimini, (A.D. 360) in which a Confession of Faith was agreed upon, which the Arians soon after boasted of as sanctioning their doctrine, and "the Church," we are told, "was astonished to find itself unexpectedly become Arian."†

The fact is, that numberless writers, both of those who

* Οὗτος . . . . . γεγραμμένος Θεὸς, ἕτερος ἐστι τοῦ τὰ πάντα ποιήσαντος Θεοῦ, ἀριθμῷ λέγω, ἀλλ' αὐ γνώμῃ; *&c.*

† See Essay VI. (Second Series), § 2. Note b.

were, and who were not, accounted heretics, being displeased, and justly, with one another's explanations of the mode of existence of the Deity, instead of taking warning aright from the errors of their neighbours, sought, each, the remedy, in some *other* explanation instead, concerning matters unrevealed and inexplicable by man. They found nothing to satisfy a metaphysical curiosity in the brief and *indistinct,* though decisive, declarations of Scripture, that "God was in Christ, reconciling the World unto Himself;" —that "in Him dwelleth all the Fulness of the Godhead, bodily;"—that "it is God that worketh in us both to will and to do of his good pleasure;"—that if we "keep Christ's saying, He dwelleth in us, and we, in Him;"—that "if any man have not the Spirit of Christ, he is none of his;"—and that "the Lord is the Spirit," *&c.** They wanted something more full, and more philosophical, than all this; and their theology accordingly was "spoiled, through philosophy and vain deceit, after the tradition of men, after the rudiments of the World, and not after Christ." Hostile as they were to each other, the grand mistake in principle was common to many in all parties.

And in later ages the Schoolmen kept up the same Spirit, and even transmitted it to Protestants. "Theology teaches," (says a passage in a Protestant work) "that there is in God, one Essence, two Processions, three Persons, four Relations, five Notions, and the Circumincession, which the Greeks call Perichoresis." . . . . What follows is still more to my purpose; but I cannot bring myself to transcribe any further. "Who is this that darkeneth counsel by words without knowledge?"

But the substance of great part of what I have been saying, has been expressed in better language than mine,

* Not, as in our version, "*that* Spirit;" Ὁ δὲ Κύριος ΤΟ πνευμά ἐστιν. In this place, and also in John i. 21, our translators were apparently looking to some version in which an attempt is made to express in Latin the force of the Greek Article.

in a late work, which displays no ordinary ability, Mr. Douglas's *Errors regarding Religion*.

"The radical mistake in all these systems, whether heretical or orthodox, which have embroiled mankind in so many scandalous disputes, and absurd and pernicious opinions, proceeds from the disposition so natural in man of being wise above what is written. They are not satisfied with believing a plain declaration of the Saviour, 'I and the Father are one.' They undertake with the utmost presumption and folly to explain in what manner the Father and the Son are one; but man might as well attempt to take up the ocean in the hollow of his hand, as endeavour, by his narrow understanding, to comprehend the manner of the Divine existence." . . . . P. 50.

"Heresies, however, are not confined to the heterodox. While the Arians and Semi-Arians were corrupting the truth by every subtilty of argument and ingenious perversion of terms, the orthodox all the while were dogmatizing about the Divine nature with a profusion of words which either had no meaning, or were gross mistakes, or inapplicable metaphors when applied to the infinite and spiritual existence of God. And not content with using such arguments against the heretics as generally produced a new heresy without refuting the former one, as soon as they obtained the power, they expelled them from the Roman empire, and sent them with all the zeal which persecution confers, and which the orthodox, from their prosperity, had lost, to spread every variety of error amongst the nations of the barbarians.

"Orthodoxy was become a very nice affair, from the rigour of its terms, and the perplexity of its creed, and very unlike the highway for the simple, which the Gospel presents. A slip in a single expression was enough to make a man a heretic. The use or omission of a single word occasioned a new rent in Christianity. Every heresy produced a new creed, and every creed a new heresy. . . . . .

Never does human folly and learned ignorance appear in a more disgusting point of view than in these disputes of Christians amongst themselves; nor does any study appear so well calculated to foster infidelity as the history of Christian sects, unless the reader be guided by light from above, and carefully distinguish the doctrines of the Bible from the miserable disputes of pretended Christians."—P. 53.

To discuss this important subject more fully (or perhaps indeed as fully as it has been here treated of) is hardly suitable to a logical work: and yet the importance of attending to the ambiguity I have now been considering, cannot be duly appreciated, without offering some remarks on the subject-matter with which that ambiguity is connected; and such remarks again, if scantily and imperfectly developed, are open to cavil or mistake. I must take the liberty therefore of referring the reader to such works, (in addition to those already mentioned) both my own, and those of others, as contain something of a fuller statement of the same views. It may be added, that the views I have taken derive confirmation, now that they have been so long before the public, from the total absence (to the best of my knowledge) of all attempts at refutation; especially when considered in conjunction with the strong objection to them which is felt by some. *E. G.* I have seen, in an argumentative work, a warning given to the reader against this very Article (by name) as containing very erroneous doctrine; of which, however, *no refutation* at all is subjoined; which one cannot but suppose any writer would have done, who had ever thought of, or heard of, any, even plausible, arguments against the doctrines censured.—See *Essays* (First Series), Essay II. § 4, and Essays IV. and V.;—Second Series, Essay VI. § 2, p. 199; VII. § 3; and IX. § 1.—Third Series, Essay II. § 1. *Archbishop King's Sermon on Predestination, &c.*, and *Encyclop. Metropol.* History, Chap. xxvii. p. 589, and Chap. xxxiv. p. 740.

xx. POSSIBLE. — This word, like the others of kindred meaning, relates sometimes to *contingency*, sometimes to *power* or liberty; and these two senses are frequently confounded. In the first sense we say, *e.g.* "it is possible this patient may recover," not meaning, that it depends on *his choice;* but that *we* are *not sure* whether the event will not be such. In the other sense it is "possible" to the best man to violate every rule of morality; since if it were out of his *power* to act so if he chose it, there would be no moral goodness in the case; though we are quite sure that such never *will* be his choice.—*See* "IMPOSSIBLE."

xxi. PREACH.—The word "preach" has "so much slid from its original sense of *proclaiming* as a herald, as to obscure the sense of every passage in which the preaching of the gospel,—(κηρύττειν τὸ εὐαγγέλιον,)—literally, 'proclaiming the good tidings,' occurs. The sacred writers constantly preserve the distinction between 'preaching' and 'teaching:'—'announcing,'—'giving *information* of an event;' and giving *instruction* to believers. And our translators have also, *almost* always, adhered to this distinction; though the word 'preach,' having in great measure acquired, in their time, its secondary sense, there is one passage in which they inadvertently so employ it. When the disciples were assembled at Troas, 'to break bread, Paul *preached* unto them, and as Paul was long *preaching*, the young man Eutychus fell down from a window, and was taken up dead:' the word διαλεγομένος should have been rendered 'discoursing.' To *disciples*, he did not, in the strict sense, *preach*. So also it is not *our* business, in the strict sense, to 'preach the gospel,' except to any who, from their tender years, or from neglected education, have never had the glad tidings announced to them of God's giving his Son for our salvation. Our ordinary occupation is not to preach (κηρύττειν) but (διδάσκειν) to teach men how to understand the Scriptures, and to apply them to their lives."—*Discourse appended to " Essays on the Dangers to Christian Faith."*—Pp. 264, 265.

xxii. PRIEST.—*See* " DISSERTATION," Book IV. Ch. iv. § 2.

Etymologically, the word answers to Presbyter, *i. e.* Elder, in the Christian Church, or Jewish Synagogue;* and is often applied to the second order of Christian Ministers at the present day. But it is remarkable that it never occurs in this sense, in our translation of the Scriptures: the word πρεσβύτερος being always rendered by Elder; and its derivative, Priest, always given as the translation of Ἱερεὺς. This latter is an office assigned to none under the Gospel-scheme, except the ONE great High Priest, of whom the Jewish Priests were types, and who offered a sacrifice (that being the most distinguishing office of a Priest in the sense of Ἱερεὺς) which is the only one under the Gospel.

It is incalculable how much confusion has arisen from confounding together the two senses of the word Priest, and thence, the two offices themselves.

I have enlarged accordingly on this subject in a Sermon, delivered before the University of Oxford, and subjoined to the last edition of the Bampton Lectures. See also *Essays,* Third Series, Essay II.

xxiii. REASON.—This word is liable to many ambiguities, of which I propose to notice only a few of the most important. Sometimes it is used to signify all the intellectual powers collectively; in which sense it can hardly be said to be altogether denied to brutes; since several of what we reckon intellectual processes in the human mind, are evidently such as some brutes are capable of.

Reason is, however, frequently employed to denote those

* See Vitringa on the Synagogue. The abridged translation, by Mr. Bernard, of this valuable work, is an important addition to our theological literature.

intellectual powers exclusively in which Man *differs* from brutes; though what these are no one has been able precisely to define. The employment at will of the faculty of Abstraction seems to be the principal; that being, at least, principally concerned in the use of Language. The Moral faculty, or power of distinguishing right from wrong, (which appears also to be closely connected with Abstraction, without which it could not exist) is one of which brutes are destitute; but then Dr. Paley and some other ethical writers deny it to Man also. The description given by that author of our discernment of good and bad conduct, (*viz.* as wholly dependent on expectation of reward and punishment,) would in a great degree apply to many of the brute-creation; especially the more intelligent of domestic animals, as dogs and horses. It is in this sense, however, that some writers speak of "*Reason*" as enabling us to judge of virtue and vice; not, as Dr. Campbell in his Philosophy of Rhetoric has understood them, in the sense of the power of *argumentation.*

Reason, however, is often used for the faculty of carrying on the "third operation" of the mind; *viz. Reasoning,* or *Ratiocination.* And it is from inattention to this ambiguity (which has been repeatedly noticed in the course of the foregoing treatise,) that some have treated of Logic as the art of rightly employing the mental faculties in general.

Reason is also employed to signify the Premiss or Premises of an Argument; especially the Minor-Premiss; and it is from Reason in this sense that the word "Reasoning" is derived.

It is also very frequently used to signify a *Cause;* as when we say, in popular language, that the "Reason of an eclipse of the sun is, that the moon is interposed between it and the earth." This should be strictly called the *cause.* On the other hand, "Because" (*i.e.* "by-Cause") is used to introduce either the Physical Cause or the Logical proof: and "Therefore," "Hence," "Since," "Follow," "Consequence," and many other kindred words, have a corresponding ambiguity: *e. g.* "the ground is wet, *because* it has rained;" or "it has rained, and hence the ground is wet;" this is the assignment of the *cause:* again, "it has rained, *because* the ground is wet;" "the ground is wet, and *therefore* it has rained:" this is assigning the logical *proof;* the wetness of the ground is the cause, not of the rain having fallen, but of *our knowing* that it has fallen. And this probably it is that has led to the ambiguous use in all languages of almost all the words relating to these two points. It is an ambiguity which has produced incalculable confusion of thought, and from which it is the harder to escape, on account of its extending to those very forms of expression which are introduced in order to clear it up.

What adds to the confusion is, that the Cause is often employed as a Proof of the Effect:* as when we infer, from a great fall of rain, that there is, or will be, a flood; which is at once the physical Effect, and the logical Conclusion. The case is just reversed, when from a flood we infer that the rain has fallen.

The more attention any one bestows on this ambiguity, the more extensive and important its results will appear.—*See* Book i. § 2. *See* also Rhetoric, Book i.

xxiv. REGENERATION.—This word is employed by some Divines to signify the actual new life and character which ought to distinguish the Christian; by others, a release from a state of condemnation:—a reconciliation to God,—adoption as his children, *&c.*,† which is a necessary *preliminary* to the entrance on such a state; (but which,

* See Fallacies. "Non causa pro causa." Book III. § 14.

† " . . . . Baptism, wherein *I was made* a member of Christ, a child of God, and an inheritor of the Kingdom of Heaven." . . . . "A death unto sin, and a new birth unto righteousness, *&c.*" . . . . "We being regenerate, and made thy children by adoption and grace, *&c.*"

unhappily, is not invariably followed by it): and these are, of course, as different things as a grain of seed sown, and "the full corn in the ear."

Much controversy has taken place as to the time at which, and the circumstances under which, "Regeneration" takes place; the greater part of which may be traced to this ambiguity.

xxv. SAME (as well as "One," "Identical," and other words derived from them) is used frequently in a sense very different from its primary one; (as applicable to a *single* object); *viz.* it is employed to denote great *similarity.* When several objects are undistinguishably alike, *One single description* will apply equally to any of them; and thence they are said to be all of *one and the same* nature, appearance, *&c.*: as *e. g.* when we say, "this house is built of the *same* stone with such another," we only mean that the stones are undistinguishable in their qualities; not that the one building was pulled down, and the other constructed with the materials. Whereas Sameness, in the primary sense, does not even necessarily imply Similarity; for if we say of any man that he is greatly altered since such a time, we understand, and indeed imply by the very expression, that he is *One person,* though different in several qualities; else it would not be *he.* It is worth observing also that "Same," in the secondary sense, admits, according to popular usage, of *degrees:* we speak of two things being *nearly* the same, but not entirely; *personal* identity does not admit of degrees.

Nothing, perhaps, has contributed more to the error of Realism than inattention to this ambiguity. When several persons are said to have *One and the Same* opinion—thought—or idea,—many men, overlooking the true simple statement of the case, which is, that they *are all thinking alike,* look for something more abstruse and mystical, and imagine there must be some *One Thing,* in the primary sense, though not an individual, which is present at once in the mind of each of these persons: and thence readily sprung Plato's theory of Ideas; each of which was, according to him, one real, eternal object, existing entire and complete in each of the individual objects that are known by one name. Hence, first in poetical mythology, and ultimately, perhaps, in popular belief, Fortune, Liberty, Prudence, (Minerva,) a Boundary, (Terminus,) and even the Mildew of Corn, (Rubigo,) *&c.*, became personified, deified, and represented by Statues; somewhat according to the process which is described by Swift, in his humorous manner, in speaking of Zeal, (in the Tale of a Tub,) "how from a notion it became a word, and from thence, in a hot summer, ripened into a tangible Substance." We find Seneca thinking it necessary gravely to combat the position of some of his Stoical predecessors, "that the Cardinal Virtues are Animals:" while the Hindoos of the present day, from observing the similar symptoms which are known by the name of Small-pox, and the communication of the like from one patient to another, do not merely call it (as we do) *one* disease, but believe (if we may credit the accounts given) that the Small-pox is a Goddess, who becomes incarnate in each infected patient. All these absurdities are in fact but the extreme and ultimate point of Realism.—*See* Dissertation, Book IV. Chap. v.

xxvi. SIN, in its ordinary acceptation, means some actual transgression, in thought, word, or deed, of the moral law, or of a positive divine precept. It has also, what may be called, a theological sense, in which it is used for that *sinfulness* or *frailty*,—that liability, or proneness, to transgression, which all men inherit from our first parents, and which is commonly denominated "original" Sin;* in which

* Of the *degree* of this depravity of our nature, various accounts are given; some representing it as amounting to a total loss of the moral faculty, or even, to a preference of evil for its own sake; others making it to consist in

sense we find such expressions as "in Sin hath my Mother conceived me." The word seems also to be still further transferred, to signify the state of *condemnation itself*, in which the children of Adam are "by nature born," in consequence of this sinful tendency in them: (or, according to some divines, in consequence of the very guilt of Adam's offence being actually imputed to each individual of his posterity.*) It must be in the sense of a "state of condemnation," that our Church, in her office for Infant Baptism, speaks of "remission of Sins," with *reference to* a child, which is no moral agent: "following the innocency of children," (*i. e.* of *actual* Sin) being mentioned within a few sentences. And as it is plain that actual Sin cannot, in the former place, be meant, so, neither can it be, in this place, man's *proneness* to Sin: since the baptismal office would not pray for, and hold out a promise of "*release*" and "*remission*" of that φρόνημα σαρκὸς which, according to the Article, "remains even in the regenerate."

Though all Theologians probably are *aware* of these distinctions, yet much confusion of thought has resulted from their not being always attended to.

xxvii. SINCERITY and SINCERE, have a twofold meaning of great moral importance. Sincerity is often used to denote mere "reality of conviction;"—that a man actually believes what he professes to believe. Sometimes again it

a certain undue preponderance of the lower propensities over the nobler sentiments, &c. But these seem to be not differences as to the *sense* of the *word*, (with which alone we are here concerned) but as to *the state of the fact*.

It is worth while to notice however the carelessness with which some are apt to express themselves, as if this frailty were *introduced* as a *consequence* of Adam's transgression; as if, supposing him *not* frail, he *would* have so transgressed.

* I must again remind the reader that I am inquiring only into the senses in which each word has *actually* been used; not into the truth or falsity of each *doctrine* in question. On the present question, see *Essays on the Difficulties in St. Paul's Writings*, Essay VI.

is used to denote "*unbiassed* conviction;" or at least an earnest endeavour to shake off all prejudices, and all undue influence of wishes and passions on the judgment, and to decide impartially.

It is in this latter sense that "sincerity" is justly regarded as so commendable a quality that many and great errors are reckoned pardonable in proportion as a man has earnestly and *sincerely* endeavoured to ascertain what is right and true: while he who has *not* acted thus, but has allowed himself to be biassed by self-interest or passion, deserves no credit for the "sincerity" (*i. e.* reality) of his conviction, even if it should happen to be in itself a right one.

It is a common mistake to suppose that the only influence of interest, party spirit, or other improper motives is to induce men to make professions contrary to their real conviction. But "a gift" as the Scriptures express it "*blinds the eyes.*" Not only the outward profession but the real convictions of the judgment are liable to be biassed by such motives. In fact "sincerity" in this sense will usually be the last stage of depravity: as Aristotle has remarked in respect of the character of the 'Ακόλαστος,—the man who from long indulgence in vice has so corrupted his principles as to feel no disapprobation of it. It is notorious that liars often bring themselves by continual repetition to "credit their own lie."* And universally any one who persists in what is wrong, and in seeking excuses to justify it, will usually in time succeed in deceiving himself into the belief that it is right,† and thus warping his conscience.

Yet the credit due to the one kind of conscientious Sincerity is often (partly through this ambiguity) bestowed on the other. But it makes all the difference whether you pursue a certain course *because you judge it right,* or judge it to be right *because you pursue it;*—whether you follow your conscience as one follows a *guide*, or as one *follows the*

* Shakespere—The Tempest.

† See Epistle to Rom. ch. i.

horses in a carriage, while he himself guides them according to his will.

xxviii. TENDENCY. "The doctrine, as mischievous as it is, I conceive, unfounded, that since there is a tendency in population to increase faster than the means of subsistence, hence, the pressure of population against subsistence may be expected to become greater and greater in each successive generation, (unless new and extraordinary remedies are resorted to,) and thus to produce a progressive diminution of human welfare;—this doctrine, which some maintain, in defiance of the fact that all civilized countries have a greater proportionate amount of wealth, (in other words, a smaller population, in proportion to the means of subsistence) now, than formerly,—may be traced chiefly to an undetected ambiguity in the word '*tendency*,' which forms a part of the middle term of the argument. By a 'tendency' towards a certain result is sometimes meant, 'the existence of a cause which, if *operating unimpeded*, would produce that result.' In this sense it may be said, with truth, that the earth, or any other body moving round a centre, has a *tendency* to fly off at a tangent; *i. e.* the centrifugal force operates in that direction, though it is controlled by the centripetal; or, again, that man has a *greater tendency* to fall prostrate than to stand erect; *i. e.* the attraction of gravitation and the position of the centre of gravity, are such that the least breath of air would overset him, but for the voluntary exertion of muscular force: and, again, that population has a *tendency* to increase beyond subsistence; *i. e.* there are in man propensities, which, if unrestrained, lead to that result.

"But sometimes, again, 'a tendency towards a certain result' is understood to mean 'the existence of such a state of things that that result *may be expected to take place*.' Now it is in these *two* senses that the word is used, in the two premises of the argument in question. But in this latter sense, the earth has a greater tendency to remain in its orbit than to fly off from it; man has a greater tendency to stand erect than to fall prostrate; and (as may be proved by comparing a more barbarous with a more civilized period in the history of any Country) in the progress of society, subsistence has a tendency to increase at a greater rate than population; or at least with a continually *diminishing inferiority*. In this Country, for instance, much as our population has increased within the last five centuries, it yet bears a far less ratio to subsistence (though still a much greater than could be wished) than it did five hundred years ago."* But many of the writers I have alluded to seem to have confounded "an *excess of increase*" with "an *increase* of the *excess*."

THEREFORE.—*See* "REASON," and "WHY."

xxix. TRUTH, in the strict logical sense, applies to Propositions, and to nothing else; and consists in the conformity of the declaration made to the actual state of the case; agreeably to Aldrich's definition of a "true" proposition—vera est, quæ *quod res est* dicit.

It would be an advantage if the word Trueness or Verity could be introduced and employed in this sense, since the word Truth is so often used to denote the "true" *Proposition itself*. "What I tell you is the *Truth;* the *Truth* of what I say shall be proved;" the term is here used in these two senses; viz., in the "concrete," and in the "abstract" sense.† In like manner Falsehood is often opposed to truth in both these senses; being commonly used to signify the quality of a false proposition. But as we have the word *Falsity*, which properly denotes this, I have thought it best, in a scientific treatise, always to employ it for that purpose.

* Pol. Econ. Lect. IX. p. 248—250.

† See Book ii. Ch. v. § 1.

In its etymological sense, Truth signifies that which the speaker "trows," or believes to be the fact. The etymology of the word ΑΛΗΘΕΣ seems to be similar; denoting *non-concealment.* In this sense it is opposed to a *Lie:* and may be called Moral, as the other may Logical, Truth. A witness therefore may comply with his oath to speak the Truth, though it so happen that he is *mistaken* in some particular of his evidence, provided he is fully convinced that the thing is as he states it.

Truth is not unfrequently applied, in loose and inaccurate language, to *arguments;* where the proper expression would be "correctness," "conclusiveness," or "validity."

Truth again, is often used in the sense of *Reality,* TO ON. People speak of the Truth or Falsity of *facts;* properly speaking, they are either *real* or *fictitious:* it is the *statement* that is "true" or "false." The "true" *cause* of any thing, is a common expression; meaning "that which may with Truth be assigned as the cause." The senses of Falsehood correspond.

"Truth" in this sense, of "reality," is also opposed to shadows,—types,—pictures, *&c.* Thus, "the Law was given by Moses, but grace and 'truth' came by Jesus Christ;" for the Law had only a "*shadow* of good things to come."

The present is an ambiguity of which advantage has been often taken,—through a deficiency either in candour or in clearness of thought—in advocating the claims of the Romish Church; the ambiguity of the word Church (which see) lending its aid to the fallacy. "Even the Protestants," they say, "dare not deny ours to be a "*true* Church;" now there can be but "*one* true Church:" (which they support by those passages of Scripture which relate to the collective Body of Christians in all those several Societies which also are called in Scripture, Churches;) "ours therefore must be the *true Church;* if you forsake us, you forsake the *truth* and the *Church,* and consequently shut yourself out from the promises of the Gospel." Those who are of a logical and accurate turn of mind will easily perceive that the sense in which the Romish Church is admitted by her opponents to be a *true* Church, is that of *reality*;—it is a *real, not a pretended Church*;—it may be *truly said* to be a Church. The sense in which the concession is sometimes made use of, is that of a *Church teaching true doctrines*; which was never conceded to the Church of Rome by Protestants; who hold, that a Church may err without ceasing to be a Church.

"The Church is *one*,* then, not, as consisting of One Society, but because the various societies or Churches were then modelled, and ought still to be so, on the same principles; and because they enjoy common privileges,—one Lord, one Spirit, one baptism. Accordingly, the Holy Ghost, through his agents the Apostles, has not left any detailed account of the formation of any Christian society; but He has very distinctly marked the great principles on which all were to be founded, whatever distinctions may exist amongst them. In short, the foundation of the Church by the Apostles was not analogous to the work of Romulus, or Solon; it was not, properly, the foundation of Christian societies which occupied them, but the establishment of the principles on which Christians in all ages might form societies for themselves.

"The above account is sufficiently established even by the mere negative circumstance of the absence of all mention in the Sacred Writings of any *one* Society on earth, having a Government and officers of its own, and recognised as the Catholic or Universal Church: especially when it is considered that the frequent mention of the particular Churches at Jerusalem, Antioch, Rome, Corinth, &c.—of the seven Churches in Asia,—and of 'the care of all the Churches' which Paul had founded, would

* See "One."

have rendered unavoidable the notice of the One Church (had there been any such) which bore rule over all the rest, either as its subjects, or as provincial departments of it."*

UNITY—*See* "ONE."

WHENCE—*See* "WHY," and "REASON."

xxx. WHY?—As an interrogative, this word is employed in three senses: *viz.* "By what proof?" (or Reason) "From what Cause?" "For what purpose?" This last is commonly called the "final cause." *E. G.* "Why is this prisoner guilty of the crime?" "Why does a stone fall to the earth?" "Why did you go to London?" Much confusion has arisen from not distinguishing these different inquiries. *See* REASON.

N.B. As the words which follow are all of them connected together in their significations, and as the explanations of their ambiguities have been furnished by the kindness of the Professor of Political Economy, it seemed advisable to place them by themselves, and in the order in which they appeared to him most naturally to arrange themselves.

The foundation of Political Economy being a few general propositions deduced from observation or from consciousness, and generally admitted as soon as stated, it might have been expected that there would be as little difference of opinion among Political-Economists as among Mathematicians;—that, being agreed in their premises, they

* "Essays on the Dangers," &c. Note A, pp. *169*, *170*.

could not differ in their conclusions, but through some error in reasoning, so palpable as to be readily detected. And if they had possessed a vocabulary of general terms as precisely defined as the mathematical, this would probably have been the case. But as the terms of this Science are drawn from common discourse, and seldom carefully defined by the writers who employ them, hardly one of them has any settled and invariable meaning, and their ambiguities are perpetually overlooked. The principal terms are only seven: *viz.* VALUE, WEALTH, LABOUR, CAPITAL, RENT, WAGES, PROFITS.

1. VALUE. As value is the only relation with which Political Economy is conversant, we might expect all Economists to be agreed as to its meaning. There is no subject as to which they are less agreed.

The popular, and far the most convenient, use of the word, is to signify the capacity of being given and received in exchange. So defined, it expresses a relation. The value of any one thing must consist in the several quantities of all other things which can be obtained in exchange for it, and never can remain fixed for an instant. Most writers admit the propriety of this definition at the outset, but they scarcely ever adhere to it.

Adam Smith defines Value to mean either the *utility* of a particular object, or the power of *purchasing other* goods which the possession of that object conveys. The first he calls "Value in use," the second "Value in exchange." But he soon afterwards says, that equal quantities of labour at all times and places are of equal Value to the labourer, whatever may be the quantity of goods he receives in return for them; and that labour never varies in its own Value. It is clear that he affixed, or thought he had affixed, some other meaning to the word; as the first of these propositions is contradictory, and the second false, whichever of his two definitions we adopt.

Mr. Ricardo appears to set out by admitting Adam Smith's *definition* of Value in exchange. But in the greater part of his "Principles of Political Economy," he uses the word as synonymous with *Cost:* and by this one ambiguity has rendered his great work a long enigma.

Mr. Malthus* defines Value to be the power of purchasing. In the very next page he distinguishes absolute from relative Value, a distinction contradictory to his definition of the term, as expressive of a *relation*.

Mr. M'Culloch† distinguishes between real and exchangeable, or relative value. And in his nomenclature, the exchangeable, or relative, Value of a commodity consists in its capacity of purchasing;—its real Value in the quantity of labour required for its production or appropriation.

All these differences appear to arise from a confusion of cause and effect. Having decided that commodities are Valuable in proportion to the labour they have respectively cost, it was natural to call that labour their Value.

2. WEALTH. Lord Lauderdale has defined Wealth to be "all that man desires." Mr. Malthus, ‡ "those *material* objects which are necessary, useful, or agreeable." Adam Smith confines the term to that portion of the results of land and labour which is capable of being accumulated. The French Economists, to the net product of land. Mr. M'Culloch § and M. Storch, || to those material products which have exchangeable value; according to Colonel Torrens¶ it consists of articles which possess

* "Measure of Value," p. 1.

† "Principles of Political Economy," Part III. sect. 1.

‡ "Principles of Political Economy," p. 28.

§ "Supplement to the Encyclopædia Britannica," Vol. VI. p. 217.

|| "Cours d'Economie Politique," Tome I. p. 91. Paris edit.

¶ "Production of Wealth," p. 1.

utility, and are produced by some portion of voluntary effort. M. Say * divides wealth into natural and social, and applies the latter term to whatever is susceptible of exchange. It will be observed that the principal difference between these definitions consists in the admission or rejection of the qualifications "exchangeable," and, "material." †

It were well if the ambiguities of this word had done no more than puzzle philosophers. One of them gave birth to the mercantile system. In common language, to grow rich is to get *money;* to diminish in fortune is to lose *money:* a rich man is said to have a great deal of *money;* a poor man, very little: and the terms Wealth and Money are in short employed as synonymous. In consequence of these popular notions (to use the words of Adam Smith) all the different nations of Europe have studied every means of accumulating gold and silver in their respective countries. This they have attempted by prohibiting the exportation of money, and by giving bounties on the exportation, and imposing restrictions on the importation, of other commodities, in the hope of producing what has been called a "favourable balance of trade;" that is, a trade in which, the imports being always of less value than the exports, the difference is paid in money. A conduct as wise as that of a tradesman who should part with his goods only for money; and instead of employing their price in paying his workmen's wages, or replacing his stock, should keep

* "Traité d'Economie Pol." Liv. II. Chap. ii.

† "In many cases, where an exchange really takes place, the fact is liable (till the attention is called to it) to be overlooked, in consequence of our not seeing any actual transfer from hand to hand of a material object. For instance, when the copyright of a book is sold to a bookseller, the article transferred is not the mere paper covered with writing, but the exclusive *privilege* of printing and publishing. It is plain, however, on a moment's thought, that the transaction is as real an exchange, as that which takes place between the bookseller and his customers who buy copies of the work."—*Introd. to. Pol. Econ.* Lect. I.

it for ever in his till. The attempt to force such a trade has been as vain, as the trade, if it could have been obtained, would have been mischievous. But the results have been fraud, punishment, and poverty at home, and discord and war without. It has made nations consider the Wealth of their customers a source of loss instead of profit; and an advantageous market a curse instead of a blessing. By inducing them to refuse to profit by the peculiar advantages in climate, soil, or industry, possessed by their neighbours, it has forced them in a great measure to give up their own. It has for centuries done more, and perhaps for centuries to come will do more, to retard the improvement of Europe than all other causes put together.

3. LABOUR. The word Labour signifies both the *act* of labouring, and the *result* of that act. It is used in the first sense when we talk of the wages of labour; in the second when we talk of accumulated labour. When used to express the act of labouring, it may appear to have a precise sense, but it is still subject to some ambiguity. Say's definition* is "action suivie, dirigée vers un bût;" Storch's,† "l'action des facultés humaines dirigée vers un bût utile." These definitions include a walk taken for the purposes of health, and even the exertions of an agreeable converser.

The great defect of Adam Smith, and of our own economists in general, is the want of definitions. There is, perhaps, no definition of Labour by any British Economist. If Adam Smith had framed one, he would probably have struck out his celebrated distinction between "productive" and "unproductive" labourers; for it is difficult to conceive any definition of Labour which will admit the epithet "unproductive" to be applied to any of its subdivisions, excepting that of *misdirected* labour. On the

* "Traité," &c. Tome II. p. 506. † "Cours," &c. Liv. 1. Chap. iv.

other hand, if Mr. M'Culloch or Mr. Mill had defined Labour they would scarcely have applied that term to the growth of a tree, or the improvement of wine in a cellar.

4. CAPITAL. This word, as might have been expected, from the complexity of the notions which it implies, has been used in very different senses.

It is, as usual, undefined by Adam Smith. The general meaning which he attached to it will however appear from his enumeration of its species. He divides it* into *Fixed* and *Circulating:* including in the first what the capitalist retains, in the second what he parts with. *Fixed* Capital he subdivides into—1. Machinery; 2. Shops and other buildings used for trade or manufacture; 3. Improvements of land; 4. Knowledge and skill. *Circulating* Capital he subdivides into—1. Money; 2. Provisions in the hands of the provision-venders; 3. Unfinished materials of manufacture; 4. Finished work in the hands of the merchant or manufacture; such as furniture in a cabinet-maker's shop, or trinkets in that of a jeweller.

The following is a list of the definitions adopted by some of the most eminent subsequent economists:

Ricardo†—" that part of the wealth of a country which is employed in production; consisting of food, clothing, tools, raw materials, machinery, *&c.*, necessary to give effect to labour."

Malthus‡—" that portion of the material possessions of a country which is destined to be employed with a view to profit."

Say§—" accumulation de valeurs soustraites à la consomption improductive." Chap. iii. " Machinery, necessaries of the workman, materials."

* Book II. Chap. i.

† " Principles of Political Economy," p. 89, 3rd edit.

‡ " Principles," &c. p. 293.

§ " Traité," &c. Tome II. p. 454.

Storch *—" un fonds de richesses destiné à la production matérielle."

M'Culloch †—" that portion of the produce of industry which can be made directly available to support human existence or facilitate production."

Mill ‡—" something produced, for the purpose of being employed as the mean towards a further production."

Torrens §—" those things on which labour has been bestowed, and which are destined, not for the immediate supply of our wants, but to aid us in obtaining other articles of utility."

It is obvious that few of these definitions exactly coincide. Adam Smith's (as implied in his use of the term; for he gives no formal definition) excludes the necessaries of the labourer, when in his own possession; all the rest (and perhaps with better reason) admit them. On the other hand, Adam Smith admits (and in that he seems to be right) those things which are incapable of productive consumption, provided they have not yet reached their consumers. All the other definitions, except perhaps that of Mr. Malthus, which is ambiguous, are subject to the inconsistency of affirming that a diamond, and the gold in which it is to be set, are Capital while the jeweller keeps them separate, but cease to be so when he has formed them into a ring; almost all of them, also, pointedly exclude knowledge and skill. The most objectionable, perhaps, is that of Mr. M'Culloch, which, while it excludes all the finished contents of a jeweller's shop, would include a racing stud.

Adam Smith, however, is far from being consistent in his use of the word; thus, in the beginning of his second book he states, that all Capitals are destined for the main-

* " Cours," &c. Liv. II. Chap. i.

† " Principles," &c. p. 92.

‡ " Elements," &c. p. 19, 3rd edit.

§ " Production of Wealth," p. 5.

tenance of productive labour only. It is difficult to see what labour is maintained by what is to be unproductively consumed.

5. RENT. 6. WAGES. 7. PROFIT.

Adam Smith first divided revenue into Rent, Wages, and Profit; and his division has been generally followed. The following definitions will best show the degree of precision with which these three terms have been employed.

Adam Smith.

1. Rent. What is paid for the licence to gather the produce of the land.—Book I. Chap. vi.

2. Wages. The price of labour.—Book I. Chap. v.

3. Profit. The revenue derived from stock by the person who manages or employs it.—Book I. Chap. vi.

Say. (*Traité d'Economie Politique.*) 4ème Edit.

1. Rent. Le profit résultant du service productif de la terre.—Tome II. p. 169.

2. Wages. Le prix de l'achat d'un service productif industriel.—Tome II. p. 503.

3. Profit. La portion de la valeur produite, retirée par le capitaliste.—Tome I. p. 71, subdivided into intérêt, profit industriel, and profit capital.

Storch. (*Cours d'Economie Politique.*) Paris, 1823.

1. Rent. Le prix qu'on paye pour l'usage d'un fonds de terre.—Tome I. p. 354.

2. Wages. Le prix du travail.—p. 283.

3. Profit. The returns to capital are considered by

Storch, under the heads, rente de capital, and profit de l'entrepreneur. The first he divides into loyer, the hire of fixed capital, and intérêt, that of circulating capital. The second he considers as composed of, 1st, remuneration for the use of capital; 2nd, assurance against risk; 3rd, remuneration for trouble.—Liv. III. Chap. ii. viii. xiii.

SISMONDI. (*Nouveau Principes, &c.*)

1. Rent. La part de la récolte annuelle du sol qui revient au propriétaire après qu'il a acquitté les frais qui l'ont fait naître; and he analyzes rent into, 1st, la compensation du travail de la terre; 2nd, le prix de monopole: 3rd, la mieux valeur que le propriétaire obtient par la comparaison d'une terre de nature supérieure à une terre inférieure: 4th, le révenu des capitaux qu'il a fixés luimême sur la terre, et ne peut plus en retirer.—Tome I. p. 280.

2. Wages. Le prix du travail.—p. 91.

3. Profit. La valeur dont l'ouvrage achevé surpasse les avances qui l'ont fait faire. L'avantage qui résulte des travaux passés. Subdivided into intérêt and profit mercantile.—p. 94, 359.

MALTHUS. (*Principles, &c.*)

1. Rent. That portion of the value of the whole produce of land which remains to the owner after payment of all the outgoings of cultivation, including average profits on the capital employed. The excess of price above wages and profits.—p. 134.

2. Wages. The remuneration of the labourer for his personal exertions.—p. 240.

3. Profit. The difference between the value of the advances necessary to produce a commodity, and the value of the commodity when produced.—p. 293.

MILL. (*Elements, &c.*) 3rd Ed.

1. Rent. The difference between the return made to the most productive, and that which is made to the least productive portion of capital employed on the land.—p. 33.

2. Wages. The price of the labourer's share of the commodity produced.—p. 41.

3. Profit. The share of the joint produce of labour and stock which is received by the owner of stock after replacing the capital consumed. The portion of the whole annual produce which remains after deducting rent and wages. Remuneration for hoarded labour.—Chap. 2, 3.

TORRENS. (*Corn Trade.*) 3rd Ed.

1. Rent. That part of the produce which is given to the land-proprietor for the use of the soil.—p. 130.

2. Wages. The articles of wealth which the labourer receives in exchange for his labour.—p. 83.

3. Profit. The excess of value which the finished work possesses above the value of the material, implements, and subsistence expended. The surplus remaining after the cost of production has been replaced. — *Production of Wealth*, p. 53.

M'CULLOCH. (*Principles, &c.*)

1. Rent. That portion of the produce of the earth which is paid by the farmer to the landlord for the use of the natural and inherent powers of the soil.—p. 265.

2. Wages. The compensation paid to labourers in return for their services.—*Essay on Rate of Wages*, p. 1.

3. Profit. The excess of the commodities produced by the expenditure of a given quantity of capital, over that quantity of capital.—*Principles*, p. 366.

RICARDO. (*Principles, &c.*) 3rd Ed.

1. Rent. That portion of the produce of the earth

which is paid to the landlord for the use of the original and indestructible powers of the soil.—p. 53.

2. Wages. The labourer's proportion of the produce.—Chap. v.

3. Profit. The capitalist's proportion of the produce.—Chap. vi.

The first observation to be made on these definitions, is, that the Rent of *land*, which is only a *species* of an extensive genus, is used as a genus, and that its cognate species are either omitted, or included under genera to which they do not properly belong. Wages and Profits are of human creation: they imply a sacrifice of ease or immediate enjoyment, and bear a ratio to that sacrifice which is indicated by the common expressions of "the rate of wages," and the "rate of profits:" a ratio which has a strong tendency to uniformity. But there is another and a very large source of revenue which is not the creation of man, but of nature; which owes its origin, not to the will of its possessor, but to accident; which implies no sacrifice, has no tendency to uniformity, and to which the term "rate" is seldom applied.

This revenue arises from the exclusive right to some instrument of production, enabling the employment of a given amount of labour or capital to be more than usually productive. The *principal* of these instruments is land; but all extraordinary powers of body or mind,—all processes in manufacture which are protected by secrecy or by law,—all peculiar advantages from situation or connexion,—in short, every instrument of production which is not universally accessible, affords a revenue distinct in its origin from Wages or Profits, and of which the Rent of land is only a species. In the classification of revenues, either Rent ought to have been omitted as a genus, and considered only as an anomalous interruption of the general uniformity of wages and profits, or all the accidental sources of revenue ought to have been included in one genus, of which the Rent of land would have formed the principal species.

Another remark is, that almost all these definitions of Profit include the *wages of the labour of the Capitalist.* The continental Economists have in general been aware of this, and have pointed it out in their analyses of the component parts of Profit. The British Economists have seldom entered into this analysis, and the want of it has been a great cause of obscurity.

On the other hand, much of what properly belongs to Profit and Rent is generally included under Wages. Almost all Economists consider the members of the liberal professions under the class of labourers. The whole subsistence of such persons, observes Mr. M'Culloch,* is derived from Wages; and they are as evidently labourers as if they handled the spade or the plough. But it should be considered, that those who are engaged in any occupation requiring more skill than that of a common husbandman, must have expended capital, more or less, on the acquisition of their skill; their education must have cost something in every case, from that of the handicraft-apprentice, to that of the legal or medical student; and a Profit on this outlay is of course looked for, as in other disbursements of capital; and the higher profit, in proportion to the risk; *viz.* the uncertainty of a man's success in his business. Part, therefore, and generally far the greater part, of what has been reckoned the wages of his labour ought more properly to be reckoned profits on the capital expended in fitting him for that particular kind of labour. And again, all the excess of gains acquired by one possessing extraordinary talents, opportunities, or patronage (since these correspond to the possession of land,—of a patent-right,—or other monopoly,—of a secret, *&c.*) may be more properly regarded as Rent than as Wages.

* "Principles," &c. p. 228.

Another most fruitful source of ambiguity arises from the use of the word Wages, sometimes as expressing a *quantity*, sometimes as expressing a *proportion*.

In ordinary language, Wages means the *amount of some commodity*, generally of silver, given to the labourer in return for a given exertion; and they rise or fall, as that amount is increased or diminished.

In the language of Mr. Ricardo, they usually mean the labourer's *proportion of what is produced*, supposing that produce to be divided between him and the Capitalist. In this sense they generally rise as the whole produce is diminished; though if the word be used in the other sense, they generally fall. If Mr. Ricardo had constantly used the word "Wages," to express a *proportion*, the only inconvenience would have been the necessity of always translating this expression into common language. But he is not consistent. When he says,* that "whatever raises the Wages of labour lowers the Profits of stock," he considers Wages as a *proportion*. When he says, † that "high Wages encourage population;" he considers wages as an *amount*. Even Mr. M'Culloch, who has clearly explained the ambiguity, has not escaped it. He has even suffered it to affect his reasonings. In his valuable essay, "on the Rate of Wages,"‡ he admits that "when Wages are high, the Capitalist has to pay a larger share of the produce of industry to his labourers." An admission utterly inconsistent with his general use of the word, as expressing the *amount* of what the labourer receives, which, as he has himself observed, § may increase while his *proportion* diminishes.

A few only have been noticed of the ambiguities which attach to the seven terms that have been selected; and these terms have been fixed on, not as the most ambiguous,

* "Principles," &c. p. 312. † Ibid. p. 83. ‡ P. 161. § P. 365.

but as the most important, in the political nomenclature. " Supply and Demand," " Productive and Unproductive," " Overtrading," and very many others, both in political economy, and in other subjects, which are often used without any more explanation, or any more suspicion of their requiring it, than the words " triangle" or " twenty," are perhaps even more liable to ambiguities than those above treated of. But it is sufficient for the purpose of this Appendix to have noticed, by way of specimens, a few of the most remarkable terms in several different branches of knowledge, in order to show both the frequency of an ambiguous use of language, and the importance of clearing up such ambiguity.

APPENDIX.

No. II.

MISCELLANEOUS EXAMPLES FOR THE EXERCISE OF LEARNERS.

N.B. In such of the following Examples as are not in a syllogistic form, it is intended that the student should practise the reduction of them into that form; those of them, that is, in which the reasoning is in itself sound: *viz.* where it is impossible to admit the Premises and deny the Conclusion. Of such as are apparent Syllogisms, the validity must be tried by logical rules, which it may be advisable to apply in the following order: 1st. Observe whether the argument be Categorical or Hypothetical; recollecting that an hypothetical Premiss does not necessarily imply an hypothetical Syllogism, unless the reasoning turns on the hypothesis. If this appear to be the case, the rules for hypothetical Syllogisms must be applied. 2dly. If the argument be categorical, count the terms. 3dly. If *only* three, observe whether the Middle be distributed. 4thly. Observe whether the Premises are both negative; (*i. e.* really, and not in appearance only,) and if one is, whether the Conclusion be negative also; or affirmative, if both Premises affirmative. 5thly. Observe what *terms* are Distributed in the conclusion, and whether the same are distributed in the Premises. 6thly. If the Syllogism is not a Categorical in the first Figure, reduce it to that form.

---

1. No one is free who is enslaved by his appetites: a sensualist is enslaved by his appetites: therefore a sensualist is not free.

2. None but Whites are civilized: the ancient Germans were Whites: therefore they were civilized.

3. None but Whites are civilized: the Hindoos are not Whites: therefore they are not civilized.

4. None but civilized people are Whites: the Gauls were Whites: therefore they were civilized.

5. No one is rich who has not enough: no miser has enough: therefore no miser is rich.

6. If penal laws against Papists were enforced, they would be aggrieved: but penal laws against them are not enforced: therefore the Papists are not aggrieved.

7. If all testimony to miracles is to be admitted, the popish legends are to be believed: but the popish legends are not to believed: therefore no testimony to miracles is to be admitted.

8. If men are not likely to be influenced in the performance of a known duty by taking an oath to perform it, the oaths commonly administered are superfluous: if they are likely to be so influenced, every one should be made to take an oath to behave rightly throughout his life; but one or the other of these must be the case: therefore either the oaths commonly administered are superfluous, or every man should be made to take an oath to behave rightly throughout his life.

9. The Scriptures must be admitted to be agreeable to truth; and the Church of England is conformable to the

Scriptures: A.B. is a divine of the Church of England; and this opinion is in accordance with his sentiments: therefore it must be presumed to be true.

10. Enoch (according to the testimony of Scripture,) pleased God; but without faith it is impossible to please Him; (for he that cometh to God must believe that He is, and that He is a rewarder of them that diligently seek Him): therefore, *&c.*

11. "If Abraham were justified by works, then had he whereof to glory [before God:] but not [any one can have whereof to glory] before God:" therefore Abraham was not justified by works.

12. "He that is of God heareth my words: ye therefore hear them not, because ye are not of God."

13. Few treatises of science convey important truths, without any intermixture of error, in a perspicuous and interesting form: and therefore, though a treatise would deserve much attention which should possess such excellence, it is plain that few treatises of science do deserve much attention.

14. We are bound to set apart one day in seven for religious duties, if the fourth commandment is obligatory on us: but we are bound to set apart one day in seven for religious duties; and hence it appears that the fourth commandment is obligatory on us.

15. Abstinence from the eating of blood had reference to the divine institution of sacrifices: one of the precepts delivered to Noah was abstinence from the eating of blood; therefore one of the precepts delivered to Noah contained the divine institution of sacrifices.

16. If expiatory sacrifices were divinely appointed before the Mosaic law, they must have been expiatory, not of ceremonial sin (which could not then exist), but of moral sin: if so, the Levitical sacrifices must have had no less efficacy; and in that case, the atonements under the Mosaic law would have "made the comers thereunto perfect as

pertaining to the conscience;" but this was not the case: therefore, *&c.* [Davison on Prophecy.]

17. The adoration of images is forbidden to Christians, if we suppose the Mosaic law designed not for the Israelites alone, but for all men: it was designed, however, for the Israelites alone, and not for all men: therefore the adoration of images is not forbidden to Christians.

18. A desire to gain by another's loss is a violation of the tenth commandment: all gaming, therefore, since it implies a desire to profit at the expense of another, involves a breach of the tenth commandment.

19. All the fish that the net inclosed were an indiscriminate mixture of various kinds: those that were set aside and saved as valuable, were fish that the net enclosed: therefore those that were set aside, and saved as valuable, were an indiscriminate mixture of various kinds.

20. All the elect are finally saved: such persons as are arbitrarily separated from the rest of mankind by the divine decree are the elect: therefore such persons as are arbitrarily separated from the rest of mankind by the divine decree, are finally saved. [The opponents of this Conclusion generally deny the Minor Premiss and admit the Major; the reverse would be the more sound and the more effectual objection.]

21. No one who lives with another on terms of confidence is justified, on any pretence, in killing him: Brutus lived on terms of confidence with Cæsar: therefore he was not justified, on the pretence he pleaded, in killing him.

22. He that destroys a man who usurps despotic power in a free country deserves well of his countrymen: Brutus destroyed Cæsar, who usurped despotic power in Rome: therefore he deserved well of the Romans.

23. If virtue is voluntary, vice is voluntary: virtue is voluntary: therefore so is vice. [Aristh. Eth. B. iii.]

24. A wise lawgiver must either recognise the rewards and punishments of a future state, or must be able to appeal to an extraordinary Providence, dispensing them

regularly in this life; Moses did not do the former: therefore he must have done the latter. [Warburton.]

25. Nothing which is of less frequent occurrence than the falsity of testimony can be fairly established by testimony: any extraordinary and unusual fact is a thing of less frequent occurrence than the falsity of testimony (that being very common): therefore no extraordinary and unusual fact can be fairly established by testimony.

26. Testimony is a kind of evidence which is very likely to be false: the evidence on which most men believe that there are pyramids in Egypt is testimony: therefore the evidence on which most men believe that there are pyramids in Egypt is very likely to be false.

27. The religion of the ancient Greeks and Romans was a tissue of extravagant fables and groundless superstitions, credited by the vulgar and the weak, and maintained by the more enlightened, from selfish or political views: the same was clearly the case with the religion of the Egyptians: the same may be said of the Brahminical worship of India, and the religion of Fo, professed by the Chinese: the same, of the romantic mythological system of the Peruvians, of the stern and bloody rites of the Mexicans, and those of the Britons and of the Saxons: hence we may conclude that all systems of religion, however varied in circumstances, agree in being superstitions kept up among the vulgar, from interested or political views in the more enlightened classes. [See Dissertation, Chap. i. § 2.]

28. No man can possess power to perform impossibilities; a miracle is an impossibility: therefore no man can possess power to perform a miracle. [See Appendix, Art. "Impossible."

29. A. B. and C. D. are each of them equal to E. F.: therefore they are equal to each other.

30. Protection from punishment is plainly due to the innocent; therefore, as you maintain that this person ought not to be punished, it appears that you are convinced of his innocence.

31. All the most bitter persecutions have been religious persecutions: among the most bitter persecutions were those which occurred in France during the revolution: therefore they must have been religious persecutions.

32. He who cannot possibly act otherwise than he does, has neither merit nor demerit in his action: a liberal and benevolent man cannot possibly act otherwise than he does in relieving the poor: therefore such a man has neither merit nor demerit in his action. [See App. Art. "Impossible."]

33. What happens every day is not improbable: some things against which the chances are many thousands to one, happen every day: therefore some things against which the chances are many thousands to one, are not improbable.

34. The early and general assignment of the Epistle to the Hebrews to Paul as its author, must have been either from its professing to be his, and containing his name, or from its really being his; since, therefore, the former of these is not the fact, the Epistle must be Paul's.

35. "With some of them God was not well pleased; for they were overthrown in the wilderness."

36. A sensualist wishes to enjoy perpetual gratifications without satiety: it is impossible to enjoy perpetual gratifications without satiety: therefore it is impossible for a sensualist to obtain his wish.

37. If Paley's system is to be received, one who has no knowledge of a future state has no means of distinguishing virtue and vice: now one who has no means of distinguishing virtue and vice can commit no sin: therefore, if Paley's system is to be received, one who has no knowledge of a future state can commit no sin.

38. The principles of justice are variable: the appointments of nature are invariable: therefore the principles of justice are no appointment of nature. [Arist. Eth. B. v.]

39. Every one desires happiness: virtue is happiness: therefore every one desires virtue. [Arist. Eth. B. iii.]

40. A story is not to be believed, the reporters of which

give contradictory accounts of it; the story of the life and exploits of Buonaparte is of this description: therefore it is not to be believed. [*See* B. i. § 3.]

41. When the observance of the first day of the week as a religious festival in commemoration of Christ's resurrection, was first introduced, it must have been a novelty: when it was a novelty, it must have attracted notice: when it attracted notice, it would lead to inquiry respecting the truth of the resurrection: when it led to this inquiry, it must have exposed the story as an imposture, supposing it not attested by living witnesses: therefore, when the observance of the first day of the week, *&c.* was first introduced, it must have exposed as an imposture the story of the resurrection, supposing it not attested by living witnesses.

42. All the miracles of Jesus would fill more books than the world could contain: the things related by the Evangelists are the miracles of Jesus: therefore the things related by the Evangelists would fill more books than the world could contain

43. If the prophecies of the Old Testament had been written without knowledge of the events of the time of Christ, they could not correspond with them exactly; and if they had been forged by Christians, they would not be preserved and acknowledged by the Jews: they are preserved and acknowledged by the Jews, and they correspond exactly with the events of the time of Christ: therefore they were neither written without knowledge of those events, nor were forged by Christians.

44. Of two evils the less is to be preferred: occasional turbulence, therefore, being a less evil than rigid despotism, is to be preferred to it.

45. According to theologians, a man must possess faith in order to be acceptable to the Deity: now he who believes all the fables of the Hindoo mythology must possess faith: therefore such an one must, according to theologians, be acceptable to the Deity.

46. If Abraham were justified, it must have been either by faith or by works: now he was not justified by faith, (according to James,) nor by works, (according to Paul): therefore Abraham was not justified.

47. No evil should be allowed that good may come of it: all punishment is an evil: therefore no punishment should be allowed that good may come of it.

48. Repentance is a good thing: wicked men abound in repentance [Arist. Eth. B. ix.]: therefore wicked men abound in what is good.

49. A person infected with the plague will (probably) die [suppose three in five of the infected die]: this man is (probably) infected with the plague [suppose it an even chance]: therefore he will (probably) die. *Query.* What is the amount of this probability? Again, suppose the probability of the major to be (instead of $\frac{3}{5}$) $\frac{4}{7}$, and of the minor, (instead of $\frac{1}{2}$) to be $\frac{2}{3}$, *Query.* What will be the probability of the conclusion?

50. It must be admitted, indeed, that a man who has been accustomed to enjoy liberty cannot be happy in the condition of a slave: many of the negroes, however, may be happy in the condition of slaves, because they have never been accustomed to enjoy liberty.

51. Whatever is dictated by Nature is allowable: devotedness to the pursuit of pleasure in youth, and to that of gain in old age, are dictated by Nature [Arist. Rhet. B. ii.]: therefore they are allowable.

52. He is the greatest lover of any one who seeks that person's greatest good: a virtuous man seeks the greatest good for himself: therefore a virtuous man is the greatest lover of himself. [Arist. Eth. B. ix.]

53. He who has a confirmed habit of any kind of action, exercises no self-denial in the practice of that action: a good man has a confirmed habit of Virtue: therefore he who exercises self-denial in the practice of Virtue is not a good man. [Arist. Eth. B. ii.]

54. That man is independent of the caprices of Fortune

who places his chief happiness in moral and intellectual excellence: a true philosopher is independent of the caprices of Fortune: therefore a true philosopher is one who places his chief happiness in moral and intellectual excellence.

55. A system of government which extends to those actions that are performed secretly, must be one which refers either to a regular divine providence in this life, or to the rewards and punishments of another world: every perfect system of government must extend to those actions which are performed secretly: no system of government therefore can be perfect, which does not refer either to a regular divine providence in this life, or to the rewards and punishments of another world. [Warburton's Divine Legation.]

56. For those who are bent on cultivating their minds by diligent study, the incitement of academical honours is unnecessary; and it is ineffectual, for the idle, and such as are indifferent to mental improvement: therefore the incitement of academical honours is either unnecessary or ineffectual.

57. He who is properly called an actor, does not endeavour to make his hearers believe that the sentiments he expresses and the feelings he exhibits, are really his own: a barrister does this: therefore he is not properly to be called an actor.

58. He who bears arms at the command of the magistrate does what is lawful for a Christian: the Swiss in the French service, and the British in the American service, bore arms at the command of the magistrate: therefore they did what was lawful for a Christian.

59. If Lord Bacon is right, it is improper to stock a new colony with the refuse of Jails: but this we must allow not to be improper, if our method of colonizing New South Wales be a wise one: if this be wise, therefore, Lord Bacon is not right.

60. Logic is indeed worthy of being cultivated, if Aris-

totle is to be regarded as infallible: but he is not: Logic therefore is not worthy of being cultivated.

61. All studies are useful which tend to advance a man in life, or to increase national and private wealth: but the course of studies pursued at Oxford has no such tendency: therefore it is not useful.

62. If the exhibition of criminals, publicly executed, tends to heighten in others the dread of undergoing the same fate, it may be expected that those soldiers who have seen the most service, should have the most dread of death in battle; but the reverse of this is the case: therefore the former is not to be believed.

63. If the everlasting favour of God is not bestowed at random, and on no principle at all, it must be bestowed either with respect to men's persons, or with respect to their conduct: but "God is no respecter of persons:" therefore his favour must be bestowed with respect to men's conduct. [Sumner's Apostolical Preaching.]

64. If transportation is not felt as a severe punishment, it is in itself ill-suited to the prevention of crime: if it is so felt, much of its severity is wasted, from its taking place at too great a distance to affect the feelings, or even come to the knowledge, of most of those whom it is designed to deter; but one or other of these must be the case: therefore transportation is not calculated to answer the purpose of preventing crime.

65. War is productive of evil: therefore peace is likely to be productive of good.

66. Some objects of great beauty answer no other perceptible purpose but to gratify the sight: many flowers have great beauty; and many of them accordingly answer no other purpose but to gratify the sight.

67. A man who deliberately devotes himself to a life of sensuality is deserving of strong reprobation: but those do not deliberately devote themselves to a life of sensuality who are hurried into excess by the impulse of the passions:

such therefore as are hurried into excess by the impulse of the passions are not deserving of strong reprobation. [Arist. Eth. B. vii.]

68. It is a difficult task to restrain all inordinate desires: to conform to the precepts of Scripture implies a restraint of all inordinate desires: therefore it is a difficult task to conform to the precepts of Scripture.

69. Any one who is candid will refrain from condemning a book without reading it: some Reviewers do not refrain from this: therefore some Reviewers are not candid.

70. If any objection that can be urged would justify a change of established laws, no laws could reasonably be maintained: but some laws can reasonably be maintained: therefore no objection that can be urged will justify a change of established laws.

71. If any complete theory could be framed, to explain the establishment of Christianity by human causes, such a theory would have been proposed before now; but none such ever has been proposed: therefore no such theory can be framed.

72. He who is content with what he has, is truly rich: a covetous man is not content with what he has: no covetous man therefore is truly rich.

73. A true prophecy coincides precisely with all the circumstances of such an event as could not be conjectured by natural reason: this is the case with the prophecies of the Messiah contained in the Old Testament: therefore these are true prophecies.

74. The connexion of soul and body cannot be comprehended or explained; but it must be believed: therefore something must be believed which cannot be comprehended or explained.

75. Lias lies above Red Sandstone; Red Sandstone lies above Coal: therefore Lias lies above Coal.

76. Cloven feet being found universally in horned animals,

we may conclude that this fossil animal, since it appears to have had cloven feet, was horned.

77. All that glitters is not gold: tinsel glitters: therefore it is not gold.

78. A negro is a man: therefore he who murders a negro murders a man.

79. Meat and drink are necessaries of life: the revenues of Vitellius were spent on Meat and Drink: therefore the revenues of Vitellius were spent on the necessaries of life.

80. Nothing is heavier than Platina: feathers are heavier than nothing: therefore feathers are heavier than Platina.

81. The child of Themistocles governed his mother: she governed her husband; he governed Athens; Athens, Greece; and Greece, the world: therefore the child of Themistocles governed the world.

82. He who calls you a man speaks truly: he who calls you a fool, calls you a man: therefore he who calls you a fool speaks truly.

83. Warm countries alone produce wines: Spain is a warm country: therefore Spain produces wines.

84. It is an intensely cold climate that is sufficient to freeze Quicksilver: the climate of Siberia is sufficient to freeze Quicksilver: therefore the climate of Siberia is intensely cold.

85. Mistleto of the oak is a vegetable excrescence which is not a plant; and every vegetable excrescence which is not a plant, is possessed of magical virtues: therefore Mistleto of the oak is possessed of magical virtues.

86. If the hour-hand of a clock be any distance (suppose a foot) before the minute-hand, this last, though moving twelve times faster, can never overtake the other; for while the minute-hand is moving over those twelve inches, the hour-hand will have moved over one inch: so that they will then be an inch apart; and while the minute-hand is moving over that one inch, the hour-hand will have moved

over $\frac{1}{12}$ inch, so that it will still be a-head; and again, while the minute-hand is passing over that space of $\frac{1}{12}$ inch which now divides them, the hour-hand will pass over $\frac{1}{144}$ inch; so that it will still be a-head, though the distance between the two is diminished; *&c. &c. &c.*, and thus it is plain we may go on for ever: therefore the minute-hand can never overtake the hour-hand. [This is one of the sophistical puzzles noticed by Aldrich (the moving bodies being Achilles and a Tortoise;) but he is not happy in his attempt at a solution. He proposes to remove the difficulty by demonstrating that, in a certain given time, Achilles *would* overtake the Tortoise: as if any one had ever doubted *that*. The very problem proposed is to surmount the difficulty of a seeming demonstration of a thing palpably impossible; to show that it *is* palpably impossible, is no solution of the problem.

I have heard the present example adduced as a proof that the pretensions of Logic are futile, since (it was said) the most perfect logical demonstration may lead from true premises to an absurd conclusion. The reverse is the truth; the example before us furnishes a confirmation of the utility of an acquaintance with the syllogistic form: *in which form the pretended demonstration in question cannot possibly be exhibited.* An attempt to do so will evince the utter want of connexion between the premises and the conclusion.]

87. Theft is a crime: theft was encouraged by the laws of Sparta: therefore the laws of Sparta encouraged crime.

88. Every hen comes from an egg: every egg comes from a hen: therefore every egg comes from an egg.

89. Jupiter was the son of Saturn: therefore the son of Jupiter was the grandson of Saturn.

90. All cold is to be expelled by heat: this person's disorder is a cold: therefore it is to be expelled by heat.

91. Wine is a stimulant: therefore in a case where stimulants are hurtful, wine is hurtful.

92. Opium is a poison: but physicians advise some of their patients to take opium: therefore physicians advise some of their patients to take poison.

93. What we eat grew in the fields: loaves of bread are what we eat: therefore loaves of bread grew in the fields.

94. Animal-food may be entirely dispensed with: (as is

shown by the practice of the Brahmins and of some monks;) and vegetable-food may be entirely dispensed with (as is plain from the example of the Esquimaux and others;) but all food consists of animal-food and vegetable-food: therefore all food may be dispensed with.

95. No trifling business will enrich those engaged in it: a mining speculation is no trifling business: therefore a mining speculation will enrich those engaged in it.

96. He who is most hungry eats most; he who eats least is most hungry: therefore he who eats least eats most. [*See* Aldrich's Compendium: Fallaciæ: where this is rightly solved.]

97. Whatever body is in motion must move either in the place where it is, or in a place where it is not: neither of these is possible: therefore there is no such thing as motion. [In this instance, as well as in the one lately noticed, Aldrich mistakes the character of the difficulty; which is, not to prove the truth of that which is self-evident, but to explain an apparent demonstration militating against that which nevertheless no one ever doubted. He says in this case, "solvitur ambulando;" but (pace tanti viri) this is no solution at all, but is the very thing which *constitutes the difficulty* in question; for it is precisely *because* we know the possibility of motion, that a seeming proof of its impossibility produces perplexity.—*See* Introduction.

98. All vegetables grow most in the increase of the moon: hair is a vegetable: therefore hair grows most in the increase of the moon.

99. Most of the studies pursued at Oxford conduce to the improvement of the mind: all the works of the most celebrated ancients are among the studies pursued at Oxford: therefore some of the works of the most celebrated ancients conduce to the improvement of the mind.

100. Some poisons are vegetable: no poisons are useful drugs: therefore some useful drugs are not vegetable.

101. A theory will speedily be exploded, if false, which appeals to the evidence of observation and experiment: Craniology appeals to this evidence: therefore, if Craniology be a false theory, it will speedily be exploded. [Let the probability of one of these premises be $\frac{7}{10}$; and of the other $\frac{4}{5}$: *Query*. What is the probability of the conclusion, and which are the terms?]

102. Wilkes was a favourite with the populace; he who is a favourite with the populace must understand how to manage them: he who understands how to manage them, must be well acquainted with their character: he who is well acquainted with their character, must hold them in contempt: therefore Wilkes must have held the populace in contempt.

103. To discover whether man has any moral sense, he should be viewed in that state in which all his faculties are most fully developed; the civilized state is that in which all man's faculties are most fully developed: therefore, to discover whether man has any moral sense, he should be viewed in a civilized state.

104. Revenge, Robbery, Adultery, Infanticide, *&c.* have been countenanced by public opinion in several countries: all the crimes we know of are Revenge, Robbery, Adultery, Infanticide, *&c.*: therefore, all the crimes we know of have been countenanced by public opinion in several countries. [Paley's Moral Philosophy.]

105. No soldiers should be brought into the field who are not well qualified to perform their part. None but veterans are well qualified to perform their part. None but veterans should be brought into the field.

106. A monopoly of the sugar-refining business is beneficial to sugar-refiners: and of the corn-trade to corn-growers: and of the silk-manufacture to silk-weavers, *&c. &c.*; and thus each class of men are benefited by some restrictions. Now all these classes of men make up the whole community; therefore a system of restrictions is beneficial to the community. [*See* Chap. iii. § 11.]

107. There are two kinds of things which we ought not to fret about: what we can help, and what we cannot. [To be stated as a Dilemma.]

108. He who believes himself to be always in the right in his opinion, lays claim to infallibility: you always believe

yourself to be in the right in your opinion: therefore you lay claim to infallibility.

109. No part of mankind can ever have received divine instruction in any of the arts of life: because the Israelites, who are said to have had a revelation made to them of religion, did not know, in the times of Solomon, that the circumference of a Circle differs from the treble of the Diameter.

110. The Epistle attributed to Barnabas is not to be reckoned among the writings of the Apostolic Fathers; because, if genuine, it is a part of Scripture, and, if spurious, it is the work of some forger of a later age.

111. If the original civilization of Mankind was not the work of a divine Instructor, some instance may be found of a nation of savages having civilized themselves. [Pol. Econ. Lect. V.]

112. The Law of Moses prohibited theft, murder, *&c.* But that Law is abolished: therefore theft, murder, *&c.* are not prohibited.

113. Agriculture might have been invented by man, without a superhuman instructor; and so might the working of metals; and so might medicine; and so might navigation, *&c.*; and in short there is no art of civilized life that can be pointed out, which might not have been invented by the natural faculties of man. Therefore the arts of civilized life might have been invented by man without any superhuman instructor.*

114. All those must disapprove of inflicting punishment on this woman who consider her as innocent: and as you disapprove of inflicting punishment on her, it is to be presumed you think her innocent.

115. If a State has a right to enforce laws, (and without this it could not subsist) it must have a right to prescribe what the religion of the People shall be. [See Book III. §. 9.]

* See Polit. Econ. Lect. V. p. 123.

116. Every man is bound in duty to aim at promoting the *good*—generally, and in all respects—of Mankind: a Civil Magistrate (or Legislator) is a man: therefore a Civil Magistrate is bound in duty to aim at promoting the good generally and in all respects—of Mankind. And hence it appears that, since true Religion is one of the greatest of goods, the Civil Magistrate is bound to enforce, by means of the power committed to him, the profession of a true Religion, and to suppress heresy. [*See* Essay I. on the "Kingdom of Christ."]

117. The month of May has no "*R*" in its name; nor has June, July, or August: all the hottest months are May, June, July and August: therefore all the hottest months are without an "*R*" in their names. [*See* Book IV. Ch. i. § 1.]

118. This man may possibly be right in his peculiar religious Creed; and the same may be said of that man: and of a third, and a fourth, &c.: therefore it is possible they may be all right.

119. When the Disciples were first called Christians, they must have received the title either from Believers, or from Jewish unbelievers, or from Pagans: but one of these suppositions is impossible; and another is negatived by the New Testament records; therefore the remaining supposition is established.

APPENDIX.

No. III.

PRAXIS OF LOGICAL ANALYSIS.

Some have expressed much contempt for the mode in which Logic is usually taught, and in which students are examined in it, as comprising no more than a mere enumeration of technical rules, and perhaps an application of them to the simplest examples, exhibited in a form already syllogistic, or nearly so. That such a description, if intended to be universal, is not correct, I am perfectly certain; though, hitherto, the indiscriminate requisition of Logic from all candidates for a degree, has confined both lectures and examinations, in a greater degree than is desirable, to this elementary character.* But the student who wishes to acquire, and to show that he has acquired, not only the elementary rules, but a facility of applying them in practice, should proceed from the study of such examples as the foregoing, to exercise himself in analysing logically, according to the rules here given, and somewhat in the manner of the subjoined specimen, some of Euclid's demonstrations,—various portions of Aristotle's works,—the opening of Warburton's "Divine Legation," (which exhibits the arguments in a form very nearly syllogistic)—several parts of Chillingworth's Defence of Protestantism,—the concluding part of Paley's Horæ Paulinæ,—Leslie's

* See Preface.

Method with the Deists,—various portions of A. Smith's Wealth of Nations,—and other argumentative Works on the most dissimilar subjects. The latter part of § 1. Chap. V. of the Dissertation on the Province of Reasoning, will furnish a convenient subject of a short analysis.

A student who should prepare himself, in this manner, in one or more such books, and present himself for this kind of examination in them, would furnish a good test for ascertaining his proficiency in practical Logic.

As the rules of Logic apply to arguments only after they have been exhibited at full length in the bare elementary form, it may be useful to subjoin some remarks on the mode of analysing and reducing to that form, any train of argument that may be presented to us: since this must in general be the first step taken in an attempt to apply logical rules.*

First then, of whatever length the reasoning may be, whether treatise, chapter, or paragraph, begin with the concluding assertion;—not necessarily the last sentence expressed, but the last point established;—and this, whether it be formally enunciated, or left to be understood. Then, tracing the reasoning backwards, observe on what ground that assertion is made. The assertion will be your Conclusion; the ground on which it rests, your Premises. The whole Syllogism thus obtained may be tried by the rules of Logic.

If no incorrectness appear in this syllogism, proceed to take the premises separately, and pursue with each the same plan as with the conclusion you first stated. A premiss must have been used as such, either because it required no proof, or because it had been proved. If it

* These directions are, in substance, and nearly, in words, extracted from the Preface to Hinds's abridged Introduction to Logic.

have not been proved, consider whether it be so self-evident as to have needed no proof. If it have been proved, you must regard it as a conclusion derived from other assertions which are premises to it: so that the process with which you set out will be repeated; *viz.* to observe on what grounds the assertion rests, to state these as premises, and to apply the proper rules to the syllogism thus obtained. Having satisfied yourself of the correctness of this, proceed, as before, to state its premises, if needful, as conclusions derived from other assertions. And thus the analysis will go on (if the whole chain of argument be correct) till you arrive at the premises with which the whole commences; which of course should be assertions requiring no proof; or, if the chain be any where faulty, the analysis will proceed till you come to some proposition, either assumed as self-evident, though requiring proof, or incorrectly deduced from other assertions.*

It will often happen that the same assertion will have been proved by many different arguments; and then, the

* Many students probably will find it a very clear and convenient mode of exhibiting the logical analysis of a course of argument, to draw it out in the form of a Tree, or Logical Division; thus,

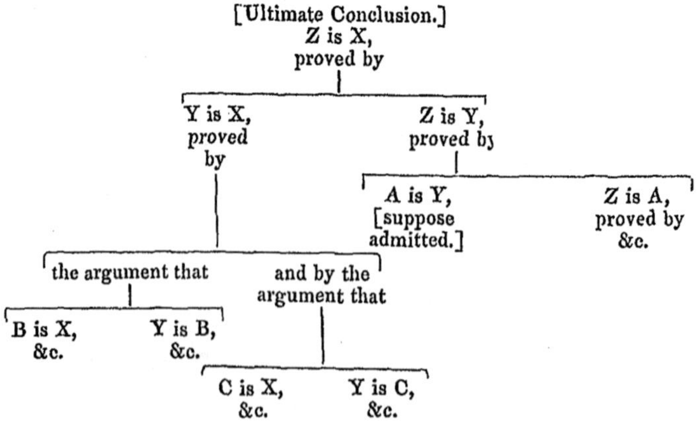

inquiry into the truth of the premises will branch out accordingly. In mathematical or other demonstrative reasoning, this will of course never take place, since absolute certainty admits of no increase: and if, as is often the case, the same truth admits of several different demonstrations, we select the simplest and clearest, and discard the rest. But in *probable* reasoning there is often a Cumulation of arguments, each proving the same conclusion; *i. e.* each proving it to be *probable.* In such cases therefore you will have first to try each argument separately; and should each of them establish the conclusion as in some degree probable, you will then have to calculate the *aggregate* probability.

In this calculation Logic only so far assists as it enables us to place the several *items* of probability in the most convenient form. As the degree of probability of each proposition that is originally *assumed,* is a point to be determined by the reasoner's own sagacity and experience as to the matter in hand, so, the degree of probability of each *conclusion,* (given, that of each of its premises,)* and also the *collective* probability resulting from several different arguments all tending to the same conclusion, is an *arithmetical* question. But the assistance afforded by logical rules in clearly stating the several items so as to prepare the way for the other operations, will not be thought lightly of by any who have observed the confusion of thought and the fallacy, which have often been introduced through the want of such a statement.

Example of Analysis applied to the first part of Paley's Evidences.

The ultimate Conclusion, that "The Christian Religion came from God" is made to rest (as far as "the direct historical evidence" is concerned) on these two premises;

* See Fallacies, § 14, near the end.

That "A Religion attested by Miracles is from God;" and that "The Christian Religion is so attested."

Of these two premises, it should be remarked, the Minor seems to have been admitted, while the Major was denied, by the unbelievers of old: whereas at present the case is reversed.*

Paley's argument therefore goes to establish the Minor premiss, about which alone, in these days, there is likely to be any question.

He states with this view, two propositions: *viz.*

Prop. I. — "That there is satisfactory evidence, that many, professing to be original witnesses of the Christian miracles, passed their lives in labours, dangers, and sufferings, voluntarily undergone in attestation of the accounts which they delivered, and solely in consequence of their belief of those accounts; and that they also submitted, from the same motives, to new rules of conduct."

Prop. II.—"That there is NOT satisfactory evidence, that persons pretending to be original witnesses of any other similar miracles, have acted in the same manner, in attestation of the accounts which they delivered, and solely in consequence of their belief of the truth of those accounts."

Of these two propositions, the latter, it will easily be perceived, is the Major premiss, stated as the *converse by*

* It is clear from the fragments remaining of the ancient arguments against Christianity, and the allusions to them in Christian writers, and also from the Jewish accounts of the life of Jesus which are still extant, (under the title of *Toldoth Jeschu*) that the original opponents of Christianity admitted that miracles were wrought, but denied that they proved the divine origin of the religion, and attributed them to Magic. This concession, in persons living so much nearer to the times assigned to the miracles, should be noticed as an important evidence; for, credulous as men were in those days respecting magic, they would hardly have resorted to this explanation, unless some, at least plausible, evidence for the miracles had been adduced. And they could not but be sensible that to prove (had that been possible) the pretended miracles to be *impostures*, would have been the most decisive course; since *that* would at once have *dis*proved the religion.

Negation (Book II. Chap. ii. § 4) of a universal affirmative: the former proposition is the Minor.

As a Syllogism in *Barbara*, therefore, the whole will stand thus:

"All miracles attested by such and such evidence, are worthy of credit:" (by conversion, "none which are not worthy of credit are so attested.")

"The Christian miracles are attested by such and such evidence:" Therefore "they are worthy of credit."

The Minor premiss is first proved by being taken as *several* distinct ones, each of which is separately established. —*See* Book II. Chap. iv. § 1.

I. It is proved that the first propagators of Christianity *suffered;* by showing,

1st. *A priori*, from the nature of the case, that they were *likely* to suffer: [because they were preachers of a religion unexpected and unwelcome: 1. to the Jews; and 2. to the Gentiles.*]

2d. From *profane testimony*.

3d. From the testimony of *Christian Writings*. [And here comes in the proof of one of the premises of this last argument; *viz.* the proof of the credibility, *as to this point* at least, of the Christian Writings.]

These arguments are *cumulative; i. e.* each separately goes to establish the probability of the one common conclusion, that "the first propagators of Christianity *suffered*."

By similar arguments it is shown that their sufferings were such as they *voluntarily* exposed themselves to.

II. It is proved that "What they suffered *for* was a *miraculous* story:" by

1st. The nature of the case; They could have had

* As Paul expresses it, "to the Jews, a *stumbling-block;* and to the Greeks, *foolishness*."

nothing but miracles on which to rest the claims of the new religion.

2d. By allusions to miracles, particularly to the Resurrection, both in Christian and in Profane Writers, as the evidence on which the religion rested.

The same course of argument goes to show that the miracles in attestation of which they suffered were such as they professed to have *witnessed*.

These arguments again are cumulative.

III. It is proved that "The miracles thus attested are what we call the *Christian* miracles:" in other words, that the story was, in the main, that which we have now in the Christian Scriptures; by

§ 1st. The nature of the case; *viz.* that it is improbable the original story should have completely died away, and a substantially new one have occupied its place;

§ 2d. by The incidental allusions of ancient writers, both Christian and profane, to accounts agreeing with those of our Scriptures, as the ones then received;

§ 3d. by The credibility of our Historical Scriptures: This is established by several distinct arguments, each separately tending to show that these books were, from the earliest ages of Christianity, well known and carefully preserved among Christians: *viz.*

§ i. They were *quoted* by ancient Christian writers.

§ ii. with peculiar *respect*.

§ iii. Collected into a *distinct volume*, and

§ iv. distinguished by appropriate names and *titles* of *respect*.

§ v. *Publicly read* and expounded, and

§ vi. had *commentaries, &c.* written on them:

§ vii. Were received by Christians of *different sects; &c. &c.**

* For some important remarks respecting the different ways in which this part of the argument is presented to different persons, *See* "Hinds on Inspiration," pp. 30—46.

The latter part of the first main proposition, branches off into two; *viz.* 1st., that the early Christians submitted to new *rules of conduct;* 2d, that they did so, *in consequence* of their belief in miracles wrought before them.

Each of these is established in various parts of the above course of argument, and by similar premises; *viz.* the nature of the case,—the accounts of heathen writers,—and the testimony of the Christian Scriptures, *&c.*

The Major premiss, that "Miracles thus attested are worthy of credit," (which must be combined with the former, in order to establish the conclusion, that "the Christian miracles are worthy of credit,") is next to be established.

Previously to his entering on the second main proposition, (which I have stated to be the Converse by negation of this Major premiss,) he draws his conclusion (Ch. x. Part I.) from the Minor premiss, in combination with the Major, resting that Major on

§ 1st. The *à priori improbability* that a false story should have been thus attested: *viz.*

"If it be so, the religion must be true.* These men could not be deceivers. By only not bearing testimony, they might have avoided all these sufferings, and have lived quietly. Would men in such circumstances pretend to have seen what they never saw; assert facts which they had no knowledge of; go about lying, to teach virtue; and, though not only convinced of Christ's being an impostor, but having seen the success of his imposture in his crucifixion, yet persist in carrying it on; and so persist, as to bring upon themselves, for nothing, and with a full knowledge of the consequence, enmity, and hatred, danger and death?"

* This is the *ultimate* conclusion deduced from the premiss, that "it is attested by real *Miracles;* which, in the present day, comes to the same thing: since those for whom he is writing, are ready at once to admit the truth of the *religion,* if convinced of the reality of the *miracles.* The ancient Jews were not.

§ 2d. That no *false* story of Miracles is *likely* to be so attested, is again proved, from the premiss that "no false story of miracles ever *has been* so attested;" and this premiss again is proved in the form of a proposition which includes it; *viz.* that "*No other* miraculous story *whatever* is so attested."

§ This assertion again, *bifurcates; viz.* it is proved respecting the several stories that are likely to be, or that have been adduced, as parallel to the Christian, that either

1 §. They are not so *attested;* or

2 §. They are not properly *miraculous; i. e.* that admitting the veracity of the narrator, it does not follow that any miracle took place; as in cases that may be explained by *false perceptions,—accidents, &c.*

In this way the learner may proceed to analyze the rest of the work, and to fill up the details of those parts of the argument which I have but slightly touched upon.*

It will be observed that, to avoid unnecessary prolixity, I have in most of the above syllogisms suppressed one premiss, which the learner will be able easily to supply for himself. *E. G.* In the early part of this analysis it will easily be seen, that the first of the series of cumulative arguments to prove that the propagators of Christianity did suffer, would at full length stand thus:

"Whoever propagated a religion unwelcome to the Jews and to the Gentiles, was likely to suffer;
The Apostles did this;
Therefore they were likely to suffer," *&c. &c.*

It is also to be observed, that the same proposition used in different syllogisms may require to be differently expressed by a substitution of some *equivalent,* in order to

* See note at the end of this Appendix.

render the argument, in each, *formally* correct. This of course is always allowable, provided great care is taken that the exact meaning be preserved: *e. g.* if the proposition be, "The persons who attested the Christian miracles underwent sufferings in attestation of them," I am authorized to state the same assertion in a different form, thus, "The Christian miracles are attested by men who suffered in attestation of their reality," *&c.*

Great care however should be used to avoid being misled by the substitution of one proposition for another, when the two are not (though perhaps they sound so) really equivalent, so that the one warrants the assumption of the other. —*See* Book iii. § 3.

Lastly, the learner is referred to the Supplement to Chap. iii. § 1, p. 97, where I have treated of the statement of a proposition as *several* distinct ones, each implying all the rest, but differing in the division of the Predicate from the Subject. Of this procedure the above analysis affords an instance.

Note referred to at page 386.

When the Student considers that the foregoing is only *one* out of many branches of evidence, all tending to the same point, and yet that there have been intelligent men who have held out against them all, he may be apt to suspect either that there must be some flaw in these arguments, which he is unable to detect, or else that there must be much stronger arguments on the other side than he has ever met with.

To enter into a discussion of the various causes leading to infidelity would be unsuitable to this occasion; but I will notice one as being more especially connected with the subject of this work, and as being very generally overlooked. "*In no other instance perhaps,*" (says Dr. Hawkins, in his valuable Essay on Tradition) "*besides that of Religion, do men commit the very illogical mistake, of first canvassing all the objections against any particular system whose pretensions to truth they would examine, before they consider the direct arguments in its favour.*" (P. 82.) But why, it may be asked, *do* they make such a mistake in *this* case? An answer, which I think would apply to a large proportion of such persons, is this: because a man having been brought up in a Christian country, has lived perhaps among such as have been accustomed from their infancy to *take for granted* the truth of their religion, and even to regard an *uninquiring* assent as a mark of commendable *faith;* and hence he has probably never even thought of proposing to himself the question,—Why should I receive Christianity as a divine revelation? Christianity being nothing *new* to him, and the *presumption* being in favour of it, while the burden of proof lies on its opponents, he is not stimulated to seek reasons for believing it, till he finds it controverted. And when it *is* controverted,—when an opponent urges—How do you reconcile this, and that, and the other, with the idea of a divine revelation? these objections *strike* by their *novelty*, by their being opposed to what is generally received. He is thus excited to inquiry; which he sets about,—naturally enough, but very unwisely,—by seeking for answers to all these objections: and fancies that unless they can all be satisfactorily solved, he ought not to receive the religion. "As if," (says the Author already cited) "there could not be truth, and truth supported by irrefragable arguments, and yet at the same time obnoxious to objections, numerous, plausible, and by no means easy of solution. There are objections (said Dr. Johnson) against a *plenum*, and objections against a *vacuum;* but one of them must be true." He adds, that "sensible men, really desirous of discovering the truth, will perceive that reason directs them to examine first the argument in favour of that side of the question, where the first presumption of truth appears. And the presumption is manifestly in favour of that religious creed already adopted by the country. . . . Their very earliest inquiry therefore must be into the direct arguments for the authority of that book on which their country rests its religion."

But reasonable as such a procedure is, there is, as I have said, a strong temptation, and one which should be carefully guarded against, to adopt the opposite course; to attend first to the objections which are brought against what is established, and which, for that very reason, rouse the mind from a state of apathy.

When Christianity was first preached, the state of things was reversed. The presumption was against it, as being a novelty. "Seeing that all these things *cannot be spoken against*, ye ought to be *quiet*," was a sentiment which favoured an indolent acquiescence in the old pagan worship. The stimulus of novelty was all on the side of those who came to overthrow this, by a new religion. The first inquiry of any one who at all attended to the subject, must have been, not,—"What are the objections to Christianity?"—but, "On what grounds do these men call on me to receive them as divine messengers?" And the same appears to be the case with the Polynesians among whom our Missionaries are labouring: they begin by inquiring, "Why should we receive this religion?" and those of them accordingly who have embraced it, appear to be Christians on much more rational and deliberate conviction than many among *us*, even of those who, in general maturity of intellect and civilization, are advanced considerably beyond those Islanders.

I am not depreciating the inestimable advantages of a religious education; but, pointing out the *peculiar* temptations which accompany it. The Jews and Pagans had, in their early prejudices, greater difficulties to surmount, than ours; but they were difficulties *of a different kind.*—See *Essays on the Dangers, &c.* Disc. i. § 3; and also *Rhet.* Part I. Ch. iii. § 1.

I have subjoined, in parallel columns, extracts from Hume's "Essay on Miracles," from two Reviews professedly Christian, but organs of two most opposite religious schools, and from Scripture. The coincidence between the first three, and the contrast they present to Scripture, being, I think, not only curious but instructive.

"Upon the whole, we may conclude that the Christian Religion not only was at first attended with miracles, but even at this day cannot be believed by any reasonable person without one. Mere reason is insufficient to convince us of its veracity; and whoever is moved by *Faith* to assent to it, is conscious of a continued miracle in his own person, which subverts all the principles of his understanding, and gives him a determination to believe what is most contrary to custom and experience."—*Hume's Essay*, (at the end.)

* * we are to be censured for having "shifted the ground of our belief from testimony to argument, and from faith to reason." * * *

In answering the question why our religion is to be believed, "The poor ignorant uninstructed peasant will probably come nearest to the answer of the Gospel. He will say, because I have been told so by those who are wiser and better than myself. My parents told me so, and the clergyman of the parish told me so; and I hear the same whenever I go to church. And I put confidence in these persons, because it is natural that I should trust my superiors. I have never had reason to suspect

"The sacred writers have none of the timidity of their modern apologists. They never sue for an assent to their doctrines, but authoritatively command the acceptance of them. They denounce unbelief as guilt, and insist on faith as a virtue of the highest order. In their catholic invitations, the intellectual not less than the social distinctions of mankind, are unheeded. Every student of their writings is aware of these facts, &c. * * * * * They presuppose that vigour of understanding may consist with feebleness of reason; and that the power of discriminating between religious truth and error does not depend chiefly on the culture or on the

"This beginning of miracles did Jesus in Cana of Galilee, and manifested his glory, and his disciples believed on Him."

"We know that thou art a teacher sent from God; for no man can do these miracles that thou doest except God be with him."

"If I had not done among them the works that none other man did, they had not had sin."

"The works that I do in my Father's name, they bear witness of me."

"Him God raised up and shewed Him openly; not to all the people, but to witnesses chosen afore of God, even to us," &c.

that they would deceive me. I hear of persons who contradict and abuse them, but they are not such persons as I would wish to follow in any other matter of life, and therefore not in religion. I was born and baptized in the church, and the Bible tells me to stay in the church, and obey its teachers: and till I have equal authority for believing that it is not the Church of Christ, as it is the Church of England, I intend to adhere to it. Now, such reasoning as this will appear to this rational age very paltry and unsatisfactory: and yet the logic is as sound as the spirit is humble. And there is nothing to compare with it either intellectually, or morally, or religiously, in all the elaborate defences and evidences which would be produced from Paley, and Grotius, and Sumner, and Chalmers."—*British Critic.*

exercise of the mere argumentative faculty. The especial patrimony of the poor and illiterate—the Gospel—has been the stay of countless millions who never framed a syllogism: of the great multitudes who, before and since the birth of Grotius, have lived in the peace and died in the consolations of our Faith, how small is the proportion of those whose convictions have been derived from the study of works like his. Of the numbers who have addicted themselves to such studies, how small is the proportion of those who have brought to the task either learning, or leisure, or industry, sufficient, &c. * * * He who lays the foundation of his faith on such evidences will too commonly end either in yielding a credulous and therefore an infirm assent, or in reposing in a self-sufficient and far more hazardous incredulity."—*Edinb. Review.*

"To Him bear all the Prophets witness."

"Be always ready to give to every one that asketh you, a reason of the hope that is in you," &c.

The coincidence between writers of such different schools is very striking, and affords matter for much reflection. They all agree in representing the "Faith" that is required of a Christian as wholly independent of *evidence*, and as necessarily, or most properly, based on feelings such as attach Pagans to their superstitions.* And they all apparently calculate on the reader's being totally ignorant of the New Testament, of which almost every chapter convicts Jesus and his followers of that "*timidity*" in appealing to the evidence of miracles and prophecies which is censured and derided. For, the passages above cited from Scripture, even if multiplied many fold, as might easily be done, would give but a very inadequate view of the case; inasmuch as the *general tenor* of all the narrative, and all the teaching, of the New Testament, *presupposes* evidence as the original ground on which belief had been all along demanded: the unbelief which it "denounces as sin" being, not as those other writers represent, the *requiring* of evidence, but—on the *contrary*,—the *rejection* of evidence.

The fallacy of representing all appeal to reason as useless in cases where the "argumentative faculty" is not *alone* sufficient—which is like denying the utility of light, because it will not enable a man to see, whose eyes are not in a state to perform their functions,—has been already noticed, Book IV. Ch. ii. § 5.

It may be a useful exercise for the learner to analyze some others of this collection of fallacies, referring to Book I. § 2, to Book II. Ch. ii. § 3, and to Appendix I. Art. "Experience."

* See Professor Powell's valuable work, "Tradition Unveiled."

INDEX

OF THE

PRINCIPAL TECHNICAL TERMS.

THE END.

R. CLAY, PRINTER, BREAD STREET HILL, LONDON.